$2 \times 3 \times 5$

① Given
- $n =$ # sub each level
- $K =$ # levels $(a \times b \times c)$
- $N =$ Total # in all levels $(K \times n)$
- $a =$ # levels of A
- b # levels b
- c # levels c

Fundamentals
of Psychological
Research

② find RS values

RS_{TOT} = square all scores + add.

RS_{ABC} = add all scores in levels $\dfrac{\square^2 \square^2 \square^2}{n}$

$$RS_{AB} = \frac{(\Sigma Xa_1b_1)^2 + (\Sigma Xa_1b_2)^2 + (\Sigma Xa_1b_3)^2 + (\Sigma Xa_2b_1)^2 + (\Sigma Xa_2b_2)^2 + (\Sigma Xa_2b_3)^2}{nc}$$

$$RS_{AC} = \frac{(\Sigma Xa_1c_1)^2 \ldots \ldots (\Sigma Xa_2c_5)^2}{nb}$$

$$RS_{BC} = \frac{(\Sigma Xb_1c_1)^2 + (\Sigma Xb_1c_2)^2 \ldots \ldots (\Sigma Xb_2c_5)^2}{na}$$

$$RS_A = \frac{(\Sigma Xa_1)^2 + (\Sigma Xa_2)^2}{nbc}$$

$$RS_b = \frac{(\Sigma Xb_1)^2 + (\Sigma Xb_2)^2 + (\Sigma Xb_3)^2}{nac}$$

$$RS_C = \frac{(\Sigma Xc_1)^2 (\Sigma Xc_2)^2 + (\Sigma Xc_3)^2 + (\Sigma Xc_4)^2 + (\Sigma Xc_5)^2}{nab}$$

$c =$ all scores in levels
cell
$$\left(\square^x \ \square^x \ \square^x \ \square^y \right)^2 \Big/ nabc$$

③ Find SS scores

SS_{TOT} $RS_{TOT} - C$

$SS_A = RS_A - C$

$SS_B = RS_B - C$

$SS_C = RS_C - C$

$SS_{AB} = RS_{AB} - C - SS_A - SS_B$

$SS_{AC} = RS_{AC} - C - SS_A - SS_C$

$SS_{BC} = RS_{BC} - C - SS_B - SS_C$

$SS_{ABC} = RS_{ABC} - C - SS_A - SS_B - SS_C - SS_{AB} - SS_{AC} - SS_{BC}$

SS_E $SS_{TOT} - SS_{Bet}(SS_A + SS_B + SS_C + SS_{AB} + SS_{AC} + SS_{BC} + SS_{ABC})$

④

Source	SS	df	ms	F
SS_A	—	$a-1$	SS_A/df	F_A
SS_B	—	$b-1$	SS_B/df	F_B
SS_C	—	$c-1$	SS_C/df	F_C
SS_{AB}	—	$df_a \cdot df_b$ SS_{ab}/df		F_{AB}
SS_{AC}	—	$df_a \cdot df_c$ SS_{ac}/df		F_{AC}
SS_{BC}	—	$df_b \cdot df_c$	"	F_{BC}
SS_{ABC}	—	df $a \cdot b \cdot c$	"	F_{ABC}
SSE	—	$k(n-1)$	"	
SS_{TOT}	—	$N-1$		

NUM
df

den
$\dfrac{k(n-1)}{(SSC)}$

CHI SQUARE

OF OBSERVED frequency
EF EXPECTED frequency

$$\chi^2 = \sum \frac{(OF - EF)^2}{EF}$$

N = TOTAL # Sub.

$EF = \dfrac{N}{k}$

k = categories

	Bush	DuPont
EF	EF=2000	EF=2000
OF	1600	2400

$k \cdot EF = N$

$$\chi^2 = \frac{(EF-OF)^2}{EF} + \frac{(EF-OF)^2}{EF} \cdot \frac{400^2}{2000} + \frac{400^2}{2000} = \left\{ \frac{160,000}{2000} \right\} \cdot 2 = 80 + 80 = \boxed{160}$$

EF_1	EF_2	
1950	2050	4000 RT_1
EF_3	EF_4	
1200	1800	3000 RT_2
3150	3850	7000
CT_1	CT_2	GT

$df = (n-1)(c-1)$

$4\,\overline{|7000}$

$EF =$

$EF_1 = \dfrac{RT_1}{GT}(CT_1)$

$EF_2 = \dfrac{RT_1}{GT}(CT_2)$

$EF_3 = \dfrac{RT_2}{GT}(CT_1)$

$EF_4 = \dfrac{RT_2}{GT}(CT_2)$

$$\frac{\left(OF_1 - \frac{RT_1}{GT}(CT_1)\right)^2}{EF_1} + \frac{\left(OF_2 - \frac{RT_1}{GT}(CT_2)\right)}{EF_2} + \frac{\left(OF_3 - \frac{RT_2}{GT}(CT_1)\right)}{EF_3} + \frac{\left(OF_4 - \frac{RT_2}{GT}(CT_2)\right)}{EF_4}$$

FUNDAMENTALS OF PSYCHOLOGICAL RESEARCH

Third Edition

Gordon Wood

Michigan State University

df (number of rows -1)(#columns -1)

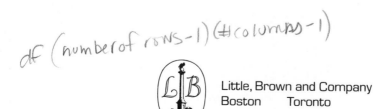

Little, Brown and Company
Boston   Toronto

Pearson R

$$r = \frac{\Sigma xy}{\sqrt{(\Sigma x^2)(\Sigma y^2)}}$$

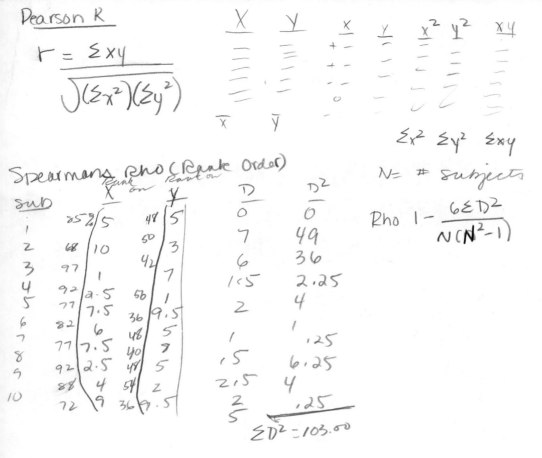

Spearmans Rho (Rank Order)

sub	Rank on X		Rank on Y		D	D²
1	85	5	48	5	0	0
2	68	10	50	3	7	49
3	97	1	42	7	6	36
4	92	2.5	56	1	1.5	2.25
5	77	7.5	36	9.5	2	4
6	82	6	48	5	1	1
7	77	7.5	40	8	.5	.25
8	92	2.5	48	5	2.5	6.25
9	88	4	54	2	2	4
10	72	9	36	9.5	.5	.25

$$\Sigma D^2 = 103.00$$

$N = \#$ subjects

$$Rho\ 1 - \frac{6\Sigma D^2}{N(N^2-1)}$$

Library of Congress Catalog Card No. 80-82550

ISBN 0-316-951692

9 8 7 6 5 4 3 2 1

MV

Published simultaneously in Canada
by Little, Brown & Company (Canada) Limited

Printed in the United States of America

Sex	Verdict	Ver.	RowTotal
F	a	b	
M	c	d	
COLT.			

TO MY MOTHER

Phi Coefficient $\dfrac{(bc - ad)}{\sqrt{(j)(k)(l)(m)}}$

abcd – frequencies in four cells by 2x2 contingency table

jklm – jk Row Totals

lm column totals

8 — Judy Parkerton

186713

Chi Square p 338
references: p 353
J Dist - 340
F Dist - 342

Describing *the* Results of Experiments 203 -
A Nominal Data 203-4
A Ordinal Data. 205-6
A Interval & Ratio Data 206-209

Summary 209 - 211.

CHAPTER 9

Computing Correlation Coefficients 214-
A Nominal Data & Phi Coef. 214 - 217
A Ordinal Data & Rank-order Correlation 217 - 219
A Interval Data & Pearson Product moment Cor. 219 - 221

CH 10

CHI SQUARE 240 NEW PRICE _____
  one Variable 240 USED PRICE ████████
Two Variables 243 BUFFALO UNIVERSITY STORE
Chi 2 + Phi Coef. 246 - 248
The Median Test : A Special Chi Square 248-9
Restrictions on the Use of Chi² 249 - 250

T-Test   T-Test
Between Groups   Within Groups

$\bar{X}_1 - \bar{X}_2$ $\bar{D}$
────────────────────   ──────────────────────────
$\sqrt{\dfrac{\Sigma x_1^2 + \Sigma x_2^2}{n_1 + n_2 - 2}} \left(\dfrac{1}{n_1} + \dfrac{1}{n_2}\right)$ $\sqrt{\dfrac{N(\Sigma D^2) - (\Sigma D)^2}{N}} \left(\dfrac{1}{N(N-1)}\right)$

$X_5 - X$ $= \dfrac{D}{}$ $\dfrac{D^2}{}$
$X_6 - \check{X}$

$\Sigma D = \bigcirc$ $\Sigma D \bigcirc$

F Ratio (Multilevel of Design) | 1 X 3 |

① Given n = # of subjects in each iv.

K = # of levels of iv

N – TOTAL # sub.

② Find R.S values

RS_{TOT} = scores² added = RS_{TOT}

RS_{BET} $\frac{scores² added}{}$

$C - \frac{(scores\ added)^2}{N}$

③ Find SS values

$SS_{TOT} = RS_{TOT} - C$

$SS_{BET}\quad RS_{BET} - C$

$SS_E = SS_{TOT} - SS_{BET}$

$\frac{Num.}{df_{BET}}\quad \frac{Den}{df_E}$

④ Summary Table

Source	SS	df	MS	F
SS_{BET}	—	$K-1$	$\frac{SS_{BET}}{df}$	$\frac{MS_{BET}}{MS_E}$
SS_E	—	$K(n-1)$	$\frac{SS_E}{df}$	
SS_{TOT}	—	$N-1$		

2x2 FACTORIAL Design

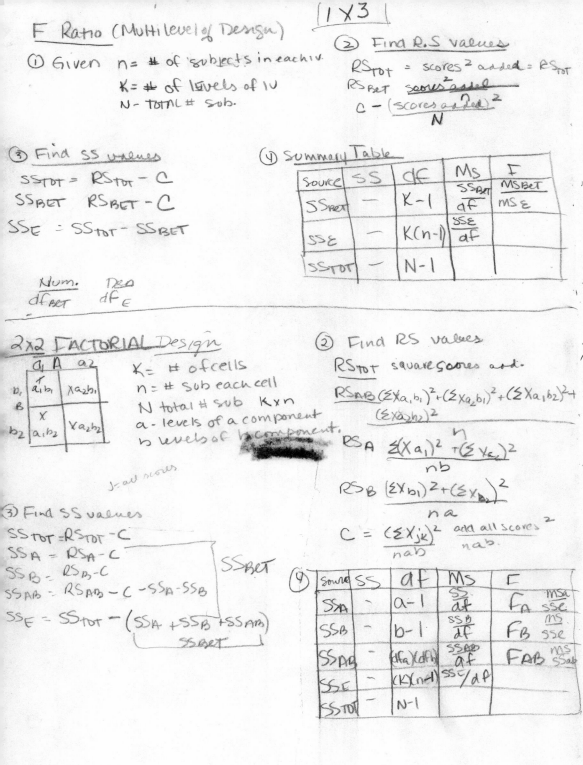

	a_1 A a_2	
b_1 B	a_1b_1	χa_2b_1
	χ	
b_2	a_1b_2	χa_2b_2

$\downarrow$ all scores

K = # of cells

n = # sub each cell

N total # sub $K \times n$

a – levels of a component

b levels of b component.

② Find RS values

RS_{TOT} square scores add.

$RS_{AB} \frac{(\Sigma X_{a_1b_1})^2 + (\Sigma X_{a_2b_1})^2 + (\Sigma X_{a_1b_2})^2 + (\Sigma X_{a_2b_2})^2}{n}$

$RS_A \frac{\Sigma(X_{a_1})^2 + (\Sigma X_{a_2})^2}{nb}$

$RS_B \frac{(\Sigma X_{b_1})^2 + (\Sigma X_{b_2})^2}{na}$

$C = \frac{(\Sigma X_{jk})^2}{nab}$ add all scores² $\quad nab.$

③ Find SS values

$SS_{TOT} = RS_{TOT} - C$

$SS_A = RS_A - C$

$SS_B = RS_B - C$ $\Big\}$ SS_{BET}

$SS_{AB} = RS_{AB} - C - SS_A - SS_B$

$SS_E = SS_{TOT} - \underbrace{(SS_A + SS_B + SS_{AB})}_{SS_{BET}}$

④

Source	SS	df	MS	F
SS_A	—	$a-1$	$\frac{SS}{df}$	$F_A \frac{ms_A}{sse}$
SS_B	—	$b-1$	$\frac{SS_B}{df}$	$F_B \frac{ms}{sse}$
SS_{AB}	—	$(df_a)(df_b)$	$\frac{SS_{AB}}{df}$	$F_{AB} \frac{ms}{ss_{ab}}$
SS_E	—	$(K)(n-1)$	SS/df	
SS_{TOT}	—	$N-1$		

Preface

Students taking their first course in methodology and statistics frequently have misconceptions about its general usefulness. Many believe that methodology and statistics are important for some areas of psychology (for example, human memory, animal behavior, or perception) but not for others (such as personality, clinical, or social psychology). The fact is, however, that investigators in diverse areas of the social sciences use similar methods and statistical techniques to evaluate ideas about behavior and mental activity. Thus this text should be as useful to the student interested in research in memory or perception as it is for the student interested in research in child development, social psychology, or even research in the various medical fields.

Many students believe that methodology and statistics are important for majors in psychology but not of particular use to students who will not pursue a major or minor in psychology. This is much too narrow a view. We are confronted daily with claims made by so-called experts and researchers in the social sciences that have important consequences for daily living. The citizen who can evaluate these claims is better able to separate good solutions from current fads. Some students also have misconceptions about how much mathematical training is needed to conduct or understand research in the social sciences. Statistics plays an important role in research, but it is not necessary to have a strong background in mathematics or statistics to evaluate or conduct psychological research. This text emphasizes the practical uses of statistics while keeping mathematical symbols to a minimum, in order to present statistical tests at a level that can be understood and used by students lacking a background in mathematics or statistics.

This edition uses the same basic format as previous editions, but a number of changes have been made to increase student appeal without sacrificing the breadth and depth of coverage attained in earlier editions. The changes include a much greater use of concrete, real life examples, the use of easier examples and problems, an increase in the number of problems and questions at the end of each chapter, and a change of emphasis in the earlier chapters from the philosophy of science to a rationale based on human bias in decision making. Students should find this edition more enjoyable, easier to read, and easier to understand.

A number of people contributed to the three editions of this text. Joyce Pennington, James V. Hindrichs, Eugene A. Lovelace, Terrence M. Allen, Christopher Hunter, Lynn Lloyd, Harold O. Kiess, Marian R. Ferguson, Jane E. Robbins, a number of anonymous reviewers, and several of my former students contributed to the first two editions. E. Eugene Schultz played an important role in the development of the Instructor's Manual for the third edition, and I am indebted to Raymond W. Frankmann, John Bull, Roland Siiter, and John Brockway for their numerous constructive criticisms that helped to shape the third edition. I would also like to thank Thomas C. Pavela, Barbara Sonnenschein, and Dana Norton for their help in carrying the third edition through to a successful conclusion.

I am indebted to the Literary Executor of the late Sir Ronald A. Fisher, F.R.S., to Dr. Frank Yates, F.R.S., and to Longman Group Ltd., London, for their permission to reprint material from Tables III and VI from their books *Statistical Methods for Research Workers* and *Statistical Tables for Biological, Agricultural and Medical Research*.

Contents

Fundamentals of Psychological Research

succeed at whatever they do. Motivation, not education, may be the important variable. Money might be responsible. Because well-educated people, as a group, make more money, it may be the availability of money that leads to fewer divorces. Couples who do not have to combat the frustrations of being poor may be happier and, as a result, satisfied with their marriage. Age could also be responsible. Since well-educated people are likely to marry at a later age, the divorce rate may be age-related. Perhaps well-educated people solve a number of their problems before getting married. In brief, we can take a simple relationship between two measures, a description, and then propose a number of plausible alternative explanations for the obtained relationship. If we can then rule out all explanations but one, we can be relatively confident that the phenomenon is explained, at least until we can develop additional plausible explanations.

Consider the phenomenon of individual differences in happiness. Some people report being happy; others indicate that they are sad, unable to control their fate, apprehensive about the future, and generally discouraged — in a word, depressed. What accounts for the fact that some people get depressed for long periods, say for a period of several months, and others have only temporary periods of depression (a day or less)? If we can account for depression (that is, individual differences in happiness) it may be possible to help depressed people. One possibility is that depressed people overreact. For example, a student may view a temporary setback (a low grade in a course) as being more important than it really is. Perhaps irrational thought patterns and a negative self-perception are responsible for depression (Beck, 1970, 1976). If we could train people to replace irrational thoughts with rational thoughts and develop a more realistic self-perception, perhaps they would no longer be depressed.

This sounds like a reasonable view and, indeed, Beck and his associates have obtained results that support the importance of thought patterns in depression. Another possibility is that depressed people have extremely accurate, perhaps too accurate, self-perceptions (Mischel, 1979). To test this possibility, Mischel had depressed and nondepressed people rate themselves. Other observers rated the behaviors of both the depressed and nondepressed participants. Although the depressed participants gave themselves lower ratings on social competency than the nondepressed, their ratings were more "realistic" than the self-ratings of the nondepressed. According to Mischel's report, depressed participants are more likely to have an accurate view of themselves than the nondepressed. The nondepressed see themselves as better than others see them. In Mischel's words, they have a "halo" or "illusory glow." As the depressed overcome their depression, they tend to rate themselves higher (Lewinsohn, Mischel, Chaplin, & Barton, 1980).

In a similar vein Myers and Ridl (1979) consider a number of research findings which support the view that most of us tend to be vain. We consider ourselves better than average. If we succeed we are likely to attribute our success to our ability and effort; if we fail we are likely to attribute the failure to bad luck or unavoidable circumstances. If we become angry, it is probably because of factors in the environment (an unreasonable college professor); if others become angry, we are more likely to view them as hotheads (Jones & Nisbett, 1972). Myers and Ridl indicate how we can demonstrate this bias. Simply ask a group of people to rate themselves anonymously in relation to their peers. Estimate, for example, the percentage of your classmates who are more honest than you are. If we compute an average for the class, the average estimate should be around 50 percent if each person's self-perception of honesty, in relation to classmates, is accurate. If the average estimate deviates considerably from 50 percent, it follows that the estimates are biased. If they are biased in the direction of an enhanced view of self, the average estimate should be below 50 percent.

Importance and Human Bias. The fact that nondepressed humans tend to judge themselves as better than average has important implications. One is that treatment for depressed people might be better directed toward more benign self-appraisal rather than realistic self-appraisal. Happiness may depend more on developing an "illusory glow" than on agreeing with the appraisals made by others. If we need to judge ourselves higher than others judge us to feel good, then there is little question that we should do so. Clearly, it is better to be happy and "out of step" with the views of others than to be depressed and "in step."

The above example also illustrates the point that there can be a number of plausible alternative explanations for a particular phenomenon, and it can make considerable difference which explanation is accepted. No claim is being made that the accuracy of self-perceptions accounts for all the phenomena of depression. The important point for our purposes is that one's explanation of a phenomenon and the course of action that results is frequently of great importance.

One reason for studying research methodology, then, is that we need to be able to describe and explain the relationships among events if we are to improve performance (for example, help people become happier). We need systematic procedures to avoid bias when evaluating alternative explanations for behavior and mental activity. If satisfactory personal adjustment requires that we maintain an "illusory glow," then obviously we do not want to eliminate this bias in our self-perceptions. However, human bias in reaching decisions about phenomena in the real world is not helpful because it may result in our selecting a plausible alternative explanation that is incorrect or not as useful as other explanations. We study research methodology to learn how to use procedures that allow us to avoid bias when deciding among alternative explanations. We can perhaps best appreciate the need for systematic procedures by pointing out some of the weaknesses of nonsystematic procedures.

Weaknesses of Nonresearch Approaches

Introspections and Self-Reports. The major reason for developing systematic procedures for describing events and evaluating plausible alternative explanations for phenomena is that our introspections, intuitions, and self-reports are subject to errors and biases. If we have an explanation for why a particular phenomenon occurs (such as why people become depressed) that differs from views held by others, we are likely to prefer our view whereas others prefer theirs. We are likely to believe that our intuitions are correct since, after all, we are above average and therefore more likely to be right than wrong. Intuitions, introspections, and self-reports would be useful if we all had the same intuitions, introspections, and self-reports, but it is clear that we do not. In cases such as depression, when the plausible alternative explanations have important implications for what should be done, we need some way of deciding whether an explanation is consistent with the facts.

Introspection is a label for the process of looking inward to examine our mental experiences (thought processes). Introspection has been used extensively by psychologists but, over the years, most psychologists have come to recognize the limitations of this approach. Introspections have not resulted in the accumulation of many interesting facts (Hebb, 1974). They are not useful for studying many aspects of mental activity because we can have mental activity in the absence of introspective knowledge of this process. Consider the tip-of-the-tongue phenomenon. You have undoubtedly had the frustrating experience of knowing you have information stored in memory, such as the name of an old friend, but being unable to retrieve the information. An hour or so after you give up in frustration, the name pops into your awareness. Why did the name pop into awareness? What mechanism made this possible? You do not have the foggiest notion, because you cannot turn your thoughts inward to examine these mental experiences.

Consider the accuracy of self-report statements. Do you know why you do the things you do? If you are asked to give reasons why you selected a particular college or dating partner, made particular purchases, or voted for a particular candidate, you will probably be able to do so. The question of interest is whether you know the *real* reasons. Do you give the real reasons or only those reasons you can think of? Typically, it is very difficult to evaluate the accuracy of our self-report statements because our thoughts, like our dreams, are private. However, we can compare the results of systematic procedures for evaluating the influence of a particular event with the self-reports of participants to assess whether the results are the same (Nisbett & Wilson, 1977).

Consider helping in a crisis. A number of different systematic investigations of helping behavior have revealed that the number of people who witness a crisis is an important consideration. We are more likely to intervene when we are the only bystander than when we are with other bystanders (Latané & Darley, 1970). For example, you are more likely to come to the aid of a stranded motorist on a deserted road than on a busy interstate. In brief, when we compare helping behavior in two situations, one bystander and more than one, we find that the number of bystanders influences helping behavior. If we also ask participants why they helped or failed to help, it is reasonable to expect some participants to mention that they felt responsible or did not feel responsible depending on whether they were the only bystander or with others. Nisbett and Wilson (1977) compared the results of self-reports with more systematic procedures and found little agreement with the results obtained from the two procedures. In a number of studies, not just studies of bystander apathy, there was little agreement between what participants considered important and what the objective measures indicated was important. Nisbett and Wilson concluded that the lack of agreement strongly suggests that self-report procedures are unlikely to tell us much about the factors that influence our decision making. At the very least, it is clear that systematic procedures yield different results from those obtained by self-report procedures. If we can demonstrate that humans have biases, then we have good reason to opt for systematic, objective procedures.

Intuitions and Biases. If we rely on our intuitions, unsystematic observations, or introspections we are likely to reach erroneous conclusions a good part of the time. As an extreme example, consider a problem taken from Anderson (1975). Imagine that you could take a large piece of paper which is .008 inches thick and fold it fifty times. Each successive fold doubles the thickness of the paper. The task is to estimate how high the paper will be after it has been folded fifty times. Make an estimate of the height before continuing. For people with considerable mathematical ability the problem may pose little or no challenge. However, those who dislike anything mathematical are left to their intuitions. Most people who rely on their intuitions make estimates of a few inches or perhaps a few feet. The height of the paper after fifty folds will be slightly more than 142,159,007 miles (that is, $H = .008 \times 2^{50}$). Our intuitions are of little use in some situations.

Imagine that we have a large urn filled with blue and green balls; 60 percent are blue and 40 percent are green. After each draw, the ball is returned to the urn and the balls are mixed before the next draw. If we play a game in which you try to predict which color ball will be drawn by some random procedure (for example, a blindfolded person selecting a ball), what strategy would you use? To make it more interesting imagine that you win a dollar every time you are correct and lose a dollar every time you are incorrect. Your best strategy would be to predict blue every time since the probability of winning is .60 when you select blue and only .40 when you select green. Some people select the optimal strategy, but many people predict blue about 60 percent of the time and green about 40 percent of the time. Why? There is no clear answer, but there are a number of possibilities.

One possibility is that many people have no understanding of probability and thus do not realize that they are more likely to lose than win every time they select the green ball. Or, more likely, they believe that they can detect a pattern in the draws. If blue has been selected for the last five times, they believe that green is long overdue, not realizing that there is no memory in the urn (each draw is an independent event). Another possibility is cognitive conceit, a discrepancy between what people actually know and what they think they know, so that they believe they know more than they know (Dawes, 1976). For this example, the participant may reason that because green has to be selected part of the time, the only way to obtain a perfect performance or near-perfect performance is to select green part of the time. They think that there is little reason to settle for 60 percent accuracy when it is possible to do better. They are conceited in that they believe they can do better than what one should expect solely on the basis of chance. After all, most of us believe that we are above average so *we* should be able to do better than chance. If we succeed we are likely to attribute it to our good judgment. If we fail, there is always bad luck.

Our view of the world influences the way we perceive it. We are more likely to note events that support our view of the world than events that contradict our view. Or it may be a memory phenomenon — we may be better able to remember events that support our position than events that do not (Tversky & Kahneman, 1973). Chapman and Chapman (1969) investigated whether we perceive events that are highly associated with each other as occurring more frequently than they actually do. If we do misperceive associated events, we are suffering from what the Chapmans label an illusory correlation: we see a relationship when, in fact, there is none.

The Chapmans used word association and draw-a-person techniques to assess whether we misperceive associated events. For the word association procedure, they asked participants to view word pairs (bacon-tiger, bacon-eggs, bacon-notebook) presented on a screen. Some of the pairs were related (bacon-eggs) and some were not (bacon-tiger). All word pairs were presented the same number of times. However, when asked to estimate the frequency of each pair, the participants substantially overestimated the related pairs. The Chapmans also demonstrated that the illusory correlation is of clinical significance in that we tend to see events that support our theories. They considered the relationship between our personality and the pictures we draw. If we are suspicious, will we draw people with big eyes? More important, if we believe suspicious people draw people with big eyes, will we see this in their drawings even though there actually is no such relationship? The Chapmans' research revealed that the answer is yes. The implications for research are clear and profound. We have a bias to maintain our theoretical views in the absence of supporting evidence, therefore we need systematic procedures to eliminate our personal biases from the decision-making process. Numerous other studies also support the view that we are biased decision makers (Wason, 1968).

Wason has demonstrated that we have a bias for positive instances. That is, we seek evidence to support (confirm) our views, not evidence to refute them. For example, people who believe in ESP, hypnosis, acupuncture, transcendental meditation, astrology, and so forth are likely to pay much attention to alleged positive instances and ignore negative instances. If you read your horoscope you are likely to find some truth in what you read. But, you are likely to read only your horoscope. If you were to read all the horoscopes, you would probably find some truth in each one of them. And, if all the horoscopes were mixed and the labels removed, it is unlikely that you would be able to select your horoscope. If people could find their own horoscope under these conditions there would be some reason to accept the view that one's birth date is important.

In sum, there is good reason to believe that we need to use systematic procedures for evaluating plausible alternative explanations for phenomena. If we are left to our own devices, we are likely to make mistakes. Although our well-being may depend on our maintaining a positive view of our abilities, it is likely that cognitive conceit is a hindrance to making decisions about the relative worth of plausible alternative explanations for phenomena. We need to replace our biases with systematic, objective procedures.

PLAUSIBLE ALTERNATIVE EXPLANATIONS

One of the basic points that we will stress throughout is that progress is made when we can propose plausible alternative explanations for phenomena, such as individual differences in happiness, and then evaluate the proposed explanations with systematic, objective procedures. Basically this is a simple notion. However, there are some complexities that arise when we consider criteria for plausible explanations and the systematic, objective procedures that we can use to evaluate our ideas. The alternatives that we propose are likely to be influenced by the positions we take on certain issues. One such issue is the relative importance of behaviorist versus cognitive approaches.

Behaviorism-Cognitivism Distinction

As there are numerous ways to view behavior and mental activity, it is not an easy matter for an investigator or student to decide which approach to select. We cannot make clear distinctions between cognitive and behaviorist approaches, but we can indicate some general ways in which the two approaches differ. Cognitive psychologists emphasize the individual whereas behaviorists emphasize the environment. Cognitive psychologists are more likely to be interested in thought processes, memory processes, decision making, and perception. Behaviorists are more likely to emphasize environmental control. For example, a behaviorist is likely to be interested in how our behavior relates to the reinforcements that we receive (the goodies of life). Thus, they study behavior by noting how environmental changes influence behavior. They are generally interested in the functional relationship between input and output variables. One can study the influence of drugs, therapies, instructional techniques, and so on without worrying about the internal state of the individual. Cognitive psychologists, on the other hand, are likely to maintain that many important aspects of behavior and mental activity (such as decision making, reading, dreaming) cannot be studied effectively without considering how humans process information.

Control. The issue of control is a basic one because it influences what you are likely to view as important and the procedures you will accept. If control is in the environment, then it is reasonable to establish the relationship between environmental influences and behavior. If control is in the individual, then one is more likely to emphasize human thought processes and the way information is represented in humans. Consider some examples.

A youngster shoots an elderly woman because, he argues, he was influenced by an episode on a television program. A rapist claims that he is not at fault because his victim was wearing a sexy dress; he could not control himself. A man stops at a bar, consumes four manhattans, and while driving home has a car accident in which three youngsters are killed. The man claims the bartender is at fault for allowing him to have four manhattans. A college student blames her parents for her inability to perform well in competitive situations; her parents were too permissive, giving her everything she wanted. Your willingness to accept such claims is likely to be a function of your view on the cognitivism-behaviorism continuum. If you believe that the environment is the important consideration, you are likely to be more accepting of the above accounts than if you stress the importance of cognitive factors.

Assumptions of Scientists. Our concern is not with legal responsibility, but, instead, with the likelihood that psychologists and other social scientists will be able to arrive at good explanations for behavior and mental activity. If control is in the environment, a reasonable strategy is to make systematic changes in the environment and then note changes, if any, in behavior. If you adopt such a view, you are also adopting, perhaps implicitly, the view that there is *order* or an overall pattern or scheme of events and that this order can be detected. The assumption that our behaviors have causes, determinants, or antecedents that can be detected is usually referred to as *determinism.* Individuals who take a behavioristic view are also likely to accept the importance of observations and experiments. People who insist that conclusions be based on observable, experimental results can be said to have adopted the assumption of *empiricism.* The assumption of empiricism implies

more than just using observable events to test plausible alternative explanations. The procedures used must be systematic and controlled. If we do not
make systematic observations, we are likely to be unduly influenced by our
own views.

What about the individual who adopts a cognitive view? If we stress the
importance of the individual, can we also adopt a systematic set of procedures
to test plausible explanations for phenomena? Although there are some exceptions, most psychologists who adopt a cognitive approach also accept the
assumptions of order, determinism, and empiricism. It is reasonable to emphasize the importance of the individual and still maintain that we can develop and test explanations for our behavior and mental activity. For example,
we can test explanations for how humans perceive (illusions, color vision,
hearing), code information (reading, use of images), remember (mnemonic
systems, retention of different kinds of information, failure of memory), and
use information (decision making, adjustment, inferences). Humans can be
viewed as complex information processors. In this view the problem is to
determine how information is processed. To find this out, we need to be able
to test plausible alternative explanations.

However, there are some psychologists who reject the view that it is useful
to propose and test alternative views of behavior and mental activity. According to this view, the individual has control, and, therefore, each individual
can do what he or she elects to do. Everyone has free will and can elect to
"grow" or not "grow." To be more specific, reconsider our earlier discussion
of depression. Clearly, there are individual differences in the extent to which
people are happy or sad. One approach is to maintain that the matter is in
the mind of each individual who chooses whether to be happy or sad, and
there is little that we can do to test different views of why people are happy
or depressed. On the other hand, we can maintain that depression and happiness are related to the accuracy of our self-perceptions. We can test this view
by noting any systematic relationship between accuracy of self-perceptions
and depression and, if one exists, take steps to see if we can eliminate depression by getting people to modify the way they perceive themselves.

The emphasis in this text is on the latter approach. We adopt this position
simply because there are so many instances of systematic relationships among
events (cognitions and depression, strategies and decision making, mnemonic
techniques and memory performance) that there is little doubt about the
feasibility of proposing and testing plausible alternative explanations for phenomena. Human behavior and mental activity are simply too important for
us to accept the very risky conclusion that we cannot develop procedures to
test plausible views of why we do what we do. Even if one does accept the
view that humans are free to do as they choose, it is clear that some have
more "freedom" than others or perceive that they have more than others.
How does one account for the fact that there are individual differences in

the amount of perceived control? Is perceived control related to what you tell yourself, your history of reinforcement, or what? We need to develop explanations for human behavior and mental activity, *and* we need to test them.

Theories

Plausible explanations are given a number of labels such as theories, ideas, views, models, notions, or hypotheses. Researchers tend to use words such as *idea, view, notion,* or *hypothesis* when they are attempting to account for a particular fact (such as the relationship between education and divorce rate) and the word *theory* when they are attempting to account for more complex phenomena. However, since all these words can refer to tentative explanations, you can expect to find them used interchangeably by some investigators.

Because our emphasis is on testing alternative explanations, any idea, view, notion, hypothesis, or theory that cannot be tested is of little use. Plausible alternatives are of importance because they guide research; we do research to test such explanations. They also enable us to organize facts. For example, the fact that most of us consider ourselves to be above average can be used to organize a number of facts, such as the relationship between depression and self-perception, attribution of success to ourselves and failures to the environment, and overprediction of high performance for self (Mischel, 1979; Myers & Ridl, 1979).

Simplicity and Generalizability

How complex do our explanations of behavior have to be? Most investigators prefer simple explanations over complex when both account equally well for the facts. They also prefer general explanations over explanations that are appropriate for only a very limited range of phenomena, but in many instances such explanations are not possible. If, for example, you study the effect of alcohol consumption on memory ability by performing an experiment with twenty college sophomores, you will like to be able to generalize your findings beyond the twenty students who actually participated. Imagine that you performed the experiment correctly and the results were clear. The students who consumed alcohol were not able to remember as well as students who did not consume alcohol. Can you say that this is a general finding, or must you limit your conclusions to the conditions of your study? If the findings apply only to low-anxiety, attractive college females, from upper-middle-class backgrounds with IQs greater than 125 who drink 3 ounces of gin at 9 A.M. on Tuesday, vote Republican, and so on, there is no way to arrive at a general understanding of the effects of alcohol on memory ability. In order to arrive at a general understanding of the relationships among events, we must be able to disregard most other variables (attractiveness, political party, IQ) when studying the effects of alcohol consumption on motor performance.

The extent to which generalization of research findings is possible depends, in part, on the research area considered. Investigators interested in physiological, perception, attention, and basic learning and memory phenomena usually do not have to be greatly concerned about the problem of generality. The phenomena that these investigators study are usually not affected by individual differences. For example, the visual system is pretty much the same for all people; differences in intelligence, beauty, socioeconomic status, personality, age, weight, and so on will not affect it. It is reasonable for these investigators to generalize their findings.

The situation appears to be considerably different for investigators interested in personality, social behavior, or instruction (see Cronbach, 1975). In these areas the effect of treatment manipulations frequently depends on the type of person participating in the experiment. For example, a new instructional technique may be effective for college students but not for high school students. The same treatment manipulation frequently produces different effects for different people. And it is usually difficult to predict an individual's behavior in a given situation unless a great deal is known about that individual. Thus, although simple theories are the goal of science, in general they do not account very well for personality, social behavior, or instructional effects. A simple theory that accounts for behavior studied under controlled conditions in the laboratory may fail to account for behavior observed in real life. Thus, investigators in these areas are usually much more cautious about generalizing their findings. They are more likely to view generalizations as assertions to be tested, not conclusions. Such investigators spend more of their experimental effort determining the generality of their findings.

Generating Explanations

Selecting a Problem Area. If you are curious, reasonably intelligent, independent, and highly motivated, you have the appropriate characteristics for research. For the most part, it is difficult to evaluate whether you have such characteristics until you have made a sincere effort to involve yourself in a research problem. Many apathetic, antiscientific individuals have developed a fondness for the scientific approach to problem solving. I suspect that most researchers were apathetic toward research until they became involved in *their* research. The first task for the experimenter is to select a problem.

How does one select a problem area for research? You need to decide what you find interesting and important. Research is no fun unless you are excited about what you are doing. The purpose of psychological research is to test ideas concerning behavior or mental activity. The individual who is interested in understanding why people become alcoholics does research on alcoholism; the individual interested in understanding the storage and re-trieval of information does research on memory process. The first important step, then, is for you to decide what interests you, be it personality, percep-tion, memory, decision making, therapy, or whatever. You may elect to do considerable reading before you select a problem area. Obviously, well-read people have an advantage because they are likely to be aware of more phenomena.

Generating Ideas. Once you select a problem *situation* of interest, you can consider the available plausible alternative explanations for the questions that interest you. There is little that we can say about this since there are so many prob-lem areas and questions of potential interest. Obviously the person interested in understanding sleep, for example, will ask very different questions, and, therefore, propose very different alternative explanations from the person interested in another problem area such as personality, memory, vision, or alcoholism. Clearly, the nature of the plausible explanations will depend on the phenomena investigators attempt to explain. Despite this diversity, how-ever, there are a number of aspects of generating and testing explanations that are shared by all investigators regardless of the area of interest. There is a basic methodology that transcends most, if not all, research areas in the social sciences and some areas beyond (medicine, epidemiology, education). In other words, the material in this text should be as useful to the person interested in studying personality or social psychology as it is for the person in-terested in studying memory processes or perception. Our basic concern will be in developing procedures to test ideas.

EVALUATING ALTERNATIVE EXPLANATIONS

Predictions About Observable Events

There are limits to the kinds of ideas that can be tested. We can say little about questions that are vaguely stated (How does the mind work? Does pornography influence the moral fiber of youths? Which therapy is best?) or explanations that do not lead to predictions about observable events. For example, we cannot test the view that smoking marijuana results in a poorly functioning brain. How do we determine when the brain is working well, and how do we tie a malfunctioning brain to a single antecedent such as smoking marijuana? We need to be more specific, and we have to deal with observable events. We could, for example, test whether smoking marijuana has an influence on our ability to memorize a list of words, perform a specific motor task such as riding a bicycle, or perform mental arithmetic problems. We could do this by comparing the performance of people who had smoked marijuana with an "equivalent" group of participants who had not. We test our ideas by making predictions about what people will do under certain circumstances, that is, predictions about observable behaviors.

Practical and Ethical Considerations

Practical constraints limit the ideas we can test and how we can test them. There are many practical constraints such as lack of facilities, money, or equipment. To study how mentally retarded children perform various tasks, you need to get the consent of parents, guardians, or institution officials. If you cannot get this approval, you will have to do something else. To test a program for treating alcoholics, it is best if you are able to determine who receives your treatment and who does not. If you do not have this authority, you will need to develop some other way of assessing the effectiveness of your program. In short, investigators have to recognize that there are a number of practical hurdles to overcome in testing ideas. A particularly sensitive consideration is ethical standards.

Ethics and the Use of Animals. Concern for the proper care and treatment of animals used in research is great. Researchers who use animals must be aware of the laws and guidelines for their care and handling. An investigator who plans to use animals should contact the local humane society and the American Humane Association, P.O. Box 1266, Denver, Colorado, 80201. The animal health regulations for each state can be obtained from the state public health office or state veterinarian. Another essential publication, available from the U.S. Department of Health and Human Services, is entitled *Guide for Laboratory Animal Facilities and Care.* Or the investigator can write to the American Psychological Association, Office of Scientific Affairs, 1200 Seventeenth Street, N.W., Washington, D.C., 20036, for the manual on the care of animals.

Additional regulations must be followed when laboratory animals are used by people not trained in their care and treatment. The American Psychological Association Committee on Precautions and Standards in Animal Experimentation has prepared guidelines on the use of animals in school science behavior projects. These are published in the *American Psychologist,* 1972, Volume 27, page 337. Although they were intended primarily for students in intermediate and secondary schools, they are also applicable to the use of animals by students in colleges and universities. The guidelines are briefly considered here, to give the reader an appreciation of the steps used to safeguard the welfare of animals.

The first four guidelines cover the proper planning and supervision of each project, the adherence to the laws of each state and to the recommendations of humane societies, and the use of small animals that are easy to maintain or of invertebrates whenever possible. The fifth guideline is that "No student shall undertake an experiment which includes the use of drugs, surgical procedures, noxious or painful stimuli such as electric shock, extreme temperature, starvation, malnutrition, ionizing radiation, etc. except under extremely close and rigorous supervision of a researcher qualified in the specific area of study." The purpose of this restriction is, of course, to ensure that there are sound reasons for any unusual treatment of animals. The sixth guideline directs researchers to make certain the animals receive proper housing, food, water, exercise, gentle handling, and so forth. It is crucial that arrangements be made for the care of the animals over vacation periods.

The seventh guideline concerns the disposition of animals at the conclusion of the experiment. Sometimes the animals are maintained as pets. In some cases they are selected so that their normal life span corresponds to the duration of the experiment. In other cases it is necessary to perform euthanasia, which should be carried out only by a trained person. In such cases, remember that most of the animals used in experiments are bred solely for the purpose of research; they would not exist otherwise.

Ethics and the Use of Human Subjects. The task of determining ethical standards governing the use of human subjects is an immense undertaking. There are so many kinds of research projects involving human subjects and so many opinions on how the rights of these participants should be protected that it is difficult to arrive at a set of principles to which all researchers can subscribe. In spite of the difficulty, the American Psychological Association appointed a Committee on Ethical Standards in Psychological Research to revise the association's 1953 code of ethics for research using human subjects. The standards that were eventually adopted were published by the American Psychological Association in 1973. The list of ethical principles is as follows:

The Ethical Principles in the Conduct of Research with Human Participants*

1. In planning a study the investigator has the personal responsibility to make a careful evaluation of its ethical acceptability, taking into account these Principles for research with human beings. To the extent that this appraisal, weighing scientific and humane values, suggests a deviation from any Principle, the investigator incurs an increasingly serious obligation to seek ethical advice and to observe more stringent safeguards to protect the rights of the human research participant.

* The principles shown above were written by the Committee on Ethical Standards in Psychological Research. Copyright 1973 by the American Psychological Association, reprinted by permission.

The final version of the committee report, entitled *Ethical Principles in the Conduct of Research with Human Participants,* has been published by the American Psychological Association (1200 Seventeenth Street, N.W., Washington, D.C. 20036) in booklet form. The booklet offers a detailed discussion of each principle, to help the reader place the issues in context. I would encourage all who plan to use human subjects in research to obtain a copy of this report.

2. Responsibility for the establishment and maintenance of acceptable ethical practice in research always remains with the individual investigator. The investigator is also responsible for the ethical treatment of research participants by collaborators, assistants, students and employees, all of whom, however, incur parallel obligations.

3. Ethical practice requires the investigator to inform the participant of all features of the research that reasonably might be expected to influence willingness to participate and to explain all other aspects of the research about which the participant inquires. Failure to make full disclosure gives added emphasis to the investigator's responsibility to protect the welfare and dignity of the research participant.

4. Openness and honesty are essential characteristics of the relationship between investigator and research participant. When the methodological requirements of a study necessitate concealment or deception, the investigator is required to ensure the participant's understanding of the reasons for his action and to restore the quality of the relationship with the investigator.

5. Ethical research practice requires the investigator to respect the individual's freedom to decline to participate in research or to discontinue participation at any time. The obligation to protect this freedom requires special vigilance when the investigator is in a position of power over the participant. The decision to limit this freedom increases the investigator's responsibility to protect the participant's dignity and welfare.

6. Ethically acceptable research begins with the establishment of a clear and fair agreement between the investigator and the research participant that clarifies the responsibilities of each. The investigator has the obligation to honor all promises and commitments included in that agreement.

7. The ethical investigator protects participants from physical and mental discomfort, harm and danger. If the risk of such consequences exists, the investigator is required to inform the participant of that fact, to secure consent before proceeding, and to take all possible measures to minimize distress. A research procedure may not be used if it is likely to cause serious and lasting harm to participants.

8. After the data are collected, ethical practice requires the investigator to provide the participant with a full clarification of the nature of the study and to remove any misconceptions that may have arisen. Where scientific or humane values justify delaying or withholding information, the investigator acquires a special responsibility to assure that there are no damaging consequences for the participant.

9. Where research procedures may result in undesirable consequences for the participant, the investigator has the responsibility to detect and remove or correct these consequences, including, where relevant, long-term after-effects.

10. Information obtained about the research participants during the course of an investigation is confidential. When the possibility exists that others may obtain access to such information, ethical research practice requires that this possibility, together with the plans for protecting confidentiality, be explained to the participants as a part of the procedure for obtaining informed consent.

Note that informed consent is the basic notion embodied in these ethical principles. The investigator has an obligation to inform the potential subject of all the features of the experiment that can reasonably be expected to influence the subject's willingness to participate. If this is impossible, then the investigator must take additional steps to ensure that the rights of the subject are not violated.

The Stuart W. Cook Committee, the group responsible for drafting the ethical principles, invited thousands of researchers to list incidents of research involving ethical issues. Some of the incidents were reported in the special issue of the *Monitor* (May 1972) in which the second draft of the standards was presented and discussed. To give you an appreciation of some of the ethical problems researchers may confront, a number of these incidents have been paraphrased in the list that follows:

Examples of Research Involving Ethical Issues*

1. An investigator is interested in the effect of manipulating the level of initial self-esteem. The proposed research would involve having two people compete for the attention of a member of the opposite sex. The experimenter would arrange the situation in such a way that one competitor would experience an embarrassing defeat while the other would be victorious. In this case there is no way to inform the subjects about the factors that may influence their willingness to participate and still make the desired manipulation. Is it possible to do this research without violating the ethical standards?

2. An investigator observes people in situations in which they do not know they are being observed. A cost-benefit rationale is offered for the invasion of privacy. The value of the findings is weighed against the possible harm to the subjects (e.g., the extent to which their privacy is violated). In cases in which the investigator has any misgivings about the ethical issue, a decision is made not to conduct the research. Furthermore, the investigator consults his colleagues before starting any research of this nature and weighs their views in arriving at a decision. The plan is to inform the subjects in full about the nature of the experiment after it is completed. If the subjects object to the study or to aspects of it, the investigator would not publish the results. Is research of this nature ethical? Are there some situations in which it would be ethical and others in which it would be unethical?

3. An investigator who was studying procedures for reducing fear of snakes had his graduate students telephone undergraduates to determine their willingness to participate. The investigator was unaware that the graduate students told the undergraduates they had to participate. What standards are violated?

4. The subjects were informed correctly regarding the basic procedures that would be used, but they were misinformed about the purpose of the experiment. They were told the experiment was designed to test the speed of

* Selected and adapted from the Special Issue of The American Psychological Association *Monitor* (May 1972).

the visual system. Actually, the experimenter was interested in testing long-term memory. The subjects were not told the real purpose because the investigator was afraid this knowledge would influence their performance. The experimenter reasoned that a subject who would participate for the stated reason would also participate for the real reason. Is this an acceptable procedure?

5. A doctoral student was interested in factors influencing cheating. The doctoral student administered an examination, collected the papers, and then photographed each one. The students were not informed about the photographing. The papers were returned unscored and the students were given the opportunity to cheat while scoring their papers. The papers were collected again and were compared with the photographs. Is this an ethical procedure?

6. A professor of psychology worked on the production line in a factory for one semester. He did not reveal his identity to his coworkers or his reasons for being there. His purpose was to study the interactions of his coworkers. The findings proved to be useful in his subsequent teaching and research. His coworkers, some of whom he became very close to, were not informed of his purpose until the observation session was completed. Is this type of data collection ethical?

7. An experimenter returned fake test scores to male college students in order to assess the effects of success and failure on a second task. The subjects were told that the test scores were related to IQ and grade point average. After the second test, the subjects were told that the scores were faked and why the false information was given. The entire experiment was executed in a single session so that any fears the subjects had could be quickly alleviated. Is this an acceptable procedure?

8. A kidney patient and his nearest relative were asked to consent to having the patient take some tests to determine cognitive functioning before and after hemodialysis. The investigators were interested in the effects of uremia on cognitive functioning. In this case there is some question whether the patient was coerced into participating since his life depended on his remaining in the program. Did the patient have a real choice? Is the procedure ethical?

9. An experiment was conducted to assess driver reaction to a stressful situation. The subject was asked to drive a car past a construction site. The experimenter rigged a human-looking dummy in such a way that it would be propelled in front of the car making it impossible for the subject to avoid it. The subjects reacted as one would expect. And, when they learned that the situation was rigged, they informed the experimenter of their displeasure. Despite their complaints, the experimenter continued testing subjects. Is this procedure ethical?

10. An investigator was interested in how children would perform a task after watching another child being punished for low performance in the task. The question of interest was whether observing a punishment scene would raise or lower the children's subsequent performance relative to children who did not observe punishment. The children were tested in pairs. The first member of each pair received a scolding for low performance. The child's task

was to drop marbles through holes. Even though the children were doing their best, they were scolded for low performance for approximately three minutes of the six-minute session. It was clear to the experimenter that most of the children were very anxious. After the session was over, the experimenter explained that he was only fooling and praised each child extensively. Most of the children seemed to understand. Is it ethical to use psychological torment in research?

11. An investigator, who was using Galvanic Skin Responding procedures, had a subject become extremely upset during a testing session. The eight-year-old subject discontinued the experiment and went home. The experimenter was unaware of the subject's reason for leaving. Later, it was determined that the subject thought that blood was being extracted from his body since the electrode wires had a red plastic covering and red ink was used in the recording pens. Was the experimenter's behavior unethical?

12. The respondents to a mailed questionnaire were told that they would not be identified with their responses. A self-addressed return envelope was included for the "convenience" of the responder. The type and location of the stamp were such that the investigator could identify 100 of the respondents to the questionnaire. Is this procedure unethical?

13. An investigator conducted a series of interviews with patients in a state mental institution. The investigator assured each patient that the taped interviews would not be heard by anyone but the other member of the research team. Under these circumstances many of the patients gave extremely candid responses. For the purpose of discussion, assume that one patient indicated a strong desire to escape from the institution for the purpose of committing sexual offenses on young children. What would you do if you were the investigator?

You can decide whether or not each of the above incidents violates the adopted standards presented in the ethical principles list. It should be kept in mind that researchers were specifically asked to provide examples of research involving ethical questions. The incidents presented are not representative of the research problems encountered by the "typical" investigator. You may want to have additional information before evaluating some of the incidents. Indeed, an important aspect of evaluation is deciding what additional information, if any, is needed.

A consideration of the list of ethical principles and the list of examples of ethical issues should provide you with an awareness of some of the ethical problems that may be raised by research. If a proposed project is in violation of these ethical standards, the investigator must either abandon the project or change it to eliminate unethical procedures. In some cases there is likely to be disagreement about whether a research project is in violation of the standards. For instance, there will probably be disagreement over whether some of the incidents described in the examples of ethical issues should be placed in the unethical or ethical category. In some of these cases it is likely that procedural changes could be made to eliminate the ethical problem.

If there is considerable difference of opinion about whether a particular procedure is in violation of the ethical standards and there is no change that can be made to eliminate the ethical problem, then the investigator is well advised to abandon the project. Fortunately, the vast majority of research projects do not pose serious ethical problems. Of course, this does not mean that ethical considerations can be taken lightly. Every investigator should evaluate his procedures carefully to determine whether they conform to the ethical standards.

MEASUREMENT

The Importance of Measurement

Measurement is the use of rules to assign numbers to properties of objects or events. The particular rules used determine the level of measurement that is obtained and, consequently, the operations that can be performed. We could, for example, assign numbers to people to indicate our assessment of their aggressiveness, using 10 for the most aggressive and 1 for the least aggressive, and the numbers 2 through 9 for intermediate levels. Or we could administer an IQ test and assign a number to each participant on the basis of his or her obtained score. In both cases we are using rules to assign numbers to people, but the rules differ. (The consequences of using different rules are discussed in Chapter 8.)

What are the advantages of using rules to assign numbers to properties of objects or events? One advantage is description. In describing aggressiveness, for example, it is easier to use numbers than to say "We have one extremely timid person, one mildly timid, two mildly assertive, four very assertive, four aggressive, and one who is obnoxiously aggressive." It is difficult to compare groups when you use verbal labels and relatively easy when you use numbers. In brief, the advantages of measurement are objectivity, comparability, and ease of communication. There is usually no problem in agreement or communication when performance is described in terms of a score (a number) on some task or test. We can be objective because the procedure for determining the number is specified, as in IQ testing, for example. We can compare the performance of individuals, and we can be clear about what the numbers indicate; that is, we can give the rule we used for assigning the number. In the final analysis, the advantage of a specific measurement depends on the rule that is used to assign numbers to objects or events. Some rules may help an investigator to understand a phenomenon and some may not. The usefulness of a rule for assigning numbers to objects or events depends on the *reliability* and *validity* of the measuring instrument (that is, the procedures or rules used to assign the numbers).

Reliability

It is useful to have a concrete example for discussing aspects of reliability and validity, so imagine that in a few years from now you find yourself in charge of admissions at a small, exclusive, liberal arts college. Our interest is in how you might select 25 students for the freshman class from a pool of 100 applicants. There are a number of possibilities, but we will consider only three: personal interviews, high school grades, and scores on the Scholastic Aptitude Test (SAT). Our first concern is the reliability of the three measures, that is, their precision or consistency. Later (Chapter 6) we will develop a precision view of reliability; here we will restrict ourselves to the notion of consistency. Our basic interest is in whether repeated measures give consistent results.

To obtain consistent measures, the property of the object or event we are interested in and our procedures for obtaining the measure (the rule we use to apply numbers to properties of objects or events) must be stable. If scholastic ability is a stable characteristic and the SAT is a reliable way of assessing it, a person who does well on the SAT is likely to do well if tested a second time; a person who does poorly the first time is likely to do poorly the second time. Thus, one way of assessing reliability is to obtain two or more separate measures on different occasions. If the participants obtain about the same score on each testing, it is reasonable to conclude that the testing instrument is reliable. Or, if all the items of a test are designed to measure a single ability and the ability is believed to be stable, we could separate the odd-numbered items and the even-numbered items to get two scores. If the test is reliable, people who score well on the odd-numbered items should also do well on the even-numbered items; those who do poorly on the odd-numbered items should do poorly on the even-numbered items. We could also assess the reliability of judges. If two judges interview each applicant and decide, independently, who should be accepted or rejected, we could compare their decisions. The extent to which they agree determines the reliability of their judgments.

Back to your role as the admissions director. We cannot assess the reliability of high school grades because this measure is only obtained once. However, your decisions will be consistent if you base them solely on high school grade point average (that is, admit the 25 applicants with the highest grade point average), provided there are no clerical errors. There should also be perfect reliability (consistency) between your decisions and those of anyone else who uses grade point average as the sole criterion for admission. Similarly, if you decide to rely solely on the SAT scores, you or any other judge should obtain the same results. In the case of SAT scores, however, it is possible to have more than one score for each student (students can retake the test). Therefore, we can test the reliability of SAT scores.

If each applicant was required to provide two SAT scores, you could base your decision on either the first or second score. Would you reach the same conclusions in both cases? The answer depends on the reliability of the SAT. If students obtain about the same score when they retake the test (that is, the test is reliable), you will make "substantially" the same decisions in both cases. If the SAT is not reliable, your decisions will be largely determined by which scores (first or second set) you elect to use. In actuality there is some debate about the reliability of the SAT. Some people (see Rice, 1979) have argued that special training can increase SAT scores whereas the Educational Testing Service maintains that a student who takes a special course designed to increase his or her SAT score is wasting both time and money. Obviously, the reliability of the test is an important consideration since it is frequently one of the criteria used for admission decisions.

Now consider the reliability of interviews. If all students are interviewed twice, an admissions decision could be based on each interview. Would the same decision be reached in each case? In this instance reliability should depend on a number of factors such as carryover effects from the first to the second interview (biases from the first carrying over to the second), who conducts each interview, whether the same questions are asked in each interview, whether the applicant acts differently during the two interviews, and so on. With a well-structured interview technique, reliable measures can be obtained, but, in general, it is fair to conclude that interviews are less reliable than more structured situations such as the SAT, particularly if different interviewers are used. Even if only one interviewer is used, it is difficult for the interviewer to treat each applicant the same. Interviewers typically have biases and the opportunity to use their "clinical" judgment during the interview. Consequently, it is not always clear what rules are used to assign numbers to the persons being interviewed.

Validity

We like to believe that we are consistent, not wishy-washy. If we make an important decision, we like to believe that it was based on more than just a momentary whim. Fortunately, we are able to assess our degree of consistency in cases in which we use measurement by making repeated measurements, comparing the decisions of different judges, and so on. However, reliability is only half the story. A measure could have perfect reliability and be useless for helping us understand behavior and mental ability. For example, we could obtain reliable measures for skull size, but if this measure is not related to anything else (such as academic performance), it is not a very useful measure. Usually, the measurement problem is of special difficulty for psychologists and other social scientists because of their interest in abilities and characteristics that cannot be directly measured, such as creativity, intelligence, altruism, and self-esteem. Thus, in addition to the problem of consistency (reliability), one typically has to deal with the question of validity, whether a measuring instrument or procedure measures what it intends to measure. We will consider three types of validity: content, predictive, and construct. All three types deal with the usefulness of measurement.

Content Validity. Content validity refers to the representativeness of the items of the measuring instrument. It is of considerable concern for instructors who prepare examinations and for the students who take them. You expect the questions on examinations to be representative of the assigned material, but, on some occasions at least, you are likely to be disappointed (angry?). The representativeness of items is a subjective matter.

Consider using high school grades, SAT scores, and interviews for making admissions decisions. Which procedure has the highest content validity? The answer depends on a number of considerations such as the specific courses the applicant took in high school (for example, "Mickey Mouse" courses or challenging courses), the type of institution the applicant is applying to, the quality of the high school curriculum, and, of course, the type of interview. If you are seeking admission to an institution or applying for a job and the interviewer asks you about the intimate details of your personal life or other matters unrelated to your ability to succeed, the interview can be said to lack content validity. It is not likely to have predictive validity either.

Predictive Validity. Predictive validity is similar to content validity; both tell us whether a test or other selection device measures what it is supposed to measure. They are determined by different procedures, however. Content validity involves a subjective judgment in most cases whereas predictive validity is determined by comparing the results of a test or selection device (such as an interview) with an external *criterion* or standard. For this reason predictive validity is sometimes called criterion-related validity. When we use high school grades, SAT scores, or interviews to select applicants for admission to a particular institution or to determine who should be given a particular job or award, we are making a prediction. We predict or expect that the people selected will do better than those who are rejected. In many instances there is no assessment of predictive validity because those who are rejected are denied the opportunity. There is no way of knowing whether they would have succeeded if given the chance. In a number of other cases, however, investigators have examined the predictive validity of different selection procedures. In particular, they have assessed how students should be selected for graduate school to ensure that the most qualified applicants are accepted. The central issue has been the relative merit of clinical versus statistical prediction.

As the admissions director of a small, exclusive, liberal arts college, you know that only a portion of the students who are accepted make it through the program. Your task is to select the students who are most likely to succeed. How do you do it? Would it be better to use a straightforward statistical procedure in which you obtain a number for each applicant by considering high school grades and SAT scores? Or should you elect to use a clinical approach in which you look at the courses taken in high school, the grades received, letters of recommendation, outside interests of the applicant, and so on? In this case you make an overall judgment based on the information you have available. You may decide, for example, that grade point average is important only when motivation is high.

Dawes (1976, 1979) has compared clinical and statistical procedures for graduate admissions by examining a number of studies. The question is one of predictive validity. Which procedure best predicts grades in graduate school, number of research articles published, number of years taken to finish graduate school, and so on. These are criteria that can be used to compare the effectiveness of clinical and statistical procedures. If the same information is available for clinical and statistical procedures, there is good support for the superiority of statistical procedures. That is, you are more likely to select applicants who will succeed (get high grades, publish articles) if you use statistical procedures. Statistical procedures appear to have higher predictive validity than clinical procedures. Why? A statistical procedure is certain to be consistent, but we are not, particularly when we have to judge hundreds of applicants. It also appears that we use relatively simple rules in making decisions that can be better obtained by using a simple formula. Although we are likely to consider a formula "dehumanizing," this is only because we think we can do better (Dawes, 1976). Perhaps what we have is merely another instance of cognitive conceit.

Construct Validity. A construct is a concept that has been invented to account for individual differences in behavior or for the reason for differences in performance. Investigators interested in construct validation assume that individuals possess stable characteristics that can be measured and used to account for performance in a number of situations. Testing a theory and validating a construct are the same except that construct validation involves testing a particular kind of theory, a theory about why individuals behave differently.

Scholastic aptitude is a construct. The logic behind the test is that there are stable individual differences in scholastic aptitude that can be reliably assessed and that predict future performance in situations that require this ability. We can consider the predictive ability of such a test, but we can also consider whether this construct allows us to account for why people differ. Psychologists have postulated a number of constructs to explain why we differ in performance, such as self-esteem, intelligence, creativity, altruism, and achievement motivation. The difficult task is to develop measures for these constructs which have reliability and construct validity.

SUMMARY

The basic rationale for studying research methodology is that we need procedures to evaluate plausible alternative explanations for behavior and mental activity. Research methodology provides a way to obtain answers to important questions that influence our daily lives, have the potential for influencing our daily lives, or pique our curiosity. We need systematic procedures because our intuitions, unsystematic observations, and biases are not satisfactory means for selecting from among plausible alternative explanations. The typical procedure is to describe a phenomenon, propose alternative explanations for it, and then use systematic procedures to test these explanations.

Introspection is a label for the process of looking inward to examine our mental experiences (thought processes). It is not useful for studying many aspects of mental activity because we can have mental activity in the absence of introspective knowledge. The self-reports we give for behaviors do not necessarily agree with the results obtained with more systematic procedures, which suggests at the very least the need for both procedures. The fact that we have many biases that influence our judgments strongly suggests that we need to rely on systematic procedures for evaluating alternative plausible explanations. What we believe influences what we perceive.

One of the basic considerations that influences the explanations that are likely to be proposed is the relative importance of environmental and individual influences. Cognitive psychologists emphasize the individual and behavorists emphasize the environment. Behaviorists and most cognitive psychologists are likely to accept the assumptions of determinism (events have causes that can be detected), order, and empiricism, and they are likely to prefer simple over complex explanations.

There is little that can be said about generating explanations because the process depends on so many considerations (motivation, interests, assumptions). Clearly, it is very important to select problems that you find interesting. There are limits to the kinds of explanations that we can test. To be testable, ideas must be clearly stated, ethical, and lead to predictions about observable events. The basic principle underlying the ethical principles for conducting research is informed consent.

Measurement is the use of rules to assign numbers to properties of objects or events. The advantages of measurement are objectivity, comparability, and ease of communication. To be useful, measures should be reliable and valid. Reliability refers to the consistency of measurement. Content validity refers to the representativeness of the items of the measuring instrument or selection procedures. Predictive validity refers to whether a test or other instrument can be used to predict performance on an external criterion (for example, SAT scores have predictive validity if they predict college grades). Construct validity refers to whether a postulated characteristic or ability (creativity, altruism, intelligence) enables us to account for individual differences in performance.

QUESTIONS

(Answers for the multiple choice questions are given in Appendix D on page 350.)

1. What aspects of behavior and mental activity would you like to know more about? That is, what questions, if answered, would have an influence on your daily life, have the potential for influencing your daily life, or pique your curiosity?
2. Why do we need to develop procedures for evaluating plausible alternative solutions?
3. The usual procedure for studying behavior and mental activity is to describe a phenomenon and then attempt to explain it. Why?
4. What are some of the implications for research methods of the finding that humans tend to judge themselves as better than average?
5. What evidence suggests that our world view influences the way we perceive the world?
6. What is the behaviorism-cognitivism distinction? Why is this distinction important?
7. What are the assumptions of determinism and empiricism?
8. Why are plausible alternative explanations (theories, ideas, notions, models, hypotheses) important for understanding behavior and mental activity?
9. Evaluate each of the examples of ethical issues on page 19 in terms of the ethical principles listed on page 17.
10. A social psychologist is interested in bystander apathy. Her research plan involves having confederates fake heart attacks in different locations (classroom, subway, street, church) while wearing different "disguises" (well dressed, poorly dressed). She wants to measure the likelihood that bystanders will come to the aid of the "victim." What are the ethical considerations? Can research of this nature be performed without violating the ethical standards?
11. What is measurement and why is it important?
12. What is reliability and how can it be assessed?
13. Why is reliability a precondition for validity?
14. Distinguish among content, predictive, and construct validity.
15. _____ is the use of rules to assign numbers to the properties of objects or events. (1) Reliability (2) Validity (3) Instrumentation (4) Measurement
16. The view that a particular event is caused by other events is an assumption of the scientific approach. This assumption is known as (1) operationism (2) parsimony (3) order (4) determinism (5) empiricism
17. The two important functions of theory are to (1) retain good solutions and reject poor solutions (2) minimize chance factors and organize facts

(3) maximize chance factors and reject poor solutions   (4) guide research and organize facts

18. The basic notion embodied in the ethical principles in the conduct of research with human participants is   (1) the end must justify the means   (2) informed consent   (3) professional judgment   (4) scientific importance takes precedence over ethical considerations

19. Scores are considered valid when they are   (1) dependable   (2) reproducible   (3) consistent over a period of time   (4) measuring what they are supposed to measure

20. An investigator who is interested in testing a theory to explain why individuals perform differently would most likely be interested in   (1) construct validity   (2) reliability   (3) content validity   (4) predictive validity

21. The view that ideas should be evaluated by making systematic, controlled observations is known as the assumption of   (1) parsimony   (2) operationism   (3) empiricism   (4) determinism

 **Methods of research**

To understand, evaluate, and conduct research, we need a good grasp of research methods. Casual reading in psychological journals may lead you to conclude that learning methodology is a gigantic task. Fortunately, however, social scientists use primarily only four basic methods to conduct their thousands of investigations of behavior and mental activity. The conclusions that can be drawn from research findings depend on the method used. A knowledge of these four approaches — observation, correlation, experimentation, and quasi-experimentation — provides a good foundation for understanding and evaluating research.

THE OBSERVATIONAL APPROACH

We are interested in making observations that will enable us to describe and understand behaviors and mental activities which we consider interesting and important. Observations play an important role in all the methods we consider because, as you will remember, we can test only explanations that yield predictions about observable events. The observational approach is not a distinct method; it is the basis for all the methods as well as a potential starting point for generating plausible alternative explanations.

The Observer

How do we observe brain activity, physiological activity during sleep, eye movements of infants and adults, parent-child interactions, or measure intelligence, anxiety, self-esteem, and shyness? Typically, we use special equipment (videotape machines, computers, microelectrodes) or develop special assessment techniques that allow us to infer a particular process or activity. There are many observations that we are unable to make with our unaided senses. However, in the final analysis, it is the human observer who evaluates observations even though elaborate equipment may have been used to obtain the measures. And in many instances, particularly in our daily observations of behavior, we do not use special equipment. Humans decide what observations to make and, once they are made, how the observations are to be interpreted. Thus, the strengths and weaknesses of humans as observers are important irrespective of how observations are made.

As we have already noted, humans are biased observers. We are selective in the information we process and it is therefore not uncommon for untrained observers of the same event to disagree about what happened. Imagine that during one of your classes two students, a male and a female, enter the classroom, go to the front of the class, and proceed to have a heated argument about each other's integrity, commitment, and sexual preferences. Class is disrupted while everyone witnesses this scene. After a few minutes, the professor asks the intruders to leave and then asks the class to write down everything that happened, including a description of the two intruders. Will you agree with your fellow students concerning the descriptions and what transpired? Not likely. Fortunately, it is possible to obtain reliable observations by deciding, in advance, what behaviors are to be observed and training observers to respond to the appropriate features of the situation.

We can view our biases and our selectivity as weaknesses, perhaps, in that they may prevent us from recording what actually takes place, but we would certainly not want to trade our abilities — biased though they are — for those of a television camera or computer. Our selectivity is a positive feature in that we can attend to only those behaviors of interest (creativity, aggression, gestures). A tape recorder, television camera, or computer cannot be programmed to record only creative, aggressive, or gestural behaviors. The final goal is to understand behavior and mental activity. Our selectivity and biases make it possible for us to interpret what we observe and offer explanations for our observations. Selectivity and biases are the grist for developing explanations that we will subsequently be able to test.

Unrestricted-Restricted Distinction

Observations can be the source of ideas as well as the means of testing ideas. We can distinguish between broad, unrestricted observations made with few, if any, preconceptions about what is important and more restricted observations used to test notions that we have about behavior and mental activity. To illustrate, imagine that you are observing young children playing; you note that males appear to be bigger risk takers than females. Males are more likely to play with sticks, climb trees, fight, and so on. This can be labeled an unrestricted observation since you had no intention, at the outset, of looking for sex differences in risk taking in young children; the notion came to you while you were observing children playing. If you are curious, you might wonder whether the sex difference you noted is a general phenomenon or limited to the one situation that you observed. It is possible that you just happened to observe some boys who were high risk takers. Or perhaps your biases, in this case a belief that boys are more aggressive, resulted in your seeing more risk taking for boys than for girls when, in fact, girls take as many risks as boys. To test your notion about risk taking, it is necessary to make more systematic, restricted observations.

One way to test your view would be to specify what you mean by risk taking in terms of behaviors that can be observed. Dueling with sticks, jumping out of trees, throwing hard objects, fighting, and so on might be behaviors that you classify as risk taking. You could then have judges who do not know your hypothesis about sex differences in risk taking observe different groups of children playing. The judges are to record instances of risk-taking behavior for each child. After you obtain this information, you can note whether restricted observations also reveal a sex difference in risk taking. Other observations are also possible. If boys are bigger risk takers than girls, we might expect that they would have more accidents. You can check accident rates (a restricted observation) to determine whether there are sex differences. If you do, you will find, among other things, that the likelihood of a young boy being killed in an accident is at least four times greater than the likelihood of a young girl being killed in an accident. Since you now have a phenomenon — sex differences in accident rates or risk taking in young children — you can consider explanations for it. Are males bigger risk takers than females regardless of how parents and others treat them? Or is the sex difference a result of parents' being more protective of their female than of their male offspring? How might you answer this question?

Another aspect of the restricted-unrestricted distinction is that we may reach the wrong conclusion because our observations are too restricted. To illustrate, imagine that you are a visitor from outer space interested in studying aggressive behavior, particularly murder, in humans. You select a street corner in a large city and observe the behavior of humans there. What is the likelihood that you will witness a murder? Despite what you may think about the amount of violence in some cities, it is highly unlikely that you will witness a murder. Thus, you are likely to go back to your planet convinced, based on your limited observations, that humans are a rather nonaggressive species. We know this is a false conclusion, of course, because we are privy to many other sources of information which reveal that humans can be very aggressive; numerous homicides are reported each year.

We know that humans are aggressive, but what about other species? Do chimpanzees commit murder, start "wars," or engage in organized killings of any sort? How would you find out? Chimpanzees do not publish accounts of aggressive acts in newspapers or report on the evening news who was killed by whom. Thus, if we want to study aggression in chimpanzees, we have to rely on our own observations of their behavior. Are we in a situation similar to that of the visitor from outer space?

In general, our observations tend to be restricted. We are not able to witness many acts of violence in humans or animals simply because, in comparison with all other behaviors that occur, violent acts such as murder are infrequent. Thus, to determine whether some behaviors occur, it may be necessary to be very patient and observe behavior over a long interval. When this is done, the likelihood of detecting unusual behaviors should increase. For example, in the case of aggression in chimpanzees, Goodall (1978) has observed "warfare" among chimpanzees; one colony of chimpanzees attacked and killed another group of male chimpanzees. The methodological point of interest is that Goodall spent considerable time among the chimpanzees before observing this particular behavior. Her patience and unrestricted observations enabled her to observe an infrequent but extremely important behavior in intraspecies warfare. Clearly, our view of the innateness of human aggression is likely to depend on whether intraspecies warfare in nonhumans occurs.

Reactive-Nonreactive Distinction

Is your behavior influenced by your awareness that others are observing you? It is likely that you can think of a number of behaviors that you might perform in private but not in public. Our behavior is also often influenced by whom we are with. Frequently our behavior with close friends is different from our behavior with strangers. It is reasonable to expect, therefore, that participants will perform differently when they are being observed by psychologists or other social scientists than when they are not being observed. From the point of view of the social scientist, then, it is important to know what effect the *measurement process* (for example, awareness of being observed) has on the behavior or mental activity being observed. If the measurement process influences the behavior or mental activity of the participant, we say that a reactive measure is obtained. If it does not, we say that a nonreactive measure has been obtained.

Personality, intelligence, and aptitude tests are clear examples of reactive measures. Since the participants are aware that their behavior is being assessed, they attempt to do as well as possible. Reactive measures are very important because in most instances (such as in assessing memory ability) useful measures simply cannot be obtained unless you have the cooperation of the participant. But, if you are concerned that participants will not give candid responses when they know they are being tested, you may elect to use nonreactive measures.

A nonreactive measure is obtained if the participants do not realize that they are being observed or assessed in any way. An entertaining book by

Webb, Campbell, Schwartz, and Sechrest (1966) is a good source of information on nonreactive measures. It contains numerous examples of how such measures can be used for research in the social sciences. For example, alcohol consumption can be measured by counting the number of alcohol bottles in the garbage. Obviously, any form of bugging device, if undetected, would provide a nonreactive measure.

At the extremes, it is easy to list examples of reactive (intelligence tests) and nonreactive measures (counting beer cans in the garbage or at redemption centers when the participants are not present), but there are also measures that are difficult to classify. In some cases we simply do not know whether the participants suspect that they are being observed, and other cases involve a combination of reactive and nonreactive procedures. Consider your memory for particular events, such as word lists. Imagine you are asked to rate a list of words for pleasantness on a scale from 1 to 5. This is a reasonable task since most people agree that some words (rose, sunset) are more pleasant than others (vomit, garbage). After you complete the task you are asked, unexpectedly, to try to recall as many of the words as you can from memory. Will a reactive or nonreactive measure be obtained?

In one sense the measure is clearly reactive because you know your memory ability is being assessed. But in another sense it is nonreactive. If you did not expect to receive a memory test following the rating task, it is unlikely that you would *consciously* do anything to store the words in memory. The subsequent memory test is a nonreactive measure in that, during presentation, you were unaware that memory performance would be assessed. Memory researchers have, in fact, varied their assessment procedures to assess whether intent to learn influences memory performance. The fuzziness of the reactive-nonreactive distinction can also be considered in terms of intervention.

Intervention-Nonintervention Distinction

A major difficulty with simple observation is that you may have to wait a very long time for the behavior you are interested in to occur. Certainly you are unlikely to learn very much about aggressive behavior if you position yourself at a street corner and wait for people to act aggressively. If you conceal yourself (bug the area and observe from a distance with concealed equipment), you could probably obtain a nonreactive measure, but you may grow to be very old before you make many relevant observations. Another possible method is to intervene. In the case of risk-taking behaviors in young children, for example, you may have young confederates ask girls and boys to join them in different play behaviors (such as climbing trees). If you simply waited for these behaviors to occur, you could spend considerable time watching young children. The cost of intervention is that the intervention may influence the behaviors observed. Using confederates to encourage youngsters to engage in dangerous play, in addition to posing serious ethical questions, may lead you to overestimate the amount of risk taking that would occur naturally. In brief, your intervention may distort the phenomenon you are trying to study.

Intervention has been used extensively by social psychologists. Social psychologists interested in observing reactions of bystanders to people in distress have used various intervention techniques. One might have a confederate fake a heart attack, a seizure, act like a drunk, or stage a fight with another confederate to assess how bystanders will react to these various crises. If the bystanders are not aware that their behaviors are being observed in these "rigged" situations, the measures obtained can be classified as nonreactive. But why should we go to the trouble of staging a fight or heart attack to assess how bystanders will react? To find out how people will react in a particular situation, all you have to do is ask them.

In some cases this is probably true. Some people who claim that they would intervene in fact would do so. However, in other cases, the self-report procedure (reactive measure) would yield a different set of results from the nonreactive measure obtained by actually staging a crisis. If you were to ask a number of people whether they would come to the aid of an elderly person being mugged, it is likely that a number of the respondents would indicate a willingness to help. We have no idea, however, whether they actually would help a victim in a real mugging. Imagine that a close relative (brother, sister) needs a kidney transplant. Would you be willing to donate one of your kidneys? Most of us are likely to say yes when the need is far distant (in a hypothetical situation). How many of us would actually give up a kidney? We simply do not know unless faced with the situation. The major point is simply that there are discrepancies between reactive and nonreactive measures, which indicates the need for both. When intervention is used, the classification of the procedures as observational, experimental, or quasi-experimental depends on the systematic nature of the intervention, a point we will say more about shortly.

THE CORRELATIONAL APPROACH

The Nature of Correlation

A *variable* is a symbol and its set of values. The variables that we will be concerned with are things or events that can be measured or manipulated. Correlation is very useful because it allows us to quantify the degree of relationship between two variables. For two of the three correlational methods considered in this text, the basic task is to determine the tendency of a person who has a high, medium, or low score on one measure to have a high, medium, or low score on a second measure. For example, if there is a high positive correlation between the rate of pupil dilation and problem-solving ability, then people with rapid dilation should tend to be good problem solvers (solve many problems in a 20-minute period), and people with slow dilation should tend to be poor problem solvers (solve few problems in a 20-minute period). If there is a high negative correlation between the two measures, then those with rapid dilation should be poor problem solvers and those with slow dilation good problem solvers. Or there may be little or no correlation between the two variables. The magnitude of a correlation coefficient can be any value from −1.00 to +1.00.

You should be careful not to misinterpret the adjectives *positive* and *negative* as used to modify *correlation*. They do not indicate a value judgment; a positive correlation is not better than a negative one. A positive correlation means only that high scores on one measure tend to go with high scores on the other, middle scores with middle scores, and low scores with low. A negative correlation means that high scores on one measure tend to go with low scores on the other, and middle scores with middle scores. The investigator often determines whether the obtained correlation is positive or negative by using a particular measuring procedure.

Let us assume that our investigator is interested in the relationship between the aggressiveness of adult male seals and the number of seals in their harems. She and another investigator observe a group of twelve adult males for a month and independently rank them for aggressiveness. The observers are in exact agreement regarding the rankings. The most aggressive seal is given the rank of 1, the next most aggressive the rank of 2, and so on. Then the animals are observed during the mating season and the size of the harem of each adult male is determined. Our investigator computes a correlation between the aggressiveness rankings and the size of harem measure and obtains a high negative correlation. This means that the seals with low numbers on the aggressiveness scale (the more aggressive seals) have larger harems. The investigator could have made the correlation positive, without changing its magnitude (or its meaning), by assigning the rank of 12 to the most aggressive male, 11 to the next most aggressive, and so on.

Correlation and Prediction

Prediction. One of the advantages to being able to specify the degree of relationship between two variables is that prediction is made possible. Predictions can be made about past as well as future events. For example, if you believe the absence of sunshine makes people depressed, you might check your notion by correlating the number of people who seek help for depression with the number of overcast days each month for the past 10 years. That is, for each month you would determine the number of overcast days and the number of people who seek help for depression. You would expect to find a significant relationship if your view is correct. The amount of depression should be high for months in which there are many overcast days and low for months in which there are few overcast days. Of course, you must make your prediction before you determine what relationship actually exists. There is no test of our *understanding* if we know the facts before making the predictions. We can make predictions to test our ideas (for example, on weather and depression) or for purely practical reasons. Predictions made for purely applied situations are usually based on correlations.

Using Correlations to Make Predictions. The accuracy of prediction increases as the magnitude of the correlation increases. Thus, if two variables are correlated and we know an individual's performance on one of the variables, we can accurately predict performance on the second. In many applied situations it is important to be able to predict an individual's performance. For example, it is possible to predict harem size for seals accurately by assessing aggressiveness or vice versa. Or, if there is a high correlation between success in graduate school and performance on a particular test, the test can be used to predict success. If there are more applicants than can be accepted, it can be used to select the ones to be admitted. Whether or not such a selection procedure is justified would depend in part on the degree of relationship between the variables. In this case, success in graduate school would be the *criterion* on which to judge how well the test predicts.

If the correlation between the test and the criterion is perfect — that is, if the person who gets the highest score is the best graduate student, the one who gets the second highest score is the second best, and so on — then we can justify using the test to screen applicants. However, if the correlation is not close to $+1.00$ or -1.00, it is more difficult to justify the procedure because the abilities that produce a high score on the test are not necessarily those that lead to academic success. If the actual correlation is .50, a person who does well on the test has a higher probability of doing well in graduate studies than one who does poorly on the test; however, some people who do well on the test will fail in graduate school and vice versa. In this case of a moderate correlation between the test and the criterion, a person's decision as to whether using the test as a screening device is justified might well depend on his or her ability to perform well on written tests. An admissions office would, with reason, most likely accept the screening device in spite of its limitations, as long as the tests do predict academic success for a significant number of applicants.

Criteria for Causality. Reservations of philosophers aside, the four criteria for causality accepted by most scientists are association, time priority, nonspurious relation, and rationale (Labovitz & Hagedorn, 1971). *Association* is the relationship between variables, frequently assessed by using correlational techniques. *Time priority* refers to which variable occurred first. (If smoking causes lung cancer, smoking should occur *before* lung cancer develops.)

Nonspurious relation refers to the fact that no third variable accounts for the observed relationship between two variables. *Rationale* is the logic or explanation for the observed relationship. Is there a theoretical justification for the observed relationship? Does the observed relationship fit in with our understanding of similar phenomena?

Two variables can be related without being causally related. A significant relationship between two variables is only one of the four criteria needed for causality. Thus, if we obtain a correlation between two variables, it may be because the variables are causally related, but a correlation by itself is not sufficient evidence for a cause-effect conclusion. Consider the relationship between how parents treat their children and characteristics of the children such as competence and self-reliance. Baumrind (1967) has demonstrated that parents who are warm, affectionate, fair, and consistent in their expectations and who respect the opinions of their children have children who are self-reliant and competent; that is, there is a relationship between parental treatment and the characteristics of children. Parents who are affectionate without making any demands on their children are less likely to have children who are self-reliant and competent. Do the child-rearing practices of the parents have a cause-effect relationship with the characteristics of their children?

Given that the two variables are related, it is reasonable to entertain the notion that a causal relationship exists. However, there are other possibilities. For example, a child's characteristics (self-reliance, competence) may be determined primarily by genetic factors. Parents who are self-reliant and competent produce children who are self-reliant and competent; parents who are not, do not. One can argue for a genetic view of development in which child-rearing practices have little influence on the child's development. It is frequently the case that there are a number of plausible alternative interpretations of why two variables are related. Frequently, the two variables are causally related, but it is important to keep in mind that this is only one possibility.

Sometimes highly correlated variables will be causally related. Many people are willing to conclude, for example, that smoking can cause lung cancer even though the evidence is almost entirely correlational. If it is necessary to make a decision about whether to stop smoking, it is reasonable to interpret the high correlation between smoking and lung cancer obtained in many studies as evidence of a causal relationship. Although this interpretation may not be correct, one can hardly question the smoker's right to make it. After all, the concern is with his lungs! Besides, temporal priority, spuriousness, and rationale all support a causal interpretation. There does not seem to be any reasonable alternative explanation, at least at the present time, for this high correlation.

Multiple Correlations and Causality. If a particular problem cannot be investigated by other methods, an investigator may decide to use the correla-

for the child who does not learn to read with "normal" instruction. What can be done for a friend who has been severely depressed for months? Are aptitude tests really unfair for members of minority groups? What can we do to help a child develop into a normal, happy, successful adult?

RATIONALE FOR STUDYING RESEARCH METHODOLOGY

The Need for Understanding

Procedures for Assessing Explanations. We study research methodology because research provides a way of assessing the validity of answers to very important questions, such as those considered above. We still have much to learn about personality, social interactions, cognitive ability, reading, alcoholism, decision making, therapy, abnormal behavior, implementing and evaluating social programs, memory processes, and so on. What is at issue is the procedure or procedures that should be adopted to assess the validity of proposed answers or solutions. For virtually every important question there are theorists who propose solutions. How do we decide which solution is the "best" when theorists disagree?

We need procedures for evaluating explanations so that we can choose from plausible alternative explanations. There are a number of ways to obtain explanations. We can rely on our intuitions, the advice of others, observations, or, depending on the question, numerous theories. Usually, however, we obtain a number of answers to the same question, and therefore we still have the task of selecting from among plausible solutions. There is good reason to believe that our decision-making abilities in selecting from among the alternatives leave a lot to be desired, particularly when we have a personal investment in one of these explanations. A set of procedures for evaluating ideas (alternative plausible explanations) allows us to avoid a number of the biases that influence our decision making. Much of this text is devoted to considering procedures for describing phenomena and evaluating plausible alternative explanations.

Description and Explanation. The usual procedure for studying behavior and mental activity is to describe a phenomenon and then attempt to explain it. It does not always work out that way, but this is a common sequence. For example, there is a relationship between education and divorce rate; more highly educated people are less likely to be divorced than less well educated people. This is a description of a relationship between two measures, education and marital longevity; nothing has been said about why this relationship exists. What might be responsible for this relationship? Are well-educated people better spouses because of the education they have received, or is education, in and of itself, unrelated to marital longevity? One might argue, for example, that people who obtain more education are highly motivated to

1 Introduction

Scientists infringe on our daily lives. They give us the carcinogenic substance of the week (cigarette smoke, nitrosamines in beer and scotch, artificial sweeteners in soft drinks), tell us how elections are going to turn out after a minuscule portion of the vote has been counted, which foods we should eat and which we should avoid, how we should exercise, the effects of vitamins on the common cold, depression, and just about everything else, and even how long we can expect to live given an average amount of "luck." Social scientists, particularly psychologists, are not timid about explaining why we do what we do or, given the opportunity, assessing our strengths and weaknesses. They create and administer intelligence, aptitude, and personality tests as well as questionnaires to assess opinion and practices on numerous issues and topics. They consider matters such as the relative merits of breast- versus bottle-feeding of infants, how best to eliminate bedwetting, and procedures for increasing self-confidence, intellectual development, and general well-being. If we are depressed, anxious, too aggressive, or disturbed in any way, we can get advice as well as therapy from psychologists and others. How do they know so much? Should scientists infringe on our daily lives?

Although we generally prefer not to hear about pollution, nuclear risks, and acts of aggression, we have little choice in the matter. We live in a complex world that is made increasingly complex as new petrochemicals, drugs, and electronic and nuclear devices are developed and programs to "solve" social problems are implemented. If you have cancer or a loved one has cancer, it soon becomes very important whether claims for cancer cures (such as laetrile) are really effective or merely a means of providing momentary hope. Programs for alcohol and drug addiction become increasingly important when we know someone who is addicted. If your eight-year-old child is unable to read, you are likely to be very concerned about the reading process, factors determining whether a child will or will not learn to read, and what can be done

Research Methodology

tional approach extensively to get "close" to a causal statement. The basic difficulty with this approach is that some variable other than the one being considered may be responsible for the obtained correlation. Let us assume, for instance, that an investigator is interested in the factors that contribute to a successful marriage. She decides to correlate the degree of childhood happiness and marital happiness and obtains a high positive correlation. A critic points out that childhood happiness may not be the important variable. He believes, rather, that the important variable is the number of siblings of each marital partner, and that the number of siblings is related both to happiness in childhood and to marital success. Thus, there are two plausible rival hypotheses for the relationship between childhood happiness and marital success. If the number of siblings is the important variable, then the relationship between childhood happiness and marital success is spurious.

To test this notion our investigator can compute correlations separately for all participants having the same number of siblings. That is, she can compute the correlation between childhood happiness and marital success for people having no siblings, for people having one sibling, and so on. If she still obtains high correlations regardless of the number of siblings, then she can discount the critic's position. There is more reason to believe that the relationship between childhood happiness and marital success is nonspurious. Other explanations can be tested by the same process. If the relationship cannot be accounted for by other variables (that is, other rival hypotheses can be eliminated), then it is reasonable to place more confidence in the initial interpretation. It does not follow necessarily that there is a causal relationship between happiness in childhood and success in marriage, but this is a good possibility. A good theoretical justification for the relationship would make it an even better possibility.

The person who is selecting a mate may decide not to consider people who had unhappy childhoods. There is little reason to ignore the correlational evidence when making a decision because the correlation may, in fact, be due to a causal relationship between the two variables. Even if a third variable is responsible, it is still possible to use the correlation to predict marital success. Although it is important theoretically to determine whether two highly correlated variables are causally related, it may not make any practical difference.

Correlation and Discovery. Correlation, like observation, can lead to the discovery of possible causal relationships, which may then become the subject of experimental investigation. The correlational technique is somewhat better than the observational in that it specifies the degree of the relationship.

One should consider a variable's effect on behavior when selecting variables for experimental investigation. For example, if correlations of fifty variables with the incidence of lung cancer lead to the discovery that some variables have high correlations with lung cancer whereas others have very low or zero correlations, then the investigator who wants to select some variables and manipulate them experimentally to assess whether they *cause* lung cancer would be well-advised to select those with high correlations.

THE EXPERIMENTAL METHOD: BASIC PROPERTIES

Intervention and Control

Earlier we noted that one weakness of the observational approach is that we may have to wait a long time for the behaviors we are interested in (such as aggressive behaviors) to occur. To overcome this weakness, investigators may intervene in the situation by using confederates. For example, you could study helping behavior by having a young child pretend that he or she is lost to determine if adults, approached by the child, will provide aid. We intervene because intervention is necessary in order to be able to study many problems of interest. The way we intervene determines whether we are using an observational technique or the experimental or quasi-experimental methods. We can view the experimental method as the "ultimate intervention" in that we set up situations that allow us to have good control over the situation and the participants. If we, as experimenters, can devise different situations and then control which participants receive each situation (condition), we should be able to test alternative views of why we do the things we do. In essence, then, there is nothing complicated about the experimental method. It is simply a way of controlling situations and the participants in those situations. Complications do arise, however, since there are limits on the conditions we can use and the control that we can exercise. It is necessary to learn some new terminology.

Independent and Dependent Variables

As we said earlier, a variable is a symbol and its set of values. For our purposes variables can be viewed as things or events that can be measured or manipulated. There are many variables that we have control over as experimenters. We can intervene to manipulate these variables in the sense that we can determine the condition a particular participant receives. We can control the nature of our intervention *independently* of what participants do. Thus, variables that we control are usually called independent or manipulated variables. There are numerous ways that we can intervene. We could, for example, determine which therapy each participant receives, which instructional technique, which drug, which vitamin, and so on. There are practical and ethical limits on our interventions, but even with these limitations there are many ways in which we can intervene. It will probably be easiest for you to maintain the distinction between independent and dependent variables if you associate *in*dependent variables with *in*tervention. The intervention is special in that we determine which participant receives which condition. You should associate dependent variables with the *observation* of participants.

The distinction between independent and dependent variables simply depends on whether the variable is controlled by the experimenter (independent) or measured by the experimenter (dependent). We use dependent variables to assess whether our interventions (independent variable manipulations) have had any influence on how participants perform. The independent variables manipulated (the nature of your interventions) can be either qualitative (two or more instructional techniques) or quantitative (the amount of protein in a diet). It can also involve comparing the presence of a thing or event with its absence (instruction versus no instruction, or protein versus no protein). Whatever can be manipulated can be used as an independent variable.

Obviously, the selection of independent variables is a very important matter. You select variables that you believe are interesting and important for understanding behavior and mental activity. If, for example, you are interested in testing different therapies for depression, you are likely to manipulate the type of therapy as your independent variable. You *intervene* by controlling which therapy each participant receives. Once you select an independent variable, you severely restrict which dependent variables you will study (that is, which behaviors you will observe). We assess the effects of our intervention by determining performance on one or more dependent measures, so obviously we need to select dependent measures that will allow us to determine whether our intervention (independent variable) has been effective. In the case of therapies for depressed people, we would select some measure of depression, for example, the score on a test designed to measure depression, to evaluate whether the different therapies had any effect on depression.

The labels *experimental* and *control* can be used to distinguish groups of participants when the independent variable (intervention) involves comparing the presence of a thing or event with its absence. The groups that receive the thing or event (therapy) are called *experimental* groups. The group that does not receive the thing or event is called the *control* group.

The Logic of the Experimental Method

The experimental method differs from the correlational method in that the experimenter manipulates one or more independent variables in an attempt to influence the behavior of participants. No attempt is made to influence the behavior of participants when the correlational method is used. We simply assess the degree of relationship between two variables. We can distinguish between the experimental method and observational techniques in terms of the nature of intervention. As we already indicated, observational techniques are a component of each of the methods. The experimental method is distinguished by the systematic nature of the intervention. Intervention and control are used to form "equivalent" groups of participants who are treated identically in all respects except one. If the performance of the two groups differs, it follows that the one respect in which the groups varied (the independent variable) is the cause of the performance difference. Used properly, the experimental method makes it possible to assess the association between variables (to determine the effect of the manipulated variable on behavior), to control time priority between variables (to make the manipulation *before* measuring behavior), and to assess nonspurious relationships, because groups are equivalent on all but manipulated variables. Thus all differences in behavior can be attributed to the planned manipulations.

A few words need to be said about the special meaning of *equivalent groups* in psychological research. Equivalent groups are not identical or equal in an absolute sense; rather, they are groups whose differences in performance can be attributed solely to chance fluctuations. The subjects in two groups can differ somewhat in performance and still be equivalent in this sense. Chance fluctuations are always present. A central question in analyzing the results of experiments is whether the performance differences between groups are due solely to chance or to chance *plus* the effect of the independent variable. Equivalent groups are formed when the procedures used for selecting and assigning subjects ensure that any differences between groups are due solely to chance.

Independent Variables and the Experimental Method

It is easy to underestimate the usefulness of the experimental method. Because we are biased information processors, it is difficult to overestimate the importance of systematic procedures for evaluating our explanations for phenomena. Without systematic procedures we are likely to attend selectively to behaviors consistent with our views and, therefore, continue to believe we are correct even in cases where there is good evidence to the contrary. It is difficult, typically, to convince someone else that their views are incorrect because we have a bias for selecting positive instances. We look for evidence to support our theories, not to refute them. With systematic procedures you are forced to consider the possibility that your views are incorrect.

Another danger is that you will underestimate the number and kinds of interventions that are possible. The experimental method is used extensively in laboratory investigations of behavior and mental activity, but you should not conclude that this is the only place the method can be used. Clearly, much research is better done in the laboratory (most drug research and vision research), but there is no compelling reason why the experimental method cannot be used in real-life situations as well as the laboratory. The basic question is whether we use systematic procedures to evaluate our ideas or whether we use our intuitions and — in many cases — biased observations. There is good reason to believe that we should rely on systematic procedures whenever possible.

Consider surgery versus antibiotic therapy for tonsillitis. Are physicians too quick to recommend tonsillectomies — an expensive operation — over treatment with antibiotics? Are you really better off having your tonsils removed than having the infection treated with antibiotics and keeping them? To answer this question, a research team obtained the consent of parents to randomly assign children with tonsillitis to have surgery or to be treated medically (see *Newsweek*, Feb. 23, 1976, p. 79). That is, a systematic procedure was used to evaluate the relative merits of antibiotic therapy and surgery.

Consider the numerous social programs conducted by local, state, and federal governments. How do we evaluate the effectiveness of these programs? Do we simply ask the people in charge of the programs to evaluate them? Should we ask the recipients of aid or the participants in the program to evaluate them? These are intervention programs. Local, state, and federal governments are intervening in the lives of citizens. Given the need to intervene and, in most cases at least, a number of plausible ways that intervention could proceed, it seems reasonable to adopt systematic procedures for evaluating intervention. Billions of dollars are spent on programs, but little money is spent on evaluating whether the programs are effective or on comparing the relative effectiveness of different programs. There is no good reason, for example, why systematic procedures could not be used to evaluate different programs for conserving energy, for rehabilitating criminals, for coping with drug abuse, or for caring for and treating the mentally ill. The major point, then, is that you should not equate the experimental method solely with laboratory research. It is a systematic procedure for evaluating alternative explanations that is restricted only by ethical and practical considerations.

Subject Variables and the Experimental Method

Subject Variable–Nonsubject Variable Distinction. The distinction between subject variables and nonsubject variables, like the distinction between independent and dependent variables, is related more to what we do (how we intervene) than to inherent differences between them. Our basic intention in using the experimental method is to intervene by manipulating independent variables and then to assess the influence of our manipulation by noting differences between conditions on one or more dependent measures. For example, we might assess the effect of reading to young children on their subsequent ability to read. In this case the independent variable would be whether participants were read to: yes for the experimental group, no for the controls. We use a systematic procedure to decide which participants are in the experimental group and which are in the control group. We assess whether reading has any effect on the subsequent ability to read by assessing the reading ability of the children several years later. Their scores on a reading ability test constitute the dependent measure. Note that in this case we can intervene and determine who is read to and who is not. The independent variable of reading to children (yes versus no) is a nonsubject variable. We have control over nonsubject variables in that we can decide whether a participant receives or does not receive the treatment.

We do not always have control over the "independent" variable. For example, height, weight, age, intelligence, anxiety level, number of siblings, beauty, hostility, and self-esteem are not directly controllable by us. We cannot arbitrarily determine, for example, who will be intelligent and who will not be. If we cannot determine whether a particular participant will be in the experimental or control condition, it is likely that the "independent" variable is a subject variable. Characteristics of participants that we cannot control (intelligence, beauty, personality) cannot be manipulated because we are unable to intervene to determine who receives a particular treatment and who does not. In general, our ability to modify characteristics of participants is limited for both practical and ethical reasons. If we had a super IQ pill that raised IQ by 50 points, then, of course, we could intervene to influence IQ. We could give the superpill to experimental participants and an inert substance, usually called a placebo, to the control participants. In the absence of such superpills or other ways of modifying the characteristics of participants without violating ethical principles, we are limited in the nature of our interventions. We cannot manipulate subject variables; we can only *select* people who have particular characteristics (high self-esteem or low self-esteem) and compare them.

The distinction between subject and nonsubject variables is an important methodological consideration. With a nonsubject variable manipulation it is possible to arrive at a cause-effect conclusion; however, with a subject variable, it is extremely difficult, if not impossible, to do so. "Manipulating" a subject variable is, for interpretational purposes, the same as correlating it with the dependent variable. One has to be careful *not* to conclude that a subject variable is the *cause* of group differences in performance on the dependent measure.

Suppose an investigator wants to test a prediction that blonde college women are likely to have more dates. The procedure could be very simple. The investigator *selects* thirty natural blondes and thirty natural redheads and tabulates the number of dates each woman has for a given period. Let us assume that blondes had significantly more dates. Can this difference be attributed to hair color? No. All one can say is that the blondes had more dates. It is unreasonable to conclude that hair color was the reason; other factors such as aggressiveness, beauty, or intelligence may have been responsible. One can only conclude that hair color is related to having dates, *not* that the relationship is causal. When a subject variable manipulation is made, one cannot form equivalent groups because the characteristics of the subject determine the group in which the subject will be placed. If it is not possible to form equivalent groups before the independent variable is introduced, then there is no way to assess its effect accurately because there is no way to manipulate just *one* independent variable. It is unreasonable to reach a cause-effect conclusion when a subject variable is manipulated. Correlational studies and subject variable manipulations are similar in that it is only possible to assess whether the variables are related, not whether they are causally related.

Classification of Subject Variable Manipulations. The fact that subject variable manipulations are similar to correlational studies with regard to causality statements, and similar to the experimental method with regard to *some* procedures, makes it difficult to arrive at a simple, completely satisfactory classification. Some investigators classify subject variable manipulation as an instance of the experimental method. The subject variable is treated as the independent variable and the performance measure as the dependent variable. There is no harm in doing this as long as one remembers that the results of such experiments should not be interpreted in cause-effect terms. In this text, we will treat subject variable manipulation as a special case of the experimental method, applying the label of independent variable to subject variables as well as to nonsubject variables. By doing so, we can combine subject variable and nonsubject variable manipulations in the same experiment.

Experimental Versus Quasi-Experimental Methods

The three approaches considered so far — observation, correlation, and experiment — are used extensively in research. A fourth approach, called quasi-experimental because of its similarity to the experimental method, is used when it is possible to utilize some but not all aspects of the experimental method (Campbell & Stanley, 1963). Quasi-experimental designs will be discussed in more detail in Chapter 6; our present goal is to distinguish between experimental and quasi-experimental methods. To do so we first need to reconsider the subject variable–nonsubject variable distinction.

We said that subject variables are characteristics of the subject that cannot be manipulated by the experimenter, such as age, sex, or intelligence. Experimenters can only *select* subjects according to their characteristics; they cannot change those characteristics. This is a crucial distinction for methodological considerations because the conclusions that can be made from an experiment depend on whether the experimenter can manipulate the independent variable. There are also some instances in which investigators are not able to manipulate *nonsubject* variables because they are limited by ethical, practical, political, or other constraints. If they have been given no constraints, investigators can, of course, manipulate virtually all nonsubject variables. Quasi-experimental designs introduce something like experimental control to data collection even though it is not possible to determine who gets the experimental treatment and who does not. They are used to investigate *nonsubject* variables.

Let us assume that you are interested in the effect of a new therapy for stuttering. For practical reasons you cannot manipulate who receives the new therapy and who does not. You are required to give the new therapy to all the available stutterers in order to get the cooperation required. Although you are not able to use the preferred method for testing (the experimental method), you may be able to use a quasi-experimental design. For example, you could perform a time-series experiment (Campbell & Stanley, 1963) in which you observe the incidence of stuttering in each participant at various intervals before and after introducing the therapy. Or you might try to find another group of stutterers, not available for therapy, who can serve as a comparison group. You could test both groups of stutterers at the same time (for example, in January), administer your therapy to the treatment group, and then test both groups at a second time (say, December).

The major point is that the experimental method is not the only acceptable way to evaluate the effects of a nonsubject variable, but it is the preferred way if practical and ethical considerations allow the investigator to intervene to control which participants receive each treatment. If we are not able to use the preferred method, we use the next best method available, correlational or quasi-experimental techniques. In some cases there is no choice to be made because only one method (for example, correlational) can be used. Although the experimental method is best if you are attempting to arrive at a cause-effect statement about two variables, the best method is the one that "fits" the particular problem you are investigating. In many instances the correlational method is the best method simply because we are not able to intervene to control the treatment each participant receives.

CLASSIFYING RESEARCH ACCORDING TO METHOD

In the beginning of this chapter we noted that social scientists use four basic methods to accumulate knowledge: observation, correlation, experiment, and quasi-experiment. It is important to be able to classify research according to method because the method employed determines, in large part, what conclusions are justified. The following examples will give you some practice in classification. Try to classify each example before reading the discussion of it. (The label for each example is the title of the article discussed.)

Example 1 — Children's Reactions to Secondhand Smoke

A study was conducted (Cameron, 1972) in which 2365 children between the ages of seven and fifteen were interviewed to determine their reaction to smoking by others. The general finding was that the children did not like being exposed to tobacco smoke. Most of them disapproved of their parents' smoking and indicated some loss of respect for their parents because they smoked.

Discussion. It should be clear that the above study is an example of the use of an observational technique. A reactive measure was obtained. The children's responses might have been influenced by the fact that they knew the investigator was interested in their reaction to smoking. For example, a child who wanted to please may have concluded that the interviewer had a negative attitude toward smoking and may have responded accordingly. There is usually some danger that the results obtained with a reactive measure may be influenced by the subject's awareness of the evaluation. The investigator's task is to determine whether the advantages of the method outweigh the bias that may result if some subjects modify their responses in an effort to please or displease her.

Example 2 — The Lesson of Twin Rivers: Feedback Works

A study was performed in Twin Rivers, New Jersey, a suburban development near Trenton, to assess the effects of feedback on energy consumption. The investigators (Darley, Seligman, & Becker, 1979) asked residents if they were interested in reducing electric consumption by decreasing their use of air conditioning. Those who agreed to participate were assigned to a control or treatment condition. The participants in the treatment condition, among other things, received feedback several times a week on the amount of electricity they used. The major finding was that feedback resulted in less consumption of electricity than for those in the control condition.

Discussion. The question of principal interest is the nature of the investigator's intervention and control. Does the investigator intervene to control the treatment each participant receives? In this case the answer is yes. The investigators decided which participants received feedback and which participants did not. Therefore, they were able to establish equivalent groups prior to the introduction of the independent variable, in this case feedback and no feedback.

Example 3 — Who Gets Ahead in America?

Yankelovich (1979) discussed a book by Jencks and eleven of his colleagues entitled *Who Gets Ahead? — The Determinants of Economic Success in America.* The findings discussed in the book were based on five national surveys of men and six additional surveys with a more restricted purpose. The major emphasis is on predicting earnings and occupational status. Jencks and his collaborators find, among other things, that family background (parents' education, earnings, and family size), test scores, number of years of school completed, and personality characteristics as a teenager (such as leadership) were related both to occupational status and to earnings. Years of schooling, for example, accounted for approximately 50 percent of the individual differences in occupational status but for only 15 to 20 percent of the individual differences in the amount earned.

Discussion. Since surveys were used, observational techniques were employed. The question of interest is whether more than observational techniques were used. An observational technique is used in virtually every study because a performance measure is needed in the correlational, experimental, or quasi-experimental method. In this case the interest is in establishing whether there is a relationship among variables. For example, does the number of years of schooling influence how much you make and the status of your occupation? When we assess the degree of relationship between variables and we are not able to intervene to control the treatment each participant receives, we are likely to use the correlational method. Correlational techniques provide a useful way of assessing the degree of relationship between variables and, as we will see later (Chapter 9), allow us to account for individual differences in performance. Both observational and correlational techniques were used.

Example 4 — Effects of Early Social Deprivation on Emotionality in Rats

The investigators (Koch & Arnold, 1972) assigned ninety-five newborn rats to four rearing conditions to assess the effect of social deprivation on emotionality. One group was reared with mother and peers; a second group with mother but without peers; a third group in incubators with peers; a fourth group in incubators in isolation. Several measures of emotionality (heart rate, frequency of urination, and so on) were obtained when the rats were 65 and 113 days old. The general finding was that maternally deprived rats showed higher emotionality.

Discussion. This study is an example of the use of the experimental method. The assignment of subjects to groups was such that the investigators could be confident that the groups were equivalent before introducing the independent variable. The independent variable was the type of early social experience, a nonsubject variable. Although early social experience is a characteristic of the subject, this is not a subject variable manipulation in the sense used in this text, because the manipulation is under the control of the experimenter. He decides which rats gets a particular early experience and which does not. Thus it is possible to manipulate just one "subject" variable — not merely to *select,* as in a typical subject variable case. It is reasonable, therefore, to conclude from this experiment that the maternal deprivation *caused* the higher emotionality.

Example 5 — Sex, Setting, and Reactions to Crowding on Sidewalks

The investigator (Dabbs, 1972) studied people's reactions to having someone stand very close to them at stoplights and bus stops. The basic procedure consisted of having a male or female confederate of the investigator approach and stand very close to a pedestrian waiting for a bus or for a traffic light to change. There were 643 pedestrians, both males and females. The extent to which each pedestrian moved away from the confederate was recorded. One finding was that male confederates induced more movement than female confederates, and female pedestrians tended to move more than male pedestrians.

Discussion. The above study can be classified as an example of an observational technique. A nonreactive measure was obtained in that the pedestrians were not given any reason to suspect that their movement was being recorded. The intervention is, of course, the presence of the confederate. It is likely that the investigator would have had to wait a long time to determine how pedestrians react to crowding if he had waited for the crowding to occur naturally. By using confederates, he could arrange the situation of interest and then observe subjects' reactions.

Some readers may object to the above classification because they believe the study is more accurately classified as experimental or quasi-experimental, with sex of the confederate, sex of the pedestrian, and location of the encounter (bus stop or stoplight) as the three independent variables. Sometimes it is possible to make a case for more than one classification, because the study has the properties of more than one method. Nonreactive measures with intervention and the quasi-experimental method are especially likely to overlap. It is frequently possible to decide between these two classifications and the experimental method by considering how the subjects were assigned to conditions. If no attempt is made to ensure that the subjects tested in each condition are equivalent before obtaining the dependent measure, it is usually more appropriate to view the research as an instance of an observational technique or a quasi-experimental design. If an effort *is* made to ensure such equivalence, then the study may be regarded as an example of the experimental method. If the investigator had used a procedure to ensure that the pedestrians approached by male confederates were equivalent to the pedestrians approached by female confederates, this study would have been a good example of the experimental method — if the sex of the confederate was the only variable manipulated. The major weakness of all studies in which procedures are not used to obtain equivalent groups before the manipulation is that it is difficult to know whether any obtained differences between conditions are due to the treatment or are simply a result of the "selection" of better or poorer subjects for the treatment than nontreatment conditions.

Example 6 — The More Sorrowful Sex

Scarf (1979), a science writer, notes that there are clear sex differences in the people treated for depression in institutions — either as inpatients or as outpatients — across the country. The numbers vary from institution to institution but in general there are two to six times as many women as men who are being treated for depression. Are these differences real or merely due to biases in the way people are categorized (labeled as depressed)? Scarf considers the possibility of a bias in using the diagnostic category of depression and rejects this view, largely because her experiences with women classified as depressed convinced her that their problems were real, not merely a bias of a psychotherapist or clinician. Scarf notes that men have higher rates of the disruptive-to-others disorders (alcoholism, drug disorders) whereas women have higher rates of passive disorders, namely depression.

It is still possible, however, that sex differences in the incidence of depression are due to procedures used for obtaining the relevant information. Women see physicians more than men do, a difference that emerges around the onset of puberty. It may be that more women are diagnosed as depressed simply because they are more likely to seek medical help than males. Not so, says Scarf. Studies by Weissman and others in which a random sample is selected from a community at large and personal interviews are conducted also reveal clear sex differences in the incidence of depression. Given that the phenomenon of sex differences in the incidence of depression is reliable, the remaining question is why. There are numerous plausible explanations. Scarf suggests that the differences are due to role expectations (greater dependency in women) and sex differences in the reaction to the disruption of emotional bonds. Disruption is typically more devastating for women than for men.

Discussion. The above example is a clear case of a subject variable being studied as an independent variable. It is a subject variable because we cannot intervene to determine sex. All we can do is compare males and females to determine if they differ on particular characteristics, such as the incidence of depression. If we do get differences and they are not accounted for by biases in the way the measures were obtained (sex differences in frequency of visits to physicians), then it is reasonable to ask why sex differences are obtained. Any time we obtain differences between groups when we select on the basis of a subject variable (such as sex), it is difficult, if not impossible, to reach a cause-effect conclusion because we cannot select just one subject variable.

Males and females differ on a number of characteristics which might account for differences in the incidence of depression (roles, aggressiveness, hormones, status). It is frequently possible, however, to use subject-variable comparison to rule out some interpretations. For example, the fact that there are still sex differences in the incidence of depression when random samples are selected from the community at large makes it possible to rule out the possibility that sex differences in depression are due solely to sex differences in the frequency of consulting physicians.

Example 7 — Ads Without Answers Make the Brain Itch

Chance (1975) reported the results of a project in Kentucky under the direction of Martin Sundel, a psychologist. The purpose of the project was to evaluate whether ads with solutions or without solutions would be more effective in getting people to evaluate their life problems. Some of the ads offered solutions to problems and some did not. For example, in one solution ad the husband was told he should listen and try to understand why his wife nagged. One of the nonsolution ads about alcohol and drug abuse ended with questions such as "How many drinks are required to bring back love?" The ads ran on seventeen radio stations and five television stations and in eighteen newspapers over a sixty-week period. The effectiveness of the ads was evaluated by surveys and the number of calls to a crisis and information center about problems mentioned in the ads. The results suggest that ads without answers are better for getting people to consider their life problems.

Discussion. Several methods are used in this case. The surveys used to evaluate the ads can be classified as reactive measures. The number of phone calls to the crisis and information center, on the other hand, is a nonreactive measure obtained with intervention (the ads). Thus, two observational techniques were used. The type of ad manipulation is probably best classified as quasi-experimental. It is not fully experimental because there is no good way to know whether the people who saw the solution ads were equivalent to the people who saw the ads without solutions. However, the fact that the ads were presented several times over the sixty weeks increases the likelihood that the different responses to the ads are attributable to the nature of the ads and not to other considerations. If the same results are obtained a number of times there is more reason to believe that the treatment has an effect. A quasi-experimental approach can be used to come close to the control obtained when using the experimental method.

The reader should now have an understanding of the four basic methods used in accumulating knowledge in the social sciences. It should be clear from the examples that many investigators used a combination of research techniques in a single study. They may also study the effect of more than one independent variable in a single study. It is frequently necessary to do so because the effect of one independent variable may be influenced by the level of a second. Although the previous discussion should have given you a general understanding of the scope of the four methods, we now need to consider the experimental method in greater detail.

THE EXPERIMENTAL METHOD: ADDITIONAL PROPERTIES

We need to consider additional properties of the experimental method because discovering the relationship between independent and dependent variables is not always a straightforward matter. We differ in how we respond to some variables. You may have noticed, for example, that some people can drink one beer and be largely unaffected whereas others drink one beer and immediately begin to show some signs of intoxication (giggling, frankness). If we want to assess the effects of a single independent variable — in this case beer versus no beer — on behavior, the result that we get will depend on the participants we use. When we compare groups drinking one beer with groups drinking no beer we could get little or no effect or a substantial effect, depending on the participants we select. The results may also depend on when you have the participants drink the beer, namely, when they are very hungry or just after they have finished a big meal. In brief, we need ways to study more complex situations so that we can assess the relationships among variables as well as the simple effects that independent variables have on dependent measures.

Experiments with One Independent Variable

We wish to consider how experiments with two independent variables differ from experiments with one independent variable. To provide a base for the discussion of experiments with two independent variables we must first consider some points about experiments with one independent variable. To simplify the task, let us assume that all subjects who receive a particular treatment attain the same level of performance on the dependent variable. That is, we will assume that all subjects have identical ability. Any difference between groups can be attributed to the effect of the treatment manipulation because we are assuming that there are no chance fluctuations.

Example 1 — Independent Variable Affects Dependent Variable. Assume that you are interested in the effectiveness of therapy for depression. Specifically, you are interested in whether a cognitive therapy that stresses the importance of eliminating irrational thought patterns influences the amount of depression (Beck & Kovacs, 1977). Since you are understaffed, you are not able to give therapy to everyone who seeks help; therefore, you decide to do an experiment to assess whether cognitive therapy really works. The people seeking help are randomly assigned to the therapy (treatment) or control

enter character

intellectual ability

Type of People - some

M & W — diff
          study women

age,

SE

stratify —
  random over time

all Cog. the time
      per 1 yr
        & B - per.

Found of per Recent
      Herley.

define ~~the~~ depression

Therapist ?
1 — 2, many

Random Assign
match groups
+ random assign
Gender ?
Control groups ?

condition. All participants are tested with a "depression questionnaire" ten weeks after they seek help to see whether there is a difference between participants who receive cognitive therapy and participants who have little contact with a therapist (control condition). This is a nonsubject variable manipulation; the investigator is able to intervene and determine which participants receive therapy and which do not. The effectiveness of the intervention (independent variable) is assessed by noting differences, if any, in the scores on the dependent measure — in this case the depression questionnaire. A high score indicates depression; a low score indicates little or no depression.

The results are clear. All participants who receive therapy have a score on the depression questionnaire of 10 following therapy. All participants who do not receive therapy have a score of 20. The therapy manipulation had an effect of 10 units, since the participants in the therapy condition had a score of 10 units lower than those in the control condition. The *effect* of the independent variable is assessed by comparing the average score on the dependent measure for the participants in the two conditions. In this case there are only two conditions; there is one independent variable (therapy or no therapy) and two levels of the independent variable. The levels of the independent variable are determined by the experimenter. One could, for example, have three levels of the independent variable (cognitive therapy, behavior therapy, control). The *effect* of an independent variable, on the other hand, is determined by performance on the dependent measure. The experimenter does not control the effect of an independent variable; he or she measures or assesses the effect of an independent variable by comparing the performance on the dependent measure of participants who receive different levels of the independent variable (different treatments). It is very important to be able to distinguish between levels (determined by experimenter) and effects (assessed by comparing the performance of participants on the dependent measure).

Example 2 — Independent Variable Has No Effect on Dependent Variable. Let us assume that you are still interested in the effectiveness of therapy, but in this case you are better staffed with therapists so that all the people seeking help for depression can receive therapy. Imagine that you have one cognitive therapist and one behavior therapist and you randomly assign the participants to one of the two therapists. In this case the independent variable is the therapist or type of therapy (cognitive versus behavioristic), and the dependent measure is each participant's score on the depression questionnaire administered ten weeks following the start of therapy. Once again the results are clear. All participants who receive cognitive therapy have a score of ten on the questionnaire, and all participants who receive behavior therapy have a score of ten. Since the scores obtained on the dependent measure are not influenced by the type of therapy, we say that the independent variable has no effect. Performance on the dependent measure determines whether the independent variable has an effect. Note that in this case we can only compare cognitive therapy with behavior therapy; we cannot say anything about the effectiveness of either therapy in relation to no therapy because we did not include a no-therapy condition.

Experiments with Two Independent Variables

As we indicated earlier, the effectiveness of a particular treatment (such as one beer versus no beer) can be dependent on the individual. It is useful to be able to study when our interventions (our independent variables) have the same effect for all participants and when they do not. It is also true that some interventions depend on other considerations. For example, there is likely to be a vast difference in the effect of drinking one beer for someone who has just taken a pain pill and for someone who has not. We need to be able to understand the effects of combinations of treatments, not simply the effects of each independent variable considered in isolation. To do so we need to do more complex experiments — experiments in which more than one independent variable is manipulated.

Example 3 — Interacting Variables. We are still interested in therapy for depression, but in this case we are also interested in whether the effectiveness of a particular therapy depends on the sex of the participant. To answer this question we use a 2 by 2 factorial design. This means that there are two independent variables and two levels of each. Therapy is one independent variable, with cognitive and behavior therapy as the two levels. Sex is the other independent variable, with male and female as the two levels. Thus, we have one nonsubject variable (therapy) and one subject variable (sex). We can intervene to control the therapy each participant receives, but we cannot intervene to control their sex. The dependent measure is the score of each participant on the depression questionnaire.

When two independent variables are studied in the same experiment, there are usually good reasons why the particular independent variables are selected. For the present example, we might be interested in whether the effectiveness of a particular therapy depends on the sex of the participant, because there are clear differences in the incidence of depression in the two sexes. Given sex differences in the incidence of depression, there may be sex differences in the causes of depression for the two sexes and, therefore, the effectiveness of a particular therapy may depend on the sex of the participant. The results of our hypothetical experiment are presented in Table 2-1. The letter X refers to any score. The symbol $\overline{X}$ (called x-bar) is a label for the mean. The scores for the ten participants in each condition are presented in the table.

A consideration of the results presented in Table 2-1 is fairly straightfor-

TABLE 2–1

The Score of Each of Forty Participants on the Depression Questionnaire as a Function of the Type of Therapy and the Sex of the Participant for Example 3 (fictitious data)

Sex	Therapy		Row mean
	Behavior	Cognitive	
Male	10 10 10 10 10 $\bar{X} = 10$ 10 10 10 10 10	20 20 20 20 20 $\bar{X} = 20$ 20 20 20 20 20	15
Female	20 20 20 20 20 $\bar{X} = 20$ 20 20 20 20 20	10 10 10 10 10 $\bar{X} = 10$ 10 10 10 10 10	15
Column mean	15	15	

ward provided we only try to do one thing at a time. We want to know whether the independent variables influenced performance on the dependent measure (that is, the scores on the depression questionnaire). To do so we compare the scores of the participants in the different conditions. We can only consider one independent variable at a time. Let us consider the therapy manipulation first. How do we determine whether the type of therapy influenced the scores on the depression questionnaire? All we need is a little imagination. We are concerned only with the comparison between cognitive and behavior therapy and we therefore ignore the sex of the participants. We pretend that the experiment was a two-group instead of a four-group experiment, with twenty participants in each group. There are ten males and ten females in each group. A mean score for each therapy group is obtained by adding all the scores for the participants in each group and then dividing by the number of participants. The mean for the cognitive therapy condition is 15; the mean for the behavior therapy condition is 15. Because the two column means are identical in this case, we say that there is no effect due to therapy.

We can use a similar procedure to assess the effect of sex. Once again we pretend that the experiment was a two-group instead of a four-group experiment. This time one group consists of all males; the other group consists of all females. The mean score for all the males is 15; the mean score for all the females is 15. A comparison of the two means reveals that there is no effect due to sex; the two means are identical. Thus, for this example we conclude that neither independent variable had any influence on the scores on the depression questionnaire. Because all the data were used to obtain them, these two effects are frequently called *main* or overall effects. There was no overall effect for sex or for therapy. There is no cause for gloom, however, because there was an *interaction* between the type of therapy and sex.

Two independent variables interact if the *effect* of one is influenced by the *level* of the other. In the present example, the effect of therapy can be assessed separately for males and females. If we consider only males, behavior therapy is better than cognitive therapy, since a low score indicates little or no depression. But, if we consider the effect of therapy for females, we find that cognitive therapy is better than behavior therapy. The two variables are said to interact because the effect of one variable (therapy) depends on the level of the other independent variable (which sex we consider). Notice that it is the independent variables themselves, therapy and sex, that interact and *not* the levels of the variables; that is, it is incorrect to say that behavior therapy interacts with males or that cognitive therapy interacts with females.

Thus, *interaction* has a special meaning when used to describe the relationship between independent variables. It means that the effect of one independent variable is influenced by the level of another. To appreciate this fact, we can imagine that the investigator studied the effect of therapy using male participants only. What conclusion would be reached? The conclusion would be that behavior therapy is better than cognitive therapy. Or, if the effect of therapy was studied using only female participants, the conclusion would be that cognitive therapy is better than behavior therapy. Taken as a whole, the results reveal that the effectiveness of cognitive and behavior therapy depend on the sex of the participant; there is an interaction, but no main effects. When there is an interaction, we must be cautious in interpreting the main effects. In this case there are no main effects because the effects of the therapy manipulation for males are exactly the opposite of the effects for females. Overall there are no differences due to the therapy manipulation, but clearly the interaction indicates that something very interesting is happening. The fact that the effect of the therapy manipulation depends on the sex of the participants might be interesting for a number of reasons, not the least of which is the practical conclusion that depressed males should be given behavior therapy and depressed females should be given cognitive therapy.

Example 4 — Noninteracting Independent Variables. The results we are considering are hypothetical (fictitious). Imagine that the scores for each of the forty participants on the depression questionnaire were as indicated in Table 2-2. Once again, we assess the effects of the independent variables one at a time. To determine the effect of the therapy manipulation, we compare the twenty participants who received behavior therapy with the twenty

TABLE 2-2

The Score of Each of Forty Participants for the Depression Questionnaire as a Function of the Type of Therapy and the Sex of the Participant for Example 4 (fictitious data)

Sex	Therapy		Row mean
	Behavior	*Cognitive*	
Male	10 10 10 10 10 $\bar{X} = 10$ 10 10 10 10 10	5 5 5 5 5 $\bar{X} = 5$ 5 5 5 5 5	7.5
Female	25 25 25 25 25 $\bar{X} = 25$ 25 25 25 25 25	20 20 20 20 20 $\bar{X} = 20$ 20 20 20 20 20	22.5
Column mean	17.5	12.5	

participants who received cognitive therapy. The type of therapy had an effect of 5 — the average performance for those who received cognitive therapy was 12.5 and thus better than the average performance of 17.5 for those who received behavior therapy. Remember that a low score indicates little or no depression. A comparison of the scores for males with the scores for females also reveals a clear difference, a mean of 7.5 and 22.5, respectively, and, thus, an effect of 15. Consequently, there is a main effect of therapy and a main effect of sex. The main effects reveal that cognitive therapy is better than behavior therapy and that females are more depressed following treatment than males. These conclusions do not have to be qualified because there is no interaction. The effect of therapy for males (in this case a difference of 5) is the same as the effect for females, a difference of 5.

By now you may be ready to conclude that there is a clear relationship between main effects and interactions. If there are no main effects, there is an interaction; if there are main effects, there is no interaction. This is *not* the case! Any outcome is possible depending, of course, on the scores obtained on the dependent measure. You can have two main effects and an interaction, no main effects or interaction, one main effect and an interaction, and so on. We will consider one last example to demonstrate that interactions and main effects are independent. For our last example, we will also consider two nonsubject variables, therapy and drug. Any combination of subject and nonsubject variables can be used as independent variables. For an experiment with two independent variables, both independent variables can be subject variables, both can be nonsubject variables, or you could have, as in our previous examples, one subject variable and one nonsubject variable.

Example 5 — Two Nonsubject Variables. For our last example, imagine that you are interested in the effectiveness of therapy and drugs for treating depression. You conduct an experiment in which you use a 2 by 2 factorial design with therapy (cognitive or control) as one independent variable and the drug used (lithium carbonate or placebo) as the other independent variable. Your dependent variable, once again, is the score of each participant on a depression questionnaire. Assume that the results presented in Table 2-3 were obtained for your hypothetical experiment. How would you describe these results?

Once again, we try to do only one thing at a time. To assess for any main effect of the therapy manipulation, we obtain the mean score for all the participants who received cognitive therapy (mean = 10) and compare it with the mean for all the participants who did not receive therapy (mean = 22.5). In this case there is a clear main effect, which supports the effectiveness of cognitive therapy. To assess whether there is a main effect due to the drug manipulation we compare the mean performance for all the participants who received lithium carbonate (mean = 15) with the mean for all the participants who did not (mean = 17.5). The results of this comparison indicate a

TABLE 2-3

The Rating of Each of Forty Participants on the Depression Questionnaire as a Function of the Type of Therapy and the Drug Manipulations for Example 5 (fictitious data)

Drug	Therapy		Row mean
	Cognitive	Control	
Lithium carbonate	10 10 10 10 10 $\bar{X} = 10$ 10 10 10 10 10	20 20 20 20 20 $\bar{X} = 20$ 20 20 20 20 20	15
Placebo	10 10 10 10 10 $\bar{X} = 10$ 10 10 10 10 10	25 25 25 25 25 $\bar{X} = 25$ 25 25 25 25 25	17.5
Column mean	10	22.5	

small effect of the drug manipulation. Finally, we ask if the effectiveness of the therapy manipulation depends on whether participants received lithium carbonate or a placebo. It does because the effect of therapy was equal to 10 for the participants who received lithium carbonate and 15 for the participants who received the placebo. Thus, the effectiveness of therapy was dependent upon whether participants received a drug or not. For our hypothetical (fictitious) example, therapy was more effective when participants were given a placebo than when they were given lithium carbonate.

The results presented in Tables 2-1, 2-2, and 2-3 may seem very artificial because all participants given the same treatment had the same score.

For the present, however, there is no harm in assuming that all participants are of identical ability, and such an assumption should make it easier to understand how the effects of independent variables and interactions are assessed. The use of concrete examples, especially your own examples, can help you to grasp the concept of main effects and interactions. There is no good substitute for generating your own examples and considering all possible outcomes. Later you will see that the same basic procedure is used to evaluate outcomes of experiments when participants in the same condition differ in ability, but then one has to be careful about concluding that an obtained difference between conditions is a result of the treatment manipulation. A difference may be due solely to the chance fluctuations that are always present. The problem of deciding when to attribute differences to the independent variable(s) plus chance, and when to attribute them solely to chance, will be considered in detail in subsequent chapters.

SUMMARY

There are four basic methods that psychologists and social scientists use to study behavior and mental activity: observation, correlation, experimentation, and quasi-experimentation. Observations play an important role in all the methods considered because we can only test explanations that yield predictions about observable events. Humans have strengths and weaknesses as observers. Without special equipment we are not able to observe many behaviors, and we are typically biased. Our selectivity and biases are also positive features, however, because they are the grist for developing explanations. We can distinguish among observations on the basis of whether they are unrestricted or restricted, reactive or nonreactive, and whether the investigator intervenes to ensure that the situation of interest occurs (that is, intervention or nonintervention).

Correlational techniques allow investigators to specify the degree of relationship between variables. Correlation can be used to predict; the accuracy of the prediction will depend on the magnitude of the correlation. Although most correlational techniques do not permit one to infer a causal relationship, the correlation may, in fact, be due to a cause-effect connection between the variables. If such a connection does exist, then the variables will be correlated. The reverse is not true, however. Thus, correlational techniques can be used to "discover" causal relationships since two highly correlated variables may prove to be causally related when subjected to experimentation.

The experimental method differs from the other approaches in that the experimenter manipulates one or more independent variables and assesses the effect of the manipulations on one or more dependent measures. The independent variable is what the investigator manipulates, that is, the treatment. The dependent variable is what he measures to assess the effect of the independent variable. The logic of the method is to treat equivalent groups identically in all respects except one. If the groups differ in performance following the introduction of the treatment, then the difference can be attributed to the effect of the treatment. Quasi-experimental designs are procedures for introducing something like experimental control in data-collection operations even though it is not possible to determine who gets the treatment and who does not.

One way of distinguishing among the four methods is by the extent to which the investigator can intervene and control the situation. If there is no intervention, only the passive observation of behavior, then an observational technique is used. Correlational techniques are procedures for assessing the degree of relationship between variables *after* observations have been made. Correlational techniques are procedures for analyzing the relationships among variables, not procedures for studying behavior and mental activity directly. There are many kinds of interventions. We can intervene to ensure that a particular situation occurs and then passively observe the behavior of bystanders (an observational technique), or we can intervene to control the treatment each participant receives. If we are able to intervene to control the treatment each participant receives, we can form equivalent groups and then manipulate one or more independent variables. If two or more independent variables are manipulated in the same experiment, we can assess how behavior and mental activity are influenced by combinations of variables. If the effect of one independent variable is influenced by the level of another, they are said to interact.

QUESTIONS

(Answers for the multiple choice questions are given in Appendix D.)

1. What are some of the advantages and disadvantages of humans as observers?
2. What are the unrestricted-restricted, reactive-nonreactive, and intervention-nonintervention distinctions? What are the advantages and disadvantages of each?
3. What is the purpose of correlation? What determines whether a positive or negative correlation will be obtained? Are positive correlations better than negative ones? What are some of the uses of correlation? *Prediction*
4. Why is it difficult, if not impossible, to demonstrate causality from correlational evidence?
5. Why does the investigator's ability to intervene and control a situation determine the method that can be used to study behavior and mental activity? What are the advantages of being able to intervene and control a situation?
6. What is the relationship between the nature of the intervention an investigator makes and the subject variable–nonsubject variable distinction?

7. Distinguish between independent and dependent variables and give an example of each.

8. What does it mean to say that two variables interact? Give an example of two that can be expected to interact and indicate why your expectation is reasonable.

9. What is the advantage of manipulating a subject variable and a nonsubject variable in the same experiment?

10. An investigation was conducted by Norris (1971) in which the crying and laughing behavior of ninety severely retarded children who were living at home was compared with that of fifteen such children who were living in an institution. The children living at home attended a training center. Those in the institution attended the institution school. The investigator observed the children for ten consecutive school days. He concluded that those who lived at home laughed more than those in the institution, but that there was no difference in crying behavior between the two groups. Describe the method used by the investigator. Be specific. For example, if the experimental method was used, indicate the independent and dependent variables. Can the differences observed be attributed to where the children lived? Why or why not?

11. Cohen, Liebson, and Faillace (1972) performed a study in which alcoholics were tested under two conditions. Each alcoholic was allowed to drink ten ounces of alcohol each day for the duration of the five-week study. Each was tested under condition A for the first, third, and fifth weeks, and condition B for the second and fourth weeks. In condition A the subject was given special privileges for drinking five or fewer ounces of alcohol each day. In condition B no such special privileges were given. The major finding was that subjects drank less per day under condition A than under condition B. What method was used in this study? Be specific. Can the differences in drinking be attributed to the special privileges manipulation? Why or why not?

12. Schusterman and Gentry (1971) studied four captive male sea lions, noting their annual weight fluctuation, food consumption, and territorial behaviors. They found that the annual weight fluctuation was related to the reproductive season. Seasonal fattening, which started at five years of age, was associated with increased signs of territoriality. What method(s) did the investigators use?

13. Imagine that an investigator was interested in the effects of alcohol and sleep deprivation on vigilance. The vigilance task involved responding (pressing a key) every time a barely audible stimulus was presented. The number of correct detections in a four-hour period was the dependent measure. There were two levels of alcohol (four ounces versus none) and two levels of sleep deprivation (thirty-six hours versus none). Indicate a set of fictitious results that would lead the investigator to conclude that there was (were):

    a. a main effect of alcohol only
    b. a main effect of sleep deprivation only
    c. an alcohol by sleep deprivation interaction only
    d. two main effects and an interaction

14. Personality, intelligence, and achievement tests are all   (1) nonreactive

measures with intervention   (2) nonreactive measures without intervention
(3) reactive measures

15. The accuracy of prediction _____ as the magnitude of the correlation increases.   (1) does not change   (2) decreases   (3) increases

16. Which value of *r* (correlation coefficient) indicates the strongest degree of relationship?   (1) + .67   (2) + .87   (3) − .05   (4) − .92

17. The major drawback with correlational data is that knowledge of the correlation typically does not   (1) allow us to predict scores from one variable to the other   (2) allow us to say anything about the magnitude of the regression effect   (3) tell us anything about a cause-effect relationship between the variables   (4) tell us anything about the degree of relationship between the two variables

18. The four criteria for causality accepted by most scientists are association, time priority, nonspurious relation, and rationale. Correlation is most useful for determining   (1) association   (2) time priority   (3) nonspurious relation   (4) rationale

19. _____ refers to whether another variable can account for the observed relationship between two variables. (1) Association   (2) Time priority   (3) Spuriousness   (4) Rationale

20. Two variables that have a high correlation   (1) are causally related   (2) are not causally related   (3) may or may not be causally related   (4) have a nonspurious relation

21. Using the experimental method properly makes it possible to   (1) assess the association between variables   (2) control time priority between variables   (3) assess nonspurious relationships   (4) all of the above

22. An investigator administers vitamin C to one group and a placebo to a second group to assess the effect of vitamin C on the common cold. The frequency of colds is the   (1) independent variable   (2) dependent variable   (3) confounding variable   (4) matching variable

23. The variable measured to assess the effect of a treatment manipulation (the difference between an experimental and control group) is called the _____ variable.   (1) subject   (2) independent   (3) nonsubject   (4) extraneous   (5) dependent

24. The group receiving the treatment is called the _____ group; the group that does not is called the _____ group.   (1) control, experimental   (2) experimental, control   (3) matched, unmatched   (4) independent, dependent   (5) dependent, independent

25. Subject variables differ from nonsubject variables in that the investigator   (1) selects nonsubject variables and manipulates subject variables   (2) is free to determine the level of the subject variable each subject receives   (3) is free to determine the level of the nonsubject variable each subject receives   (4) can only use subject variables as dependent measures

26. There is a special meaning for the term *equivalent groups* in psychological research. Groups are equivalent   (1) only if their means are identical   (2) if group differences can be attributed solely to chance fluctuations   (3) if there are no chance fluctuations   (4) if there are chance fluctuations plus the effect of a treatment

27. It is possible to form equivalent groups prior to the introduction of the independent variable if the independent variable is a(n) _____ variable.
(1) subject   (2) nonsubject   (3) quasi-experimental   (4) organismic

28. In which case is the investigator, all else being equal, most likely to reach a cause-effect conclusion?   (1) a correlation study   (2) a nonsubject variable manipulation with experimental design   (3) a subject variable selected as independent variable   (4) a quasi-experimental design

29. _____ designs are procedures for introducing something like experimental control in data-collection operations even though it is not possible to determine who gets the experimental treatment and who doesn't.
(1) Nonexperimental   (2) Quasi-experimental   (3) Correlational   (4) Between-subject

30. The effect of an independent variable is assessed by   (1) comparing performance on the dependent variable for the levels of the independent variable   (2) comparing performance on the independent variable for the levels of the independent variable   (3) comparing performance on the matching variable   (4) assessing performance on intervening variables

31. The experimenter has control over the   (1) effect of the independent variable   (2) levels of the independent variable   (3) levels of the dependent variable   (4) effect of the dependent variable

32. A main effect is   (1) the effect of one independent variable on the level of a second independent variable   (2) the effect of one independent variable on another independent variable   (3) the effect of one independent variable on a dependent variable   (4) caused by the interaction of independent variables

33. An investigator compared the effectiveness of two instructional techniques (A and B) in two classrooms (high school and college). Technique A was significantly better than technique B for high school students, but technique B was significantly better than technique A for college students. Performance on the final exam was the dependent measure. It is safe to assume that the investigator found   (1) two significant main effects and no interaction   (2) a significant interaction   (3) one significant main effect and one interaction   (4) no significant interactions

Motivation

	Low	High
A	$\bar{X} = 50$	$\bar{X} = 30$
B	$\bar{X} = 50$	$\bar{X} = 10$

Method (label for rows A and B)

34. The above results were obtained in an experiment in which the motivation of the participants and the instructional method were the two independent variables. The mean scores on the dependent measure for all four conditions are presented in the table. Assume that any obtained differences are signifi-

cant. The results reveal (1) a main effect of method (2) a main effect of motivation (3) a significant interaction (④) all of the above

Sex of subject

	Male	Female
Method A	$\bar{X} = 30$	$\bar{X} = 30$
B	$\bar{X} = 50$	$\bar{X} = 10$

35. The above results were obtained in an experiment in which the sex of the subjects and the instructional method were the two independent variables. The mean scores on the dependent measure for all four conditions are presented in the table. Assume that any obtained differences are significant. The results reveal (1) a main effect of method only (2) a main effect of sex only (3) a main effect of method and a significant interaction (④) a main effect of sex and a significant interaction

36. In a 2 by 2 factorial design an interaction is obtained if (1) the level of one independent variable depends on the effect of the other independent variable (2) the effect of one independent variable depends on the effect of the other independent variable (3) the level of one independent variable depends on the level of the other independent variable (④) the effect of one independent variable depends on the level of the other independent variable

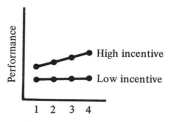

Stage of practice

37. The above figure indicates the results of an experiment in which a 2 by 4 factorial design was used. Incentive (high versus low) and stage of practice (1–4) are the two independent variables. Performance on the dependent measure is plotted on the vertical axis. An examination of the figure suggests that (1) there is a main effect due to incentive (2) there is a main effect due to stage of practice (3) there is an interaction between incentive and stage of practice (④) all of the above

38. In a 2 by 2 factorial design (1) there are four independent variables (②) there are two levels of each of the two independent variables (3) there

are two independent variables and two dependent variables   (4) there are two levels of each of the two dependent variables

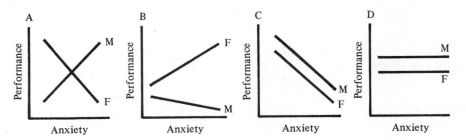

39. In which of the above figures would all effects be significant given that any differences are significant differences? The two independent variables are sex (male and female) and anxiety (high and low).   (1) A   (2) B   (3) C   (4) D

3 Estimation and hypothesis testing

We use estimation to draw inferences about quantities that cannot be tested directly, usually for practical reasons. For example, political candidates may assess how the voters stand on particular issues before they develop their own positions. Businesses may estimate how well a particular product will sell before making a large financial commitment. Social scientists are interested in knowing the opinions of the general population on a number of topics such as abortion, the effectiveness of the judicial system, collective bargaining for public employees, sexual practices, friendship, drug use, amount of exercise, as well as numerous other matters. It is not practical, however, to obtain measures on a large number of participants even though we would like to be able to make general statements about the opinions, preferences, or practices of a large number of people. We need, then, systematic procedures that allow us to estimate values (such as opinions, characteristics) for a large number of individuals after making observations on a small number of individuals. Systematic procedures need to be used because, without them, we are not likely to obtain precise estimates. One of our goals in this chapter is to consider how we can obtain precise estimates and what we mean by precision.

Investigators are frequently interested in testing their explanations for phenomena (sex differences in accident rates, depression, individual differences in cognitive ability), and the effectiveness of various treatments (different instructional approaches, therapies, strategies). A tentative explanation (a plausible alternative explanation) is frequently called a hypothesis. The process of testing hypotheses, ideas, views, theories, or notions is usually labeled hypothesis testing. We need to have systematic procedures because, without them, we are likely to allow our biases to determine the conclusions that we reach. Our first task is to consider the importance of randomization for eliminating systematic biases.

RANDOMIZATION

Random Sampling

Imagine that you would like to determine the opinions of your fellow students on a number of issues (the death penalty, foreign aid, government guarantees for business loans), but you have a very tight budget. You only have fifty questionnaires. You would like to obtain the opinions of fifty students who are representative of the entire student body at your institution; that is, you want a representative sample of the population being studied. The *sample* is usually a small portion (in this case fifty) of the participants who could have been selected; the larger group of potential participants (in this case the entire student body) is called the *population*.

How might you obtain a representative sample? Can you simply select your friends, the first fifty people you meet on a particular day, fifty students in a particular class, drinkers at a local pub, or students in your dormitory wing? What determines whether a sample is representative? Must the sample have the same characteristics as the population? For example, if the student body is 60 percent female and 40 percent male, must your sample have thirty females and twenty males? Should your sample have the same proportion of blondes as the general population, the same proportion of left-handers, blacks, tall people, Protestants, late sleepers, early risers, and so on?

Definition of a Random Sample. A little reflection should convince you that you will not be able to obtain a sample that matches the population in every detail. All we can do, and all we *need* to do, is use a procedure that eliminates any *systematic* bias in the selection process. The solution is to select a random sample. We define a random sample as one in which each subject (each participant in the case of selecting humans) in the population being considered has an equal chance of being selected and the selection of one subject does not influence the selection or nonselection of another. All conceivable samples should be equally likely.

Sometimes investigators place restrictions on the sampling process in order to obtain a sample with specific characteristics. For example, if a random sample of 1000 participants were selected from the United States population, it might not contain the same proportion of blacks as found in the general population, even though it is likely to be very close in most instances. If it is important to have a number of representatives of a particular minority group, your sampling can be random with the restriction that a specified proportion should consist of minorities. Later we will see why it is useful to place some restrictions on random selection.

Obtaining a Random Sample. Assume that you want to select a random sample of 50 students from a college having an enrollment of 980. One way of selecting them would be to print each student's name on a piece of paper, throw all the pieces into a large basket, mix them up, and then draw out fifty pieces of paper while you are blindfolded. You would obtain a random sample because each student, and any combination of 50 students, could be selected. However, this procedure would be very time-consuming if a sample is being selected from a large population.

Instead of printing all the names on separate pieces of paper, you may decide to use the student directory, which provides an alphabetical listing of the 980 students. You assign a number to each student from 1 to 980 by using the alphabetical listing; that is, the first student in the listing receives the number 1 and the last student in the listing receives the number 980. Then you turn to Appendix C-9 to select fifty numbers from 1 to 980 from the table or random numbers. To select the fifty numbers you first select a starting number in a haphazard manner and then block off successive digits in groups of three (you want numbers between 1 and 980). Once you select your three-digit starting number you simply continue to select successive *three-digit* numbers by going either vertically or horizontally (but not both) in the table. For example, if your haphazard method for entering the table gave you the twenty-first row and the twenty-seventh column on page 348 as a starting point, your starting digit is zero. (Caution: the columns are grouped by twos. Thus, the number 5, of the twenty-first row, is in the first column, 3 is in the second column, and so forth.) Going across (so that we will finish the twenty-first row before starting the twenty-second row), the first three-digit number is 002. The next ten three-digit numbers would be 035, 553, 151, 510, 083, 632, 255, 407, 666, and 268. You continue until you have obtained fifty numbers from 1 to 980. The students who have numbers corresponding to the fifty numbers selected from the table constitute a random sample. Each student and any combination of students had an equal chance of being selected for the sample.

Human Bias and Random Sampling. Much of the material that we will consider is based on the use of systematic procedures which avoid bias. In selecting a sample, we avoid bias by using random selection procedures which ensure that only chance determines who is selected for the sample. You might object because you believe you could select a sample without introducing systematic bias. You may believe, for example, that you could select a representative sample of students at your university or college by using your own judgment about the representativeness of each person for the sample. This is highly unlikely because, among other things, it assumes that you already know the characteristics of the student population. This is backwards; we select samples because we are interested in using the characteristics of the subjects in the sample to *estimate* the characteristics of the population. We also need to consider your ability to select a "random" sample without using systematic procedures.

Imagine that there are ten balls in an urn and each ball has a different single digit from 0 to 9. After the balls are well mixed, a blindfolded person draws a ball. You record the number of the ball, return the ball to the urn, mix the balls, and then have the blindfolded person draw another ball. You continue this process until you have obtained thirty numbers. With this procedure we will obtain a random string of thirty single-digit numbers. Instead of going through this laborious procedure of selecting balls from an urn, simply write down the results that you might obtain if you were to use a balls-and-urn procedure. That is, your task is simply to generate a string of single-digit numbers, thirty in all. For this example to be useful, it is necessary for you to generate a string of digits before proceeding.

After you have completed this task examine your string of thirty digits and count the number of times, if any, that you repeat a number immediately (the same number occupies consecutive positions in the string). For example, the digit series 8, 7, 3, 3, 5, 6, 8, 4, 8, 9, 1, 1, and 6 has two digits which occupy consecutive positions in the string, 3 and 1. After counting the number of times you repeat a digit immediately, refer to the table of Random Numbers in Appendix C-9, select a string of thirty consecutive digits in the table in some haphazard fashion, and then count the number of times a digit is repeated immediately. If you are like most people, you will find that there are more digits repeated consecutively in the table than in the string you generated. Most of us have a bias against repeating digits in consecutive positions. If we are unable to generate a string of random digits, how can we expect to select a random sample of participants from a population? We are likely to have more biases about people (who is representative and who is not) than we have about numbers.

Importance of Random Sampling. The goal of *estimation* is to determine characteristics of a population by determining the characteristics of a small portion of that population (a sample). The crucial step in this process is obtaining a representative sample. Values for the sample (the sample mean) are called *statistics.* Values for the population (the population mean) are called *parameters.* Thus, statistics describe samples, and parameters describe populations. If a representative (random) sample is selected, statistics can be obtained to estimate parameters. For example, if you select a random sample of twenty-five college students from a small liberal arts college, the population is all students at the college. The mean intelligence score for your sample (a statistic) could be used to estimate the mean for the population (a parameter).

Investigators interested in estimating population parameters from statistics are concerned with the properties of their estimators (statistics) and the different kinds of estimates that can be made. They are also interested in the precision of their predictions, a matter which we will consider in more detail shortly when we discuss sampling distributions.

Random Assignment

It is important to distinguish between random sampling and random assignment. The purpose of random sampling is to obtain a sample that is representative of a larger population so that the properties of the population can be estimated. The purpose of random assignment of subjects is to obtain equivalent groups before introducing the independent variable so that the effect of that variable can be estimated.

Importance of Random Assignment. It is difficult to overestimate the importance of random assignment procedures. It is a systematic procedure for avoiding bias in the assignment of participants to conditions. If we can avoid biases in assigning participants to conditions, then we can assert that any differences between groups (conditions) prior to the introduction of the independent variable are due solely to chance. Our principal concern will be whether differences between groups (conditions) *after* the introduction of the independent variable are due solely to chance fluctuations or to the effect of the independent variable plus chance fluctuations.

Consider a concrete, unrealistic example. Imagine that you develop a new drug that you believe will make humans much more intelligent. You decide to do an experiment in which one group of participants receives your new drug and the other group receives a placebo. You have 200 volunteers who you randomly assign to the two conditions with the only restriction being that there be 100 participants in each group. Only chance determines whether a particular participant is assigned to the drug or placebo condition. If you obtained the average IQ for the participants in the drug condition and the participants in the placebo condition *prior* to the introduction of the drug (before the participants are treated differently in any way), should you expect to find large differences? No, you should expect the mean IQs for the two groups to be similar (within one or two points). In fact, it is likely that we would not even bother to measure IQ prior to introducing the drug and the placebo because we are confident that random assignment will produce roughly equivalent groups. Imagine that you determine the mean IQs following the introduction of the treatment and find that the mean IQ of the drug group is 40 points higher than for the placebo group. How would you account for this difference? Is it due to chance fluctuation only, or to chance fluctuation plus the effect of the independent variable?

You will probably agree that a mean difference as large as 40 IQ points is extremely unlikely if only chance is operating, particularly when you have 100 participants in each condition; therefore, it is much more likely that the drug manipulation is responsible for most of the obtained differences in the average IQ between groups. With such a large difference, there can be little argument about the influence of the independent variable. What happens, however, when a much smaller difference (10, 5, or 2 IQ points) is obtained between groups? To answer, we would need to know something about how large a difference we might expect between groups if only chance were operating. If we know what to expect if only chance is operating then we can make a decision about whether only chance is operating or whether the obtained differences are better attributed to chance fluctuations plus the effect of the independent variable. The size of chance fluctuations is a matter that we will consider shortly.

Random Assignment Procedure. There are many acceptable random assignment procedures. The only restriction is that chance alone should determine the particular treatment a participant receives. However, it is not unusual for investigators to place additional restrictions on their random assignment procedures. There are statistical and methodological advantages to randomly assigning the subjects to groups with the restriction that there be an equal number of subjects in each group. A simple way to ensure this is to use the table of random permutations of the first eight digits, found in Appendix C-1. The table contains 280 random sequences of the eight numbers. It is very useful whenever you have eight or fewer treatment conditions.

Imagine that you want to assign sixty participants to three conditions so that there are twenty in each condition. You can do this by using twenty of the sequences of eight numbers in Appendix C-1. The first step is to select a starting sequence by some random procedure. For example, you could put each of the numbers from 0 to 9 on a piece of paper, put the papers in a hat, and draw one number at a time, returning and mixing after each draw, until you get an acceptable number (from 1 to 280). Assume that you select 163 as the starting sequence.

After the starting sequence is selected and located in the table, it is only necessary to note the ordering of the numbers 1, 2, and 3 in each sequence, because only three groups of subjects are needed; the other five numbers in each sequence are ignored. The order in the first sequence (sequence 163) is found to be 2, 3, 1, so the first subject is assigned to condition 2, the second to condition 3, and the third to condition 1. The same procedure is followed, using the next nineteen consecutive sequences to assign the other fifty-seven subjects to the three conditions. The next sequence (164) is used for the next set of three subjects, and so on. When twenty sequences have been used there will be twenty subjects in each condition. The subjects will be randomly assigned to the three conditions with the restriction that there be an equal number in each condition. Any differences obtained between the three conditions *prior* to the introduction of an independent variable can be attributed solely to chance fluctuations, provided, of course, that the participants in each condition are treated the same. A matter of considerable importance is the magnitude of chance fluctuations as they relate to the probability of a particular experimental outcome and the precision of estimation.

PROBABILITY

Probability can be an extremely complicated topic to consider; therefore, we will try to keep the discussion as simple as possible by dealing with equally likely outcomes and relatively simple examples. For example, we assume that each card in a well-shuffled, standard deck of playing cards has an equal chance of being selected or that each of the numbers 1 to 6 has an equal chance of occurring when you roll a single die. There are trick or biased decks of cards and "loaded" dice, but we will not deal with these possibilities. In most instances you can be confident that the "equally likely" assumption is valid. For example, if you go to Las Vegas to gamble, you can be confident that the dice and cards are "fair" in the sense that the laws of probability will do a good job of predicting how much the gambling casinos will win for each of their games of chance over the long haul. Gambling casino managers do not have to rely on loaded dice or trick cards to win; they understand the laws of probability for the games of chance in their casinos. Gamblers who do not understand the probability of winning for the different games of chance are at a distinct disadvantage because, in their ignorance, they are likely to make sucker bets. A knowledge of probability can have numerous applications beyond the social sciences.

Definition of Probability

The probability of an outcome can be defined as the ratio of the number of favorable outcomes to the total number of possible outcomes. The only effect that is assumed to operate is *chance*. Therefore, there is the same likelihood that each outcome will occur. A few examples should help to clarify the notion of probability. Consider the probability of drawing the ace of spades from a standard deck of well-shuffled playing cards. Since there is only one favorable outcome, the ace of spades, and fifty-two possible outcomes, the probability is 1/52 or .019. If only chance is operating, then each card has the same probability of being drawn. Consider the probability of drawing any spade. In this case there are thirteen favorable outcomes (thirteen spades) and fifty-two cards in all, so the probability is 13/52 or .25.

The computation of the ratio of favorable outcomes to total possible outcomes to determine the probability of a particular outcome is a simple procedure as long as one considers simple phenomena such as drawing a particular card or rolling a single number with a single die. Complexity increases as the number of possible outcomes increases. For example, there is only one way to roll a "two" with two dice, but there are six ways to roll a "seven." The probability of rolling a two is 1/36 while the probability of rolling a seven is 6/36 or 1/6. We can enumerate the thirty-six possible outcomes when rolling two dice because there are six possible outcomes for each die.

All we need to do is consider all possible combinations that can be obtained (see Table 3-1). As the phenomena become more complicated or the number of possible outcomes increases, other procedures are needed to determine the number of favorable outcomes and the total number of possible outcomes, but the general principle remains the same. In brief, the view of probability as the number of favorable outcomes divided by the number of total possible outcomes is very useful for social scientists, statisticians, gamblers, and others.

Frequency Distributions

A distribution is a set of values or scores for a particular attribute or variable. There are many kinds of distributions. One could obtain a distribution of scores on a final examination, a distribution of annual salaries for all truck drivers in Minnesota, a distribution of the weights of all college professors in Indiana, and so on. A frequency distribution is obtained, typically, by obtaining one number for each individual participant and counting the number of times each score is obtained. When we make observations, we are usually interested in quantifying our measurements by assigning numbers to objects or events according to a particular rule. For example, we might quantify anxiety by developing an anxiety questionnaire. Since each participant takes the questionnaire, we can obtain an anxiety score for each participant. Consider a hypothetical distribution of scores obtained by administering an anxiety questionnaire to thirty students. The scores are: 10, 42, 18, 38, 42, 39, 65, 55, 40, 35, 38, 45, 41, 25, 53, 44, 39, 43, 29, 38, 44, 46, 37, 42, 43, 43, 41, 37, 49, and 35.

TABLE 3-1

The Thirty-six Possible Outcomes for Two Dice

Second die	First die					
	1	2	3	4	5	6
1	2	3	4	5	6	7
2	3	4	5	6	7	8
3	4	5	6	7	8	9
4	5	6	7	8	9	10
5	6	7	8	9	10	11
6	7	8	9	10	11	12

Note: A particular number (for example, 7) can be rolled a number of different ways.

It is difficult to describe this set of scores as it now stands. About all one can do is read the entire set. A frequency distribution can be obtained by simply arranging the scores in ascending or descending order and counting the number of times each occurs; that is, one determines the frequency of each score in the distribution. A frequency distribution for this set is presented in Table 3-2. A frequency distribution provides a clearer description of the scores. Usually an even clearer description is possible when the scores are grouped into categories as in Table 3-3. Although Table 3-3 is somewhat easier to read than Table 3-2, some information was lost in going from the frequency distribution to the grouped frequency distribution. It is not possible to determine how many participants obtained each score by referring to the grouped frequency distribution.

Frequency distributions are a useful way of describing a set of observations. We can quickly note, for example, that a score of 10 is an unusually low score, a score of 65 is an unusually high score, and that scores in the thirties and forties are relatively common. If a participant is selected at random, we might expect that he or she would be more likely to have a score

TABLE 3–2

The Frequency Distribution for the Thirty Scores on the Anxiety Questionnaire

Scores	Frequency
10	1
18	1
25	1
29	1
35	2
37	2
38	3
39	2
40	1
41	2
42	3
43	3
44	2
45	1
46	1
49	1
53	1
55	1
65	1

TABLE 3-3

*The Grouped Frequency
Distribution for the Thirty
Scores on the Anxiety
Questionnaire*

Scores	Frequency
10–19	2
20–29	2
30–39	9
40–49	14
50–59	2
60–69	1

in the thirties or forties than in the teens or sixties simply because the former is a more common outcome, based on our distribution of outcomes, than the latter possibilities. Frequency distributions can give us some information, then, about the likelihood of different outcomes. However, our major interest is in distributions of outcomes when only chance is operating.

Consider the table of random numbers in Appendix C-9. We are interested in the single-digit numbers from 0 through 9. Since these numbers were obtained by a random procedure, what distribution of numbers should we obtain if we enter the table at a random location and simply count the number of times each digit occurs? That is, we want to obtain a frequency distribution for the digits from 0 through 9. Since only chance determines which digit occurs, we might expect that each digit will occur *about* the same number of times. Our interest here is in just how closely a frequency distribution obtained by counting the number of times each digit occurs in the table matches what we should expect if only chance is operating. To make this determination, we can use a random procedure to select a starting point in the table, the seventeenth row and eleventh column on page 349, proceed across the page (numbers 4, 8, 6, 2, 1, 1, and so on), and continue on to the next row until we obtain a distribution of 300 numbers. The distribution of these numbers is presented in Table 3-4.

An examination of Table 3-4 reveals that for the block of 300 digits considered, some digits (such as the number 6) appeared more frequently than the others whereas some (the 0 digit) appeared less frequently. The fact that only chance determines which digit is selected does not mean that each digit will appear equally often. It only means that each digit has the same probability of being selected. Most of the digits occurred *around* thirty times each, but there was some deviation from this. Another way of saying the

TABLE 3-4

Frequency Distribution of
300 Digits Taken from the
Table of Random Numbers

Digit	Frequency
0	18
1	26
2	33
3	30
4	33
5	37
6	43
7	28
8	28
9	24
	Total 300

same thing is that there are *chance fluctuations* when random sampling or random assignment procedures are used. If the probability of an outcome determined the number of times each digit occurred, then each digit should have occurred exactly thirty times. Each digit did not occur exactly thirty times, but most occurred *around* thirty times; therefore, considering probability enables us to make a good guess about the number of times a particular outcome will be obtained.

Imagine that we repeat the above exercise, but with a new starting number. What is your best guess concerning the number of times each digit will occur? Given that each of the 10 digits has an equal chance of occurring and that 300 digits are considered, we should expect each digit to occur *around* thirty times. It is highly unlikely that each digit will occur exactly thirty times, but thirty is clearly the best guess. It is reasonable to bet, for example, that the digit 0 will occur as often as the digit 6. Now reconsider the frequency distribution presented in Table 3-4. Given these results, would you be willing to bet that a single number selected from the 300 numbers used to obtain this distribution is as likely to be the digit 0 as the digit 6? Clearly this is not the case. Once the digits have been selected we know the number of favorable outcomes for each digit — in this case eighteen for the digit 0 and forty-three for the digit 6.

Knowing the probability of a particular outcome allows us to make a good guess about the actual outcome that will be obtained when only chance is operating, but the predicted results are not likely to be *exactly* the same as the obtained results. We have to expect *some* difference between what we predict and what we obtain. How *much* difference should we expect? Can we do anything to control the amount of the difference between what we predict, based on the probability of an outcome, and the results that will be obtained if only chance is operating? The answer is yes! To consider this answer we need to discuss sampling distributions.

Sampling Distributions

Distinction Between Frequency and Sampling Distributions. For frequency distributions we count the number of times each score is obtained. Typically, we obtain a single number from each participant and then determine the frequency for each score. We obtain a distribution of frequencies, as in Table 3-4. Frequency distributions are a very useful way of describing a set of scores (annual salaries, weights, final examination grades) and of calculating the probability of a particular outcome when we use random selection procedures to select a particular outcome, but frequency distributions are not very useful for estimation and hypothesis testing. Frequency distributions are not useful in these situations because we rarely estimate the characteristics of a population by making a single observation, *and,* when assessing the effectiveness of a particular independent variable, we typically test a number of participants in each treatment condition or obtain many scores for a few participants. Thus, we need distributions for sample values, not individual scores.

The major distinction between frequency and sampling distributions, then, is in the unit of analysis. For frequency distributions we count the number of times each score is obtained. For sampling distributions we compute a single measure which describes the sample (average performance for the participants in the sample) so that we have a single number for each *sample.* To have a sampling distribution we must have two or more samples. For example, if we randomly select three groups of ten participants each, administer an IQ test to each participant, and then compute the average (mean) IQ for each group, we have a single score (in this case the mean) for each group. Since we have three groups, we have three sample values. We have a distribution of sample values, or a sampling distribution based on three samples.

Precision and Sample Size. As we indicated earlier, investigators interested in estimation make observations on a small number of participants (sample) in order to estimate the characteristics (parameters) of the population. Frequently, the interest is in estimating mean performance (average annual income for a family of four, percent who suffer from depression) or measures of individual differences (differences in annual income or the severity of depression). For these estimates to be very useful, we need to know something about the precision of the estimates. What do we mean by precision and how do we assess it? We consider precision in the context of random selection procedures. Our interest is in the size of chance fluctuations when statistics are used to estimate parameters. How do we assess the size of chance fluctuations so that we can say something about the precision of our estimate?

The precision of our estimate is related to the size of the sample we select. This is an extremely important notion, but, unfortunately, a difficult one for most people to understand and appreciate. The first step is to convince you that the precision of estimates does improve as sample size increases. We will once again use the table of random numbers in Appendix C-9, even though this is not a population of values one would typically be interested in. We use it because chance alone determined what digits occur; we are interested in what happens when only chance is operating. In this case, the probability for each outcome (each individual digit from 0 to 9) is equal. Typically, this is not the case when we consider real-world events (heights, weights, income) because there are usually many more scores *around* the average value (the mean) than there are extreme values. For example, using random selection procedures, you are more likely to select a male who is 71 inches tall than a male who is 80 inches tall simply because there are many more males who are 71 than 80 inches tall. With random selection you are more likely to select an average value than an extreme value. Although our example is unusual, it is ideal in the sense that it demonstrates that increasing sample size increases precision even when all outcomes are equally likely.

For our example, we are interested in estimating the mean value for the population, which we will define as all the single-digit numbers in the table of random numbers in Appendix C-9. If you were to add all the single-digit numbers in the table and then divide by the number of digits added, you should obtain a value of around 4.5. We will not bother to do this. Instead, we will consider random samples taken from the table. We will compute a mean value for each sample and use that mean to estimate the value for the population. Our concern is the precision of our estimates. We will use 300 numbers in each case, but we will vary the size of the samples we select. Using the same starting point we used previously (the seventeenth row and eleventh column on page 349), we first select samples of size 2.

For each sample we take two numbers in the table, add them, and divide by 2. Thus, the first two digits, 4 and 8, are added to get 12, and divided by 2 to get a mean of 6. The next two digits, 6 and 2, are added to get 8, and divided by 2 to get a mean of 4. We continue this process until we use 300 numbers and obtain 150 means. The results of this procedure are presented in Table 3-5. As you can see, many of the sample means are close to 4.5, whereas a few are quite extreme (2 and below or 8 and above). What happens to the precision of our estimates as we increase sample size? If you compare Table 3-5 with Table 3-4, and consider each score (Table 3-4) as an estimate of the population mean of 4.5 and each sample mean (Table 3-5) as an estimate of the population mean of 4.5, it is clear that the estimates are closer to the actual population parameter in the second case. What happens if we increase sample size further?

The point of interest is that the precision of our estimate of a population value increases as our sample size increases. To demonstrate this point, we obtain estimates of the population mean for the table of random numbers using samples of size 4, 10, 20, and 100 in addition to the sample size of 2 already considered. Except for changing the sample size, we use the same procedure; that is, we use the same starting point in the table and the same 300 numbers. Thus, with a sample size of 4, we obtain 75 sample means; with a sample size of 10, we obtain 30 sample means; with a sample size of 20, we obtain 15 sample means; with a sample size of 100, we obtain 3 sample means. In order to make a rough comparison of the precision of our estimates, we calculate the percentage or our sample values (means) that fall into each of nine categories. Since we know that the mean for the popu-

TABLE 3-5

Sampling Distribution of Mean Based on 150 Samples of Size 2 Taken from the Table of Random Numbers

Sample mean	Frequency
.5	2
1.0	7
1.5	3
2.0	5
2.5	7
3.0	10
3.5	14
4.0	12
4.5	21
5.0	10
5.5	13
6.0	10
6.5	18
7.0	7
7.5	4
8.0	5
8.5	1
9.0	1
	Total 150

lation should be around 4.5, our precision increases as the percentage of the estimates around 4.5 increases. The results of this demonstration are presented in Table 3-6. The important point to note is that as sample size increases a greater percentage of the estimates are around 4.5. For example, the percent of the sample means in the 4.00 to 4.99 category generally increases as sample size increases whereas the percent of the sample mean in the extreme categories (.00 to .99 and 8.00 to 9.00) decreases as sample size increases.

What does this have to do with estimation and hypothesis testing? The implications for estimation are straightforward. If the precision of estimation increases as sample size increases, we can have more confidence in an estimate based on a large sample than in an estimate based on a small sample, provided that appropriate procedures (random selection) were used to obtain the samples. At the extreme, we can compare the results obtained when we make one observation (select one person or one digit) with the results when we make 100 observations and compute a single sample value based on 100 observations. Our goal in both cases is to estimate the mean for the population. A comparison of Table 3-4 with the last column of Table 3-6 should leave little doubt about the powerful influence of sample size. The probability of obtaining a sample mean having a value between 4.00 and 4.99 is very high when the sample size is 100.

There is also a very important applied implication for gamblers or would-be

TABLE 3–6

The Percent of the Estimates (Sample Means) in Each Category as a Function of Sample Size

| Sample mean | Number of digits used to obtain each sample mean | | | | |
	2	4	10	20	100
.00–.99	1.3	0.0	0.0	0.0	0.0
1.00–1.99	6.7	2.7	0.0	0.0	0.0
2.00–2.99	8.0	9.3	6.7	0.0	0.0
3.00–3.99	16.0	16.0	20.0	6.7	0.0
4.00–4.99	22.0	26.7	40.0	66.7	100.0
5.00–5.99	15.3	26.7	23.3	20.0	0.0
6.00–6.99	18.7	13.3	6.7	6.7	0.0
7.00–7.99	7.3	5.3	3.3	0.0	0.0
8.00–9.00	4.7	0.0	0.0	0.0	0.0

Note: Because the mean value for all the numbers in the table of random numbers is very close to 4.5, precision increases as the percent in the 4.00 to 5.99 category increases.

gamblers. For games of pure chance (roulette, craps, keno, slot machines), it is possible to calculate the cost to the bettor — how much you should expect to lose if you have average luck or if you play for a very long time. For example, a roulette player with average luck can expect to lose slightly more than 5 percent of the amount he or she bets. A knowledgeable crap player can expect to lose slightly less than 1 percent of the amount he or she bets, given average luck. We can consider these values as the population values for the two games. The results for a single gambler can be viewed as a sample. The point is simply that a gambler who gambles a great deal has a very large sample (many observations are obtained), and so the sample statistic is likely to be very close to the population parameter. Managers of gambling establishments know that, over the long haul, they are going to get their 1, 5, or 11 percent, depending on the game, because, as sample size increases, the value for the sample closely approximates the value for the population. The point that most people do not appreciate is that sample size does not have to be very large before successive samples yield very similar estimates and, therefore, there is little chance fluctuation among the samples. As fluctuation of the sample values decreases, precision increases.

The relationship between the precision of estimation and sample size is also important for hypothesis testing. When we randomly assign individuals to conditions, we can be confident that any obtained differences between the groups are due to chance fluctuations only. And we know what to expect if only chance is operating; that is, we know the distribution of possible outcomes if only chance is operating. For example, obtaining a sample mean between .00 and .99 is highly unlikely if we have a sample size of 100, but much more likely if we have a sample size of 2 (see Table 3-6). The sampling distributions obtained in Table 3-6 are based on a relatively small number of samples. It is possible to obtain sampling distributions for a number of situations when chance alone is operating. It is possible to do this because there is a clear relationship between the precision of measurement (estimation) and sample size.

Empirical Sampling Distributions. Let us assume that we are performing a pseudo-experiment in which random assignment is used to form two groups of ten subjects each. (The experiment is a pseudo-experiment in that no independent variable is manipulated.) The subjects in each group are a *sample* from a larger set of potential subjects. We call our groups group 1 and group 2. The groups are treated identically. After forming our groups we obtain a score on the dependent variable for each subject. Then a mean score is computed for each group, and the group 2 mean is subtracted from the group 1 mean to obtain the difference between the two group means. If this procedure were repeated until the pseudo-experiment had been conducted 100,000 times, the result would be 100,000 numbers. Each number would represent the difference between a group 1 and a group 2 mean.

A distribution using these 100,000 numbers could be made by plotting the frequency with which each mean difference was obtained. However, since this is a distribution of sample values, the difference between sample means, it is called a sampling distribution instead of a frequency distribution. Because an independent variable is *not* manipulated, the sampling distribution obtained must reflect *chance fluctuations*. Chance fluctuations are differences between scores which are due solely to chance, not to treatment effects. As we will see shortly, it is important to know how large a difference we can expect between two groups if only chance is operating.

The sampling distribution just considered is a sampling distribution of the difference between two means because we always subtracted one group mean from the other (obtained a difference score) for each of the scores represented in the sampling distribution. This is only one of many kinds of sampling distributions. We can obtain an empirical sampling distribution simply by taking a number of random samples of the same size from a population.

Let us assume that you are interested in determining the average weight of all female students at a large midwestern university. It would be too difficult to get this information for all the female students so you decide to select a *random sample* of 100 from the *population* of 15,000 female students at the university. You select your sample, obtain the weight of each person in the sample, and then compute the mean weight for the sample by adding all 100 weights and dividing by 100. If you have no information about the population mean (the mean weight for all 15,000 female students), the sample mean is the best estimate of the population mean. Because you used random sampling your sample is representative of the population. You do not have a sampling distribution, of course, because you selected only one sample. In order to obtain a sampling distribution you have to repeat the above procedure.

Although it is not practical to obtain empirical sampling distributions, let us *imagine* that you repeat the above procedure until you have 500 samples of 100 female students. A student could be in more than one sample because the total population that you are sampling is only 15,000 students. You now have 500 sample means each based on 100 observations (female students). Do you think that all 500 sample means will be the same? On one hand we might expect them to all be about the same because each sample was chosen to be representative of the population. On the other hand we must expect chance fluctuations because it is likely that some samples will include more heavy or light female students than other samples. The sampling distribution for the 500 estimates will tell us how much chance fluctuation we can expect among the estimates.

The amount of chance fluctuation among sample means is related to the size of the sample. Imagine that you obtain two empirical sampling distributions for the population of 15,000 female students just considered. The first sampling distribution is obtained by selecting 500 samples of 3 students each. The second sampling distribution is obtaining by selecting 500 samples of *150* students each. Thus, we have 500 estimates of the population mean based on 3 people in each sample, and we have 500 estimates of the population mean based on 150 people in each sample. Do you expect the 500 estimates based on 3 people in each sample to be the same? Do you expect the 500 estimates based on 150 people in each sample to be the same? In which case do you expect more chance fluctuation among the 500 estimates (more imprecise estimates)? If you remember our earlier discussion of precision and sample size, you should expect much more sample means fluctuation among the small samples than among the large samples. The sampling distribution based on the 500 samples of 3 students will tell us how much fluctuation of the sample means we can expect for this sample size. And the sampling distribution based on the 500 samples of 150 each will tell us how much chance fluctuation of the sample means we can expect for this sample size. Sampling distributions are important because they tell us how much fluctuation to expect between sample values (sample means) if only chance is operating, as is the case when randomization procedures are used and no independent variable is manipulated.

The above examples are all empirical sampling distributions of *means* because sample means or the differences between sample means were plotted to yield the distribution of sample values. There are other sampling distributions not based on sample means. For example, we could randomly select 100 students from a larger population of 20,000 students, determine the weight and height of each student, and then compute the correlation between weight and height for all 100 students. This procedure would yield one number, between −1.00 and +1.00, for the sample. We could repeat the procedure until we had 700 correlations and then plot their frequency. We would then have an empirical sampling distribution because each correlation is a *sample* value. We can expect the sample values to be *about* the same, since each sample correlation is an *estimate* of the correlation in the population (the correlation you would get if all 20,000 students were considered). Yet there would be some fluctuation among the values because only chance determines who is selected for each sample.

In sum, it is possible to obtain an empirical sampling distribution by taking a number of random samples of the same size from a population, determining a single value for each sample (for example, mean or correlation), and then plotting the distribution of the sample values. There are numerous sampling distributions because the size of the samples selected and the sample statistic obtained (such as mean or correlation) determine the properties of the sampling distribution. The crucial point is that sampling distributions obtained with random sampling procedures are useful because they tell us how much fluctuation to expect among sample values if only chance is operating. This is important information for estimation and hypothesis testing.

It would be too difficult to obtain sampling distributions empirically. The above examples were presented only to give you an understanding of the general nature and usefulness of sampling distributions. It is not necessary to obtain sampling distributions empirically because they can be obtained by using mathematics.

Mathematical Sampling Distributions. The sampling distributions obtained by using mathematics are essentially the same as empirical distributions if each empirical sampling distribution is based on an extremely large number of samples (for example, 100,000). The mathematical sampling distributions are distributions that would be obtained if an *infinite* number of empirical samples were selected. Although the mathematical derivation of sampling distributions is beyond the scope of this text, you should remember that it is possible to use mathematics to obtain sampling distributions that indicate the amount of fluctuation (the precision of estimation) that we can expect if chance alone is operating. The sampling distributions are available. Our concern will be with how we can use them.

Rare and Common Outcomes

Sampling distributions are useful because they allow us to determine whether a particular outcome is rare or common if only chance is operating. To demonstrate this point, reconsider Table 3-6. Imagine that our task is to decide whether a particular sample was selected randomly from the table of random numbers (that is, only chance determined the particular outcome) or a biased procedure was used. We are simply playing a game in which our task is to decide whether a particular outcome is rare or common if only chance is operating. For the first example, you are told that a sample of two digits was selected and a mean of 6.50 was obtained. Is this a rare or common outcome? An examination of Table 3-6 reveals that it is relatively common since 18.7 percent of the samples are in the 6.00 to 6.99 category. What if you are told that a sample of 100 digits was selected and a mean of 6.50 was obtained? In this case you note that this outcome is unlikely if only chance is operating since the sampling distribution based on 100 digits per sample does not contain any samples in the 6.00 to 6.99 category. If we have a sampling distribution based on an infinite number of samples there might be some in this category, but there are not likely to be many. Thus, obtaining a mean of 6.50 when you have a random sample of 100 digits is a rare outcome if only chance is operating. If asked to determine whether the sample was obtained randomly or whether it is a biased sample, you might be willing to conclude that it is biased. It might have been obtained by using a random selection procedure, but the probability of this occurring when chance only is operating is so small that you are willing to conclude that more than chance is operating, that is, a biased selection procedure was used.

The situation is similar when we use sampling distributions to make a decision about a particular experimental outcome. We use random assignment procedures to assign participants to conditions and then we introduce an independent variable. Our concern is whether group differences (the difference in mean performance for the treatment conditions) on the dependent measure should be attributed to chance fluctuation only (a common outcome if only chance is operating) or to chance plus the effect of the treatment. To determine this we compare our experimental outcome with the distribution of possible outcomes. The distribution of possible outcomes is obtained by examining the appropriate *mathematical* sampling distribution. A rare outcome is a large difference between groups where *large* is defined in terms of the likelihood of the difference being obtained if only chance were operating. Small differences are common since, if only chance is operating, we expect two samples selected from the same population to provide us with about the same estimate of the population value. A pictorial representation of a sampling distribution for the difference between two means is presented in Figure 3-1.

We need to note a few characteristics of the distribution of possible outcomes when only chance is operating (sampling distributions) because knowing these characteristics will be useful later. For the distribution plotted in Figure 3-1, we have an infinite number of pairs of samples, all of the same size. Participants are randomly assigned to two groups and we compare the mean performance of the two groups on a dependent measure. For each two samples we obtain one number, the difference between the two means. If only chance is operating, we should obtain a sampling distribution like the one depicted in Figure 3-1 if an infinite number of pairs of samples are considered. The difference between means is plotted on the horizontal axis, and the frequency of each mean difference is plotted on the vertical axis. The height of the curve indicates the relative frequency.

The important point to note is that most of the time we should expect the difference between the two means to be *about* 0, indicated by the fact that the curve is highest over the 0. As the size of the difference between the means increases, the likelihood that this outcome will be obtained decreases. A large difference between means is defined in terms of the likelihood of obtaining such a difference if only chance is operating. If the likelihood is small (only 5 percent of the time), we say that the outcome is rare if only chance is operating. In Figure 3-1, we are interested in extreme outcomes (in this case large mean differences), the "tails" of the distribution. We are not interested in common outcomes if only chance is operating but in rare outcomes if only chance is operating.

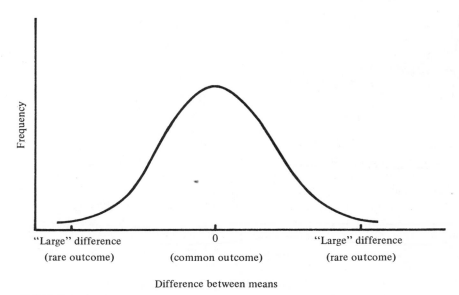

FIGURE 3-1

Sampling distribution for the difference between means

You probably noted that no numbers except 0 are plotted on the horizontal axis. All we have done is to indicate that the difference between means should be about 0, most of the time, if only chance is operating. Why not fill in values to indicate just how large a difference we need to get in order to have a rare outcome if only chance is operating? The reason, as you probably realize, is that the actual difference needed to have a rare outcome depends on a number of factors, primarily the size of the sample. If you doubt this, you can, once again, refer to Table 3-6. A particular outcome may be a common occurrence if small samples are selected but a rare outcome if large samples are selected. Thus, we can only define rare or common outcomes in terms of a particular sampling distribution.

THE LOGIC BEHIND THE STATISTICAL ANALYSIS OF EXPERIMENTS

Conducting an Experiment

Testing Hypotheses. We do experiments to test our hypotheses about the relationships among variables. The excitement of research is related to the quality of our ideas. If you have trivial thoughts, you will probably only do trivial research; if you have interesting and important ideas to test, your research should be interesting and important. For the purpose of presenting the logic behind the statistical analysis of experiments and terminology that investigators use, imagine that you are interested in the effects of jogging on anxiety. You have heard many testimonials from joggers who claim that jogging has beneficial effects, including a reduction in anxiety. You decide to do a two-group experiment to assess the effects of jogging on anxiety.

Earlier we noted the distinction between independent and dependent variables. The independent variable is determined by the experimenter. In this case you decide to manipulate jogging. Some of your participants will jog and some will not; *you* decide who jogs and who does not. You need some measure that will allow you to evaluate whether the independent variable has had any effect (a dependent measure). You decide to use heartbeats per minute in a "standard" waiting situation designed to promote anxiety. We will not be concerned with the details of how the measure is obtained or with the details of conducting the experiment. You use a random assignment procedure to determine which participants jog and which participants do not. Sometime later (say, four months) you obtain a measure of heartbeats per minute in your standard waiting situation. Your interest is in whether jogging is related to heartbeat rate.

Research and Null Hypotheses. Investigators distinguish between two kinds of hypotheses: research and null. A *research hypothesis* is an assertion about a particular phenomenon (whether sex differences in accident rates among children are genetically determined) or the relationship among variables (whether jogging reduces anxiety). For our particular example, your research hypothesis is that jogging reduces anxiety; therefore, you expect the mean heartbeats per minute for the joggers to be lower than for the nonjoggers. The research hypothesis (usually indicated by the symbol H_1) will be of scientific interest if it is supported by your experimental results. The *null hypothesis* (usually indicated by the symbol H_0) is the statement that the treatment manipulation will *not* have any effect — that there is zero effect due to the independent variable. If the null hypothesis is true, then the observed differences in performance on the dependent measure (heartbeat rate per minute) are due solely to chance fluctuations. If the research hypothesis is true, then the differences between treatment conditions are due to chance fluctuations *plus* the effect of the independent variable.

Why do we have to bother with a research hypothesis–null hypothesis distinction when, clearly, our interest is in the research hypothesis? The reason is that the null hypothesis is the only hypothesis that we can test directly. The null hypothesis is the assertion that only chance is operating. We know the distribution of possible outcomes (sampling distributions) when only chance is operating, so we can compare our particular result (the result of our experiment) with the distribution we can expect if only chance is operating to decide whether chance alone or more than chance is operating. We formulate our research hypothesis and null hypothesis so that they both cannot be correct. If the null hypothesis is rejected, then we accept the research hypothesis. This is a reasonable strategy provided our experiment is methodologically sound.

Experimental Design and Results. The experimental or quasi-experimental design is the plan used to test whether a manipulation has had an effect. We will discuss these designs in subsequent units. Here we need only point out that the various experimental designs (but not quasi-experimental designs) can be viewed as different procedures for obtaining equivalent groups. In the present example, we used random assignment of participants to obtain equivalent groups prior to the introduction of the treatment. We will assume that the experiment was conducted properly and the results presented in Table 3-7 were obtained. Does jogging influence the number of heartbeats per minute or are the obtained results due to chance fluctuations only? To determine whether obtained differences are due to the effect of the independent variable or only to chance, we need to perform statistical tests.

Statistical Tests

The task is to determine whether the results obtained in Table 3-7 represent a common or rare outcome if only chance is operating (jogging has no effect on heartbeats per minute in a standard waiting situation). Is this particular outcome rare or common if only chance is operating? An examination

TABLE 3-7

*Heartbeats per Minute During "Standard" Waiting
Situation for Participants in the Jogging and Nonjogging Condition (fictitious data)*

	Jogging condition	Nonjogging condition
	69	75
	69	71
	75	79
	70	76
	73	76
	70	73
Total	426	450
$\bar{X}$	71	75

of the results reveals that the mean for the participants in the nonjogging condition is higher than for the participants in the jogging condition, but is this mean difference of 4 large enough to warrant concluding that jogging has actually had an effect? How likely is it that we could obtain a mean difference of 4 solely on the basis of chance? To answer this question we need to compare this experimental outcome with the appropriate sampling distribution.

In order to get our results in the appropriate form to make this comparison, we perform a statistical test. All the statistical tests to be considered in the second section of this text deal with the probability of a particular outcome occurring by chance. The essential question is whether the results obtained are a common or rare occurrence when only chance is operating. The end result of each statistical test is a single number, which is then compared with a number found by referring to the appropriate statistical table. The statistical tables are based on sampling distributions. This comparison lets us decide whether a particular experimental outcome is rare or common *when the null hypothesis is true*. If the outcome is rare, we conclude that more than chance is operating. We reject the null hypothesis and accept the research hypothesis. If the outcome is not rare, the null hypothesis is not rejected.

Significant Differences. The obtained differences between groups are said to be *significant if the results* are unlikely to occur on the basis of chance. If a particular experimental outcome is rare when chance only is operating, it is reasonable to assert that *more than* chance is operating and to reject the null hypothesis and accept the research hypothesis. In this case the investigator asserts that the differences between the treatments were not due solely to chance fluctuations, but to chance *plus* the effect of the independent variable. If the results are such that the null hypothesis can be rejected, the obtained differences are said to be significant. Statistical tests are often called *significance tests* because they are designed to determine whether obtained differences are rare, and therefore a significant outcome, or common, and therefore insignificant.

Significance Level. The curious reader is probably wondering how rare an outcome must be to be called significant. That is, how rare does an experimental outcome have to be, assuming that chance only is operating, before the investigator will reject the null hypothesis and accept the research hypothesis? The actual level varies somewhat depending on the research area, but most investigators will accept an outcome that has a probability of .05 or less as rare. If the probability of an outcome is .05, it can be expected to occur 5 times in every 100 if only chance is operating. The level used to define a rare outcome is called the *significance level.* The name follows from the fact that the obtained differences are significant, that is, attributable to the effect of chance *plus* the effect of the independent variable, if the probability of the experimental outcome is less than the significance level.

The significance level that is adopted defines what is meant by a rare outcome *and* what is meant by equivalent groups. Groups are said to be equivalent if the probability of the obtained outcome is greater than the significance level, assuming that chance only is operating. If an investigator selects the .001 significance level, then the probability of rejecting the null hypothesis when the null hypothesis is true is 1 in 1000. In this case a rare outcome is defined as an outcome with a probability of .001 if only chance is operating. The probability of obtaining equivalent groups *before* the independent variable is introduced is .999 if chance only determines the assignment of participants to groups.

The sum of the probability of a rare outcome and the probability of obtaining equivalent groups must be 1.00 because these are the only two possibilities. If the .05 significance level is adopted and the null hypothesis is true, then the probability of a rare outcome is .05 and the probability of obtaining equivalent groups is .95. If the independent variable does not have any effect (the null hypothesis is true), the probability of obtaining equivalent groups *after* the introduction of the independent variable is the same as the probability of obtaining equivalent groups *before* its introduction. Thus, if chance only is operating, it is highly likely that "small" mean differences will be obtained on the dependent measure after the introduction of the independent variable; therefore, the investigator will probably be unable to reject the null hypothesis. Since it is possible to obtain "large" mean differences solely on the basis of chance, an investigator may occasionally reject the null hypothesis when the null hypothesis is true. However, most of the time when the null hypothesis is rejected it will, in fact, be false — that is, in most cases "large" mean differences between groups are due to the effects of chance fluctuations *plus* the independent variable.

In short, the crucial consideration in performing a statistical test is whether the outcome of an experiment is rare or common if the null hypothesis is true. The likelihood of a particular outcome is determined by comparing the obtained outcome with the distribution of possible outcomes. The distribution of possible outcomes is obtained from sampling distributions.

Correct Decisions and Errors

Consider your attempt to assess the effects of jogging on anxiety once again. You obtain your results (see Table 3-7) and analyze them to determine whether your experimental outcome is a rare or common occurrence if only chance is operating. If the outcome is rare, provided only chance is operating, you reject the null hypothesis and accept the research hypothesis. If the outcome is common, provided only chance is operating, you are unable to reject the null hypothesis. Thus, you do one of two things: you either reject the null hypothesis or fail to reject it. Our concern here is whether you will make a correct decision or an error.

Four Outcomes When Evaluating an Independent Variable. The four outcomes when evaluating an independent variable are presented in Table 3-8. There are two important considerations: your decision and the true state of nature. We do not know the true state of nature in an absolute sense; we do experiments to reach conclusions about it. Sometimes our decisions are correct, and sometimes they are incorrect. As you can see from the table, there are two ways you can make a correct decision. You can reject the null hypothesis (accept the research hypothesis), when the research hypothesis is true (jogging does have an effect on anxiety); or you can fail to reject the null hypothesis when the null hypothesis is true (jogging has no effect on anxiety). The likelihood of making the correct decision depends on a number of factors such as the use of systematic procedures to avoid bias and the real relationship between the variables you are studying. For example, you are more likely to detect an effect due to jogging if jogging has an extremely powerful effect (lowers heartbeat by an average of 12 beats per minute) than if it has a very weak effect (lowers heartbeat by an average of 1 beat per minute). Even though we do not know the true state of nature, we can appreciate the fact that the absolute relationship that exists in nature (the strength of the relationship) will influence our ability to detect it. Of course, there is no good substitute for the use of systematic procedures that avoid bias. We do not want to claim that variables are related when, in fact, they are not, and we want to detect relationships when they actually exist. Therefore, we need to pay special attention to the errors we can make when reaching a decision about the effectiveness of an independent variable.

Type 1 and Type 2 Errors. If we assert that the independent variable has an effect (we reject the null hypothesis and accept the research hypothesis)

TABLE 3-8

The Four Outcomes When Evaluating an Independent Variable

		Investigator's decision	
		H_0 *(Fails to reject null hypothesis)*	H_1 *(Rejects null hypothesis)*
State of nature	H_0 *is true (Jogging has no effect on anxiety)*	Correct decision (Probability = $1 - \alpha$)	Type 1 error (Probability = α)
	H_1 *is true (Jogging has an effect on anxiety)*	Type 2 error (Probability = β)	Correct decision (Probability = $1 - \beta$)

when in fact it does not, we commit an error. This is called a Type 1 error, and the probability of committing it is equal to the significance level (also called the alpha level) that we have adopted. You have control over the probability of making a Type 1 error in that you can decide how rare an outcome has to be before you will reject the null hypothesis. You can adopt a very stringent significance level such as .001. (This can be represented as $p < .001$; the p stands for probability.) If the obtained differences are so large that the results are significant at the .001 level, there is less than 1 chance in 1000 that the results are due solely to chance. Thus, if you adopt the .001 significance level and obtain a significant result (a very large mean difference), you can reject the null hypothesis. You realize that there is a 1 in 1000 chance that you might be wrong (perhaps only chance is operating). However, you know that it is more likely that such a large difference is due to chance plus the effect of your treatment (jogging) than just to chance. The main point here is that the possibility of being wrong when rejecting the null hypothesis cannot be eliminated, but the probability can be controlled. The probability is equal to the significance level adopted. If we only had three outcomes to consider, two ways to be correct and Type 1 errors, the problem would be simple. All we would have to do would be to adopt a very stringent significance level. We would only reject the null hypothesis when we obtained very large (rare) differences between groups. We do not do this, however, because if we insist on extremely large differences, we are likely to commit a large number of Type 2 errors.

If we assert that the independent variable does not have an effect (fail to reject the null hypothesis) when it does have an effect (jogging does reduce anxiety), we are committing a Type 2 error. The Greek letter beta (β) is used to indicate the probability of making a Type 2 error. The probability of making a Type 2 error is considerably more difficult to calculate than for a Type 1 error because it depends on the procedures used and the *real* effect of the independent variable. The probability decreases as the real effect of the independent variable increases. This is just the "other side" of the point we made earlier — we are more likely to detect an effect of a powerful independent variable (assume jogging decreases anxiety by a large amount) than a weak independent variable (assume jogging decreases anxiety by only a small amount).

Relationship Between Type 1 and Type 2 Errors. The probability of making a Type 1 error is equal to the significance level that is adopted, so adopting a more stringent significance level decreases the probability of making a Type 1 error. If this were the only consideration, it would be a good idea to adopt a very stringent significance level. However, investigators are also concerned about making Type 2 errors, and the probability of making a Type 2 error is also related to the significance level. Adopting a more stringent significance level increases the probability of making a Type 2 error. The investigator who is more interested in avoiding Type 1 errors is likely to adopt a stringent significance level. The one who wants to avoid Type 2 errors is likely to adopt a lenient significance level. Most investigators are interested in avoiding Type 1 and Type 2 errors about equally so they take a middle position and select the .05 significance level.

One-Tailed Versus Two-Tailed Tests

As we know, if the null hypothesis is true, the independent variable has no influence on the dependent measure, and if the research hypothesis is true, the independent variable does have an influence. Now in some cases an investigator may want to be more specific about the effect of the independent variable on the dependent variable. Instead of simply asserting that the independent variable has an effect she may want to specify the direction of the effect. For example, if a two-group experiment is conducted the investigator may predict that the experimental subjects will be better than control subjects. The research hypothesis is supported only if the experimental subjects are better. The null hypothesis is accepted if control subjects are better than experimental subjects regardless of the magnitude of the difference between the two conditions.

Advantages of a One-Tailed Test. The reason for the labels one-tailed and two-tailed can be appreciated by referring to the null hypothesis sampling distribution presented in Figure 3-2. For this demonstration, assume that the control group mean is always subtracted from the experimental group mean. The investigator making a two-tailed test rejects the null hypothesis whenever there is a large difference between the two means regardless of whether the experimental mean is more or less than the control mean. He is interested in both tails, or extremes, of the sampling distribution curve. If the investigator selects the .05 significance level, 2.5 percent of the area under the curve at each tail is designated as the rejection area.

The "advantage" of making a one-tailed test is that 5 percent of the area under the curve at only one extreme is selected. If the 5 percent is selected at the right extreme only, then a smaller mean difference is needed to reject the null hypothesis if the results are in the predicted direction. Thus if the results are in the predicted direction, the probability of rejecting the null hypothesis is greater with a one-tailed than with a two-tailed test. Unfortunately, some investigators misuse one-tailed tests.

Misuse of One-Tailed Tests. An investigator predicts that the experimental subjects will be better than control subjects. Since a directional prediction is made, the investigator plans to use a one-tailed test. Assume that the investigator who adopts the .05 significance level can reject the null hypothesis if a mean difference of 4 or more is obtained, provided the results are in the predicted direction. Unfortunately, the results are in the opposite direction. The control group mean is 6 more than the experimental group mean. In this

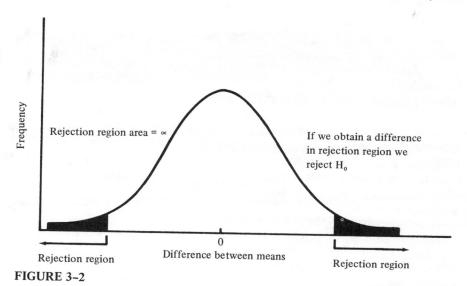

FIGURE 3–2

The null hypothesis sampling distribution for the difference between two means

case the experimenter should not reject the null hypothesis. The prediction was in the wrong direction so he should not benefit from the fact that the obtained difference exceeded the difference needed for a one-tailed, or even a two-tailed, test of the prediction. If the experimenter switches to a two-tailed test after the results are obtained and reports the results as significant, then he has actually used a two-tailed test and accepted the .075 level of significance (5 percent at one tail and 2.5 percent at the other).

Selecting a One- or Two-Tailed Test. To use a one-tailed test correctly it is necessary to make the prediction prior to collecting the data. If the results are in the opposite direction to that predicted, then the null hypothesis cannot be rejected even though large differences are obtained. An investigator who reports as significant results that are in the direction opposite to what he predicted is using a two-tailed test. Before deciding to use a one-tailed test you should ask yourself whether you are willing to accept the null hypothesis if the results are in the opposite direction and large differences are obtained. If you are not willing to do this, you should not use a one-tailed test. You would only be deceiving yourself about the significance level you have adopted. Most investigators always use the two-tailed test.

SUMMARY

Social scientists are interested in making inferences about quantities that cannot be tested directly and in testing hypotheses about behavior and mental activity. Randomization techniques are important for estimation and hypothesis testing. The purpose of random sampling is to obtain a sample that is representative of the larger population being studied so that sample values (statistics) can be used to estimate population values (parameters). The purpose of random assignment is to obtain equivalent groups prior to the introduction of the independent variable.

To make estimates and test hypotheses it is necessary to have some understanding of probability. The probability of an outcome can be defined as the ratio of the number of favorable outcomes to the total number of possible outcomes. The only factor that is assumed to operate is chance. Sampling distributions are important because they tell us how much fluctuation to expect among sample values if chance only is operating. We can determine the probability of a particular experimental outcome if we have the distribution of possible outcomes when chance only is operating.

The overall logic of hypothesis testing is rather simple. One starts with an idea that can be tested by making predictions about observable outcomes. In many cases this means that an experimenter predicts that an independent variable will have an influence on performance. Such an assertion is called the research hypothesis. The null hypothesis is the assertion that the independent variable will not have an effect. The testing procedure usually involves obtaining groups that are likely to be equivalent and then introducing the independent variable. The effect of the independent variable is assessed by comparing the way the participants in the various conditions perform on the dependent variable.

After the results are obtained the outcome is determined and compared with a distribution of possible outcomes based on the assumption that the null hypothesis is true. If the outcome is rare when compared with the appropriate null hypothesis sampling distribution, then the null hypothesis is rejected. The experimenter has reason to believe that the particular outcome is not rare; instead, he attributes the obtained differences to the effect of the independent manipulation. Experimenters attempt to reject the null hypothesis and, in general, are not interested in accepting it. They know the probability of being wrong when they reject the null hypothesis but they do not know the probability of being wrong if they accept it.

QUESTIONS

(Answers for the multiple choice questions are given in Appendix D.)
1. Distinguish between the following terms:
   a. estimation and hypothesis testing
   b. sample and population
   c. statistic and parameter
   d. random sampling and random assignment
   e. research hypothesis and null hypothesis

f. frequency distributions and sampling distributions

g. one-tailed and two-tailed tests

h. Type 1 and Type 2 errors

2. How would you select a random sample of 50 students from your college or university? How would you select a random sample of 100 people from your state or province?

3. What procedure would you use to randomly assign the members of your class to five groups?

4. How do we determine the probability of any event's occurring if chance only is operating?

5. Consider the following proposition: The task is to draw an ace from a standard deck of playing cards. You pay a dime if you fail to draw an ace and receive a dollar if you succeed. The cards are shuffled after every draw. Would you accept this proposition? Why or why not? Would you accept the proposition if each draw cost only a nickel?

6. Consider the following proposition: A roulette wheel has nine slots numbered 0 through 8. You can pick any number or all the even numbers or all the odd numbers. If you select even numbers or odd numbers and win, you win the same amount that you bet. On this type of bet you lose, of course, if the little ball ends up in the 0 hole. If you select any single number from 0 through 8 and win, you receive seven times what you bet. Assuming that you have a strong urge to gamble, would you pick a single number, odd numbers, or even numbers? Does it make any difference? Do you expect to win or lose?

7. What are sampling distributions and why are they important?

8. How are null hypothesis sampling distributions obtained?

9. Why is it important to state the research hypothesis in such a way that only either the null hypothesis or the research hypothesis is correct?

10. What are "equivalent groups"? How does the significance level you adopt affect the meaning of equivalent groups?

11. What determines the probability of making a Type 1 error? What determines the probability of making a Type 2 error?

12. What is the relationship between the significance level and the probability of making a Type 1 or Type 2 error? That is, what is the effect of decreasing the significance level (.01 instead of .05) on each of these errors?

13. Explain why investigators attempt to reject the null hypothesis and, in general, are not interested in accepting it.

14. Why is it better to use a two-tailed than a one-tailed test?

15. _____ is used to make inferences about quantities that cannot, usually for practical reasons, be tested directly. (1) Estimation (2) Hypothesis testing (3) Random assignment (4) A parameter

16. The purpose of _____ is to obtain a sample that is representative of the larger population so that the properties of the population can be estimated. (1) random assignment (2) random assignment with restriction (3) random sampling (4) hypothesis testing

17. A sample is a small portion of the subjects who could have been selected; the larger group of potential subjects is called the (1) parameter (2) statistic (3) distribution (4) population

18. The probability of drawing the ace of spades from a well-shuffled deck of fifty-two cards is _____, assuming that chance only is operating. (1) 1.00   (2) 0   (3) 1/51   (4) 1/52

19. Successive samples are drawn at random from a population and the mean of each sample is computed and recorded. The distribution of these means is called a   (1) population parameter   (2) population of means   (3) frequency distribution   (4) sampling distribution

20. You randomly select 100 students from a population of 40,000 students, determine each student's weight, and then compute the mean weight for the sample. You repeat this same procedure 500 times to obtain 500 means based on 500 random samples. You should expect   (1) all the means to be identical   (2) some fluctuations of the means due to chance   (3) large fluctuations of the means due to treatment plus chance   (4) larger fluctuations of the means than would be obtained if there were only 20 students in each of the 500 samples

21. As sample size increases, the variability in the distribution of randomly selected sample means (the null hypothesis sampling distribution) will most likely   (1) increase   (2) decrease   (3) remain the same

22. _____ describe samples, and _____ describe populations. (1) Parameters, statistics   (2) Statistics, parameters   (3) Means, variances (4) Variances, means

23. The assertion that a particular independent variable will have an effect on a dependent measure is usually referred to as the _____ hypothesis. (1) null   (2) treatment   (3) Type 1   (4) research

24. In statistical work a significant difference is one that is large enough   (1) to be meaningful to the experimenter   (2) that chance cannot affect it (3) that it leads to acceptance of the null hypothesis   (4) that it would rarely be expected to occur solely by chance

25. The significance level is equal to the probability of   (1) rejecting the research hypothesis when in fact it is true   (2) accepting the research hypothesis when in fact it is true   (3) accepting the null hypothesis when in fact it is false   (4) rejecting the null hypothesis when in fact it is true

26. The significance level defines what is meant by   (1) a rare event   (2) the research hypothesis   (3) equivalent groups   (4) both 1 and 3

27. A Type 1 error is made if the investigator   (1) rejects the null hypothesis when it is true   (2) rejects the null hypothesis when it is false   (3) accepts the research hypothesis   (4) fails to reject the null hypothesis when it is false

28. A Type 2 error is made if the investigator   (1) rejects the null hypothesis when it is true   (2) rejects the null hypothesis when it is false   (3) accepts the research hypothesis   (4) fails to reject the null hypothesis when it is false

29. If an investigator set her significance level at .05, then the probability of making a Type 1 error would be   (1) .05   (2) .95   (3) less than it would be if the .01 level had been adopted if the null hypothesis is true   (4) less than it would be if the .01 level had been adopted if the null hypothesis is false

Between-subject designs

The task for this and the two subsequent chapters is to consider experimental and quasi-experimental designs. Designs are nothing more than plans that allow us to eliminate bias, or, if this is not possible, to keep the amount of bias as small as possible. Humans are biased information processors; what we believe influences what we see. If we are to determine the true state of nature (the real relationship among events), we must have systematic procedures for testing our hypotheses. There are two important ingredients for successful research: important, testable ideas and systematic procedures which avoid bias to test them. We know very little about the process of generating important, testable ideas, but we do know systematic procedures for avoiding bias.

In a between-subject design each subject receives only one level of each independent variable. For example, to assess the effects of reward on motor performance each participant would either receive the reward or not receive it. The treatment is between subjects in that the performance of different participants is compared to assess the effect of the independent variable. If there is more than one independent variable, each subject gets only one combination of levels. For example, if there were two levels of one independent variable (low and high incentive) and three levels of a second variable (drug A, B, C), each participant would receive either high or low incentive and drug A, B, or C. No participant would receive both high and low incentive or more than one drug. For a between-subject design we compare the performance of different subjects in order to assess whether our treatment has had an effect.

The word *between* in the label between-subject designs indicates that the comparisons of interest are between (involving different) subjects. The word *subject* in the name of the designs may lead you to conclude that only humans and animals are used as subjects. Although social scientists typically use humans or animals, the systematic procedures we will consider can be used for other subjects as well, either inanimate or animate. The subject is the object or organism that receives the treatment. If your interest is in comparing automobile paints, you could use different automobiles as subjects. If you are interested in comparing fertilizers, rose bushes could be your subjects. We use the words subject and participant interchangeably when humans are subjects simply because participant seems like a more appropriate term for people who give their informed consent before participating. Rose bushes do not have a choice in the matter.

The major plan, procedure, or design that we use to avoid bias is to rely on random selection or random assignment. As we stated earlier, if random procedures are used, differences between conditions *prior* to the introduction of the independent variable should reflect chance fluctuation only. And, if the treatment or treatments we introduce have no influence on the dependent measure, differences between conditions on the dependent measure *after* treatment should also reflect chance fluctuation only. To assess the effectiveness of treatments, we need ways to decide whether differences between treatments are better attributed to chance alone or to chance plus the effect of the treatment. The analysis of variance provides us with a procedure for making this decision.

THE USEFULNESS OF ANALYSIS OF VARIANCE

The Concept of Variance

The concept of variance is not as difficult as it at first seems. We want to measure the extent to which scores vary, and to do this it is convenient to have a reference point. The *mean* is that reference point. It is computed by adding all the scores and dividing the sum by the number of scores. For example, if we measured the heartbeat rate of five children we might obtain the following five scores: 83, 68, 65, 75, 74. To obtain the mean we add the five scores (total = 365) and divide by 5, the number of scores. This calculation gives us a mean of 73. We can then find the difference between each score and the mean, and add up the difference scores. That is, we can determine how much, if any, each score *deviates* from the mean by subtracting the score from the mean or the mean from the score. If this is done for each score and these deviations from the mean are added, the sum will be equal to zero. This computation is presented in Table 4-1.

The sum of the deviations from the mean is not a suitable measure of variability (the extent to which scores differ or fluctuate) because it will always be zero; the sum of the positive deviations is always equal to the sum of the negative deviations. The problem could be "solved" by ignoring the minus sign and adding all the deviations regardless of sign. Although this

TABLE 4–1

The Heartbeat Rate for Five Children and the Computation of the Variance of These Scores

Heartbeat score (X)	Deviation score $(X - \bar{X})$	Squared deviation score $(X - \bar{X})^2$
83	10	100
68	−5	25
65	−8	64
75	2	4
74	1	1
Sum = 365	Sum = 0	Sum = 194

$$\bar{X} = 73 \qquad \text{Variance} = \frac{\text{Sum of the squared deviation scores}}{\text{Number of scores minus 1}}$$

$$\text{Variance} = \frac{194}{4} = 48.50$$

Note: The deviation scores are obtained by subtracting the mean from each score.

procedure would yield a measure of variability, there are statistical and practical reasons for using, instead, a measure obtained by squaring each deviation from the mean. The number obtained by taking the sum of the squared deviation scores and dividing by the number of scores minus one is called the *variance*.

You will probably remember that sample values can be used to estimate population values when the sample is selected randomly from the population. The sample values are called statistics, and the population values are called parameters. If the five children were selected randomly from a large population of children (all third-grade students in Peoria, Illinois) we could use the sample results to estimate the population values. The sample mean would be the best estimate of the population mean, and the sample variance would be the best estimate of the population variance. Sometimes all the scores for the population may be available. In this case there would be no need for estimation; the mean for the population would be computed by summing all the scores and dividing by the number of scores (the size of the population). The computation of variance, on the other hand, differs for populations and samples.

The variance of a population is the sum of the squared deviations from the mean divided by the number of scores. In computing the variance for a sample of fewer than thirty scores from a population, the sum of the squared deviations is divided by the number of scores minus one. The purpose of this is to obtain a more accurate estimate of population variance. Over the long haul, the sum of the squared deviations divided by the number of scores minus one provides a better estimate than the sum of the squared deviations divided by the total number of scores. If there are more than thirty scores, however, the variance is not influenced very much by which divisor is used.

Some investigators divide by the number of scores if their sole concern is *describing* the scores, and they divide by the number of scores minus one if their concern is *estimating* population variance. Since variance is usually computed for small samples (fewer than thirty scores per group or sample) and not for the entire population, most investigators always divide by the number of scores minus one. That is, they do not bother to distinguish between a variance for description and one for estimation; the variance for estimation fulfills both functions. In this text, variance will always be computed by dividing by the number of scores minus one, regardless of the size of the sample. The symbol s^2 is usually used for sample variance.

You are encouraged to study the example in Table 4-1 until it is clear that variance is nothing more than a measure of the extent to which scores differ from the mean. Or you may wish to compute the variance for each of the following three sets of scores. Set A is 5, 5, 5, 5, 5, 5. Set B is 4, 6, 4, 6, 4, 6. Set C is 1, 9, 1, 9, 1, 9. By computing the three variances you will see that the variance provides a measure of the extent to which scores differ from a mean. If the variance is computed for a sample, the sample variance can be used to estimate population variance. The analysis of variance provides us with a way to obtain two independent estimates of population variance.

Obtaining Two Estimates of Population Variance

One estimate of population variance can be obtained by determining the variability in performance *within* each group. The variability in performance within each group provides an estimate, so there are as many estimates as there are groups. We need only one estimate based on fluctuations of scores within groups, so we take an average of the sample variances as the best within-group estimate of population variance. The other estimate of population variance is based on group means. If the null hypothesis is true, the group means can be regarded as a distribution of sample means from the same population. This distribution of sample means can be used to obtain another estimate of population variance. Because this second estimate is based on group means, it is a between-group estimate of population variance. The first estimate of population variance is influenced by fluctuations within each group, and the second, which is based on differences between means, is influenced by differences between groups (between means). Examples should help us to clarify the point that two independent estimates of population variance can be obtained.

Example 1 — Large Treatment Effect. Let us assume that an investigator was interested in comparing the effects of two drugs on problem-solving behavior. The dependent measure was the number of minutes required to solve the problem. The independent variable was the type of drug, A or B. The results of the experiment are presented in Table 4-2. Our task is to consider how two independent estimates of population variance can be obtained. Later we will consider how these estimates can be compared in order to make statements about the effects of treatments.

First we need to compute the variance for each group separately. Remember that this calculation is made by computing the mean for each group, subtracting the group mean from each score, squaring each deviation score, summing the squared deviation scores, and then dividing the sum of the squared deviation scores by the number of scores minus one. The letter n is used as a symbol for the number of scores in each condition. For the two conditions in the first example, the variance for the group receiving drug A is .80 and the variance for drug B is .80. The estimate of population variance based on within-group variance is also .80 because the two sample estimates are equal. We can obtain the within-group estimate of population variance by adding the individual estimates and dividing by the number of estimates. These computations are presented in Table 4-2.

We can also obtain an estimate of population variance by considering between-group fluctuations (the extent to which the group means differ). In this case we use means instead of individual scores. If we are going to determine the extent to which means fluctuate, we need a reference point. The *overall mean* or *grand mean* will be our reference point. The overall mean is obtained by adding all the scores (sum = 72) and dividing by the number of scores, twelve in this case. The overall mean is 6 ($72/12 = 6$). The estimate of population variance based on between-group fluctuation is obtained by subtracting the overall mean from the group mean, squaring the difference, summing the squared difference scores, multiplying by the number of scores in each condition, and then dividing by the number of groups minus one. This computation is also presented in Table 4-2.

For the example just considered, the between-group and within-group estimates of population variance are markedly different (.80 for the within-group estimate and 48 for the between-group estimate). It is reasonable to ask, therefore, which estimate is the better estimate of population variance. The within-group estimate is better; it should reflect only chance fluctuation because all subjects within a group are treated the same. The between-group estimate should reflect chance fluctuations *plus* any effect of the independent variable; if the independent variable has an effect, the between-group estimate should be larger than the within-group estimate. If chance only is operating

TABLE 4-2

The Results and Analysis of the Experiment Used as Example 1 (fictitious data)

Drug A	$(X - \bar{X})$	$(X - \bar{X})^2$	Drug B	$(X - \bar{X})$	$(X - \bar{X})^2$
3	-1	1	7	-1	1
4	0	0	8	0	0
5	1	1	9	1	1
3	-1	1	7	-1	1
4	0	0	8	0	0
5	1	1	9	1	1
Sum 24	0	4	Sum 48	0	4

$$\bar{X} = 4 \qquad\qquad \bar{X} = 8$$

Computation of within-group variance

Variance (s^2) for drug A condition

$$s^2 = \frac{\text{sum } (X - \bar{X})^2}{n - 1} = \frac{4}{5} = .80 \qquad \text{where } n = \text{number of scores (subjects) in each group, in this case } n = 6$$

Variance for drug B condition

$$s^2 = \frac{\text{sum } (X - \bar{X})^2}{n - 1} = \frac{4}{5} = .80$$

Within-group estimate of population variance

$$\frac{\text{Sample 1 estimate + Sample 2 estimate}}{2} = \frac{.80 + .80}{2} = .80$$

Computation of between-group variance

Drug A condition	Drug B condition	
$\bar{X} = 4$	$\bar{X} = 8$	Overall mean $= \dfrac{24 + 48}{12} = 6$

Between-group estimate $= \dfrac{n \; \text{sum(group mean} - \text{overall mean)}^2}{k - 1}$ where k = number of groups

$$n[x_1 - \text{OM}]^2 + [x_2 - \text{OM}]^2$$

Between-group estimate $= \dfrac{6[(4 - 6)^2 + (8 - 6)^2]}{2 - 1}$

Between-group estimate $= \dfrac{6(8)}{1} = 48$

(there is no effect due to the independent variable) the two estimates should be about the same. We obtain two independent estimates of population variance so that we can compare the estimates to assess the effects of treatment manipulations.

We said that the between-group estimate should be larger than the within-group estimate if there is a treatment effect. If the independent variable does not have an effect, then the group means can be considered sample means, which are estimates of the same population mean. However, when it does have an effect the group means will not all be estimates of the same mean because the independent variable will result in an increase or decrease in one or more of the group means. In short, there should be greater fluctuations between the group means when the independent variable has an effect than when it does not. But there is no reason to expect within-group fluctuations to increase if the independent variable has an effect.

In sum, the analysis of variance test compares the between-group and within-group estimates of population variance. If the two estimates are about the same, there is no reason to reject the null hypothesis. If the between-group estimate is considerably larger than the within-group estimate, then the null hypothesis can be rejected. To conclude that the independent variable has an effect, the within-group fluctuations must be smaller than the between-group fluctuations.

Example 2 — No Treatment Effect. Let us assume that an investigator compared the effects of two drugs on problem-solving behavior. The dependent variable was the number of minutes required to solve the problem. The independent variable was the type of drug, C or D. Assume that the results presented in Table 4-3 were obtained and that the investigator computed the two estimates of population variance, a between-group and a within-group estimate, as presented in Table 4-3. The procedure used to obtain the two estimates is identical to the procedure used for example 1. Since the between-group and within-group estimates are identical in this case, there is no basis for rejecting the null hypothesis. To reject the null hypothesis the between-group estimate has to be *significantly* larger than the within-group estimate. We will consider procedures for determining whether the between-group estimate is significantly larger than the within-group estimate in later chapters. Here we want to demonstrate that two independent variance estimates can be obtained and then compared to evaluate whether a treatment (independent variable) influenced performance on the dependent measure.

The example in Table 4-3 is somewhat unusual in that the two estimates of population variance are identical. This can happen, of course, but it is more likely that the two estimates will vary somewhat even when there is no treatment effect. If chance only is operating, the between-group estimate can be smaller than, equal to, or larger than the within-group estimate. We reject the null hypothesis only when the between-group estimate is *significantly* larger than the within-group estimate.

TABLE 4-3

The Results and Analysis of the Experiment Used as Example 2 (fictitious data)

Drug C	$(X - \bar{X})$	$(X - \bar{X})^2$	Drug D	$(X - \bar{X})$	$(X - \bar{X})^2$
5	-9	81	15	-5	25
25	11	121	35	15	225
25	11	121	15	-5	25
10	-4	16	15	-5	25
5	-9	81	20	0	0
Sum 70	0	420	Sum 100	0	300
$\bar{X} = 14$			$\bar{X} = 20$		

Computation of within-group variance

Variance for drug C condition

$$s^2 = \frac{\text{sum } (X - \bar{X})^2}{n - 1} = \frac{420}{4} = 105$$

Variance for drug D condition

$$s^2 = \frac{\text{sum } (X - \bar{X})^2}{n - 1} = \frac{300}{4} = 75$$

Within-group estimate of population variance

$$\frac{\text{Sample 1 estimate} + \text{Sample 2 estimate}}{2} = \frac{105 + 75}{2} = 90$$

Computation of between-group variance

Drug C condition   *Drug D condition*

$\bar{X} = 14$ $\bar{X} = 20$ Overall mean $= \dfrac{70 + 100}{10} = 17$

Between-group estimate $= \dfrac{n \text{ sum(group mean} - \text{overall mean)}^2}{k - 1}$

Between-group estimate $= \dfrac{5[(14 - 17)^2 + (20 - 17)^2]}{2 - 1}$

Between-group estimate $= \dfrac{5(18)}{1} = 90$

THE RANDOM-GROUPS DESIGN

Imagine that you and I and sixteen others decide to have a friendly game of baseball; the losing team buys the beer. You are one team captain and I am the other. The problem is to assign the remaining sixteen players to one or the other of the two teams. What procedure should we use to make these assignments? Suppose that I, after claiming to be unbiased (after all, it is a "friendly" game), offer to make the assignments. What would you do? Unless you get more pleasure from losing than winning, you should protest. If you did not, you would most likely lose because I get more pleasure from winning than losing. I am likely to be biased in making the assignments. The usual procedure for obtaining "equal" teams is to use some chance procedure (flip a coin) to determine who gets the first choice and then alternate choices. If we are about equal in our ability to judge the baseball skills of the remaining sixteen players, we should arrive at approximately equal teams. We want the assignment procedure to be fair so that each team has a chance to win.

Now consider the task of assigning participants to treatment conditions to evaluate the effectiveness of a particular independent variable (such as laetrile as a cancer cure, jogging to reduce anxiety, intervention programs for juvenile delinquents). Should the individual investigator be allowed to use *any* procedure he or she deems appropriate to make the assignment of participants to conditions? Clearly, the answer is no. You may believe that you can make assignments in an unbiased manner, but it is not likely that you would, in fact, be able to do so, particularly if the results have important personal consequences (prestige, financial rewards).

The Logic of the Random-Groups Design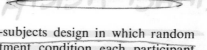

The random-groups design is a between-subjects design in which random assignment is used to determine the treatment condition each participant receives. The random assignment procedure is meant to ensure that between-group differences before the introduction of the independent variable will be due solely to chance fluctuations. If only chance determines the assignment of subjects to conditions, then the significance level that is adopted will determine the probability of obtaining equivalent groups before the introduction of the independent variable.

Consider an example in which we know that only chance is operating, the table of random numbers in Appendix C-9. Suppose that we use random assignment to place successive two-digit numbers in the table to either group 1 or group 2. That is, we use both the number tables for random assignment in Appendix C-1 and the table of random numbers in Appendix C-9. By a random procedure I selected the starting sequence of 33 in Appendix C-1 and the sixth row, column 1 on page 348 for Appendix C-9. The results of this selection procedure are presented in Table 4-4. Successive pairs of two-digit numbers were assigned randomly to either group 1 or group 2.

The question of interest is whether this random assignment procedure yields equivalent groups. Is the difference between groups obtained in Table 4-4 a rare or common outcome if only chance is operating? If we adopt the .05 significance level, we have a 5 percent chance of obtaining a rare outcome and a 95 percent chance of obtaining a common outcome since, in this case, we know that only chance is operating. Later you will be able to do the appropriate statistical analysis to convince yourself that the results presented in Table 4-4 represent a common outcome, given that only chance is operating. You could compute the between-group and within-group estimates of population variance, as we did earlier, but it would be a laborious procedure. There are easier ways, which will be considered in Section II, to obtain these values.

Now consider our earlier example of jogging and heartbeat rate. Further assume that, unknown to you, redheads have faster heartbeats than nonredheads. Will the random assignment procedure result in groups with approximately the same number of redheads so that group differences will not be attributable to having too many redheads in one group? If the .05 significance level is adopted, you can be confident that random assignment will yield

TABLE 4-4

The Random Assignment of Two-Digit Numbers from the Table of Random Numbers to Two Groups

Sequence number from Appendix C-1	Order of assign- ment	Group 1	Group 2
33	1,2	93	22
34	2,1	64	53
35	1,2	39	7
36	2,1	63	10
37	1,2	76	35
38	1,2	87	3
39	1,2	4	79
40	2,1	8	88
41	2,1	13	13
42	2,1	85	51
		Total = 532	361
		$\bar{X}$ = 53.20	36.10

equivalent groups prior to the introduction of the independent variable approximately 95 percent of the time. Therefore, if significant differences between groups are found *after* the introduction of the independent variable, it is reasonable to assert that these differences are due to chance *plus* the effect of the independent variable, since the probability that they are due to chance alone is known to be small (.05). This probability is known to be small *because* the random assignment procedure was used to ensure that only chance determined the assignment of subjects to conditions.

Experiments with One Independent Variable

The random-groups design can be used whenever it is possible to randomly assign subjects to groups and then introduce the independent variable. It follows, therefore, that this design can be used to test essentially all independent variables except subject variables.

It is possible, for instance, to assess the effect of a new drug by using a random-groups design. The subjects are randomly assigned to either the experimental or control condition. Then the treatment is administered, and the effect of the treatment on some dependent variable is assessed. If the performance of the experimental subjects on the dependent variable differs significantly from that of the control subjects, the difference can be attributed to the effect of the treatment. The control subjects should be treated the same as the experimental subjects except for the intended manipulation. To ensure that the use of the drug is the only manipulation, the subjects must not be given any information about the treatment conditions. The control subjects are given a placebo; the experimental subjects are given the drug. Neither the subjects nor the person administering the treatments should know which treatment a subject receives. Experiments in which both the subjects and the person administering the treatments are kept unaware of the nature of the manipulation are frequently called *double-blind* experiments.

Although a two-group experiment can be used to assess the effect of a particular manipulation, investigators frequently prefer to use more than two levels for an independent variable. The use of additional levels of an independent variable allows them to answer additional questions. For example, an investigator interested in the effect of a new drug may manipulate the amount of the drug administered. In this case a three-group random-groups design could be used. One group would receive a high dose, a second group a low dose, and the third a placebo. The investigator would be able to determine whether the drug has an effect *and* whether the dosage has an effect.

It is difficult to overstate the importance of the random-groups design because it is useful for a wide variety of research problems. It is an extremely powerful design because there are so many independent variables that can be introduced after subjects have been randomly assigned to conditions. Investigators interested in all areas of human information processing, development, and social behavior use this design extensively. Instructors frequently have their students perform experiments in which one independent variable is manipulated by using the random-groups design. The beginning student, in particular, should find it useful, because it is an excellent vehicle for learning about research methodology. Because an understanding of this design is the basis for more complicated experiments, it needs to be studied extensively. Let us consider another example.

Imagine that you are interested in the effect of diet on intellectual development; you believe that adequate protein is extremely important, particularly during the early years. For ethical, practical, and legal reasons you are not able to use human subjects in your experiment, so you use rhesus monkeys. Assume that a reliable and valid test of intellectual development is available and that the test can be administered to all subjects when they mature at four years of age. This test is the dependent measure; the diet of each subject is the manipulated variable. You give a high protein diet to one group and a low protein diet to the other. Because diet is a nonsubject variable you can evaluate its effect by using the random-groups design; that is, you can randomly assign each subject to one of the two groups and then introduce the diet manipulation. The diet manipulation must be the only variable that is manipulated systematically because you want to attribute any between-group differences (any significant differences) to the diet. It is extremely important, then, that the groups be treated alike.

If the groups are not treated alike except for the intended manipulation, the experiment would be _confounded_. An experiment is confounded when it is not clear whether the results are due to the independent variable manipulation or to some other unintended manipulation. For example, if the subjects receiving high protein diets were given more stimulation than subjects receiving low protein, there would not be any way to determine whether any obtained differences in intellectual performance were due to protein or stimulation.

The experiment can be criticized because it lacks a control group. One could argue that a normal diet group should have been used in addition to low and high protein groups. If the control condition had been included there would have been three levels of diet (low protein, normal protein, and high protein). Without a control group, even if you obtain a protein effect, you will not be able to determine whether low protein retards intellectual development or high protein facilitates it. You can indicate the difference between low and high protein, but you cannot make any assertions about low and high protein relative to the normal diet. You must limit the conclusion to the levels of the independent variable used.

Some highly sophisticated designs allow one to make statements about levels of an independent variable other than the levels in the experiment. Our discussion is limited to what are called *fixed effects models* — designs in which it is necessary to limit conclusions to the levels of the independent variable manipulated.

Experiments with Two Independent Variables

Experiments in which more than one independent variable is manipulated allow the investigator to determine the interaction of independent variables and the main effects of each independent variable. Since it is necessary to have a minimum of two levels of each independent variable, a minimum of four groups is required each time two independent variables are investigated with a random-groups design. We can, for example, randomly assign subjects (indicated by $S_1, S_2, \ldots S_{40}$ in Table 4-5) to four groups and then introduce two independent variables, as demonstrated in Table 4-5. Each subject receives only one combination of levels, so there are four independent groups in this experiment. No subject can be assigned to more than one group when a random-groups design is used.

Two examples should demonstrate the usefulness of the factorial random-groups design. For the first example, a 2 by 3 factorial design, assume that you are interested in ways to persuade people to stop smoking. You obtain the cooperation of 150 smokers and randomly assign them to six groups so that you have 25 smokers in each group. You then introduce your two independent variables, incentive (five dollars versus nothing) and the type of

TABLE 4-5

A 2 by 2 Factorial, Random-Groups Design

		Independent variable 1	
		Level 1	Level 2
Independent variable 2	Level A	S_1 S_2 . . . S_{10}	S_{21} S_{22} . . . S_{30}
	Level B	S_{11} S_{12} . . . S_{20}	S_{31} S_{32} . . . S_{40}

antismoking campaign (emotional appeal, practical appeal, control). This design is presented in Table 4-6. It is a 2 by 3 factorial design because there are two levels of one independent variable and three levels of the other. For the incentive manipulation, subjects either get five dollars for every day they do not smoke or they get nothing. The antismoking campaigns differ in that some subjects (controls) are simply told to stop smoking, others (practical appeal) are given specific procedures to use when they have the urge to smoke, and others (emotional appeal) are shown in graphic detail the misery and pain that can accompany lung cancer. The dependent measure is the average number of cigarettes each subject smokes per day.

The results of the above experiment should provide interesting information about the effects of incentive, type of antismoking campaign, and the interaction of these two independent variables. For example, the effect of the antismoking campaigns may depend on the level of incentive; there may be larger differences among the three levels of the antismoking manipulation when there is no incentive than when there is.

There are likely to be some problems with the above experiment because subjects given five dollars per day to stop smoking may not be as truthful about reporting their smoking behaviors as are subjects who are not paid to stop smoking. You would have to take steps to ensure that the reports were accurate before evaluating the incentive manipulation. And you would need to make sure that the smokers were treated identically except for the intended manipulations. Obviously, we would not want the emotional appeal to take twice as long to administer as the practical appeal because the amount of contact with the smoker, and not the content of the appeal, could be responsible for any change in smoking behavior. Similarly, you should spend as much time with the control subjects as the other subjects to make sure that any obtained differences are attributable to the content of the message (type

TABLE 4-6

A 2 by 3 Factorial, Random-Groups Design in Which Incentive and Antismoking Campaigns Are the Independent Variables Manipulated

		Type of antismoking campaign		
		Emotional appeal	*Practical appeal*	*Control*
Incentive	*$5/day*			
	Nothing			

of antismoking campaign) and not merely to the amount of social interaction between the investigator and the subjects.

You may want to consider different possible outcomes for the above experiment to increase your understanding of main effects and interactions. Factorial random-groups designs are useful in many research areas because it is frequently necessary to know how independent variables interact as well as what their main effects are. Social psychologists use factorial designs extensively because there is considerable evidence to suggest that the effects of many independent variables manipulated by social psychologists (credibility of the communicator, physical presence of others, content of the communication) depend on the social context in which they are investigated. Drug researchers also have considerable use for factorial, random-groups designs because it is well known that drugs interact (Hussar, 1973). Drug interactions are obtained when the effect of one drug is influenced by the prior or concurrent administration of another drug. The effects of many drugs are influenced greatly by the amount of alcohol consumed by the patient; therefore, it is very important to know which drugs interact with alcohol and which do not. It is not enough simply to tell patients not to drink when they are taking medication, because many patients faced with a choice between taking their medication or drinking will decide not to take their medication. Some drugs given in combination can lead to overdose, which would not result if the drugs were administered singly. In short, there is ample reason to believe that factorial, random-groups designs will continue to play an important role in medical and psychological research.

Subject and Nonsubject Variable Experiments

It is common for investigators to use the random-groups design to assess the effects of two or more independent variables in the same experiment. It is also possible to combine the investigation of a subject variable with a nonsubject variable in the same experiment. The random-groups design can be used for the nonsubject variable manipulation but not for the subject variable manipulation.

Let us consider an experiment in which the two types of variables are investigated. Imagine that you are interested in the effect of programmed instruction on performance in introductory psychology courses. You decide to compare programmed instruction with the more traditional lecture-discussion approach. You are also concerned about the possible generality of any effect, so you decide to test your manipulation of instruction with different kinds of subjects — low achievers and high achievers. You *select* a group of low achievers and high achievers by examining grade point averages of all subjects available for the experiment. Thus, prior achievement is your subject variable. You randomly assign all the low achievers to the two instructional conditions, and then you randomly assign all the high achievers to the two instructional conditions. You now have one subject variable (achievement level) and one nonsubject variable (type of instructional program). The design of this experiment is presented in Table 4-7.

You are not particularly interested in comparing the performance of low and high achievers. These subjects were not assigned randomly to the two achievement conditions, so there is no way of knowing what nonmanipulated variables may be responsible for performance differences. However, since you were able to use a random assignment procedure for the type of instructional program manipulation, you can attribute significant differences between the programmed approach and lecture-discussion to the manipulation. That is, because each low achiever was randomly assigned to one of the two instructional conditions, and each high achiever was randomly assigned to one of the two instructional conditions, you can be reasonably confident that the subjects in the programmed instruction and lecture-discussion conditions were equivalent before the independent variable was introduced.

The major reason for combining the manipulation of the nonsubject variable with the selection of different subjects is to assess whether the effect, if any, of the nonsubject variable depends on the type of subject. This knowledge can be valuable. If a variable such as instructional method has an influence on course performance, it is important to determine the circumstances under which it has an effect. Or, if there are sex differences in the causes of depression, we might expect the effectiveness of a particular treatment for depression to interact with the sex of the participant. The effectiveness of a particular training program (Erhard Seminars Training, transcendental meditation, assertiveness training) also may depend on the characteristics of the participants.

TABLE 4-7

A 2 by 2 Factorial Design in Which a Subject Variable and a Nonsubject Variable Are Investigated

| | | *Type of instructional program* | |
		Programmed instruction	*Lecture-discussion*
Achievement	*Low*		
	High		

Note: The subjects at each achievement level are randomly assigned to the programmed or lecture-discussion conditions.

MATCHED-GROUPS DESIGNS

Let us return to the playing-baseball-for-fun-and-beer example. If we flip a coin to determine who gets the first choice of players and then alternate choices, we are not using a random procedure to assign players to teams. We have placed some constraints on the assignment procedure. If you know that two of the players are clearly better than the other fourteen, you are going to make certain that you get at least one on your team. If you know that two of the players are clearly inferior to the other fourteen, you are going to be certain that you get one at most on your team. In brief, you use your knowledge of the participants to select the best team possible within the constraints of the selection procedures.

If the two captains are about equal in their assessment skills, it is likely that the teams will be "matched" according to ability. In fact, the teams are likely to be about equal in ability a greater percentage of the time with a "matching" procedure than with a random assignment procedure. With random assignment it is possible that the two best players could be assigned to one team and the two worst to the other team. With matching, we would not allow this to happen. Does this mean, then, that matching is a good procedure for assigning participants to conditions when attempting to evaluate the effect of an independent variable? The answer depends on a number of considerations.

A matched-groups design is a between-subject design in which the groups are "equated" on one or more matching variables (such as intelligence). Matching variables are subject variables. If a nonsubject variable is held constant for all conditions instead of being manipulated as the independent variable, it is said to be controlled. For example, if the experimental subjects and control subjects are given the same amount of time to complete their tasks, the time variable is controlled. Time is, of course, a nonsubject variable. Investigators *match* groups on subject variables and *control* nonsubject variables. The reasons for matching and the procedures used depend on whether the independent variable is a subject or nonsubject variable.

Nonsubject Variables as Independent Variables

If you are interested in studying the effect of a nonsubject variable (type of drug, therapy, strategy) on performance (some dependent measure), you usually have control over the situation. In most cases you can decide who gets the treatment and who does not. If this is true, you could use random assignment procedures or you could use random assignment with restrictions which result in the groups being matched on one or more subject variables. Is it worth our time and effort to attempt to equate our groups on one or more subject variables prior to introducing the independent variable? One consideration is whether there are subject variables that are suitable variables for matching.

Prerequisite for Matching. The investigator who is considering whether or not to use a matched-groups design should first consider whether there is a suitable matching variable. A suitable matching variable is a subject variable that is correlated with performance on the dependent measure. Subject variables that have a high correlation with the dependent measure are more suitable than ones that have a low correlation. For example, if an experiment is to be performed to assess the effects of transcendental meditation training on motor performance, motor performance would be the dependent measure. Assume that the correlation between the motor performance test and intelligence is .05, whereas the correlation between a dexterity test and motor performance is .85. In this case the dexterity test would be a far better matching variable than the intelligence test.

There is no reason for matching unless the matching variable is related to the *dependent* measure. Matched-groups designs are used to exert some control over the subjects' performance on the dependent measure. If the matching variable is unrelated to the dependent variable, then matching will have no effect. This fact is important but it frequently escapes the beginning researcher, as evidenced by the many studies in which the matching variable was unrelated to the dependent variable. For example, several decades ago most investigators routinely matched on intelligence. Apparently they believed that intelligence is related to just about every conceivable dependent variable. It isn't. Having a subject variable that correlates with the dependent measure is a *prerequisite* for using a matched-groups design.

If there is a subject variable that correlates highly with the dependent variable, you can consider whether it is feasible to match on this variable — that is, whether the advantages to be gained are great enough to justify the time and effort needed for matching. One reason for matching when a nonsubject variable is manipulated as the independent variable is to provide greater assurance that the groups will be equivalent before introducing the independent variable. The second reason for matching is to obtain a more powerful design (to increase the probability that you will detect an effect of the independent variable if, in fact, there is a real effect).

Matching and Equivalent Groups. Consider our jogging example once again. You have complete control over which participants are assigned to the jogging condition and which are assigned to the nonjogging conditions since all participants have agreed to follow your instructions. You could use a random-groups design. If you do, the probability of making a Type 1 error (rejecting the null hypothesis when there is no effect of the independent variable) is equal to the significance level that you adopt. If you want to minimize the likelihood of making a Type 1 error, you could adopt a very stringent alpha level (say .001 instead of the usual .05). Another plan, which is not recommended, is to use matching to provide further assurance that the two groups are equivalent prior to the introduction of the jogging–no jogging manipulation. Since you plan to study the effects of jogging on heartbeat rate in a "standard" waiting situation, you may reason that it would be important to make sure that the groups are equated on this measure prior to introducing the independent variable.

To achieve this end, you test all participants on the dependent measure *prior* to introducing the independent variable. In this case, then, the matching variable is the dependent measure. You select this measure because you believe that the correlation between the heartbeat measures obtained prior to and after the introduction of the independent variable will be very high. We will assume that this is, indeed, the case. After you obtain the heartbeat measure, you assign the participants to two conditions using random assignment procedures *with the restriction* that the mean heartbeat rates are equal for the two groups. Because you are now confident that your groups are equivalent, you introduce your independent variable and, after the three-month period needed to make the manipulation, you once again assess heartbeat rates. If you obtain a significant difference between groups on this final measure, you reject the null hypothesis.

This procedure has little to recommend it. It may appear attractive because you actually assess whether the groups are equivalent prior to the introduction of the jogging–no jogging manipulation. An investigator who does not have faith in random-groups designs may prefer to match whenever possible to obtain equivalent groups. This accomplishes very little, however, in that it only reduces the probability of making a Type 1 error (in this case concluding that jogging has an effect when in fact it does not). A much simpler way to reduce the probability of making a Type 1 error is to adopt a more stringent significance level (say .01 instead of .05). Why go to all the trouble of matching your groups when the same result can be obtained more simply? As we indicated earlier, there is a cost for reducing the probability of making a Type 1 error. The cost is that we increase the probability of making a Type 2 error (failing to detect a real effect of an independent variable). This is the case whether we use matching to provide further assurance that the groups are equivalent prior to the introduction of the independent variable or simply adopt a more stringent significance level.

Matching and Variance. If you can recall our earlier discussion of the usefulness of the analysis of variance, you know that we can evaluate the effectiveness of a treatment manipulation when a between-subjects design is used by obtaining two estimates of population variance, one based on within-group fluctuations, and the other based on between-group fluctuations. If only chance is operating (the treatment has no effect), we expect the two estimates will be about the same. If the treatment has an effect, we expect the between-group estimate to be "considerably greater" than the within-group estimate. Given this fact, it should be easy to see what happens if we use a matching procedure that reduces between-group differences prior to the introduction of the independent variable. Such a procedure increases the likelihood of making a Type 2 error. We want our between-groups estimate of population to be large, not small, in relation to the within-group estimate. We have a better chance of this happening — in the cases in which the independent variable actually has an effect — when the two estimates are approximately equal prior to the introduction of the independent variable than when we use matching to make the between-group estimate small compared with the within-group estimate.

Matching That Increases Power. The probability of making a correct decision when the research hypothesis is true (that is, the independent variable has an effect) is called the power of the test. Power is equal to one minus the probability of making a Type 2 error (beta). Our concern here is whether there are procedures that allow us to increase power without also increasing the probability of making a Type 1 error. One way is to reduce the size of the fluctuations between *and* within groups prior to the introduction of the independent variable.

If we know that a particular subject variable (say intelligence) is highly correlated with performance on the dependent measure, we can use this information to reduce both between- and within-group fluctuations prior to the introduction of the independent measure. If people with high IQs get high scores on the dependent measure and people with low IQs get low scores, we can reduce variance on the dependent measure by selecting people who have the same IQ score. If we use only participants who have an IQ score of 120, the variance of the scores on the dependent measure should be smaller than if we use people who have widely different IQ scores. For the purpose of illustration, imagine that the two variance estimates (between-group estimate and within-group estimate) are 10 when we use homogeneous participants (IQs of 120) and 100 when we use heterogeneous participants (people of widely different IQs). Assume further, that the effect of the independent variable is to increase the between-group estimate of population variance by 60. For our experiment with homogeneous participants, the between-group estimate will be seven times as large as the within-group estimate (that is, 60 added to 10 divided by 10). For our experiment with heterogeneous participants, the between-group estimate will be 1.6 times as large as the within-group estimate (60 added to 100 divided by 100). Clearly, if there is a real effect of the independent variable, we are more likely to detect it if we can keep both between- and within-group fluctuations small prior to the introduction of the independent variable.

There is a cost. If we select participants on the basis of their scores on a particular subject variable, we restrict the generality of the findings. In the above case, one might argue that the results apply only to people who have an IQ of 120. If IQ and the independent variable are both used as independent variables, the two may interact. The effect of the independent variable (the nonsubject variable) may be dependent on the level of the second independent variable (in this case IQ level). One way to avoid the cost and still retain the benefit is to manipulate the subject variable as an independent variable instead of using it as a matching variable. We still keep within-group fluctuations small and we assess whether the subject variable and nonsubject variable interact. If there is a main effect of the nonsubject variable and no interaction, we have dealt with the question of generality, at least for the subject variable considered.

We could quibble about whether selecting participants who have the same score on a subject variable is really matching. It is in the sense that we have bothered to equate our groups on a particular subject variable. If this procedure reduces within-group variance in comparison with results if participants could not be restricted, we will increase the power of our experiment. Another way to increase the power of the experiment without restricting who can participate is to match by obtaining pairs or sets of subjects who are equal on the matching variable. Such a procedure makes it possible to use a within-subject instead of a between-subject analysis. For example, assume that an investigator wants to match the groups on weight before investigating the effectiveness of three dieting programs. There are two treatment conditions and one control condition. He recruits three people who weigh the same and randomly assigns one subject to each condition. This is repeated for successive sets of three people. The use of this procedure will allow the investigator to analyze the results so that fluctuations due to initial weight will not be included when the size of the chance fluctuations is determined. If the matching is carried out in this way, the design is similar to the within-subject designs discussed in the next chapter.

Subject Variables as Independent Variables

As you know, one useful way of studying subject variables is to manipulate them factorially with nonsubject variables to assess whether the effect of the nonsubject variable depends on the characteristics of the subjects. This is useful information in many instances, and it avoids the problem inherent in not having control over subject variables. Suppose, however, that you are interested solely in subject variables, not in possible interactions between subject and nonsubject variables. Is there any way to establish that a particular subject variable (height, anxiety, assertiveness) is responsible for performance? Can we ever reach cause-effect conclusions about subject variables?

There are a number of important issues that involve the assessment of cause-effect relationships between subject variables and performance. Consider, for example, the question of intelligence and achievement. Does intelligence cause achievement or does achievement cause intelligence? If you believe that intelligence causes achievement and that intelligence is a relatively stable subject variable, you might be more willing to use intelligence tests to assign students to different educational experiences (children with very low scores might be assigned to classes for the mentally retarded). However, if you believe that the quality of the educational experience determines intelligence, you would probably oppose using IQ test results to assign students to educational experiences. Or consider the causes of alcoholism. If you believe that the quality of the parent-child relationship is important for determining whether the child will later become an alcoholic, your approach to the prevention of alcoholism is likely to be considerably different from that of someone who believes parent-child interactions have little influence. But how do we decide whether there is an influence or not?

In some cases repeated observations with long time intervals between them allow us to reach cause-effect conclusions about subject variables (Crano, Kenny, & Campbell, 1972), whereas in other cases we might use extensive matching in an effort to at least "come close" to a cause-effect conclusion.

Assume that you are interested in assessing whether early parent-child relationships are related to alcoholism. To be more specific, you believe that children raised in homes in which there is little love and affection displayed between parents and between parents and children are more likely later to become alcoholics than children raised in homes in which there is considerable love and affection. In order to test this view, you administer a number of questionnaires to 8000 participants. You first use your results to identify 500 children from "warm" homes and 500 from "cold" homes. Then the results are used to select 200 participants each from the warm and cold groups who are matched on a number of variables, such as intelligence, wealth of parents, number of siblings, past achievement, drinking habits of parents, and so on. After a twenty-year period, you assess the drinking habits of all 400 participants, assuming they all survive the twenty-year period, and find a significant difference in alcohol consumption. The participants from cold homes are heavier drinkers. Can you conclude that the early home environment is responsible for subsequent drinking behavior?

Researchers are likely to disagree somewhat on the answer to this question. Most would probably argue that the evidence for a causal relationship is not compelling. Many would reject the evidence because a particular variable (occupational stress) was not used as a matching variable. However, if given a choice between this procedure and a procedure that did not involve matching, most would prefer the matching procedure. With matching we can eliminate a number of alternative plausible hypotheses (such as drinking habits of parents) that we would not be able to eliminate without matching.

If the use of the matching procedure is the best method available for studying the effects of a particular subject variable, there is little choice but to use it. Note that this use of a matched-groups design is essentially the same as computing a correlation between two variables while holding other variables constant. You will recall that the manipulation of a subject variable is similar to the use of a correlational technique in that cause-effect conclusions are, from a theoretical point of view, almost never warranted.

SUMMARY

The analysis of variance of results obtained with a random-groups design enables us to obtain two independent estimates of population variance. One estimate can be obtained by determining within-group variance, which is a measure of the extent to which subjects in the same treatment condition perform alike on the dependent measure. The other estimate is the between-group variance, based on group means. The two estimates of population variance tend to be about the same if the null hypothesis is true. If the independent variable has an effect, the between-group estimate should be considerably larger than the within-group estimate.

In a between-subject design each subject receives only one level of each independent variable. The random-groups design is a between-subject design in which random assignment is used in an effort to ensure that the groups are equivalent before the independent variable is introduced. Equivalence of groups permits subsequent differences in performance to be attributed to the effect of the independent variable. The random-groups design can be used whenever it is possible to randomly assign subjects to groups before introducing the independent variable.

A matched-groups design is a between-subject design in which the groups are equated on one or more matching variables. Matching variables are subject variables. Several considerations are involved in the question of whether to use a matched-groups design when a nonsubject variable is manipulated as the independent variable. There is little justification for matching if the sole purpose is to provide greater assurance that the groups will be equivalent prior to the introduction of the independent variable. Such matching merely decreases the probability of making a Type 1 error and increases the probability of making a Type 2 error. The same result can be accomplished much more easily by adopting a more stringent significance level. Matching is justified, however, if procedures are used that reduce fluctuations within groups (selecting homogeneous participants) or allow a within-subject rather than a between-subject analysis. Within-group fluctuations can also be reduced by "converting" the matching variable to an independent variable. This last plan has the added advantage of allowing the investigator to assess whether the subject variable interacts with the nonsubject variable used as the other independent variable. Matched-groups designs are used when only one subject variable is studied in an effort to equate the groups on the relevant subject variables that are not being investigated.

QUESTIONS

(Answers for the multiple choice questions are given in Appendix D.)

1. Assume that the following results were obtained in an experiment investigating the effects of incentive on motor performance. The dependent measure was the number of errors. Calculate the within-group and between-group estimates of population variance.

Incentive group	Control group
4	10
5	8
6	9
6	10
4	9
5	8

2. What is the usefulness of the analysis of variance — that is, why is it important to obtain two independent estimates of population variance?

3. A biochemist claims to have developed a pill that will increase IQ by five points for every pill administered. To test this claim you do an experiment in which you randomly assign subjects to a 0, 1, 2, or 4 pills condition. All subjects in one group get no pills, all subjects in another get one pill, and so on. What will be the effect of the independent variable on within-group and between-group fluctuations if the biochemist is correct?

4. What is the logic of the random-groups design? Does the random assignment of subjects to conditions guarantee that the groups are equivalent prior to the introduction of the independent variable? Why?

5. When can you use the random-groups design?

6. What is the advantage of manipulating a subject variable and a nonsubject variable in the same experiment?

7. Why are matched-groups designs used when a subject variable manipulation is made? How is this design useful for evaluating subject variables?

8. What are the advantages and disadvantages of using a matched-groups design when assessing the effect of a nonsubject variable?

9. The _____ is the reference point used when computing variance.
   (1) mode   (2) range   (3) mean   (4) median   (5) standard deviation

10. Compare the variance for the following three sets of scores: set A: 5, 5, 5, 5, 5, 5; set B: 4, 6, 4, 6, 4, 6; set C: 1, 9, 1, 9, 1, 9. The variance is
   (1) the same for all three sets   (2) greater for set A than set B   (3) greatest for set C   (4) greatest for set A

11. The _____ is the reference point used to obtain an estimate of

population variance based on between-group fluctuations. (1) median (2) mode (3) overall or grand mean (4) group mean

12. The _____ estimate of population variance reflects chance fluctuations plus any effect of the independent variable. (1) within-group (2) between-group (3) matched-group (4) random-groups

13. The _____ estimate of population variance reflects chance fluctuations only. (1) within-group (2) between-group (3) matched-group (4) random-groups

14. The logic of the random-groups design is that the probability that random assignment will produce equivalent groups prior to the introduction of the independent variable is equal to (1) 1.0 (2) the significance level that is adopted (3) one minus the significance level that is adopted (4) the probability of making a Type 2 error

15. The random-groups design can be used (1) to study subject variables (2) when it is possible to randomly assign subjects to conditions and then introduce the independent variable (3) to ensure that groups will be equivalent following the introduction of the independent variable (4) to ensure that groups will be equivalent prior to the introduction of the independent variable

16. A suitable variable for matching is a _____ variable that _____ with performance on the dependent measure. (1) nonsubject, does not correlate (2) nonsubject, correlates (3) subject, correlates (4) subject, does not correlate

17. An investigator conducts a factorial design experiment in which one of the independent variables is a subject variable and the other is a nonsubject variable. The investigator may have decided to use this design in order to (1) determine whether the effect of the nonsubject variable depends on the level of the subject variable (2) assess whether the level of one independent variable depends on the level of the other independent variable (3) increase the power of the design (4) both 1 and 3

5 Within-subject designs

The fact that between-subject designs can be used for so many research problems may lead the student to conclude that there is little need for additional designs. But although the between-subject designs are very broad in scope, research problems frequently arise for which the use of these designs is difficult, impractical, or impossible. The relative importance of between- and within-subject designs varies greatly from problem area to problem area and from investigator to investigator. In some areas the research methodology is based almost entirely on one of the two designs. Yet in other areas investigators switch back and forth between the two, depending on the hypothesis under investigation. This chapter should give you a better understanding of why investigators use the designs they do and will help you determine the relative usefulness of between- and within-subject designs for your area of personal interest.

PROPERTIES OF WITHIN-SUBJECT DESIGNS

Within-Subject Manipulations

The label *within-subject* is appropriate in that sometimes one can obtain a good estimate of the effectiveness of the independent variable from the data of a single subject. For example, to use a within-subject design to compare the effectiveness of two brands of car paint, you would paint your car with both paints by alternating strips of Paint A and Paint B. Then you could evaluate the paints at a later date. The appearance of the paint would be the dependent measure. The single subject in this case is, of course, your car. By comparing the appearance of Paint A strips with that of Paint B strips, you can assess the effectiveness of the two paints within a single subject. For a between-subject design it would be necessary to compare different subjects (different cars) to assess the effect of the independent variable (type of paint). The major distinguishing feature of a within-subject design is that each subject gets more than one level of each independent variable. In all the examples of within-subject designs in this text, each subject receives all levels of each independent variable, as illustrated in Table 5-1. The table suggests that fewer subjects are needed to evaluate the effect of an independent variable if a within-subject design is used than if a between-subject design is used. This is usually the case. In fact, since each subject can provide information about the effect of the independent variable when a within-subject design is used, you may be willing to conclude that, except for the problem of the generality of the finding, one subject is all that is needed to make the evaluation. In rare instances this is true, but usually it is necessary to obtain data from more than one subject. The label *within-subject* should not be interpreted to mean that one subject is enough.

Nonsubject Variable Manipulations

Within-subject designs can be used to evaluate the effectiveness of non-subject variables only. It is, of course, impossible to manipulate subject variable characteristics such as age, intelligence, or number of siblings in a within-subject design. However, as is true with between-subject designs, it is possible to study a subject variable and nonsubject variable manipulation in the same experiment. A within-subject design can be used for the nonsubject

TABLE 5-1

An Example to Demonstrate the Distinguishing Feature of Between- and Within-Subject Designs

Type of design			
Between-subject		Within-subject	
Condition A	Condition B	Condition A	Condition B
Fred	Larry	Harry	Harry
Sam	Joel	Pete	Pete
Bob	Jack	Joan	Joan
Helen	Bert	Mary	Mary
Gary	Tom	Mark	Mark
Glenn	Jim	Rose	Rose
Ray	Stan	Lauren	Lauren

variable manipulation, allowing us to assess whether the effect of the manipulation depends on the type of subject tested. If a between-subject variable (a subject variable) and a within-subject manipulation are studied in the same experiment, the design is mixed. That is, since both types of design are used in the same experiment, the design for the entire experiment is called a *mixed* design.

Unfortunately, it is not really possible to specify the exact conditions under which a particular design should be chosen. Within-subject designs can be used for many of the same purposes as between-subject designs. Although it is frequently *possible* to use either one, a thorough analysis of methodological, practical, and statistical considerations should lead the investigator to conclude that one design is better than another for the intended purpose. To make a thorough analysis, one must be aware of the advantages and limitations of within-subject designs.

ADVANTAGES OF WITHIN-SUBJECT DESIGNS

Practical Considerations

Imagine that you have just accepted a position with a small beer company that has a young, vigorous, and ambitious management team. Management is interested in selling more of its beer, Best Brew. Management is not a bit modest about making claims for its brew, but realizes that it is an uphill battle to capture a sizable portion of the beer market. Management realizes that many people walk around with "Pabst Blue Ribbon on their mind" or a tune about the King of Beers. Few people even know about Best Brew. Your task is to establish that Best Brew is, in fact, the best; you are to compare Best Brew with the other beers and report your results to management within thirty days. How should you proceed?

The answer depends on a number of considerations, including how important it is that you keep your job, whether you are really interested in determining how Best Brew compares with other beers, the availability of participants who will compare beers for you, the amount of money you have for the project, and so on. Assume, at least at the outset, that you are genuinely interested in determining how Best Brew fares when compared with other beers. If it does not fare well, you can still propose advertising strategies for management that will lead consumers to conclude that Best Brew is the best. First, however, we want to establish how Best Brew actually compares with other beers.

The basic question is whether to use a between-subject or within-subject design. The independent variable, of course, is the brand of beer. The dependent measure you select is the rating, on a scale from 1 to 10, that the participant gives each beer, with 1 being the lowest (worst beer I ever tasted) and 10 being the highest (best beer I ever tasted). Practical considerations favor the use of a within-subject design. Since it does not take very long for a participant to taste a beer and give a rating from 1 to 10, you get more information from each participant if you have them rate two or more beers than if they rate only one. If recruiting participants is difficult, you are well-advised to use a within-subject design if possible.

Although the number of participants needed will be fewer if you can use a within-subject design instead of a between-subject design, the exact number that you need depends on what you are trying to accomplish. If you want to compare ten beers, you will need more participants than if you only want to compare two. If each participant rates each beer more than once, you will need fewer participants than if each participant can rate each beer only once. In the case of beer tasting, you would need to give serious consideration to the number of beers each participant rates and the number of times each is rated. If your participants actually swallow the beer — something beer drinkers are prone to do — you would need to limit the number of beers each participant rates and probably only obtain one rating for each beer the participant tastes. A drunk participant or even a slightly intoxicated participant may give different ratings from a sober participant. That is, the brand of beer variable may interact with the alcoholic state (sober or intoxicated) of the participants. Assume you elect to use sober participants only.

Practical considerations typically favor the use of a within-subject design over a between-subject design, but there are exceptions. In some cases there are large numbers of participants available, all conditions can be tested at the same time if different participants are assigned to each condition, and the amount of time it takes each participant to complete the experiment is long (say forty minutes or more). In instances such as these (completing questionnaires in which the nature of the questionnaire is the independent variable, comparing therapies, strategies for remembering, or methods for teaching reading), practical considerations usually dictate the use of a between-subject design. As we will soon see, methodological, interpretational, and practical considerations may dictate the use of a between-subject design. If all else is equal, you should opt for the within-subject design because of its greater efficiency.

Efficiency of Within-Subject Designs

Let us return to our beer-comparing example and consider the results presented in Table 5-2. The task is to compare the results obtained from a between-subject design (random-groups) with those obtained from a within-subject design. Consider first the ratings of the twenty participants who rated only one beer (the between-subject design). Is the hypothetical outcome presented in the table a rare or common outcome if only chance is operating?

TABLE 5–2

The Ratings on a Scale from 1 to 10 for Two Beers for the Twenty Participants Tested with a Between-Subject Design and the Ten Participants Tested with a Within-Subject Design (fictitious data)

		Type of design		
Between-subject		Within-subject		
Best Brew	Pabst	Participant	Best Brew	Pabst
3	2	A	1	2
8	3	B	6	7
4	10	C	9	10
9	4	D	2	3
1	10	E	3	4
3	9	F	3	5
6	3	G	8	9
2	5	H	7	10
7	3	I	3	3
3	7	J	4	3
ΣX 46	56		46	56
$\bar{X}$ 4.6	5.6		4.6	5.6

Overall, the ratings are somewhat higher for Pabst than for Best Brew, but there is also a considerable amount of within-group fluctuation. If we were to do an analysis of variance, would the between-group estimate of population variance be "considerably larger" than our within-group estimate? Later you will be equipped to perform the appropriate analyses. (If you evaluate the results for the between-subject design, you will have to conclude that the groups are equivalent, that is, a common outcome if only chance is operating.)

Now consider the results obtained from the within-subject design in which each participant rated each beer. A comparison of the ratings of the two beers for each participant reveals that eight of the ten rated Pabst higher, one gave tie ratings, and one preferred Best Brew. Clearly, if you work for Best Brew Brewery, this result is greater cause for concern than the results obtained with the between-subject design. The most reasonable conclusion for the between-subject design outcome is that participants do not show a preference, a much better outcome, from your point of view, than the conclusion that only one person in ten prefers Best Brew to Pabst. (The results for the within-subject design are, in fact, significant, a rare outcome if only chance is operating.) Before considering how you resolve your dilemma, we need to say a little more about design efficiency.

The power or efficiency of a design is analogous to the power of a microscope or telescope. Increasing the power of a microscope enables the observer to see smaller objects. Similarly, the use of a within-subject design sometimes allows the investigator to detect effects that cannot be detected with a between-subject design. It allows him to determine whether the mean differences in treatments are greater than might be expected on the basis of chance fluctuations within individuals. Chance fluctuations within individuals tend to be smaller than those between individuals. That is, the performances of the same person at two different times tend to be more alike than the performances of two people at the same time when some subject variable, known or unknown, is correlated with the performance measure.

When a within-subject design is used, the chance fluctuations in performance within *individuals*, not the fluctuations within *groups*, are used to assess the effect of the independent variable. Thus, a different statistical analysis is required for within-subject than for between-subject designs — because chance fluctuations in the performance of one person at two points in time tend to be smaller than the fluctuations of two people at the same time. Assume that an investigator has developed two tasks, A and B, of *identical* difficulty. You are tested on task A and then on task B, with ample time for rest between the two sessions. Two other people are randomly selected and then tested on task A only. The question is whether your two scores will be more alike than the two scores obtained by the other two subjects. That is, do within-subject chance fluctuations tend to be greater or smaller than between-subject chance fluctuations? The answer depends on whether any subject variables are correlated with performance on the tasks. For example, if intelligence correlates highly with task performance, then your scores should be more alike than the two scores of the other subjects since you have, presumably, the same IQ when you perform task A as when you perform task B. It is unlikely that two people selected at random would be of equal intelligence, so their scores would be more likely to vary.

Efficiency is defined in terms of the size of the chance fluctuations used to evaluate the effect of the independent variable (the variance of the null hypothesis sampling distribution). The smaller the chance fluctuations, the greater the efficiency. Earlier we noted that the magnitude of the chance fluctuations (precision of estimation) is related to sample size (see Table 3-6 if you have forgotten how precision of estimation is related to sample size). Here, we note that the type of design also determines efficiency because chance fluctuations within subjects tend to be smaller than those between subjects. Thus, the likelihood of rejecting the null hypothesis tends to be greater, all things being equal, for a within-subject design if the independent variable has an effect.

In some cases it is an understatement to say that there is a statistical advantage to using a within-subject design. The advantage of such a design is so marked under some conditions that there is little or no need for statistics. If it is possible to obtain a stable rate of responding, introduce the independent variable, and obtain a change in responding, there may be no need for statistical techniques. This is particularly true if it is possible to modify the level of responding at will by alternating the presence and absence of the treatment manipulation, as in many operant conditioning experiments.

Back to your dilemma. Given the results obtained with either design, you cannot make a strong case that Best Brew is better. Your within-subject design results suggest that it is not as good as Pabst. Your between-subject design revealed lower ratings for Best Brew than Pabst, but since the outcome is a common one if only chance is operating, you cannot reject the null hypothesis that there are no differences. Fortunately for you, the typical consumer does not care very much about the results of well-controlled experimental research in which beers are compared. Or, even if they do, you do not have an obligation to give all your results. You can be selective. Your goal is to help your company sell Best Brew. To do this, you can present commercials in which you ask a participant to compare Best Brew with another beer (say Pabst). You cover the containers so the actual identity is unknown to each participant, and you do nothing that would enable the participant to detect which beer you favor. Of course, in the commercial you only use the participants who actually selected Best Brew. Even if only one in ten prefers Best Brew, you can obtain a large number of participants for your commercials. You want people to accept the view that Best Brew is the best. If you only show positive instances, you might succeed. Most people have a bias for positive instances, so a positive instance confirms; they see little need to search for negative instances.

Research with One Subject

The basic task in using the experimental method is the same regardless of the number of subjects tested; it is to determine whether the treatment manipulation influences behavior. When only one subject is used and it is impossible to repeat the manipulation numerous times, it is necessary to obtain fairly stable behavior in order to do research.

Let us assume that an investigator wants to assess the effect of the withdrawal of attention on the temper tantrums of a four-year-old boy. It is necessary to establish how many times a day the child has a temper tantrum under "normal" conditions. Say that he has had seven to ten tantrums per day during the two weeks before the treatment manipulation. The treatment is to ignore the boy every time he has a tantrum. In all other respects, the investigator maintains the same relationship with him. If there is a sharp drop in the number of tantrums (to zero or one per day for the second week of treatment), it is reasonable to conclude that withdrawal of attention was responsible for the change in behavior (which is also to say that attention *reinforced* the tantrums).

Should the investigator want to be even more convinced that the manipulation was effective he could reinstate the "normal" conditions (paying attention to the child during a tantrum) to see if the child will resume the tantrum behavior. Let us assume that over the period of one week the child gradually returns to having seven to ten temper tantrums per day. If the withdrawal of reinforcement treatment is reinstated and the tantrum behavior quickly drops to zero again there can be little doubt that the manipulation was effective (see Wolf & Risley, 1971).

You should not conclude from this example that there are few, if any, problems in doing applied research with a small number of subjects. An interesting and informative account of some of the problems involved in such research is given by Wolf and Risley (1971). These authors emphasize the fact that it may be necessary to introduce the treatment manipulation more than once to make sure that the results are not due to a confounding variable. In the above experiment, for example, the investigator attributed the reduction in tantrum behavior to the manipulation. Yet it is possible that the little boy stopped having tantrums for other reasons. Perhaps the little girl next door gave him a long, wet kiss as a means of providing consolation. The boy, a keen observer of behavioral contingencies, noted the tantrum/kissing contingency and decided to discontinue tantrums. This alternative explanation can be rejected if the investigator withdraws reinforcement on a number of occasions and obtains a marked reduction in tantrums each time.

Research with Established Baselines

The use of within-subject designs with a small number of subjects is likely to be effective only if the experimenter has enough control over the situation to obtain a stable rate of responding or a stable response (as in some studies of sensation and perception). Or, in some cases, he can make use of the fact that a stable rate of responding exists even though he has little control. For example, a drug addict or alcoholic may have a stable rate of using drugs or drinking. It may, therefore, be possible to assess the effects of different treatments and still avoid the ethical problems involved in using a control group. In order to use the random-groups design to assess the effectiveness of a particular treatment for alcoholism or drug addiction, one must assign the subjects to treatment and no-treatment conditions. Many investigators and practitioners are unwilling to do this because they believe it is unethical to deny treatment to anyone. This difficulty can be avoided with a within-subject design because in such a design it is possible to treat everyone and compare the level of response before and after treatment. Although this approach has advantages, it has a few disadvantages too. One particularly troublesome difficulty is that participants and patients try, in general, to do what experimenters and therapists want them to do. This makes it difficult to isolate the effects attributable to the treatment.

METHODOLOGICAL AND INTERPRETATIONAL CONSIDERATIONS

Limitations of Within-Subject Designs

Inappropriateness of the Design for Some Problems. The use of a within-subject design is not appropriate for some experiments because it is not feasible to administer all the treatments to a single subject. For example, an investigator interested in the effect of a particular training technique should not test subjects in both the trained and nontrained condition because the use of one treatment precludes the use of the other. Once a subject is trained it is not possible to untrain him. Testing all the subjects in the untrained condition first is not an acceptable solution because any obtained differences may be due to either the ordering of the treatments or their nature.

Demand Characteristics. Another limitation of within-subject designs is that demand characteristics are likely to be a bigger problem than with a between-subject design. Demand characteristics are those aspects of the experiment that allow a subject to make a good guess about what the experimenter "wants." The results of the experiment may be drastically influenced if a subject can determine what it is all about or how the experimenter would like him to respond. He may attempt to please the experimenter and provide what he believes to be the desired results. Human subjects are more likely to be able to figure out the experimenter's expectations when a within-subject design is used because they experience all the levels of the independent variable.

Controlling Nonmanipulated Variables. The problem of controlling non-manipulated variables tends to be greater with within-subject designs because the subjects are always tested at two or more points in time. Therefore, the experimenter has to take steps to ensure that time-related variables such as the ordering of the treatments or practice and fatigue effects are not responsible for any obtained differences between the treatment conditions. Time-related variables may limit the use of within-subject designs because it is sometimes difficult or impossible to control these effects.

Counterbalancing

Nature and Purpose of Counterbalancing. Counterbalancing refers to the use of procedures that distribute the effects of nonmanipulated variables over the treatment conditions so that obtained differences can be attributed to chance and the treatment manipulation and not to the nonmanipulated variables. (It is *not* used to eliminate chance fluctuations.) Counterbalancing is accomplished by varying the order of treatments within or between subjects. It is important to control the effects of ordering because a subject may become practiced or fatigued as the experiment progresses. If each subject gets each treatment a number of times, then it is possible to balance out the effects of time-related variables by presenting the treatments in a random order. If each subject receives each treatment only once, then more than one subject is needed to balance out time-related variables. For example, when there are two treatments, A and B, and all subjects receive treatment A followed by treatment B, it is not possible to attribute any obtained differences to the effect of the treatment; perhaps the ordering of the two treatments was the important consideration. But if half the subjects receive treatment B followed by treatment A, the results obtained from all subjects can be combined to balance out the effect of the order of presentation (if there is equal transfer from A to B and B to A, a point that will be considered in detail later).

Table 5-3 shows an experiment with and without counterbalancing; the order of treatments was balanced in one case but not the other. Imagine that you were interested in comparing the preferences of participants for two beers, Best Brew (condition A) and Budweiser (condition B). In both cases we can compare the A and B treatments by obtaining a mean score on the dependent measure for each of the treatments. The two procedures differ in that differences between the two treatments are interpretable with counter-

TABLE 5-3

An Experiment With and Without Counterbalancing

With counterbalancing			Without counterbalancing		
Subject	Order of treatments		Subject	Order of treatments	
1	A	B	1	A	B
2	B	A	2	A	B
3	A	B	3	A	B
4	A	B	4	A	B
5	B	A	5	A	B
6	B	A	6	A	B
7	A	B	7	A	B
8	B	A	8	A	B
9	A	B	9	A	B
10	B	A	10	A	B

balancing but not without counterbalancing. If all subjects are given treat-ment A and then treatment B there is no way to determine whether any obtained difference is due to the actual treatment or to time-related effects such as practice, fatigue, or, in the present example, mild intoxication. Without counterbalancing, the experiment would be confounded.

The purpose of counterbalancing is to compensate for the effects of time-related variables. The procedures used depend on the number of subjects available and the number of treatment conditions. When complete counterbalancing is used, every treatment is presented in each position an equal number of times and every treatment follows every other an equal number of times.

Complete Counterbalancing. There are a number of examples that you might consider. If you prefer alcoholic examples, you might imagine that you are interested in comparing four quality wines. You work for the editor of a "food and wine" magazine who instructs you to evaluate the best white wine produced at each of four wineries. For those who prefer nonalcoholic examples, imagine that the task is to judge four soft drinks (Pepsi, Coca Cola, Seven-Up, and Tab). Participants are blindfolded so that they cannot use color when judging quality. Or, for those interested in reading, we can assess the effect of four kinds of print (pica, elite, script, great primer) on speed of oral reading. For convenience in exposition, the four conditions of your experiment, whether wines, soft drinks, or print type, are identified as A, B, C, and D. Our concern is how we can administer all four treatments to participants in such a way that we can balance out effects due to practice, fatigue, or mild intoxication.

To completely counterbalance the order of the treatments (A, B, C, D) it would be necessary to have twenty-four subjects, each getting one of the twenty-four different orders of the four treatments. The twenty-four possible orders are presented in Table 5-4; note that each treatment is presented in each sequential position six times. Each subject is randomly assigned one sequence from 1 to 24; the sequences are not used in the same order in which they are presented in the table. Only chance determines which sequence each subject receives.

Let us assume that the twenty-four subjects are randomly assigned to the twenty-four possible sequences with the restriction that each sequence be used only once. The subjects are tested and the results analyzed. The analysis reveals that there are significant differences among the four treatment conditions. If this is the case, it is not reasonable to attribute the results to the order in which the treatments were presented because all possible orders were used.

Partial Counterbalancing. When many treatments are given it is no longer feasible to use complete counterbalancing because there are so many possible orderings of the conditions. For example, there are 120 presentation

TABLE 5-4

The Twenty-four Possible Sequences of Treatments for the Experiment Investigating the Effect of Kind of Print on Speed of Reading; Comparing Four Wines; or Comparing Four Soft Drinks

Sequence number	Order of treatment	Sequence number	Order of treatment
1	A B C D	13	C A B D
2	A B D C	14	C A D B
3	A C B D	15	C B A D
4	A C D B	16	C B D A
5	A D B C	17	C D A B
6	A D C B	18	C D B A
7	B A C D	19	D A B C
8	B A D C	20	D A C B
9	B C A D	21	D B A C
10	B C D A	22	D B C A
11	B D A C	23	D C A B
12	B D C A	24	D C B A

orders of five conditions, thereby requiring 120 subjects. With a large number of treatments or a limited number of subjects, it is necessary to use partial counterbalancing.

Assume that you are unable to get the cooperation of twenty-four participants who will serve in all four of the conditions of your experiment. This is unlikely if you are comparing wines, or even soft drinks, but a reasonable possibility if you are studying the effect of print on reading speed. Many people are sensitive about their reading speed, perhaps because they believe that others read much faster than they do. Considering that the average reading speed is between 250 and 300 words per minute (Gibson & Levin, 1975), the concerns of many are likely to be unjustified.

Let us assume that only twelve subjects are available instead of twenty-four. The twelve subjects are randomly assigned to twelve of the twenty-four sequences such that each treatment (A, B, C, D) is presented in each position three times. Most investigators would probably accept this counterbalancing procedure and not be concerned about any confounding effects due to treatments and presentation order even though each treatment did not precede and follow every other treatment an equal number of times. Evaluation of the adequacy of a counterbalancing procedure comes down to a question of belief. Do other investigators believe the controls are adequate? It is unlikely that many investigators would accept the counterbalancing procedures if, say, only two sequences were randomly selected and six subjects were tested in one sequence and six in the other. But as the number of sequences used is increased, the likelihood of adequately controlling for possible confounding effects is also increased.

There is no absolute point at which one can say the counterbalancing is adequate (say, seven or more sequences) because some investigators will be more concerned about the adequacy than others. You should do the best job that conditions allow. If you can obtain twenty-four subjects, there is little reason not to use complete counterbalancing. If you can only obtain twelve subjects, you have to settle for a less than complete procedure, but if you are able to present each treatment in each position in the presentation sequence an equal number of times (if four people taste Pepsi first, another four taste it second, another four taste it third, and another four taste it fourth), you should convince most investigators that you had counterbalanced adequately. Obviously, if conditions are too unfavorable (you can only recruit two participants), you should not do an experiment that requires extensive counterbalancing between subjects in order to control the effects of time-related variables.

Similar procedures can be used if each subject receives each condition more than once. For example, if there are two conditions, A and B, and each subject is to receive each condition twice, then half the subjects could receive an ABBA, ABBA sequence, and the other half could receive a BAAB, BAAB sequence.

Differential Transfer

Counterbalancing the order in which treatments are presented is a very useful way of controlling for ordering effects — but it does not always work. It may not balance out presentation order effects if there are differential carry-over effects from one treatment condition to the next. If the results obtained with condition B are different when C precedes B from when A precedes B, there is differential transfer. When there are such transfer effects, it may be impossible to counterbalance the order of treatments to control position effects.

Differential transfer is of considerable interest for both methodological and theoretical reasons. To illustrate, imagine that you are interested in problem solving, specifically the strategies that participants report using for different tasks. To accomplish this end you develop three tasks which, it turns out, differ considerably in difficulty. We will label the very easy task as A, the very difficult task as C, and the task of moderate difficulty as B. We will consider performance on task B only. Is performance on task B higher when B is preceded by task A than when B is preceded by task C? If this is the case it can be attributed to the carryover of expectations, skills, or sets from one task to the next. If there are differential carryover effects from one condition to the next, the conclusions you reach about the effect of a particular treatment are likely to depend on the design. That is, our conclusion about the three treatments might be different depending on whether we use a between-subject design or a within-subject design, particularly if we are not able to use complete counterbalancing. For example, if C precedes B more often than A precedes B, our estimate of the difficulty of B is likely to be higher with a within- than with a between-subject design. If there is reason to suspect that carryover effects will make it difficult to interpret the treatment manipulation, it is a good idea to opt for the random-groups design.

On a more optimistic note, transfer effects can be viewed as phenomena of considerable interest which need to be explained. Why is it that performance on a task of moderate difficulty is lower when preceded by a difficult task than by an easy task? One explanation offered by Seligman and others (Seligman, 1975; Maier & Seligman, 1976; Alloy & Seligman, 1979) is learned helplessness. The basic notion is that repeated failure results in the development of a perceptual bias or expectation which influences future performance. A person who has a history of failure may conclude that whatever he or she does will not have an effect, so there is little point in trying. The person has learned to be helpless. Seligman argues that learned helplessness is a very important concept which influences development, whether a person becomes depressed, and even death. In his view it is a very useful way of viewing motivation. People who have developed learned helplessness simply do not try.

The point of interest here is that there may be good reasons why one type of design yields different results from another type of design. One can bemoan the fact that different methods occasionally yield different results or one can view the findings as phenomena to be explained. Clearly, the view of learned helplessness, and, if you prefer, the opposite side of the coin, which is self-esteem (self-efficacy), are based in no small part on laboratory studies of transfer effects. That is, the phenomenon of learned helplessness can be produced in the laboratory with either humans or lower animals as participants. The phenomenon is typically studied in the laboratory by examining differential transfer.

Generality of Research Findings

Interest in Establishing Generalities. It is possible to manipulate subject and nonsubject variables in the same experiment regardless of whether a between- or within-subject design is used to assess the effect of the nonsubject variable manipulation. Manipulating both kinds of variables enables the experimenter to determine whether the effect of the nonsubject variable manipulation depends on the type of subject being used. If it does not, then the finding can be said to have greater generality.

Investigators differ considerably about their interest in demonstrating the generality of a finding. Some of them assume that it is unnecessary because they believe in the generality of behavioral laws. They believe one should not worry about a separate set of laws for each type of subject. It follows from this view that a manipulation that is effective with one subject should be effective with others; some investigators will accept a finding that has been obtained by testing one subject in a within-subject design.

On the other hand, some investigators are unwilling to generalize such evidence much beyond the one or two subjects tested. If the effect of a non-subject variable manipulation *does* depend on the characteristics of subjects, and if only one or two subjects are used, the experimenter may have happened to use only the type of subject who shows the desired effect. Some investigators place less weight on the evidence obtained in this way because a generalization of such results tends to deny the importance of subject variables.

There is something to be said for both points of view. Obviously, we need to know when subject variables are important and when they are not. If subject variables are relatively unimportant for many nonsubject-variable manipulations, then much time and effort can be wasted in the attempt to demonstrate the generality of particular findings. There can be little question that the generality of very important findings should be determined by such methods as using different types of subjects. However, it seems unreasonable to insist that each experiment contain a large sample of subjects so that the pervasiveness of an effect can be determined; it is simply more economical to determine, first, whether the effect exists.

Design and Generality. You may wonder what the relationship is between design and generality. Specifically, which of the two basic designs yields findings of greater generality? There is no clear answer to this question because each design has an advantage and a disadvantage. The advantage of a between-subject design is that more subjects are tested. The greater the number of subjects tested, all things being equal, the greater the generality of the results. The disadvantage of this design is that the effect of the independent variable cannot be assessed for each subject but only for the group. However, if the effect is very large (if the worst subject in the experimental condition is better than the best subject in the control condition), it is probably fair to conclude that the independent variable influenced every experimental subject.

The situation is reversed in a within-subject design. Usually fewer subjects are used, but it is frequently possible to assess the effect of the independent variable for each. If all subjects tested demonstrate the same effect and many subjects are tested, then most investigators would be very willing to generalize the finding. Usually, however, the number of subjects tested is quite small when the effect of the independent variable can be assessed for each. In sum, the generality of a research finding tends to be independent of the type of design used. Findings of little and of considerable generality can be obtained with each type.

Selecting a Within-Subject Design

We have now reached the point where it is possible to discuss generally the selection of a within-subject design. The task for the investigator is to weigh the advantages and disadvantages of each type of design and then select the one that will provide the best test of the effectiveness of the independent variable.

The major factors to consider are the nature of the independent variable, the number of subjects available, the resources available, and the statistical advantages. The most important consideration is the independent variable because its nature will frequently dictate the type of design. In some cases within-subject designs are ruled out because testing each subject in more than one treatment condition would be impossible, or would result in differential transfer, destroy the intended manipulation, or alert subjects to the "real" purpose of the experiment. Yet when a limited number of subjects are available, or when subjects can be tested in all treatment conditions, the investigator should give serious consideration to the within-subject design. Methodological and practical considerations may suggest the use of one type of design over the other; if not, the decision can be based on statistical considerations. Since the within-subject design is the more efficient, it is preferred.

In sum, there is no list of rules that an investigator can apply when selecting a design. In general, however, within-subject designs should be seriously considered whenever a small number of subjects are available, extensive training or testing is required, differential transfer does not loom as a confounding variable, or the magnitude of the effect of the independent variable is believed to be small — that is, when an efficient design is needed.

SUMMARY

The major distinguishing feature of a within-subject design is that each subject gets more than one level of each independent variable. In a between-subject design each subject receives only one level of each independent variable. Within-subject designs can be used to evaluate nonsubject variables only. Since the two types of designs can be used for many of the same purposes, it is frequently possible to use either one to investigate a particular effect.

The advantages of the within-subject design are that fewer subjects are needed and the design is usually more efficient than a between-subject design because the independent variable is assessed in terms of chance fluctuations within subjects. Chance fluctuations within subjects are typically smaller than those between subjects.

Within-subject designs are simply not appropriate for some experiments. It is not always feasible to administer all the treatments to a single subject.

Demand characteristics are likely to be a bigger problem in these designs because the participant has a better chance of determining what results the experimenter wants if he is tested in all treatment conditions. Also, it is necessary to control time-related variables because subjects are tested at two or more points in time.

The major methodological problems involved in within-subject designs are counterbalancing the effects of time-related variables and determining whether there is differential transfer between the various treatment conditions. The problem of the generality of the research findings does not appear to be any greater than it is in between-subject designs.

The nature of the independent variable, the availability of subjects and resources, and statistical considerations are the principal factors to consider when selecting a design. The nature of the independent variable is the most important consideration because its manipulation will frequently dictate the choice of the design. Within-subject designs are useful in a wide variety of areas. They are especially useful in applied research because the effectiveness of treatment manipulations can be assessed with one subject, allowing the investigator to give the treatment to all subjects.

QUESTIONS

(Answers for the multiple choice questions are given in Appendix D.)

1. Distinguish between within- and between-subject designs and give an example of each.
2. What is the purpose of counterbalancing? Why is counterbalancing used extensively when within-subject designs are used?
3. How would you counterbalance if you had three treatments, a within-subject design, and twelve subjects?
4. What is differential transfer? Give an example of an independent variable that you believe would produce differential transfer effects. Give an example of one that you believe would not produce such effects. How would you determine whether or not you were correct in your judgments?
5. What are the advantages and limitations of within-subject designs?
6. Explain why a within-subject design is likely to be more efficient than a between-subject design. How is efficiency defined in this regard?
7. Assume that an investigator is interested in the effect of a physical disability on inducing compliance behavior. The independent variable is whether the experimenter's confederate wears an eye patch or not. The dependent variable is the number of letters, if any, that the subject agrees to write to aid the confederate's "Help Save the Redwoods" campaign. Each subject is led to believe that the confederate is another subject serving in the same experiment. The experiment is actually conducted while both "subjects" are sup-

posedly waiting for the investigator. What type of research design should be used? Why?

8. Assume that you are given the responsibility for evaluating the effect of a new rehabilitation program in a state prison system on the rate of recidivism. You have the authority to decide whether a prisoner is assigned to the new or old program, or both. What type of design would you use? Why?

9. Assume that a new drug has been developed to reduce hypertension. The independent variable is whether the drug or a placebo is administered to the subjects. The dependent measure is blood pressure. What type of design would you use? Why?

10. Assume that you have been hired by the state to evaluate the claims made by the advocates of a speed-reading course. You have the cooperation of the people who conduct the course. What type of design would you use to evaluate it? Why? What would you use as the dependent measure?

11. Let us assume that you want to test the view that the ability to discriminate among fine wines is developed as a result of experience — that people who have consumed a number of fine wines develop their powers of discrimination. Assume that large quantities of wine and time are available. What type of design would you use to test the view that there is a causal relationship between consumption and the ability to discriminate among wines? Why? What treatment conditions would you use? Would you use a double-blind procedure for the testing stage?

12. How would you evaluate the effectiveness of heroin substitutes such as methadone for reducing drug addiction?

13. How would you evaluate the effectiveness of two different fabric softeners, reading instruction programs, hand lotions, soaps, lipsticks, coffeepots, paints, or fertilizers?

14. The major distinguishing feature of a within-subject design is that each subject gets (1) only one level of each independent variable (2) only one combination of treatments when a factorial design is used (3) more than one level of each independent variable (4) only one level of each dependent variable

15. Chance fluctuations within individuals tend to be _____ those between individuals. (1) smaller than (2) larger than (3) the same as

16. One advantage of the within-subject design over the between-subject design is that the within-subject design has greater efficiency. Efficiency refers to the (1) number of subjects needed per condition (2) number of experimenters needed to execute the experiment (3) size of the chance fluctuations used to assess the effect of the independent variable (4) amount of data obtained from each subject for a given unit of time

17. All else being equal, demand characteristics are likely to be _____ problem for within- than for between-subject designs. (1) a bigger (2) less of a (3) an equally difficult

18. Counterbalancing is used to (1) eliminate chance fluctuations (2) balance out the effects of time-related variables (3) reduce within-group fluctuations (4) control for the effects of nonmanipulated subject variables

19. If the results obtained with condition B are different when C precedes

B from when A precedes B, there is   (1) only partial counterbalancing
(2) complete counterbalancing   (3) differential transfer   (4) zero transfer

20. The minimum number of subjects needed to assess the effect of an independent variable with a within-subject design under optimal conditions is
(1) the number needed for complete counterbalancing   (2) the number needed for partial counterbalancing   (3) ten   (4) one

6 Nonexperimental and quasi-experimental designs

Imagine that you have a wealthy friend who has recently participated in a weekend "training" session for which she paid $300. Your friend is ecstatic about the benefits she received, claiming, among other things, that the experience has changed her entire life. You have no idea what it means to have your entire life changed, but you listen as she attempts to persuade you to take the training. You respond that $300 is a lot of money, that you do not have $300, and that you have little faith that the "training" will have a lasting effect, except to make you poorer. Your friend persists, even offers to contribute $250 of the $300 for your training. You suddenly become more interested. You could afford the weekend if you took the money you had been saving for a new coat. After pondering the decision for a few minutes, you happen to notice an article about the training program in the newspaper you had been reading. The article reports the results of a well-controlled experiment in which the effectiveness of the training procedure was evaluated. The major conclusion of the study is that there was no clear evidence that training resulted in significant changes in behavior, but, when interviewed, some of the participants in the training session were very enthusiastic about the benefits of training. What are you likely to do?

The answer depends on a number of considerations such as your preference for well-controlled studies over self-reports and whether you have ever taken the advice of your friend on previous occasions. There is reason to believe that you would follow the advice of your friend if she has given you good advice on previous occasions. If we take someone's advice and have a pleasant experience as a result, we are likely to listen carefully the next time he or she makes a recommendation. If not, we should know better the next time. If a close friend has a good experience, why shouldn't we also have a good experience? If we believe that humans are similar, we might expect them to agree in their evaluation of the training session. We base most of our daily decisions on nonexperimental evidence (advice of friends, reviewers, intuitions). There is little choice in the matter since we cannot do an elaborate experiment every time we have to choose between two or more alternatives. In fact, we appear to have a bias for deciding on the basis of previous experience, presumably because in most instances that is all there is. In one sense this is a reasonable bias; clearly some information is better than none when deciding among alternatives. Something that worked well in the past may have worked well because, in fact, it is a good solution. However, it is important to recognize that making personal decisions by relying on friends, intuitions, or reviewers is drastically different from relying on experimental evidence or quasi-experimental evidence. One goal of this chapter is to indicate why this is the case.

In this chapter we will consider nonexperimental and quasi-experimental designs. Quasi-experimental designs are discussed because they can be very useful for studying problems when experimental designs are not suitable. Nonexperimental designs are considered because they are *not* useful for research purposes (even though many of our daily decisions are based on them). We need to know why they are not useful so that we will avoid them.

NONEXPERIMENTAL DESIGNS

We present three examples of nonexperimental designs that have some plausibility (some similarity with the everyday procedures we use to make decisions) and then consider why the designs are not useful for research purposes. It should be a helpful exercise for you to evaluate each of the examples presented prior to reading about the factors that influence design adequacy. If you do this you are likely to generate many of the criticisms of nonexperimental designs, but not all. Unfortunately, it is one thing to generate criticisms of a particular research plan when specifically asked to do so and quite another to recognize weaknesses in research studies that you are personally involved in or that you find particularly interesting because the conclusions square with your personal biases. The critical evaluation of procedures can become a general attitude to apply in your daily living and not merely a strategy you use when asked to evaluate a few nonexperimental designs.

Three Nonexperimental Designs

Single Group—Observed Once Design. Often a treatment is introduced to a single group and then a performance measure is obtained. There is no control or comparison group and there is no comparison of performance before and after treatment. For example, one could evaluate the effect of a therapy by interviewing patients after such therapy. Should we accept at face value the patient's claim that the therapy was successful? Should we pay $300 for a weekend of training because a close friend claims that the experience changed her life? It is tempting to accept this procedure because we obtain most of our information about particular treatments, products, performances, and so on in exactly this way. Testimonials of users or alleged users are undoubtedly the most common way of advertising products and services. When used for research purposes, this is sometimes referred to as the one-shot case study (Campbell, 1957). One-shot refers to the fact that only one observation is made (patients are only asked to evaluate their treatment once).

Clearly, it is convenient for us to take the advice of others about particular events, products, and services for our daily living if objectively better information is not available, but this is not a satisfactory way to accumulate knowledge. We are biased processors of information; we need systematic procedures to eliminate bias. What are the biases that might be present when a single group–observed once design is used? If participants generally give a positive account (praise) for the treatment they received, this may be because the treatment actually was effective, but there are other explanations as well. What are some of them?

Single-Group, Pretest-Posttest Design. The major problem with the single group–observed once design is that there is no way to evaluate whether the treatment is related to performance on the dependent measure. We need a way to assess whether the introduction of a treatment produces a *change* in performance. Thus, one might argue that it is necessary to have two performance measures, one taken before administering the treatment and one following treatment. Then the two performance measures can be compared to evaluate the treatment. If there is a significant difference between the pretest and posttest scores, it is tempting to conclude that the treatment was responsible for the change.

The single-group, pretest-posttest design has considerable intuitive appeal. One measures behavior, administers a treatment, and then measures behavior again. If there is a change, such change must be a result of the treatment. There *appears* to be little reason to bother with a control group when it is possible to measure the behavior of interest immediately before and after treatment. The design is attractive for another reason; one is able to select subjects on the basis of the pretest. Thus it is only necessary to administer the treatment to subjects who can be expected to benefit from it.

Let us assume that you are interested in evaluating a therapy for reducing anxiety. You prefer to treat people who are anxious; nonanxious people do not need the therapy. To find anxious people you administer an anxiety test to a large class of introductory psychology students ($n = 600$). You use the results of the pretest to select the twenty-five most anxious students; then you

administer the therapy to them (assume they cooperate) and give them an anxiety posttest that is equivalent to the pretest to determine whether the treatment had any effect. If there is a significant decrease in the anxiety scores from the pretest to the posttest, can the difference be attributed to the therapy?

For a second example, let us assume that you teach remedial reading. You would like to evaluate a new remedial reading program, so you administer a reading test to a large number of third-grade students in a large metropolitan elementary school. You select the fifty students who have the lowest reading scores for your remedial reading program. After they complete the eight-week reading program they are retested to assess the effects of the reading program. If there is a significant increase in the scores from pretest to posttest, should you attribute this change to the effect of the reading program?

Is a single-group, pretest-posttest design better than a single group– observed once design? That is, are there more problems with one design than the other? In order to generate what weaknesses a design might have, you should imagine that the design was used and significant differences were obtained (pretest-posttest differences) or, in the case of the single group– observed once design, "favorable" results were obtained. What might account for the favorable results other than an effective treatment? If you can generate other explanations, it may be because the design has not enabled you to eliminate sources of bias.

The Static-Groups Design. The static-groups design is most similar to a subject-variable comparison. About the only difference is that the groups are already formed in the case of the static-groups design. For a subject variable comparison, you may need to do considerable work to select the participants you want to compare. For example, you may develop a test to identify participants who are assertive or nonassertive. For static-groups comparisons we take groups that are already formed. We might compare the incidence of cancer in industrial and nonindustrial communities. If there is a higher incidence in industrial communities, we might conclude, perhaps erroneously, that the "treatment" (presence of industry) is responsible for the higher incidence of cancer. Or we might compare communities in which there is a high incidence of unwed, pregnant teenagers with a community in which the incidence is very low in an effort to relate the difference to other variables.

The basic logic of the static-groups comparison is that differences between groups that differ on a particular variable *may* be due to the variable. The difficult problem is determining whether the "treatment" is responsible for any obtained differences in performance. Since it is not possible to assign participants to groups before introducing the "treatment," it is difficult to rule out other factors as being responsible for any obtained differences between groups. To evaluate the suitability of this design, you might compare it with subject-variable comparisons not based on intact groups. What advantages, if any, might you obtain by not being restricted to intact groups?

Factors Influencing Design Adequacy

As you know, we use designs or plans when testing our ideas in an effort to avoid bias. Thus, the central concern in evaluating the adequacy of a design is whether the systematic procedures that are used allow us to avoid bias. If the plan does not enable us to rule out alternative explanations for the results (factors other than the treatment may be responsible for any obtained difference in performance on the dependent measure), then the design is not completely satisfactory. Nonexperimental designs are unsatisfactory because it is usually possible to list a *number* of factors, in addition to the treatment, that may be responsible for any obtained performance differences. We will consider seven factors, using special labels for each. It is likely that you were able to generate the first factors we will consider. In fact, there is some danger that you will conclude, erroneously, that understanding design adequacy is little more than common sense. Having common sense is certainly useful, but it is not enough. To evaluate your common sense, you need to try to list seven factors that influence design adequacy before reading about them.

History and Maturation. You undoubtedly recognized that events other than the treatment that occur between testings in a pretest-posttest situation or before testing in a single group–observed once design might be responsible for the results. The term *maturation* refers to events that take place within the individual. Maturation effects are relatively independent of environmental stimulation. They are time-related processes — neurological development, aging, fatigue, sexual arousal, and so on (Campbell & Stanley, 1963). History effects, on the other hand, are related directly to environmental stimulation; they depend on the participant's situation. For example, a person in college has different experiences from one who is not in college, but their maturational changes are probably similar.

We can reconsider our single-group, pretest-posttest design example in which twenty-five anxious students underwent therapy for anxiety as a means of demonstrating the history factor. If there is a significant decrease in the anxiety scores from the pretest to the posttest, can we attribute the difference to the therapy? It is not reasonable to conclude that the therapy was responsible because there are several other factors that may be responsible for a decrease in the anxiety score. For example, if the investigator administered the first anxiety test to students during their first week at college, it is likely that the scores would be high. New students tend to be anxious; as they develop new friendships, pass examinations, and become acquainted with their professors, their anxiety usually decreases. These events, not the treatment, may be responsible for any reduction in anxiety. Or it may be that the therapy per se had no effect on anxiety, but the events associated with therapy did; for example, maybe the pretest-posttest difference can be attributed to the attention paid to the student independent of the therapy given. The same reduction might occur by taking each of the twenty-five students for coffee, coke, or beer once a week instead of administering therapy. In short, several events that may occur between the pretest and posttest could change the test scores. A control group that is identical to the no-treatment condition except for the treatment manipulation is needed.

To demonstrate the maturation factor, we can reconsider our single-group, pretest-posttest example in which fifty third-grade students are given an eight-week remedial reading program. Perhaps neurological development during the eight weeks is responsible for the increase in reading scores. Maturation effects can be very powerful, particularly when there is a long period of time between the two tests. For example, a depressed person may seek help for his or her depression. If the depression is related to unusual hormonal activity (such as menopause) that gradually stabilizes with time, improvement may be due to maturational effects and not to the treatment obtained. It is tempting to believe that the treatment was actually responsible because it is likely to be the most salient change (expensive, requiring trips to the therapist), but this may not be the case. In evaluating research it is important not to stop after you have generated one plausible explanation (the treatment) because there may be many others.

Selection. The selection factor becomes an important consideration any time you do not have control over who receives the treatment and who does not. Thus, it is a problem for all between-subject designs that do not allow us to form equivalent groups before introducing the independent variable. We may introduce bias in the selection process if we cannot use random assignment or random selection procedures when forming groups. It is an obvious problem any time we have static-groups comparisons or subject-variable comparisons. It may also be a problem when within-subject comparisons are made.

Consider the task of evaluating special training programs when you do not have control over the selection of participants. If you have a self-selection process (people willing to pay $300 for training), the people who participate may be unusual in a number of respects (wealth, trust, depression). It is important to recognize that people who select themselves for a particular treatment may do so at an unusual time for them. Typically, we seek help when we believe we need it. If we do not bother to seek help, we may find that we feel better after a few days without treatment. If we seek it, we are likely to attribute any change to our treatment, regardless of its actual effectiveness. The major point is simply that we cannot expect self-selected groups to be representative of the larger population. At best this means that the effectiveness of a treatment demonstrated by using self-selected participants should not be generalized.

Sensitization, Measurement, and Demand Characteristics. Sensitization, measurement, and demand characteristics all refer to interpretational problems arising from the procedures used to assess a treatment effect. Sensitization and measurement refer to the fact that the assessment process may change the subject's behavior. If a single-group, pretest-posttest design is used, any difference between the two scores may be a function of the procedure and not the treatment; the pretest may *sensitize* the subject to the treatment effect.

It is possible to demonstrate sensitization by performing a 2 by 2 factorial, random-groups design, as shown in Table 6-1. One variable is the treatment (yes versus no), and the other variable is the presence of a pretest (yes versus no). We can determine whether there is a treatment effect for the subjects who get the pretest, *and* we can determine whether there is a treatment effect for the subjects who do not get the pretest. We use the performance on the dependent measure, of course, to assess the treatment effect. If a treatment effect is obtained for subjects who took the pretest, and *no* treatment effect is obtained for those who did not, we have evidence of sensitization. A treatment effect is obtained only if a pretest is given.

The *measurement* factor can refer to the facts that a test may change the subjects, and different results may be obtained with reactive and nonreactive measures. You will remember that reactive and nonreactive measures differ; nonreactive measures are obtained in such a way that the observees are not aware that their behavior is being recorded. If the effect of a treatment depends on the type of dependent measure (reactive versus nonreactive), there is a measurement factor.

Demand characteristics are cues available to a participant in an experiment that may enable him to determine the "purpose" of the experiment. A participant who knows what the experimenter wants may respond to please or

TABLE 6–1

An Example to Demonstrate That the Effect of a Treatment May Depend on the Use of a Pretest

		Treatment	
		Yes	No
Pretest	Yes	$\bar{X} = 40$	$\bar{X} = 20$
	No	$\bar{X} = 20$	$\bar{X} = 20$

displease the experimenter. Obviously, we can expect demand characteristics to pose a greater interpretational problem if the subject has several cues about the purpose of the experiment (for example, pretest and reactive measures) than if he has none. Because demand characteristics pose interpretational problems for experimental as well as nonexperimental designs, we will discuss them in more detail in the next chapter.

You need not be concerned about fine distinctions among sensitization, measurement, and demand characteristics, because the distinction among these factors is, at best, blurred. Sensitization and measurement can probably be classified as examples of the demand characteristic factor since both of these factors can be viewed as cue effects. That is, sensitization may occur because subjects use the pretest to determine what the experimenter hopes to accomplish with the treatment. And a difference between reactive and nonreactive measures may be obtained because the subject is able to determine what the experimenter wants when a reactive measure is used and respond accordingly. We can call all three factors demand characteristics or we can use all three labels. It is probably better to remember all three labels because all three are used in research articles in the social sciences.

Regression. When a single-group, pretest-posttest design is used, differences between the two scores for each subject may be due to regression and not to the effect of the treatment manipulation. To discuss what is meant by regression and why regression is an important methodological consideration, it is first necessary to reconsider the concept of reliability.

Reliability can mean either consistency of measurement or precision of measurement. When considering reliability in terms of precision, we view each individual's score as having two unobservable components, a true score and an error score; that is, we *theorize* that there is a true score and an error score component. It might help you to appreciate the distinction if you view the true score as due to skill and the error score as due to chance (either good, bad, or average luck). The true score components tap stable characteristics of the individuals (differences in skill). None changes over time unless there are basic changes in individuals. The error component, on the other hand, does change over time. This component represents all the chance factors that are likely to influence performance at one time. Chance can increase the score, decrease the score, or leave it unchanged. Reliability is determined by the relative variances of the true scores and error scores. If the error score variance is much smaller than the true score variance, then chance fluctuations over time are small and, as a result, the observed score on each testing occasion will be determined primarily by the true score. In this case successive measurements will be consistent (they will yield about the same score) because the scores will be determined largely by the participant's stable characteristics. If, on the other hand, there is large error score variance, scores for repeated testings of the same individual are likely to vary widely. The scores will frequently be far from the true score and inconsistent because performance is determined largely by chance.

Let us consider what results might be obtained if each subject is given two tests and the tests are highly reliable or unreliable. If the tests have perfect reliability, then each test is tapping the same stable characteristics; the scores should not change from the first test to the second. This result is given in Table 6-2. Notice that all subjects have the same score for each test because we have assumed that there is no error component for each score. If we select subjects on the basis of their score on the first test we should not expect their scores on the second test to change unless we introduce a treatment that has a real effect between the first and second test.

Now let us use the same scores to demonstrate what might happen if the two tests are unreliable. If the scores reflect chance fluctuations only, then we should not expect each subject to achieve the same score for both tests. Each subject's score is assumed to reflect chance fluctuations only. We can *simulate* what might happen if only chance determines the score by using the same scores presented in Table 6-2. In this case, however, we will randomly assign the scores to subjects by placing each score on a piece of paper and blindly drawing them out of a hat. The first number is assigned to the first subject, the second to the second subject, and so on. We do this twice, once for each

TABLE 6–2

Scores for a Group of Subjects on Two Equivalent Tests Having Perfect Reliability

Subject	Test 1 score	Test 2 score
1	130	130
2	63	63
3	89	89
4	46	46
5	113	113
6	79	79
7	103	103
8	99	99
9	116	116
10	61	61
11	80	80
12	89	89
13	125	125
14	55	55
15	92	92

test. The results of such a random selection of numbers are presented in Table 6-3.

To understand the methodological implications of unreliability we need to imagine that a single-group, pretest-posttest design is used and there is no treatment effect. Should we expect the mean pretest and posttest scores to differ? The answer to this question depends on two considerations — the reliability of the test and the selection of subjects. If the two tests correlate perfectly then the situation is comparable to the one depicted in Table 6-2. We should not expect the mean pretest score to differ from the mean posttest score, regardless of which subjects are selected for the experiment, because the tests are tapping the subjects' stable characteristics only. However, we can expect a marked change in the pretest and posttest scores if the subjects who have high pretest scores are selected *and* the pretest-posttest reliability is low.

We can simulate the second situation by selecting the five subjects who have the highest pretest scores from Table 6-3. The five highest scores are 113, 125, 116, 103, and 130 (subjects 3, 8, 12, 13, and 15); the mean of these five scores is 117.40. Now if we consider the five posttest scores for the *same* subjects we find that their scores are 125, 103, 89, 46, and 99; the mean is 92.40. We find that there is a marked change from pretest to posttest for subjects who have high scores on the pretest when chance factors deter-

TABLE 6-3

Scores for a Group of Subjects on Two Tests Having Low Reliability

Subject	Test 1 score	Test 2 score
1	99	92
2	55	113
3	113	125
4	80	80
5	61	55
6	63	89
7	46	130
8	125	103
9	89	63
10	89	116
11	79	79
12	116	89
13	103	46
14	92	61
15	130	99

mine each score because we *selected* those subjects who had high scores on the pretest. If their high scores were obtained by chance (they were lucky), there is no guarantee that they will also obtain high scores on the posttest (they may not be lucky again). In general, then, we can expect scores to decrease from pretest to posttest if subjects who have high scores on the pretest are selected and there is less than perfect pretest-posttest reliability.

The methodological implication of the above discussion should be clear. Rarely, if ever, do tests have perfect reliability; therefore, we can expect chance fluctuations to have at least some influence on each subject's score. If we select subjects with high pretest scores, we should expect their posttest scores to be lower, even if there is no treatment effect. Therefore, if we get a change from pretest to posttest we do not know whether to attribute it to the treatment or to the unreliability of our measuring instruments. The same situation holds if we select subjects who have low pretest scores, except that the posttest scores should increase. That is, if the pretest scores are used to select subjects who, by chance, had low scores, there is no guarantee that they will obtain low scores on the second test as well.

A change should be expected from pretest to posttest, even if there is no treatment effect, as long as the subjects selected have extreme pretest scores and the two tests lack perfect reliability. This change is called *regression*. The change from the pretest to the posttest is a tendency for the extreme scores to change in the direction of the mean score. To regress, in this case, means to approach or revert to the mean performance. The amount of regression will be related to the reliability of the two tests; it should increase as the correlation (reliability) of the two tests decreases.

The implication for the single-group, pretest-posttest design is straightforward. We rarely, if ever, have a perfect correlation between two tests, even if the same test is given twice. Thus if we select subjects who have extreme pretest scores, we must expect to get regression effects. One solution is to select only those subjects who have average scores on the pretest. In this case, we believe that we should not get regression effects if we start with average scores. Although this is true, we may not be able to select those people who have average scores on the pretest since, for the purpose of determining regression effects, it is best to define average in terms of the *population* mean. If our sample mean turns out to be an accurate estimate of the population mean, the procedure should eliminate any regression *toward* the mean. A better solution is to use a control group that is given both the pre- and posttest but not the independent variable. The use of a control group allows us to study only those subjects who have extreme scores on the pretest (for example, high anxiety or low reading scores). In many cases we want to study subjects with extreme scores. It is necessary, of course, to make sure that the experimental and control groups are equivalent before introducing the treatment to the experimental group.

The importance of understanding regression and many of the other factors (such as demand characteristics) extends beyond questions of experimental design. We need to recognize that these factors may help us account for a number of behaviors. Clearly, there is good reason to believe that we pick up cues that help us to decide how others expect us to behave, that hormonal and other maturational factors influence the way we respond, and that the behaviors we obtain are related, at least in part, to the subjects we observe. Regression effects, however, may have subtle effects that are frequently not appreciated. For example, if an athlete has an outstanding year in 1981, what do you predict for that athlete in 1982? You should expect some regression toward the mean, provided there is some chance component to performance; that is, the outstanding year in 1981 was probably due to considerable skill plus some good luck. The skill will probably remain for 1982, provided the athlete is not "over the hill," but we cannot expect the good luck to remain. We should expect lower performance. Since most people do not appreciate the influence of regression effects, you can use your knowledge to your own advantage. For example, the optimal time to propose a wager is after your prospective opponent has completed an outstanding match, round, or whatever it is you are playing, and you were terrible. Obviously, you have to adjust the wager for the differences in your respective abilities. Given the adjustment and regression toward the mean, you should win more times than you lose.

Evaluation of Nonexperimental Designs

Nonexperimental designs are inadequate because it is difficult to determine whether performance is influenced by the treatment or other confounding factors. The single group–observed once design is confounded by history, maturation, selection, and possibly by demand characteristics. The single-group, pretest-posttest design is confounded by history, maturation, measurement, regression, and possibly by sensitization. The static-groups design is confounded by the need for selection (see Campbell & Stanley, 1963). In short, these designs are simply not very good. Fortunately, we can usually avoid them because experimental designs are widely applicable. Sometimes, however, experimental designs are not suitable. If experimental designs are not appropriate, the student is encouraged to consider using a quasi-experimental approach before opting for a nonexperimental procedure. Nonexperimental designs should be used only as a last resort because their scientific usefulness is, at best, limited.

QUASI-EXPERIMENTAL DESIGNS

The basic logic behind the use of quasi-experimental designs is very simple. Because we cannot always form equivalent groups before introducing the treatment, we need procedures that allow us to eliminate or minimize the influence of confounding factors. If we can rule out confounding variables, then we can conclude, with reasonable assurance, that the treatment is responsible for a significant difference in performance. We are usually not able to reach conclusions about treatment effects with nonexperimental designs because there are usually a number of confounding factors. Quasi-experiments are an improvement over nonexperiments because we can rule out most, if not all, confounding effects.

Consider how we evaluate social programs, legislative actions, and educational practices. In most cases there is little or no formal evaluation. Rather, we typically try a particular procedure and stay with it until someone gets tired of it and is willing to seek change. Examples are sex education programs in the schools, the legal age for purchasing alcoholic beverages, punishments for the possession of marijuana, and rehabilitation programs for juvenile delinquents. Can we use systematic procedures to avoid bias when attempting to evaluate the effectiveness of various programs, or are we forced to simply try various approaches without being concerned about evaluation?

A strong case can be made for using experimental procedures. If there is a need for government intervention *and* there are a number of ways to intervene, it should be possible to use systematic procedures to eliminate bias from the evaluation process. For example, if your interest is in the comparison of a new program for juvenile delinquents with the current program, random assignment could be used to determine which program each delinquent receives. The expectation, of course, is that the new program is as good as or better than the old program. If you can establish that it is better by using evaluation procedures that eliminate systematic bias, then there is good reason to advocate a change to the new system. If the two systems are equally effective, there is little reason to switch systems unless other considerations (such as costs) distinguish the programs.

One argument against the use of systematic procedures is that ethical considerations preclude the random assignment of participants to programs. This is a valid argument in cases in which it is known that one program is better than another. Of course, if it is already well known that one is better than the other, there is no need for evaluation in the first place. We should expect the use of experimental procedures to increase as more people come to realize the importance of developing systematic procedures to avoid bias when evaluating different courses of action. Yet, it is unlikely that experimental procedures will quickly replace nonexperimental and quasi-experimental procedures simply because many people do not believe in systematic evaluation.

Consider sex education in the schools. It is a hot issue for parents, teachers, school board members, and administrators. Many believe that the schools have no business including this topic in the curriculum. They argue that it is better handled in the home. The difficulty, as you undoubtedly realize, is that leaving it up to the parents can result in its being left undone. As a result many teenagers may have little real understanding of sex. The basic question is whether schools should play any role in sex education. We could do an experiment to evaluate sex education programs in the schools, but it is unlikely that we would be able to obtain the necessary cooperation. The ideal way to evaluate the programs would be to use random assignment to determine which students receive the sex education program and which do not. Imagine the response, however, at a PTA meeting convened to discuss sex education if you advocated random assignment to determine which students would receive the sex education program.

It is highly unlikely that society will soon approve of systematic procedures for the evaluation of sex education programs, legal drinking age, capital punishment, and so on, but this does not mean that we have to rely solely on non-experimental evidence. Instead, we can use quasi-experimental procedures. Quasi-experimental procedures are ways of avoiding some of the interpretational problems inherent in using nonexperimental procedures. In this sense, quasi-experimental procedures lie between nonexperimental and experimental procedures, typically closer to the experimental. We will consider only two quasi-experimental approaches, but there are many others (see Campbell & Stanley, 1963).

Time-Series Design

The time-series design is similar to the single-group, pretest-posttest non-experiment design in that performance is assessed before and after the treatment is introduced. The difference between the two designs is that performance is assessed *several* times before and after treatment with the time-series design. What is gained by making periodic measurements of performance before and after treatment?

Let us assume that a school system in a large metropolitan area initiated a sex education program to begin in early January of 1981. Our concern will be the effect of this program on teenage pregnancy. Imagine that we examine the incidence of teenage pregnancy in 1981 and 1982 and detect a drop in the rate. Can we attribute the decrease in pregnancy to the sex education program? The results are presented in Figure 6-1. You may conclude, at least initially, that the evidence supports the view that sex education programs are effective, but this may not be the case. There are a number of possible explanations for the drop indicated in Figure 6-1, such as chance fluctuation, continuation of a previous trend, regression, and history (for example, economic conditions). If we know the incidence of teenage pregnancy for several years before and after the start of the sex education program, we are better equipped to evaluate its effectiveness. Four hypothetical patterns of results of a time-series analysis are presented in Figure 6-2.

Figure 6-2A suggests that the sex education program did not have any

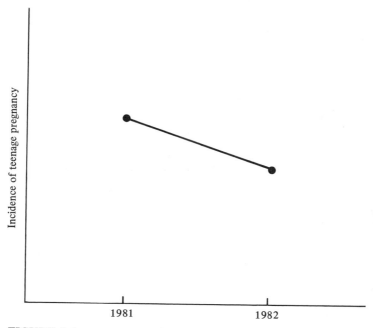

FIGURE 6-1

Incidence of teenage pregnancy for 1981 and 1982 (fictitious data)

effect on teenage pregnancy. The decrease from 1981 to 1982 appears to be simply a continuation of a trend that started a few years earlier. The results presented in Figure 6-2B also fail to support the importance of the sex education program. In this case 1981 appears to have been an unusual year for teenage pregnancy. Perhaps a number of "chance occurrences" (blackouts, increased alcohol consumption, balmy evenings) during 1981 resulted in more teenage pregnancies. The reduction from 1981 to 1982 may be simply a regression effect. That is, if we have an unusual year we should expect a change in the direction of average performance (regression toward the mean) in the following year. One problem in evaluating social change is that change is likely to be initiated during unusual times (Crano & Brewer, 1973). For example, a period of high teenage pregnancy may convince school boards that sex education in the schools is necessary. If action is taken during an unusual year, the regression to the average rate the following year may be misinterpreted as being due to the sex education program.

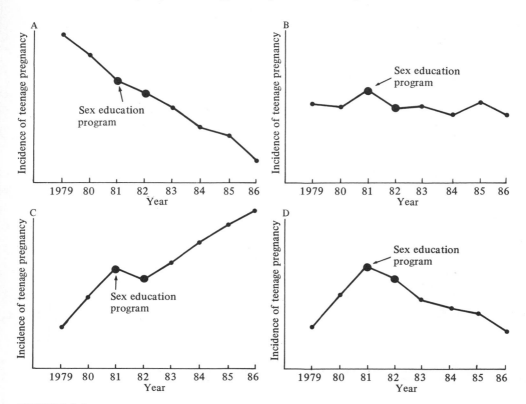

FIGURE 6-2

Four possible outcomes (hypothetical) of a time-series analysis

The results presented in Figures 6-2C and D are consistent with the view that the sex education program had an effect on the incidence of teenage pregnancy. Figure 6-2C suggests a temporary effect whereas 6-2D suggests a strong, long-lasting effect. There are other possible interpretations for the results presented in the last two figures. The important point is that these results are consistent with (they do not contradict) the view that the sex education program has an effect.

Considering the incidence of pregnancy over a number of years is clearly better than considering only the results for 1981 and 1982. However, the time-series design does have some limitations. One difficulty is that since the investigator typically does not control the time at which the treatment is introduced, the treatment may be introduced at an unusual time. If a change is introduced at an unusual time (for example, in response to publicity about teenage pregnancy), a number of changes may be implemented at the same time to alleviate an undesirable situation. For example, publicity about teenage pregnancy may have led teenagers to seek information about contraceptive devices. Or perhaps the publicity convinced a number of parents that they should take responsibility for the sex education of their children. If all these events occur at about the same time that a new sex education program is initiated, it is difficult to determine the actual cause of the lower pregnancy rate. If the investigator can decide when the treatment will be introduced, she can reduce the probability that another important event will occur (be introduced) at the same time. Thus, there should be fewer rival hypotheses to consider if the investigator can control when the treatment is introduced.

The time-series design is useful for many situations. As the previous example indicates, it can be used to assess treatment effects in real situations. In this case it may be possible to generate rival hypotheses (other than the treatment) to account for the obtained result. Yet it is also possible to use the time-series design in situations where other events are not allowed to occur — for example, in laboratory experiments. In the laboratory the time-series design is very similar to some of the within-subject experimental designs considered in Chapter 5. For example, investigators who study operant conditioning frequently determine the response rate of subjects for a long period of time, introduce the treatment, and then determine the response rate for another long interval. If the response changes after the treatment, they are likely to conclude that the treatment was responsible. This conclusion is usually reasonable because investigators try to minimize the possibility that any other event was introduced along with the treatment. The same logic applies for experiments conducted in more real-life situations except that there is a greater likelihood that some other event besides the treatment was responsible for the results.

Nonequivalent, Control-Group Design

There are many instances in which you do not have control over who gets a particular treatment and who does not because you cannot randomly assign participants to conditions. For example, instructors typically have little or no control over which students enroll in their classes. Thus, an instructor interested in comparing the effectiveness of two teaching methods has no clear way of obtaining equivalent groups prior to introducing the independent variable. However, this should not be a critical deterrent because it is possible to use a nonequivalent, control-group design.

Let us assume that a foreign language instructor is interested in evaluating the effect of a new program for teaching the second-year German course. She teaches the same course twice, once at 9:00 A.M. and once at 2:00 P.M. The classes are not likely to be equivalent because students can select their classes. Therefore the students who enroll in the 9:00 class may already know more German or may be brighter than students who enroll in the 2:00 class. Although she cannot randomly assign the students to the two classes, the instructor can control the teaching approach that she uses for each class. She decides to use the new technique for the 2:00 class and the old technique for the 9:00 class. She administers the same German test to both classes on the first day of class and another test to both classes on the last day of class. She can then compare the amount of change from pretest to posttest for each group to evaluate the new instructional method relative to the old method. She has used a nonequivalent, control-group design.

The methodological issue is whether this design is adequate. If the 2:00 class has a significantly greater increase from pretest to posttest than the 9:00 class, can we conclude that the new instructional technique is better than the old technique? The answer depends on several considerations. It is necessary to assume that the experiment was conducted properly; that is, the instructor should be equally enthusiastic for the two classes, assign the same amount of homework, proceed at the same pace, and so on. If the experiment was performed properly, the next task is to consider rival hypotheses. Are there other explanations besides the treatment manipulation for the obtained results?

The evaluation of a design is a relative matter. We need to compare the strengths and weaknesses of this approach with those of other approaches. The design is clearly better than the single-group, pretest-posttest design because we can compare the amount of change for the treatment group with the amount for the control group. Events other than the treatment that occur between the pretest and posttest should influence the two groups equally, and we do not have to be particularly concerned with ability differences between the two groups because we are interested in how the two groups change over a period of time. We should be able to evaluate the relative changes even though the groups are of unequal ability. Although history and maturation are confounding variables for the single-group, pretest-posttest design, and the need for selection can confound the static-groups design, these factors do not *usually* pose interpretational problems for the nonequivalent, control-group design. Yet, that design is not without weaknesses.

The nonequivalent, control-group design does not have general weaknesses, but interpretational problems may arise under some circumstances. For example, if there are large differences between the treatment and control groups before the treatment is introduced, there may be *differential regression* in the two conditions. To understand this point it is necessary to remember that the amount of regression is related to the selection of subjects. If subjects in the treatment group have extreme scores (very low scores) on the pretest and the subjects in the control group do not, there may be more regression for the treatment group than for the control group. Similarly, if an experiment is conducted with young children and there are large differences between the treatment group and control group on the pretest, differences in the amount of change from pretest to posttest could be the result of maturational instead of treatment effects. Exceptionally bright children may develop faster than average children, so both groups should have similar pretest performance levels.

We have said that the pretest may sensitize the subjects in the treatment condition to the treatment; a treatment effect may be obtained only if a pretest is given. Sensitization or demand characteristics pose greater interpretational problems in some areas than others. There is usually not much of a problem in research on teaching methods, for example, because the tests used can be identical or very similar to the tests normally given. Investigators interested in opinion or attitude change, however, need to be more concerned about this interpretational problem, because a pretest about opinions or attitudes may make the subject very sensitive to the treatment manipulation.

COMPARISON OF THE DESIGNS

Experimental, quasi-experimental, and nonexperimental designs have various strengths and weaknesses in relation to each other. Before considering the strengths and weaknesses of the three classes of designs, we need to discuss whether the classifications themselves are reliable.

Classification of Designs

The ease of classifying designs depends, at least in part, on whether between-subject or within-subject comparisons are made. When we make between-subject comparisons we can distinguish experimental designs from others on the basis of how groups are formed. If subjects are randomly assigned to conditions before the treatment is introduced and the groups are treated identically except for the treatment, we have an experimental design. Matched-groups designs in which subjects are randomly assigned to conditions after matching are one type of experimental design. Between-subject comparisons that do not involve random assignment of subjects to groups at some point are either quasi-experimental, nonexperimental, or subject-variable designs. The distinction between quasi-experimental and nonexperimental designs can be made on the basis of the number of confounding factors that are present. If there are several possible confounding factors (history, maturation, selection), the design is nonexperimental. In general it is usually fairly easy to classify between-subject comparisons according to the type of design used. Within-subject comparisons are more difficult.

It is frequently difficult to classify designs involving within-subject comparisons because there is no clear procedural difference between the classes of designs; we do not use random assignment procedures to assign subjects to the conditions when we make within-subject comparisons. One solution is to distinguish experimental, quasi-experimental, and nonexperimental designs on the basis of the number of confounding factors present. If it is unlikely that there are any confounding factors, the experimental label is appropriate. If there are several confounding factors, the nonexperimental label is appropriate. If there is a possibility that there is one or more confounding factors, the quasi-experimental label is appropriate. In short, the classification of a design can be determined by the amount of control the investigator has over nonmanipulated variables. Thus, within-subject comparisons made in well-controlled laboratory situations can usually be classified as experimental, whereas within-subject comparisons made in real-life situations are more likely to be classified as quasi-experimental or nonexperimental. Although there is no simple rule for putting within-subject designs into categories, it does not matter greatly how a design is classified as long as you know what, if any, confounding factors are present. As we have stressed repeatedly, the important consideration is whether you can use systematic procedures that will eliminate or at least minimize bias.

Internal and External Validity

Validity can refer to experiments as well as to measurement. Internal validity refers to whether the effect was due to the treatment administered in a specific experiment. External validity refers to whether a treatment effect can be generalized. A treatment effect that cannot be generalized beyond the specific experimental conditions lacks external validity. A treatment effect that can be obtained in the real world (in different settings, with different populations of subjects, and so forth) has external validity (see Campbell, 1957). Internal validity is a precondition for external validity. A treatment that has external validity also has internal validity. It does not necessarily follow, however, that a treatment that has an effect in the laboratory (has internal validity) will also have an effect in real-world situations. We can usually establish internal validity by use of appropriate designs and by controlling for potential confounding variables, but establishing external validity is a matter of degree. External validity refers to the generality of a finding; it will not be established merely because a treatment is administered in a realistic setting. We cannot establish external validity completely because there are so many different situations in which a treatment can be evaluated.

The strengths and weaknesses of the different types of designs can be discussed in terms of internal and external validity. Because nonexperimental designs lack internal validity, they usually have little or no usefulness. Nonexperimental designs rarely enable one to determine the effectiveness of a treatment, so there is no sound basis for discussing the generality of the treatment effect. In short, nonexperimental designs are not very useful for establishing internal or external validity.

Experimental designs provide the best way of establishing internal validity, but in a number of instances they are not as useful as quasi-experimental designs for establishing external validity in real-life situations. Quasi-experimental designs can often be used to assess treatment effects when it is not practical or feasible to use experimental designs. They may be useful when research is performed in real-life situations such as classrooms, medical clinics, and so forth. One should not conclude, however, that it is always impossible to use experimental designs in real-life situations. This is clearly not the case. If either a quasi-experimental or experimental approach can be used, the investigator should, all else being equal, adopt the experimental approach. Quasi-experimental approaches are valuable when it is not possible to use an experimental approach, but they should not be selected without first considering whether an experimental design can be used. The use of experimental designs in real-life situations should increase as more people discover that these designs can be very useful for investigating applied problems.

SUMMARY

Three nonexperimental designs were considered to give the reader an understanding of what factors influence design adequacy. The factors that have an influence are history, maturation, selection, measurement, demand characteristics, sensitization, and regression. History and maturation refer to events (other than the treatment) that many account for differences in performance. The history factor includes only those events that are specific to the situation being investigated. Maturation refers to time-related processes within the individual that may influence performance. Selection refers to the fact that some designs do not allow the investigator to form equivalent groups before introducing the independent variable. Measurement and sensitization refer to the fact that the assessment process may change the subject's behavior. Demand characteristics are those cues available to a subject that may enable him to determine the purpose of the experiment. Regression is a change from pretest to posttest that results if the pretest-posttest measures are not perfectly reliable and subjects with extreme pretest scores are selected. Nonexperimental designs are inadequate because it is difficult to determine whether performance is influenced by the treatment or by one or more of the above confounding factors.

The basic logic behind the use of quasi-experimental designs is very simple. Because it is not always possible to form equivalent groups before introducing the treatment, we need procedures that allow us to eliminate or minimize the influence of confounding factors; quasi-experimental designs provide such procedures. The influence of confounding factors can be minimized by assessing performance several times before and after the experimental treatment (time-series design) or by using a nonequivalent, control-group design. The nonequivalent, control-group design involves a comparison of groups that are *not* equivalent before introducing the treatment. Each group is given a pretest and a posttest, so it is possible to evaluate whether the pretest-posttest change for the treatment group is different from that for the control group.

An experiment has internal validity if a treatment has an effect. It has external validity if a treatment effect can be generalized. Internal and external validity are related since internal validity is a precondition for external validity. Nonexperimental designs are not useful for establishing internal or external validity. Experimental designs provide the best way of establishing internal validity, but they are frequently not as useful as quasi-experimental designs for establishing external validity because investigators are *usually* not free to use random assignment procedures in real-life situations. Quasi-experimental designs are useful because they can frequently be used to assess treatment effects when it is not feasible to use experimental designs.

QUESTIONS

(Answers for the multiple choice questions are given in Appendix D.)

1. Give examples, other than the ones mentioned in the text, of the following nonexperimental designs. To what extent, if any, are these designs "used" in your everyday decision making? What are the weaknesses of each?
   a. single group–observed once
   b. single-group, pretest-posttest
   c. static-groups
2. Distinguish between the history and maturation factor.
3. In what way, if any, does a static-groups design differ from a subject-variable experiment in which subjects are assigned to conditions on the basis of a personal characteristic (such as shyness)?
4. How could you determine whether there is a sensitization effect?
5. Why is it necessary to understand regression effects? What influences the magnitude of regression?
6. What is the logic behind quasi-experimental designs?
7. Give examples, other than the ones mentioned in the text, of a time-series design and a nonequivalent, control-group design. Why are these designs useful?
8. Distinguish between internal and external validity.
9. Why should the use of experimental designs in real-life situations be encouraged?

10. Evaluating the effect of therapy by interviewing patients following therapy is an example of a (1) single group–observed once design (2) single-group, pretest-posttest design (3) static-groups design (4) time-series design

11. You are interested in evaluating a treatment for claustrophobia. You administer your test for claustrophobia, give the treatment, and then give the test again. You have used a _____ design. (1) time-series (2) equivalent control-group (3) single-group, pretest-posttest (4) single group–observed once

12. The interpretational problems confronted when studying a subject variable are most similar to the problems confronted when using a (1) single-group, pretest-posttest design (2) time-series design (3) nonequivalent, control-group design (4) static-groups design

13. The major problem with nonexperimental designs is that (1) the treatment cannot be responsible for any obtained differences (2) they lack external validity (3) they are confounded (4) they are too costly to use

14. When the results of a treatment manipulation depend on whether subjects are given a pretest, we say there is a _____ factor present. (1) sensitization (2) regression (3) history (4) selection

15. _____ refer(s) to those cues available to a subject in an experiment that may enable him or her to determine the "purpose" of the experiment. (1) Measurement (2) Sensitization (3) Demand characteristics (4) Regression

16. Reliability is determined by the (1) relative variances of the true score and error score components (2) true score component (3) error score component (4) size of the measurement factor

17. Imagine that a single-group, pretest-posttest design is used and there is no treatment effect. We should expect to obtain a large regression effect if (1) the pretest and posttest scores are correlated perfectly (2) the pretest and posttest scores have a low or 0 correlation (3) subjects are selected who have extreme scores on the pretest and the correlation between the pre- and posttest scores is perfect (4) subjects are selected who have extreme scores on the pretest and the correlation between the pre- and posttest scores is 0 (5) subjects are selected who have average scores on the pretest and the correlation between the pre- and posttest scores is 0

18. The advantage of a time-series over a single-group, pretest-posttest design is that the time-series design allows us to (1) rule out most, if not all, confounding effects (2) form equivalent groups prior to the introduction of the independent variable (3) eliminate chance fluctuations (4) increase the regression effect

Collecting data

In this chapter we consider some of the problems that may be encountered when collecting data. Clearly, investigators face different problems depending on their areas of interest. The survey researcher has very different preparation and data-collection problems from the neuropsychologist recording the activity of cells in the hypothalamus of the rat. However, all investigators need to make preparations, obtain subjects, and, at least in most instances, adopt testing procedures to obtain data. Our goal is to consider general aspects of data collection so that you will be better equipped to evaluate the research of others, appreciate some of the problems of collecting data, and, if you elect to do your own research project, avoid some of the pitfalls of data collection.

PREPARATIONS

Relevant Knowledge

Previous Research. How much time should you spend reading about the research that has already been done in a particular problem area before you prepare to collect data for a project? The answer depends largely on what you hope to gain from doing a research project. If your interest is in gaining some experience about how research is conducted so that you can better appreciate and evaluate research in the social sciences, the answer is "very little," particularly if you do not have the time or interest to do the reading. You can learn a great deal about research by doing your own project even if you are unaware of what others have already accomplished. If, however, your goal is to increase understanding (for example, establish a relationship between variables, test a theory that has never been tested), you are well advised to examine the previous literature on the topic of interest.

For most experienced researchers, examining the literature is an ongoing process. Reading the research reports of others can help us to get ideas for our own research as well as help us to avoid mistakes in logic, design, data collection, and analysis. If we know what has already been done, we are better able to go beyond this and thus make a contribution. Finally, it may be that we do not even have to bother collecting data because data are already available. Another researcher may have collected the information you need but not examined it in the way you want to examine it. In such a case, you may be able to obtain the data and perform the analyses you are interested in.

Data Files. There is little point in collecting data if they are already available, and a tremendous amount of data are available. Millions of college students have taken examinations as a precondition for admission to a college or university; elementary and secondary schools have also given millions (probably billions) of tests. The local, state, and, especially, the federal governments have amassed an enormous amount of data on numerous topics such as crime rates, juvenile delinquency, alcoholism, integration, incomes, birth rates, life expectancy, mental illness, suicide rates, and so forth. In some cases the information is confidential, so you cannot gain access to it, but in many other cases it is not. When data collection is extremely expensive and time-consuming (such as recording the verbal interactions of parents with their very young children in an effort to better understand language development), the data are frequently made available to others. One who reads the research of others is likely to be aware of the data files that exist.

Methods. Clearly, an understanding of methods used in a particular research area is crucial before data collection is initiated. For example, someone interested in assessing public opinion should know the advantages and disadvantages of the various methods (mail survey, personal interviews, telephone interviews) of collecting the data. Personal interviews typically allow you to obtain precise estimates of population values in that you are much more likely to obtain information from each person you select for your sample. Many people do not reply to mail questionnaires, and therefore you have little way of knowing whether the replies you get are representative. The way in which questions are asked, whether in a personal interview or a mail questionnaire, can have strong effects on the replies. And, of course, random sampling procedures should be used to avoid bias in the selection of participants. It would certainly be easier to obtain the opinions of people in an intact group (students in a class, workers in a particular company) or to ask the readers of a particular journal or magazine (such as *Psychology Today*) to reply to a questionnaire printed in an issue, but there would be little justification for generalizing the result obtained. Reading the research of others should provide you with a methodological sophistication that you would not otherwise have.

Facilities, Special Skills, and Equipment

Obviously, what you need to know depends on what you plan to do. If you plan to do brain research with lower animals, you will undoubtedly need to know much about the physiology and anatomy of subjects and numerous techniques for studying brain functioning. You will probably use sophisticated equipment, have some understanding of biochemistry, and perhaps be knowledgeable about computers and microprocessors. If, on the other hand, you are interested in assessing public opinion through the use of personal interviews, you need to understand the strengths and weaknesses of the interview so that you can avoid introducing bias. If you are going to develop a questionnaire, you need to know how the results can be influenced by the wording of the questions.

Computers have become increasingly important in psychological research in recent years simply because they are useful for so many purposes. Many experiments can be automated so that the participant interacts with a computer and not a human experimenter. This is a very useful way of avoiding possible biases as well as increasing the efficiency of data collection. Computers make it possible to do many experiments that would be impossible to do without them; other experiments are better done with computers. For example, computers are particularly useful when it is important to base the presentation of material on the past responses of the participants. Computers can be programmed to evaluate the past responses very quickly using, in many cases, complex analyses that would be impossible without the computer.

Computers are also used in developing ideas for experiments; sometimes a researcher will develop ideas about behavior by noting and testing similarities between computers and humans. For example, a scientist interested in understanding how humans make sense of auditory input might try to build a machine that interprets what it hears. Is it possible to develop a machine that can type out whatever you say? Or, is it possible to develop a machine that will sort mail by analyzing the handwritten addresses on letters? The theorist who considers the problems involved in building a machine (programming a computer) to perform human functions is forced to consider a number of difficult problems. By wrestling with these problems he may develop ideas about human functioning. In brief, computers are frequently used in all aspects of research from formulating ideas to preparing the final manuscript with the aid of word processors. Many kinds of data analysis would be virtually impossible without the use of a computer.

However, a sophisticated laboratory is not a prerequisite for many research problems. Although a well-equipped laboratory makes it easier to do research and some problems can only be studied if special equipment is available, many problems can be studied without special skills and equipment. Consider the looking behavior of infants. You can study the looking behavior of infants by using a large piece of cardboard. You place a peephole in the cardboard so that you can see the infant's eyes without the infant seeing you. You can study the infant's preferences for different stimuli by presenting pairs of stimuli on the infant's side of the cardboard, one to the right of the peephole and one to the left. You note which way the infant looks by observing through the peephole. This is a crude but effective way of studying the preferences of infants.

Now consider eye movements while reading. If you wish to study the role of eye movements in reading (how much information we process in a single eye fixation, factors that determine where we fixate while reading, whether we can process information during a saccade or only when the eye is fixated, the relationship between reading difficulty and the number of fixations), it is very useful to have complex equipment that allows you to note individual eye fixations, record the duration of each fixation, and change the reading text as a function of where the reader is looking. To accomplish this, one needs computer control. Eye movements are simply too fast (3 to 5 per second, typically) to observe without sophisticated equipment. We rarely know exactly where we are fixating while reading, much less where anyone else is fixating. To know and to control the reading material in interesting ways, we need special equipment and skills (Rayner, 1978). Since equipment of this nature is extremely expensive, money is a crucial consideration for some kinds of research. Much of the money for research is provided by educational institutions (such as colleges and universities) and the federal government (National Science Foundation, National Institutes of Health).

The facilities you need for collecting data depend on the problem area. If you are interested in studying eye movements while reading, you will ask participants to come to your laboratory because it would be difficult for you to go to them. If, on the other hand, you are doing survey research, you may collect your data in the homes of the participants. There are few limits on where and how data can be collected. Data can be collected in a classroom, home, shopping mall, hospital, bar, laboratory, and elsewhere. The only limits on data collection are ethical, practical, and methodological. The methodological concern is that you avoid introducing bias.

SUBJECTS

Human Participants

College Students. Undoubtedly more psychological research has been conducted using college students as participants than any other type of subject. The reason is availability and costs. Most of the psychological research is conducted at colleges and universities, and often money is not available to pay participants for their time. The most common solution is to ask students in introductory psychology courses to be participants. When this is done the ethical problems involved in recruiting participants from classes are considerable. Psychology departments and instructors typically use a variety of procedures to ensure that the rights of participants are not violated. From the experimenter's point of view, the crucial considerations are obtaining the participant's informed consent whenever possible and treating the participant with respect and dignity. Experimenters should resolve any ethical issues before testing subjects. (The ethical principles for conducting research are presented in Chapter 1.)

Typically, additional procedures are used to protect the rights of participants. Participants are informed of their rights and asked to sign a consent form before proceeding. For institutions receiving research support from the federal government, it is common practice for a committee to screen research proposals to determine whether all ethical matters have been resolved before experimenters are allowed to gain access to the participants; that is, there is usually a process that must be followed (you need someone's approval) before you can recruit participants for your research. These people (course instructors, review committees, and others) are frequently called gatekeepers.

Infants, Preschoolers, and School Children. If you are interested in human development, you are likely to prefer infants, preschoolers, or school children as participants. How do you recruit young children or infants for your research? The gatekeepers in most cases are the parents. If you are interested in testing very young infants, you might read the birth notices in the local papers. Then you can write to the parents to explain your proposition in a way that you hope they will find attractive. If you have an interesting project or can make it appear interesting, or if you can provide a monetary reward, you should be able to get good cooperation. In general, parents tend to be interested in learning more about their infants and therefore many are very cooperative even when you can offer little more than your appreciation. Gatekeepers typically want assurance that researchers know what they are doing before giving consent, so success in most instances will depend on your own qualifications (such as degrees) or your affiliation with qualified professionals (developmental psychologists, pediatricians).

Another way to gain access is through day-care centers, laboratory preschools, and elementary, junior high, and high schools. If you have the proper qualifications or affiliations, you may be able to win the cooperation of the administrators at these various centers or schools in order to test participants using their facilities, provided that the parents approve. The point is that research with human participants typically involves a considerable amount of time and effort for recruiting participants. Success in obtaining participants depends on a number of factors, including the merit of your project, your ability to convince others of the merit, past relationships between school administrators and researchers, and so forth.

Other Populations. There are actually few limits on the availability of participants if you have the energy to seek them out. If you want to do research with the elderly, you can attempt to find participants through the administrators of retirement homes or local and state institutions, or perhaps by advertising in newspapers. If you want to study special populations (such as autistic children, alcoholics, child abusers, depressed people, juvenile delinquents), you will undoubtedly need to make special arrangements with the gatekeepers who have direct contact with the potential participants. Gaining the informed consent of participants can be a very time-consuming, difficult process, particularly when you have little to offer in return besides your appreciation. Clearly, people who have direct contact with special participants (clinical psychologists, for example) have a much better chance of obtaining informed consent than "outsiders" who do not have the enthusiastic support of the gatekeeper.

It helps to have money to pay your participants. If you do, there are many ways to obtain participants. You can place ads in newspapers, make arrangements with different organizations, or perhaps even set up a booth at a shopping mall. You will not obtain a random sample with these procedures, but you can use random assignment to ensure that only chance determines the assignment of participants to conditions. Later, when we consider testing procedures, we will say more about sampling. Here we are only concerned with recruiting participants and treating them according to the research plan (random assignment, within-subjects comparison, simple reactive measures); we are not concerned with estimating population values.

Some researchers may be fortunate enough to have several subject populations available and, therefore, may decide to compare them. If the only interest is in comparing two subject populations on some dependent variable, the only possible conclusion will be that one population does better at the task than the other. It is not reasonable to attribute the difference to any specific variable because there is no way of knowing all the variables on which the two populations differ. Of course, there are many occasions when it is important to know which population will do better at a particular task. The investigator may want to compare the populations for practical reasons or to determine whether there is a phenomenon to investigate further. If he obtains differences between populations, then he can design additional studies in an attempt to discover the reasons for the differences (such as sex differences in accident rates, sex differences in depression, age differences in memory ability).

Lower Animals

Researchers use lower animals as research subjects for a variety of reasons. Many researchers are interested in why animals do the things they do without having any special interest in generalizing the results to human behavior. Our furry and feathered friends are certainly worthy of study in their own right. Others select lower animals for subjects for practical or ethical reasons because the manipulations they want to make would be impossible or unethical with humans. Genetic studies and physiological studies, for example, typically must be done, or are better done, with lower animals as subjects.

From the researcher's point of view, there are a number of advantages to working with lower animals. If money is available, a number of lower animals (rats, pigeons, cats, monkeys, cockroaches) can be purchased from laboratories that breed animals for research purposes. Availability of subjects is not a problem, provided you have money. The disadvantage to using lower animals is that they have to be cared for twenty-four hours a day, seven days a week, in accordance with the ethical codes for animal care discussed in Chapter 1. If you do not have money to purchase animals, you may be able to get them in other ways. If you are fleet of foot, you may be able to trap the animals of your choice in the wild; more likely, you may be able to borrow them from researchers or others with a surplus. As a student in a comparative psychology course, I was able to obtain South American cockroaches (they are huge!) from a physiology professor, bees from a beekeeper, and chickens from a chicken breeder (a company that raised chickens for research). None of the three studies made a contribution to knowledge. Either chickens are among the dumbest of animals or I asked the wrong question. For the other two studies, I know I asked the wrong question. But it was an interesting and worthwhile experience because it forced me to consider numerous aspects of psychological research.

TESTING PROCEDURES

Avoiding Bias When Collecting Data

Demand Characteristics. Assume that you are engaged in doing research on a problem in which you have great personal interest. In addition, you may have a considerable amount of bias. It would probably be gratifying to you to have any prediction you might make supported by experimental results. But you should want the results to reflect the true state of affairs and not your bias; therefore, it is important to minimize the likelihood that your biases will affect the results. The work of Orne (1959, 1962) and Rosenthal (1963, 1966) has demonstrated that the experimenter's expectations or biases can influence the results of psychological experiments. Orne points out that a human subject will, generally, attempt to determine the purpose of the experiment and then do what is necessary to make it succeed.

As we saw in the last chapter, each experiment has *demand characteristics* from the point of view of the subject. Subjects are sometimes able to determine what the experimenter wants and respond accordingly. Moreover, the effect of finding out what the experimenter wants may be influenced markedly by the treatment condition the subject is in, because experimenters rarely want the same performance from subjects in different treatment conditions. If the subject detects that he is in the "special" group, his interest and performance level may increase; if he detects that he is in the "control" group, his interest and performance may decrease. Such an experiment is confounded because there is no way of knowing whether the results are due to the independent variable or to the effect of demand characteristics.

It is also possible, of course, that the subjects will determine what the experimenter wants and then respond in just the opposite way. Yet most subjects tend to be cooperative. You can assess whether a subject is cooperative by asking him to hold a large chunk of ice. If you return forty minutes later and the subject is sitting in a puddle of water clutching a small chunk of ice, you have a cooperative subject (Hanley, 1969).

You should do whatever is necessary to eliminate or at least minimize the effect of demand characteristics. When you provide cues that enable the subjects to discern what results you want, you have a confounded experiment. Any significant mean differences could be attributed to the effect of the independent variable or to the demand characteristics. Perhaps the subjects were only trying to please you by doing what you wanted them to do.

The extent to which demand characteristics confound an experiment will depend on the nature of the problem. For example, in studying the experimental control of dreaming, one should take precautions to eliminate or minimize the effects of demand characteristics. Direct instruction or hypnosis can be used to attempt to influence dream content, but it is difficult to determine the success of such an attempt. Perhaps the subjects will react to the demand characteristics of the experiment and report the type of dream they think the investigator wants them to report, regardless of their actual dreams. Patients in psychoanalysis tend to report having the type of dreams that their analysts expect. Patients of Adlerians have Adlerian dreams, patients of Freudians have Freudian dreams, and so on. Is this because the analysts are controlling the dream content? Or is the effect due to demand characteristics?

At the opposite extreme, in a study in which all conditions are tested at the same time, the experimenter does not have any knowledge of what condition each subject is being tested in, and the subjects are not able to detect whether they are in an experimental or control condition, there is little reason to be concerned with the confounding effects of demand characteristics.

If you select a problem in which demand characteristics could be a problem you should design your experiment in such a way that the effects of these characteristics can be assessed. For example, if one group of subjects is more likely to detect the real purpose of the experiment than the other group, you may try to manipulate the cooperativeness of the subjects (by providing incentives or by adopting a gentle, considerate manner for only one group) as an additional independent variable. If you are able to manipulate cooperativeness and if the other independent variable produces the predicted effect for both cooperative and uncooperative subjects, you may reasonably conclude that the results are not due to demand characteristics.

Even if there is little reason to think that subjects can discern the purpose of the experiment or detect how you "want" them to perform, you should take precautions against demand characteristics; subjects may be very perceptive. Sometimes it is possible to test them without knowing the particular condition to which each is assigned. When subjects are tested individually, however, it is usually impossible for the experimenter not to know the condition of each. In such a case it may help to have them tested by another experimenter who is unaware of the purpose of the experiment. Care should be taken to ensure that he is unbiased. In some cases, it is feasible to "bias" experimenters in opposite directions and analyze for the effect of biasing.

In short, you should be aware that subjects may determine what you are trying to do and may perform accordingly. The danger of confounding the experiment in this way is present in both between-subject and within-subject designs but is usually a greater threat in within-subject designs. In fact, a consideration of demand characteristics may lead you to choose a between-subject design if testing each subject in all conditions would disclose the purpose of the experiment. Also, it may lead you to automate the experiment as much as possible. For example, the instructions could be tape recorded to minimize the possibility that the experimenter, while reading the instructions, would provide differential cues to subjects in the various conditions.

Selecting Subjects. Imagine that your task is to sample the opinions of twenty other college students. You do not have the time or interest in obtaining a real random sample by using the student directory and a table of random numbers, primarily because you realize that it would be difficult to find and then obtain the cooperation of the people selected. You decide, instead, to select the first person you see at half-hour intervals from 1:00 P.M. until 5:00 P.M. each day for as many days as it takes to obtain twenty participants. If the person you select refuses to cooperate, you wait a half hour before selecting another participant. Clearly, this procedure will not yield a random sample, but will it be "relatively unbiased"? It would appear to be more representative than if you simply asked twenty of your friends, but there is actually no way of knowing the factors that will influence where you happen to be when you select and how you will choose a participant if there is more than one person in the immediate vicinity. You might, for example, have a bias for selecting people who are well dressed and attractive. The point is simply that you should not deceive yourself into believing that, since *you* are an unbiased person, you need not bother with random selection or random assignment procedures. It is likely that you are not aware of many of your biases.

A confounding feature that is specific to between-subject designs is the failure to obtain equivalent groups. As you recall, each subject receives only one level of each independent variable for a between-subject design. It is important that there be a high probability of obtaining equivalent groups before the independent variable is introduced. Therefore, except for the limits of the design and procedure, it is necessary to assign subjects to conditions on a random basis. If a matched-groups design is used, subjects should be assigned randomly with the restriction that the groups be equated on the matching variable. As long as the independent variable is something other than a subject variable manipulation, there should be little difficulty in obtaining equivalent groups *most of the time* through the use of random assignment.

If your interest is in selecting a sample so that you can estimate values (parameters) for the population, you need to use random selection procedures. However, you can place some restrictions on the sample you select. This is frequently done when you want to know values for subgroups in the population (minority groups, very wealthy people, and so on) which are not likely to be sampled in sufficient numbers if random sampling is used. For example, if you want to assess the views of a particular minority group (such as blacks) as well as the general population, you may select a random sample of 300 with the restriction that 100 of the participants will be blacks. Random selection is used except for this restriction. Although you know that the minority group composition of your sample does not match that of the population, you are willing to make this sacrifice to get a good (large enough) sample of black citizens so that you can be relatively confident that your sample value will be precise (that is, close to the population value for black citizens). The added advantage is that you can compare the views of blacks and nonblacks on specific issues.

When we divide the population into groups or strata prior to sampling and then obtain a random sample from each group, we have a stratified random sample. When we do this it is likely that some groups will be over-represented in our sample, but we are willing to accept this in order to get precise estimates for each group. If the Internal Revenue Service is interested in the accuracy of income tax returns, they may use a stratified sampling procedure to obtain estimates of the population values. They may do this because they believe the cheating rate is likely to be higher for people with large incomes than for those with small incomes. Thus, they divide the population into groups or levels of income with a range of $10,000 in each category. People who make less than $10,000 are in one stratum; people who make between $10,000 and $19,999 are in the second stratum; and so on until we reach people who make over $200,000. We take a random sample of 100 from each category so that we can estimate the accuracy of income tax returns as a function of income level. This is more useful than a random sample procedure, from the Internal Revenue Service's point of view, because if the estimates vary for the different strata, appropriate action can be taken. Thus, they are more likely to audit taxpayers who make a lot of money if the results indicate that people of high income are more likely to file inaccurate returns. If you took a simple random sample (no division into categories) rather than a stratified random sample, you would probably have too few people in the $200,000 and over category to obtain a precise estimate for the population value for this category.

Inadvertent Destruction of Equivalent Groups. Even when equivalent groups have been obtained by the use of random assignment, the nature of the independent variable may destroy their equivalence. For example, assume that you are interested in how performance on a task is influenced by the difficulty of the preceding task. Your concern is with the concept of learned helplessness and, in particular, with whether helplessness "acquired" on one day will carry over to the next day. To see if your view is correct, you test whether a participant is more likely to perform at a higher level if the earlier laboratory experience was easy or if it was difficult. The subjects are randomly assigned to the two conditions. The experiment requires that each subject participate in two separate sessions on successive days. All subjects are given the same task on day 2. On day 1, one group of subjects is given a fairly easy task and the other group a more difficult task. After the subjects complete their tasks, you thank them and ask them to return the next day for another session. Unfortunately, all the subjects do not return the second day. Of the twenty subjects who had easy tasks, eighteen return for the second day. Of the twenty who had difficult tasks only twelve return.

You are a little disturbed by the fact that some of the subjects did not return for the second session, but you analyze the data for those who did. You find that the subjects who performed difficult tasks on day 1 have a higher mean performance on day 2 than those who performed easy tasks even though all subjects were given the same task for day 2. You conclude that, at least for this task, subjects tend to perform better if their previous laboratory experience was difficult than if it was easy. Is this conclusion justified?

It should be clear that the nature of the independent variable may have resulted in the destruction of equivalent groups. One could argue that the group differences are a result of nonequivalent groups. Is it plausible that the eight subjects with difficult tasks who did not return for day 2 were unlike the twelve who did return. More specifically, they may have responded to the difficult situation by becoming helpless whereas those who returned responded with increased effort. Or perhaps the eight who did not return were, on the average, duller than the twelve who did return. If you form equivalent groups and then introduce a treatment that "weeds out" the dull participants in one group but not in the other, your equivalent groups have been destroyed.

The destruction of equivalent groups can also be a serious methodological problem in making a survey. Assume that you select a stratified random sample in which you have a number of strata based on income level. You then send a mail questionnaire to the 100 people you have selected at each level. If everyone returned the mail questionnaire there would be nothing to worry about, but this will not happen. If the return rate is related to level, your stratified random sample has been destroyed. You cannot regain your random sampling by selecting participants to replace those lost in each category because there may be something special about the people who refused to return the questionnaire.

Failure to Control Nonmanipulated Variables. At the risk of laboring the obvious, let us point out again that investigators must control for the effects of nonmanipulated variables. The experimenter should make every effort to see that the groups differ only with respect to the intended manipulation. For example, if an investigator is studying a new drug's effects on humans, it is important to treat the subjects in all groups alike except for the drug. This means that control subjects should be given seemingly identical injections or pills. The person giving the treatments should not know who gets the real drug and who gets the placebo. If subjects were told what treatment they were to receive, there would be no way of determining whether the effects were due to the drug or to the fact that subjects knew they were receiving a special treatment.

There are a number of ways that an experiment can be confounded by failure to control nonmanipulated variables. For example, if the independent variable is the type of strategy subjects are asked to employ, the experimenter should take care not to sound more encouraging in one condition than another. He should also make sure that all subjects are given the same amount of time to perform the task that is used to assess the independent variable. In short, the investigator should examine the procedures carefully to make sure that only the intended manipulation is made. It is necessary to control for nonmanipulated variables regardless of whether a between-subject or within-subject design is used.

The principal problem of confounding with a within-subject design is failure to counterbalance for practice and time-related effects. As you remember, each subject receives every level of the independent variable in a within-subject design. Since it is not possible to present all the levels of the independent variable at the same time, it is necessary to control for the effects of practice and time by making sure that each treatment is presented at each stage of practice an equal number of times. In addition, in some cases it is a good idea to have each treatment precede and follow every other treatment an equal number of times. This is particularly important if there is reason to believe that the effect of a treatment will be influenced by the immediately preceding treatment.

Increasing Power and Precision

Size of Sample. As we indicated earlier, there is a relationship between sample size and the precision of estimates — precision increases as sample size increases. The advantage of random sampling in estimating is that your samples do not have to be very large before you can obtain precise estimates. For example, it is relatively common to estimate voter preferences for political candidates seeking national office by sampling fewer than 1000 voters.

Number of Subjects per Condition. A similar point holds for the number of subjects that should be tested in each condition when using an experimental design. The number tested in each condition should depend on the anticipated effect of the independent variable, the type of design, and whether you are interested in detecting small effects. The likelihood of detecting a real effect (that is, concluding that the treatment has an effect when, in truth, it does) increases as the number of subjects tested in each condition increases. The issue of how many subjects to test boils down to a question of belief.

The task is to convince the scientific community that the results of the experiment are attributable to the independent variable and not solely to chance, or worse, to a nonmanipulated but confounding variable. The purpose of conducting and analyzing experiments is to convince others and yourself of the effectiveness or ineffectiveness of a particular manipulation. Thus, the astute approach is to determine what would convince other investigators and then to meet or better their criteria. For any experiment there are usually computational advantages to having an equal number of subjects in each condition.

Minimizing Chance Fluctuations. Precision of estimation and the power of a statistical analysis are related to the distribution of possible outcomes if only chance is operating. We want to keep chance fluctuations as small as possible so that if more than chance is operating we will be better able to notice the effect. There are a number of ways of accomplishing this in addition to increasing the sample size. As we indicated earlier, within-subject designs are typically more efficient (have greater power) than between-subject designs because chance fluctuations within individuals are smaller than between individuals. If our participants are relatively similar (all college students), chance fluctuations within groups are likely to be smaller than if the participants are not similar (selected from the general population). The size of within-group fluctuations is the estimate of chance fluctuations when a between-group design is used; therefore, anything that keeps this estimate small helps to improve efficiency.

Procedures that reduce fluctuations within individuals, except for possible treatment effects, also increase efficiency. Thus, when a single participant is tested in a number of conditions, it is a common practice to provide the subject with a few practice or warm-up trials prior to the actual test. This is done simply to help ensure that performance at different times during the experiment will be about the same if there are no real treatment effects. The situation is analogous to trying to keep within-group fluctuations small so that you can detect any real effects of the independent variable. In this case, you want to keep within-individual chance fluctuations small; therefore, you make an effort to have the participant perform optimally when tested in each treatment condition.

SUMMARY

You can learn a great deal about research by doing your own project even if you are largely unaware of earlier research in the same problem area. However, the quality of your research and, thus, the chances of your making a real contribution are increased markedly if you know about the earlier research. Such knowledge will enable you to avoid methodological pitfalls and repeating what has already been done, and will alert you to information (data files) which might save you much time and effort. Obviously, what you need to know to collect data depends on what you hope to accomplish. Some problems require special skills and equipment; others do not.

Obtaining subjects for your research can be a complicated process in which you have to gain the cooperation of one or more gatekeepers. College students are frequently used as subjects because of their availability and, in most cases, willingness to cooperate. Obtaining the cooperation of other subject populations (infants, elderly persons, alcoholics) is frequently more difficult, but certainly possible for the researcher with the appropriate qualifications or contacts. The advantages of using lower animals is that they can usually be purchased commercially and they can be used for genetic, physiological, and other kinds of research that cannot be done with humans.

Two major concerns when collecting data are avoiding bias and increasing the power or precision of results. The experimenter's biases or expectations can influence the results of an experiment if participants detect these biases or if the biases influence the behavior of participants in any way. Biases may also occur as a result of using improper procedures for assigning subjects to conditions or for selecting samples. Once equivalent groups are obtained or random samples are selected, the task is to avoid the introduction of bias or the inadvertent destruction of equivalence.

The power of an experiment and the precision of an estimate are related to sample size and the number of subjects per condition. A critical consideration for determining power and efficiency is the nature of the distribution of possible outcomes if only chance is operating. Chance fluctuations are related to the type of design used, characteristics of participants, and specific testing procedures.

QUESTIONS

(Answers for the multiple choice questions are given in Appendix D.)

1. What are the advantages of reading about the research that has already been done in a particular problem area before doing research in the same area?
2. Under what conditions might you avoid the data-collection phase of doing research?
3. Defend or refute the view that complex equipment and computer skills are crucial for psychological research.
4. What procedures are used to obtain participants for psychological research? Why is it important to understand the role of gatekeepers?
5. Do you believe school administrators should cooperate with researchers? Why or why not?
6. What are demand characteristics and why are they an important methodological consideration?
7. What are stratified random samples and why are they important?
8. Indicate how the equivalence of groups could be destroyed during the course of data collection.
9. Indicate how the randomness of a stratified random sample could be destroyed during the course of data collection.
10. Why is the failure to control nonmanipulated variables such an important methodological consideration?
11. What is the relationship between sample size and precision? Power?
12. What procedures might you use to minimize chance fluctuations and thus increase the power of your experiment?
13. An investigator was interested in the effect of experiences at a university on the stands students take on controversial issues. She obtained a random sample of 100 freshmen, 100 sophomores, 100 juniors, and 100 seniors at a large state university. All 400 students agreed to take a test. The investigator found a direct relationship between the number of years at the institution and the score on the test. Freshmen tended to be conservative, and seniors tended to be liberal. Assume that the test was reliable and valid. The investigator concluded that the experiences at the university caused the students to become more liberal. Do you agree with her conclusions? Why?
14. An investigator was interested in the effect of violence in movies on the amount of violence reported in dreams. He randomly assigned a group of 100 subjects to two groups so that there were an equal number of subjects in each group. Each subject agreed to attend the movie of the investigator's choice if the investigator provided the ticket. One group viewed a very violent movie and the other group viewed a nonviolent movie. The subjects also agreed to record any dreams that they remembered having during the night

immediately following the movie. The investigator analyzed the dreams for violent content and found there was a significantly higher incidence of violence for the subjects who saw the violent movie. He concluded that viewing a violent movie has a tendency to cause one to have violent dreams. Do you agree with this conclusion? Why?

15. All else being equal, the probability of detecting a real effect (obtaining significant differences when the independent variable actually has an effect) _____ as the number of subjects per condition increases. (1) decreases (2) increases (3) remains the same

16. The major confounding problem for between-group designs is (1) the failure to counterbalance for time-related variables (2) the use of nonsubject variables (3) the failure to obtain equivalent groups or their destruction (4) none of the above

17. The principal problem of confounding with a within-subject design is (1) the failure to counterbalance for time-related variables (2) the use of nonsubject variables (3) the failure to obtain equivalent groups or their destruction (4) none of the above

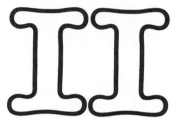

Describing, Analyzing, and Reporting Results

8 Methods and procedures for describing results

As we noted in Chapter 1, measurement is the use of rules to assign numbers to the properties of objects and events. Our concern in the first section was with the procedures used to obtain numbers, specifically, systematic procedures that avoid bias. Without systematic procedures, our observations may be the product of our personal view of the world rather than its real state. Thus, if we are interested in what *really* causes what or what *really* goes with what, we need to eliminate or at least minimize our personal biases. A similar problem exists for the description and analysis of results. After we obtain numbers, we need to know what to do with them so that our descriptions and comparisons of objects and events reflect the real state of the world and not our personal views. For this, we must first know something about the rules that are used to assign numbers to the properties of objects and events.

LEVEL OF MEASUREMENT AND PERFORMANCE VARIABLES

The term dependent measure frequently refers to the variable used for assessing the effect of one or more independent variables, and the terms performance measure and behavioral measure usually refer to results obtained with other methods. However, since these labels are interchanged by some investigators and since in describing results it makes little difference whether scores are called performance measures or dependent measures, we will not maintain this distinction. Our interest is in the description and analysis of results. The rules followed determine the level of measurement that is obtained, and, consequently, the operations that can be performed on the numbers. We will see later, for example, that it is necessary to classify the dependent variable according to the level of measurement obtained in order to select an appropriate statistical test. The four levels of measurement are nominal, ordinal, interval, and ratio.

Nominal or Categorical Measurement

A nominal classification system is one in which the classes (categories) are qualitatively related. Brands of soap or beer are examples of such a system. There is no single, quantitative variable that can be used to distinguish different brands. The differences between categories of a nominal system are of kind, not of degree. They are qualitative, not quantitative.

It is fairly easy to construct nominal classification systems because the primary task is to select categories that are qualitatively related. Social scientists and laymen have not been reluctant to create such systems. You probably have at least a tendency to place people in categories. For example, you may classify them as right-handed or left-handed, male or female, workers or politicians, introverted or extraverted, warm or cold, assertive or timid. If the categories are qualitatively different, they belong to a nominal system. For many research problems it is important to be able to determine the number of individuals in each category so that the factors influencing the assignment to categories and the relationship between classification systems can be determined.

Ordinal Measurement

For nominal data it is assumed that differences between categories are of kind, not degree. However, a single continuum will frequently underlie a particular classification system. For example, the categories of normal, neurotic, and psychotic all describe degrees of maladjustment. If there is good reason to believe that a single dimension underlies a classification system, it may be useful to rank the categories and treat the results as ordinal rather than nominal data. People in the normal, neurotic, and psychotic categories can be given the scores of 0, 1, and 2, respectively. The numbers indicate the *relative* amount of maladjustment. The difference in maladjustment between individuals in the 0 and 1 categories is not necessarily the same as the difference between those in the 1 and 2 categories. Of course, assignment to these categories must be reliable if the system is to be useful.

Since it is usually possible to argue that subjects in different categories differ on one or more quantitative variables, you may conclude that it is good strategy to "convert" nominal measurement to ordinal by "detecting" an underlying quantitative dimension. This is not necessarily a good idea, however, because there is often no sound basis for selecting a quantitative dimension.

Consider, for example, the classification of people according to political party. It can be argued that several factors, such as income, status, values, and occupation, underlie this classification. We would not want to substitute one of the underlying factors (wealth) for political party, however, because wealth and political party are not always related. For instance, Republicans tend to be wealthier than Democrats, but there are also very wealthy Democrats and very poor Republicans. The use of income (a quantitative measure) is not a good substitute for political party. There appears to be no single quantitative variable that can be used to classify people accurately according to their political preferences. Therefore it is better to remain at the nominal level of measurement. If subjects in different categories differ in a number of ways, it is more reasonable to maintain a nominal classification than to attempt to rank the categories (such as Republican, Democrat, Independent) on the basis of a single quantitative variable.

The point is that an ordinal scale represents a quantitative difference, whereas a nominal classification system does not. Ordinal data can be obtained whenever it is possible to rank subjects or events along a single dimension. For example, if you rank individuals according to physical strength or performance on a midterm you are using an ordinal scale. An ordinal scale is one in which the scale values are quantitatively related, but the differences between successive values are not necessarily equal.

When numbers are used to indicate the amount of a particular characteristic but the differences between successive units of measurement are not necessarily equal, ordinal data are obtained. For example, if the members of a class are ranked according to leadership ability, the difference in ability between members 4 and 8 is not necessarily the same as the difference between members 16 and 20. But if a dependent measure does have equal intervals between successive units on the scale, then *interval* data are obtained.

Interval and Ratio Measurement

For interval data the scale values are related by a single, underlying quantitative dimension, and there are equal intervals between successive values. Fahrenheit temperature is a good example of an interval scale. The units reflect a quantitative difference and the intervals between successive units are equal. For example, the difference between 80° and 100° Fahrenheit is the same as the difference between 40° and 60°F. These are *equal volumetric changes* in the thermometer. But the Fahrenheit scale is not a ratio scale because the ratio obtained by dividing one temperature by another is not meaningful. It is meaningless to say that 50° is twice as warm as 25°. This is the case because 0°F does not signify the complete absence of heat. The absolute zero for temperature (that is, complete absence of heat) is equal to approximately −459.60°F or approximately −273.16°C.

A ratio scale has equal intervals between successive units *and* an absolute zero. If a scale has these two features, it is meaningful to consider the ratio of two numbers on the scale. Weight is a good example of a ratio scale; it has an absolute zero and equal intervals between successive units. It is meaningful to say that a 200-pound person weighs twice as much as a 100-pound person, assuming normal gravitational force. We are referring here to a physical, not a psychological dimension (scale). For example, if you are asked to judge the weights of a number of objects, it is unlikely that you will judge a 4-pound object to be exactly twice as heavy as a 2-pound object, a 10-pound object to be exactly twice as heavy as a 5-pound object, and so on. Brightness, perhaps, is a better example. The difference in *perceived* intensity between a 50-watt and 100-watt bulb is very noticeable, but the difference between a 200-watt and 250-watt bulb is much less noticeable.

The study of the relationship between physical stimulus intensity and our perception of intensity (magnitude) is known as psychophysics. We might, for example, attempt to relate happiness (a psychological response) to money (a physical dimension). Imagine how happy you would be if, when you turned the next page, you found a fifty-dollar bill. The publisher refused to put a fifty-dollar bill in each book, but you can imagine how happy you would feel if there was one in your book. Now that you have estimated how happy you would feel, consider how much money it would take for you to be twice as happy. For most people there is not a one-to-one relationship between money and happiness. One hundred dollars probably would not make you twice as happy as $50, but $200 or $300 might (Lindsay & Norman, 1977). We will be dealing with both physical and psychological scales, but we will not be discussing the extensive research in psychophysics. Rather, our interest is in the relationship between the level of measurement and the procedures we can use to describe and analyze numbers.

Determining the Level of Measurement

It is usually easy to determine whether the level of measurement is nominal because one can readily assess whether values on a scale are quantitatively or qualitatively related. And for our purposes it makes no difference whether measurement is at the interval or ratio level. In fact, we will use the term interval to mean interval or better (interval or ratio). The major task is to decide whether the performance measure is interval or ordinal.

Unfortunately that task is not always simple. For example, scores on questionnaires, intelligence tests, and achievement tests are frequently viewed as interval data, but this view can be disputed. If the items are not homogeneous, one can argue that the differences between successive units are not equal. Often it is unclear whether they are equal; then the investigator has to decide whether to regard the measurement as ordinal or interval. There are advantages to having interval data, so when in doubt most investigators treat their data as interval.

DESCRIPTIVE MEASURES

The level of measurement determines the descriptive measures that can be computed. Description is straightforward with nominal data; it is only necessary to indicate the number of cases in each category. Each subject provides the same amount of data, namely, one case in a particular category. However, if ordinal or interval data are obtained, the subjects will almost certainly attain different scores. Therefore it is more difficult to describe performance on the dependent measure. It is necessary to obtain average scores, and the way they are obtained will usually differ for ordinal and interval data because interval scores are additive and ordinal scores are not. It makes sense to add scores to obtain averages only if the differences between successive units on the scale are equal (that is, they mean the same thing).

Our major goal in this section is to consider how interval data can be described. Because some of the measures to be discussed do not involve the addition or subtraction of individual scores, they are applicable to ordinal data as well. The steps in obtaining the various descriptive measures can be studied in the context of an example.

Let us assume that the performance measure is the number of strokes needed to complete a round of golf. The first step is to decide the level of the performance measure. It is clearly not nominal because the scores have a quantitative rather than a qualitative relationship. A slight case could be made for regarding the scores as ordinal data; one could argue that the difference between successive units is not necessarily equal. For example, the difference between a 2 and a 5 on a par 4 hole may appear to you, if you are a golfer, to be much greater than the difference between a 7 and a 10 on the same hole. However, since most investigators and golfers would probably conclude that a stroke counts as a stroke regardless of quality, the scores can be viewed as interval measures. (That is, we will treat data as interval if there is some doubt about whether the scores are instances of ordinal or of interval measurement). Now that we have determined that the level of measurement of the performance variable is interval, the next task is to describe the scores. There are two basic sets of descriptive measures for interval data: measures of central tendency and measures of variability.

Measures of Central Tendency

We fluctuate. Our performance varies with time of day, amount of sleep, level of interest, and so on. If the task is to decide who is better at a particular activity, such as golf, one should be reluctant to base the decision on limited information. To illustrate, assume that you decide to determine whether you are a better golfer than Dana, one of your friends. You both agree to play eighteen holes of golf per day for ten consecutive days.

After playing the tenth round you adjourn to a local pub to analyze the data. The question boils down, you both believe, to assessing who has the better *average* performance. Measures of central tendency must be computed in order to describe your average performance. Since you both want to appear fair, you agree to compute three different measures of central tendency: the mode, median, and mean. The scores for the ten rounds of golf for each player are presented in Table 8-1.

The Mode. The mode is the most frequently occurring score. An examination of Table 8-1 reveals that neither player had any total more than once. Therefore it is not possible to determine a modal score for each player. To compute a modal score at least one score has to be obtained more than once. For example, if a golfer has rounds of 73, 73, 74, 75, 76, 79, 82, 88, 88, and 88, her modal score would be 88 — not a good measure of her average performance. The mode can be very misleading because only the most frequent score is used; the mode does not provide any information about the other scores. The median and the mean make greater use of the evidence available.

The Median. The median is the value that divides the distribution in half after the scores are placed in ascending or descending order. The first step, then, is to place the scores in Table 8-1 in ascending order. The order for Dana is 82, 84, 85, 86, 88, 89, 90, 91, 92, and 93. The ascending order for

TABLE 8–1

The Scores for Each of Ten Rounds of Golf for Dana and You (fictitious data)

Day	You	Dana
1	80	90
2	85	84
3	87	82
4	99	85
5	116	91
6	86	89
7	82	93
8	84	92
9	92	86
10	79	88

your rounds is 79, 80, 82, 84, 85, 86, 87, 92, 99, and 116. Because there are ten scores, the middle score is half-way between the fifth and sixth. You have a median of 85.5 and Dana has a median of 88.5. You are pleased with the median scores as they indicate that, on the average, you are three strokes better than Dana. She argues that the median is not a satisfactory measure because it does not utilize all the available information. For example, even if your four lowest scores were reduced by 20, the median would be unaffected. The median is simply not sensitive to changes in extreme scores. In this case, Dana argues, the mean is a better measure. Note that the median score is useful with ordinal as well as interval data because it is not necessary to add or subtract scores to compute this measure.

The Mean. The mean is computed by adding all the scores and dividing by the number of scores. To compute the mean total score for the ten rounds of golf, the individual round totals are added and then divided by the number of scores used to obtain the total (10). Your total number of strokes for the ten rounds was 890. You divide this by 10 to obtain a mean score of 89. The symbol $\overline{X}$ (called *x*-bar) is used as a label for the mean. Dana has a mean of 88 (880 divided by 10). She can argue that, on the average, you are one stroke poorer. You reply that you are three strokes better if median performance is considered.

Dana insists that the mean is much better than the median because all the scores are used in making the computation. You answer that this is not necessarily a favorable characteristic. You believe that extreme scores should be discounted instead of being emphasized. The days you scored 79, 99, and 116 were very unusual days for you emotionally. You scored 99 on the day you heard your mother was coming for a visit, 116 on the day of her arrival, and 79 on the day she left. Obviously, you argue, such extreme scores should not be used to compute typical performance. The mean is influenced unduly by extremes.

Less debatable examples can be used to demonstrate the influence of extreme scores on the mean. Let us assume that a woman is seeking employment with a company and the president of the company informs her that the average annual salary for executive personnel is $84,000. She is impressed but skeptical. On further inquiry she finds that the figure represents the mean salary. The president makes $300,000 a year, and the other four executives each make $30,000 a year. The mean for the five executives is $84,000. In this case, however, the median salary of $30,000 is, from the prospective executive's point of view, a much more useful measure of central tendency, and the choice of the median measure over the mean is clear-cut. The same point applies if we have one or more extremely low scores. For example, if your exam grades are 0 (you missed the exam), 94, and 96, your mean score is 63.3, whereas your median score is 94. From your point of view the median is a far better measure of your average performance.

The effort to determine the better golfer, however, is at an impasse. The two major measures of central tendency yield conflicting results, and there is no ultimate authority that you can appeal to for truth. The argument that extreme scores should not be used to determine performance can be countered by asserting that good golfers are consistent. Their scores rarely deviate much from their typical performance. A good golfer should not have a bad day just because her mother is coming to visit.

By now you should be ready to concede that the question is not soluble. The measures used to assess central tendency may not be in agreement. The important issue, of course, is what the measures of central tendency reveal about the obtained scores, not which of the three is best. The suitability of the measures depends on the distribution of the scores. Although we enjoy making value judgments, there is little to be gained by doing so for measures of central tendency. It is more important to understand the strengths and weaknesses of each.

The mode is simply the most frequently occurring score, so it usually has limited usefulness. The mean utilizes more of the available information than the median, but it is not appropriate for describing ordinal data. If there are extreme scores, you may prefer the median because the mean is greatly influenced by extremes.

Measures of Variability

The Range. If you want to measure the extent to which scores vary you will find that the range is the simplest measure but that it is usually inadequate. The range is the difference score obtained by subtracting the smallest score from the largest. Although the computation is very easy, the measure is usually inadequate because it is based entirely on two scores. For the golf match example, you have a range of 37 (116 minus 79) and Dana has a range of 11 (93 minus 82). If there are only a few extreme scores, the range may give an unsatisfactory description of the variability of the scores. The variance is far more precise because all the scores are used in its computation.

Variance. The concept of variance is extremely important. You will remember that we can analyze variance (that is, compare between- and within-group estimates of population variance) to assess treatment effects. In later chapters we will see that by analyzing variance we can also explain individual differences in behavior. Before we can analyze variance, we need to have a firm understanding of how variance is computed. Let us review and expand our discussion of the computation of variance as we presented it in Chapter 4.

In measuring the extent to which scores vary it is convenient to have a reference point, the mean. It is then possible to find the difference between each score and the mean and to add up the difference scores. That is, one can determine how much, if any, each score *deviates* from the mean by subtracting the score from the mean or the mean from the score. If this is done for each score and these deviations from the mean are added, the sum will be equal to zero.

The sum of the deviations from the mean is not a suitable measure of variability because it will always be zero; the sum of the positive deviations is always equal to the sum of the negative deviations. The problem could be solved by ignoring the minus sign and adding all the deviations regardless of sign. Although this procedure would yield a measure of variability, there are statistical and practical reasons for using, instead, a measure obtained by squaring each deviation from the mean.

The variance of a population is the sum of the squared deviations from the mean divided by the number of scores. In computing the variance for a sample of less than thirty scores from a population, the sum of the squared deviations is divided by the number of scores minus one. The reason for subtracting one is to obtain a more accurate estimate of population variance. Over the long haul, the sum of the squared deviations divided by the number of scores minus one provides a better estimate than the sum of the squared deviations divided by the total number of scores. If there are more than thirty scores, however, the variance is not influenced very much by which divisor is used.

Some investigators divide by the number of scores if their sole concern is *describing* the scores, and they divide by the number of scores minus one if their concern is *estimating* population variance. Since variance is usually computed for small samples (less than thirty scores per group or sample) and not for the entire population, many investigators always divide by the number of scores minus one. They do not bother to distinguish between a variance for description and one for estimation; the variance for estimation fulfills both functions. In this text variance will always be computed by dividing by the number of scores minus one, regardless of the size of the sample. The symbol s^2 is usually used for sample variance.

The scores from the golf match example are used to demonstrate the computation of variance. The scores for your ten rounds of golf and the variance computation are presented in Table 8-2. If you are unclear about how to use the deviation method you should study this table further. Then, take Dana's golf scores (82, 84, 85, 86, 88, 89, 90, 91, 92, and 93) and compute the variance using the deviation method. If your computation is correct you will obtain a variance of 13.33. Notice that your scores are considerably more variable than Dana's.

Using the deviation method should give you a good understanding of variance. It should be clear from the computation that the variance is nothing more than a measure of the extent to which scores differ from the mean score. However, this method of computation becomes cumbersome as the number of scores increases, particularly if the mean is not a whole number.

TABLE 8-2

The Total Scores for Each of Ten Rounds of Golf and the Computation of the Variance of These Scores

Golf score (X)	Deviation score (X - $\bar{X}$)	Squared deviation score (X - $\bar{X})^2$
79	− 10	100
80	− 9	81
82	− 7	49
84	− 5	25
85	− 4	16
86	− 3	9
87	− 2	4
92	+ 3	9
99	+ 10	100
116	+ 27	729
Sum = 890	Sum = 0	Sum = 1122

$$\bar{X} = 89 \qquad s^2 = \frac{\text{Sum of the squared deviation scores}}{\text{Number of scores minus 1}}$$

$$s^2 = \frac{1122}{9} = 124.67$$

Note: The deviation scores are obtained by subtracting the mean from each score.

An example is presented in Table 8-3 to demonstrate both the deviation method and a computational method for computing the variance. The *X* refers to any score. The symbol $\bar{X}$ is used for the mean. The sigma (Σ) sign indicates the summing operation; the numbers denoted by the symbol following the sigma are *added*. Thus, the first term in the numerator for the computational formula is obtained by squaring each score and then summing the squared scores. It is important to note that the scores are squared *before* they are added. The *T* in the formula refers to the total of all the scores, and the *n* refers to the number of scores. The second term in the numerator for the computational formula is obtained by squaring the total and dividing by the number of scores. The denominator is simply the number of scores minus one. A comparison of the two formulas reveals that the denominators are the same and the numerators are mathematically equal. The numerator of the computational formula is simply another way to calculate the sum of the squared deviation scores. It should be clear that the calculation of variance is easier with the computational formula, particularly if a calculator is available. (If you do not have ready access to a calculator, you should give serious

TABLE 8-3

An Example of the Calculation of the Variance by the Deviational and Computational Formulas

	Deviational method		Computational method
Scores	$(X - \bar{X})$	$(X - \bar{X})^2$	Scores
38	− 5.25	27.56	38
55	11.75	138.06	55
62	18.75	351.56	62
25	−18.25	333.06	25
31	−12.25	150.06	31
46	2.75	7.56	46
45	1.75	3.06	45
50	6.75	45.56	50
42	− 1.25	1.56	42
39	− 4.25	18.06	39
41	− 2.25	5.06	41
45	1.75	3.06	45
	Sum = 0	Sum = 1084.22	$T = 519$

$$\bar{X} = 43.25$$

$$s^2 = \frac{\Sigma(X - \bar{X})^2}{n - 1}$$

$$s^2 = \frac{1084.22}{11}$$

$$s^2 = 98.57$$

$$\Sigma X^2 = 23,531$$

$$s^2 = \frac{\Sigma X^2 - \frac{(T)^2}{n}}{n - 1}$$

$$s^2 = \frac{23,531 - \frac{269,361}{12}}{11}$$

$$s^2 = \frac{1084.25}{11}$$

$$s^2 = 98.57$$

consideration to purchasing one. They are excellent bargains, one of the few items that have decreased in price over the years.) There is no substitute for actually working problems to increase your understanding of statistics, and having a calculator available simplifies this task considerably.

Standard Deviation. The computation of the standard deviation is easy if the variance has already been computed because the standard deviation is equal to the square root of the variance. (Most calculators make the task of obtaining the square root of a number extremely easy.) The standard deviation is a more useful *descriptive* measure than the variance because it is in the same units as the mean, whereas the variance is in different units from the mean. The fact that the variance is essentially an average *squared* deviation from the mean makes it somewhat unsatisfactory as a descriptive measure. In considering the difference between two means it is useful to have a variability measure that is in the same units as the means. This measure can be obtained by taking the square root of the variance. The resulting standard deviation is used extensively as a measure of variability and can also be used as a unit of measurement. The symbol *s* is used to denote the standard deviation of a sample.

STANDARD DEVIATION
AS A UNIT OF MEASUREMENT

Z-scores

The standard deviation can be used as a unit of measurement. An individual can determine how many standard deviation units she is above or below the mean by determining the difference between the mean and the obtained score and then dividing the difference by the standard deviation for the total set of scores. For example, let us assume that you obtain a score of 84 on a history midterm. The mean for the class was 74 and the standard deviation was 10. If you subtract the mean score for the history exam from your score you obtain a difference of 10. You then divide this difference by the standard deviation of 10 and obtain a quotient of 1 — you were one standard deviation unit above the mean on the history exam. The formula for computing a z-score is:

$$z = \frac{X - \overline{X}}{s}$$

where X refers to any score, $\overline{X}$ is the mean for the sample, and s is the standard deviation for the sample.

Z-scores can be used to compare scores from different distributions to determine a person's relative standing in each distribution. For example, assume that you are enrolled in a large psychology class and a large history class. As indicated in the above example, you obtain a score of 84 on the history exam. The mean is 74 and the standard deviation is 10. Your score on the psychology midterm is 69. The mean score was 60 and the standard deviation was 3. The question is whether your performance, relative to the other members of each class, was higher on the psychology or history exam. As we indicated previously, you were 1 standard deviation unit above the mean on the history exam, $z = +1$. Your z-score for the psychology exam is equal to +3 [(69 − 60)/3 = 3]. Even though you were ten points above the mean on the history exam and only nine points above on the psychology, your performance relative to other members of each class was far better in psychology than in history.

Z-scores and Normal Distributions

Need for a Frame of Reference. Scores in isolation do not tell very much. In order to interpret scores in a meaningful way we need a frame of reference. We can interpret a particular score if we know the distribution of scores. Consider a person who weighs 60 pounds. If the person is a first-grade student, the score is not particularly unusual. We do not know how common or how unusual it is unless we have the distribution of weights of first-graders as a frame of reference. However, most of us have seen enough first-graders to know that this is a relatively common score. If the person is a college senior, however, we have a very different situation. You have probably seen few, if any, college seniors who weigh only 60 pounds, so you know that this is an extreme score. You do not know just how extreme a score this is because you do not have the distribution of weights of college seniors. If you did, you would be able to say more about the likelihood of an individual who is a college senior weighing only 60 pounds.

Properties of Normal Distributions. Consider the distribution of scores you would obtain if various rules were used to assign numbers to the properties of different objects or events (for example, weights of first-graders, IQ scores for 19-year-olds, self-esteem of college students, income per year of 40-year-old males in Wisconsin, time to run the 100-yard dash for 20-year-old female college students, and so on). If you had all the numbers (scores) for each of these distributions, would you expect, for any one distribution, to find the mean, median, and mode to be about the same? If you compared the number of scores close to the mean with the number of scores at a "considerable" distance from the mean, which would be more frequent? Do you expect scores to pile up around the mean and decline symmetrically on both sides of the mean so that there are about as many scores above as below the mean? If we compute the standard deviation and mean for each distribution, do you expect that the percentage of scores within plus or minus 1 standard deviation of the mean will be about the same regardless of the distribution considered?

For many distributions that we might consider, the answers to the above questions are yes, because the distribution is normal or nearly normal. A pictorial representation of a normal distribution is presented in Figure 8-1. An examination of the figure reveals a "bell-shaped" distribution (that is, a symmetrical distribution with the same mean, median, and mode, scores piled up around the mean, and fewer scores as the distance from the mean

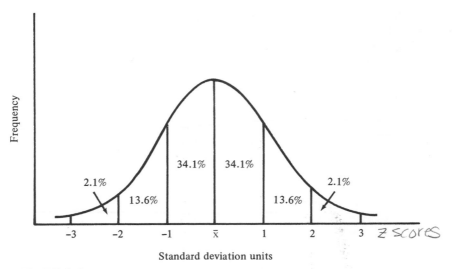

FIGURE 8–1

The standard normal distribution has the properties of a normal distribution, a mean of 0, and a standard deviation equal to 1.

increases). If a distribution is normal approximately 68 percent of the scores are within 1 standard deviation (plus or minus) of the mean, 95 percent are within 2 standard deviations, and 99 percent are within 3 standard deviations. The critical values that we need to know are the mean and the standard deviation. If we know these values and we know that the distribution is normal or nearly normal, we have a very useful frame of reference for describing scores. We know, for example, that the probability of obtaining a particular score decreases as the difference between the score and the mean increases, as indicated in Figure 8-1.

Figure 8-1 can be used to show why a score of 3 standard deviations above the mean is considerably better than a score of 1 standard deviation above. The height of the curve indicates the relative frequency of each score. The area under the curve can be used to determine the probability of obtaining a score greater or less than a particular score. It can be readily seen that the probability of obtaining a score of 3 standard deviations above the mean is considerably less than the probability of obtaining a score of 1 standard deviation above. If 99.6 percent of the scores fall within 3 standard deviations of the mean, a score that is 3 or more standard deviations above the mean is considerably higher (less likely to occur if only chance is operating) than a score which is 1 or more standard deviations above the mean. We can expect a score of 1 or more standard deviations above the mean to occur about 16 percent of the time.

Standard Normal Distribution. If the distribution we are considering is normal and we transfer each score in the distribution to a z-score, the distribution will be identical to the distribution in Figure 8-1 except that the mean will be equal to 0. This distribution is called the standard normal distribution. It is very useful because scores from normal distributions can be transformed to a *single* distribution having a mean of 0 and a standard deviation of 1. This transformation allows us to compare scores from normal distributions that have different means and variances.

The Importance of Normal Distributions. It is frequently difficult for the beginning student to appreciate the importance of knowing the properties of the standard normal distribution. Part of the difficulty may be the unwillingness to accept the conclusion that many distributions are, in fact, normal. Why should this be the case when there is little similarity in the scores obtained when different measures are taken (for example, score on a depression test as one measure and weight as the second)? If you can appreciate the fact that the standard deviation is a measure of fluctuation, as is variance, you might be better able to accept the conclusion that many distributions are normal (that is, the percentage of the scores within 1 standard deviation of the mean is relatively constant at about 68 percent). For some distributions the standard deviation may be very large (for example, 100) and in other cases it may be very small (such as .15). If it is very large, the obtained scores vary greatly, but with a large standard deviation (100) many of the scores (say 68 percent) will still be within 1 standard deviation of the mean. In fact, 60 to 70 percent of the scores are typically within 1 standard deviation of the mean even when the distribution is not normal. It is very difficult to appreciate the importance of the normal distribution without also understanding that standard deviations are fluctuation units; they tell us how much scores vary.

But, you may protest, many distributions are not normal. Consider the yearly income of adults. There are some adults who make a disgusting amount of money each year ($1 million), and therefore the distribution of scores (yearly income) is skewed (nonnormal). We expect skewness because extreme scores influence the mean more than the median. If the mean and median are different, the distribution is not normal (see Figure 8-2). Clearly, there is no doubt that many frequency distributions are not normal. However, in many instances we are not interested in frequency distributions but in sampling distributions.

Imagine that we draw a sample of 100 adults and then compute the mean income for our sample. Will our estimate be identical to the mean value for the population? Probably not, but we should expect it to be reasonably close. Now, if we repeat the procedure (select new random samples) several hundred times, we have several hundred estimates of the population mean. What will our distribution of sample values look like? Is this distribution likely to

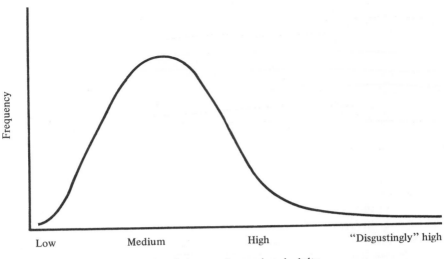

FIGURE 8–2

Frequency distribution for the yearly income of employed adults

be normal even though we sampled from a nonnormal distribution? The answer is yes — a fact, usually referred to as the *central limits theorem*, of immense importance for theorists interested in using mathematics to calculate distributions of possible outcomes when only chance is operating.

Z-scores and Other Derived Scores

Frame of Reference. Raw scores are the scores obtained on a test or performance measure. If you answer 83 out of 113 questions on a psychology final exam, your raw score is 83. The raw score, in isolation, does not convey very much information. We do not know whether this score is average or lower or higher than the other scores. Derived scores such as z-scores are useful because they provide a frame of reference. Much more information is conveyed by giving the z-score that corresponds to a raw score of 83 than by simply giving the raw score. If, for example, the z-score is +2, we know that the person's relative standing is high. Although z-scores are very useful for conveying relative standing, there are some minor inconveniences in using these derived scores. In many cases they are not useful for communication and they frequently require the use of negative numbers and decimals. Decimals are necessary because too much information would be lost if z-scores were rounded to the nearest whole number. There is considerable difference between a z-score of 2 and one of 2.49. Z-scores cannot always be used for communicating information about a person's standing because many people do not know what they are.

Equivalence of Scores. Some derived scores are based on z-scores. The logic behind many derived scores is that scores are *equivalent* if they are the same number of standard deviations above or below the mean in their respective distributions. (Note that we are interested in the equivalence of *scores*. Equivalence has a different meaning when used in reference to groups.) For example, scores that are 2.3 standard deviations above the mean in both distributions are equivalent. Given this definition of equivalence we can convert scores to any new distribution. We can *arbitrarily* decide what we want the mean and standard deviation for the new distribution to be.

Let us assume that we want to convert a raw score of 72 obtained from a distribution having a mean of 80 and a standard deviation of 4 to an equivalent score in a distribution that has a mean of 500 and a standard deviation of 100. Our task is to make sure that the score is the same number of standard deviations above or below the mean in both distributions. The first task is to determine the z-score for the old distribution. We use the z-score formula and insert the values for X, $\overline{X}$, and s. The result of our calculation gives us a z-score of −2.

$$z = \frac{X - \overline{X}}{s}$$

$$z = \frac{72 - 80}{4}$$

$$z = -2$$

Our score is 2 standard deviations below the mean. The next task is to determine what score is equivalent to this score in a new distribution having a mean of 500 and a standard deviation of 100. The answer, of course, is 300 because 300 is also 2 standard deviations below the mean. In short, the fact that equivalence can be defined in terms of standard deviations makes it possible to convert a distribution (set) of scores to a new distribution having a specified mean and standard deviation. Transformations of this sort are useful because they allow us to avoid the minor inconveniences associated with z-scores (communication, negative numbers, and decimals). The scores of most standardized tests (such as Graduate Record Examination, Army General Classification Test, Wechsler Adult Intelligence Scale) are transformed so that the scores are easy to interpret. It is, for example, easier to interpret a score (communicate relative standing) if the mean is 100 and the standard deviation is 10 than if the mean is 89 and the standard deviation is 7.

Linear and Nonlinear Transformations. Transforming raw scores to z-scores does not change the distribution of scores. If the original distribution (the raw scores) is skewed, the distribution of z-scores will be skewed. This transformation is linear, which means that there is a straight-line relationship between the original scores and the transformed scores. We can demonstrate this fact by taking any set of raw scores (such as the scores in Table 8-3) and computing the z-score for each raw score. The raw score of 38, for example (see Table 8-3), is equal to a z-score of −.53 given that the mean is 43.25 and the standard deviation is equal to 9.93. Now if we compute the z-score for each of the raw scores and then plot the raw scores on the horizontal axis and the z-scores on the vertical axis, we will find that all the points fall on a straight line (see Figure 8-3). The major point is simply that we really do not change anything when we make a z-score transformation because we do not change the original distribution.

Percentile Rank. Some transformations do change the original distribution, at least in most cases. The transformation that you are probably most familiar with is percentile. It is a useful descriptive measure because it provides an easily understood frame of reference. The percentile rank of a score is obtained by finding the percentage of scores that are smaller. For example, if you obtain a score of 89 and this turns out to be the 320th score in a set of 431 scores (that is, 430 people took the same test you did), there are 319 people who scored lower than you did. Your percentile rank is 74

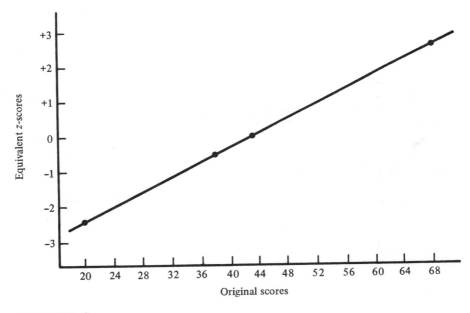

FIGURE 8-3

The plot of a z-score transformation for the raw scores presented in Table 8-3

because 74 percent of the scores (319 divided by 431) are lower than yours. Although the measure is easily understood, it is usually a nonlinear transformation. That is, converting raw scores to percentile ranks changes the original distribution in most cases. You can appreciate this fact by examining the normal distribution presented in Figure 8-1.

If the original distribution is normal, or nearly so, then a score equal to the mean score corresponds to a percentile rank of 50, and a score 1 standard deviation above the mean corresponds to a percentile rank of approximately 84. Thus, an increase of 1 standard deviation at this part of the distribution corresponds to 34 points on the percentile scale. How about the difference between a score that is 2 standard deviations above and a score that is 3 standard deviations above the mean? An increase of 1 standard deviation at this part of the distribution corresponds to an increase of approximately 2 points on the percentile scale. Clearly, if a 1 standard deviation increase corresponds to 34 percentile points in one case and 2 percentile points in another, the transformation is nonlinear. You can plot z-scores on the horizontal axis and percentile rank on the vertical axis to determine the shape of the transformation when the original distribution is normal, as in Figure 8-1.

DESCRIBING THE RESULTS OF EXPERIMENTS

In this last section we consider how measures of central tendency and variability can be used to describe the results of research. We will also consider when they are not needed. You should view these measures as tools. To use them effectively, you need to know when they are useful and when they are not; their usefulness depends on the level of measurement. We need to consider examples of research in which nominal, ordinal, and interval data are obtained.

Nominal Data

Consider the attitude of citizens toward people who chew tobacco. For many of you, chewing tobacco is absolutely disgusting. Imagine, however, that the economy is in bad shape — not a very difficult thing to imagine — and a tobacco company offers you an extremely attractive position. They want you to assess the effectiveness of different campaigns to change the public's view of the practice of chewing tobacco. You decide to accept their offer.

We can view the attitude toward people who chew tobacco as a nominal (qualitative) classification. People are asked whether they favor or oppose the practice, not how much they favor or oppose it. A random sample of 200 adults from a relatively small town is selected, and each person in the sample is asked whether he or she opposes or favors the practice of chewing tobacco in public places. After those data are collected, a campaign is initiated to convince the adults in this town that chewing tobacco is not necessarily a disgusting practice. The advertising campaign consists of testimonials of celebrities stressing the positive features of chewing (no secondhand smoke, discreetness). After the campaign is concluded, you take another sample of 200 adults from the same town. The sample is random with the restriction that anyone selected in the first sample is not used in the second. Once again, you ask each person in the sample to indicate whether he or she is opposed to or in favor of the practice of chewing tobacco. How should these results be described?

There is no need to compute measures of central tendency or variability because each person selected contributes the same score; that is, each must indicate whether he favors or opposes the practice of chewing tobacco. Therefore, it is easy to describe the results. All that is needed is the number of people who favor and the number who oppose the practice of chewing tobacco. Of course, the results are calculated separately for the two samples so that the effect of the advertising campaign can be assessed. These results are presented in Table 8-4. Notice that the table's title gives a fairly complete explanation of the table's contents. The title should be as complete as possible so the reader does not have to "discover" what information is in the table by reading the text.

It is not necessary to present the results in the form of a table. It would have been sufficient simply to state the number of adults who favor and the number who oppose prior to and after the advertising campaign. When there are only a few numbers, there is no compelling reason to present them in a table. However, as the amount of data to report increases, it frequently becomes necessary to use a table or figure to present the results. You will be prepared to analyze the results presented in Table 8-4 after reading Chapter 10.

TABLE 8-4

The Number of People in Each Sample of 200 Who Oppose and Favor the Practice of Chewing Tobacco Before and After the Advertising Campaign to Stress the Positive Features of Chewing Tobacco (fictitious data)

Nature of sample	*Opinion about chewing tobacco in public places*	
	Oppose	*Favor*
Selected before the campaign	160	40
Selected after the campaign	120	80

Ordinal Data

Let us assume that the problem is to assess the effects of a plan to develop leaders. The independent variable is whether or not the subject has participated in the plan. The dependent measure is the ranking of the experimental and control participants according to leadership ability. The proponents of the plan claim that people who complete the leadership course have a greater probability of being successful leaders than those who do not. The random-groups design is used. Thirty participants are randomly assigned to the experimental and control conditions, with fifteen participants in each. The experimental participants receive a "Learn How to Be a Leader" course and the control participants do not. Five years after completion of the course an evaluation team that is unaware of the purpose of the experiment obtains enough information to rank the thirty participants according to degree of success. The most successful person is given the rank of 30 and the least successful the rank of 1. How should the experimenter describe the results of this experiment?

Each participant's rank and treatment condition are given in Table 8-5. All the facts are presented in this way so that the reader can consider how best to describe the results. It is not correct to conclude that the results

TABLE 8-5

The Rank of Each Participant in the Experimental (E) and Control (C) Conditions for the "Learn to Be a Leader" Experiment (fictitious data)

Subject	Condition	Rank	Subject	Condition	Rank
F. T.	C	1	K. S.	C	16
D. J.	C	2	D. A.	E	17
W. L.	C	3	W. H.	E	18
T. J.	C	4	A. M.	C	19
D. B.	C	5	R. M.	E	20
R. T.	C	6	R. W.	C	21
T. A.	C	7	G. V.	E	22
D. A.	E	8	M. K.	C	23
C. N.	C	9	L. W.	E	24
S. S.	E	10	J. S.	E	25
C. W.	C	11	T. S.	E	26
S. J.	C	12	C. G.	E	27
R. C.	E	13	T. B.	E	28
F. H.	C	14	H. B.	E	29
M. F.	E	15	B. C.	E	30

Note: The rank of 1 indicates the least successful subject; the rank of 30 indicates the most successful subject.

should be described as they are in Table 8-5. In most cases it is not necessary to present the rank for each participant. Usually, the principal concern is with whether the independent variable has an effect.

The effect of the independent variable is assessed by comparing the rankings of the experimental and control participants. Since the level of measurement is ordinal, it is not permissible to add the ranks of the participants in each group to obtain average scores. Adding the ranks for descriptive purposes is not defensible unless there is reason to believe that the differences between successive ranks are equal. In this case there is no reason to believe that the data are any more than ordinal. You should not conclude, however, that ranks are never added; some statistical tests with ordinal data require adding rank scores.

Probably the best way to describe the data in Table 8-5 is to indicate the number of participants in each condition who are above the median rank. If the results are attributable to chance, the number of experimental and control participants above the median rank of 15.5 should be approximately equal. The fact that eleven of the fifteen participants above the median are experimental participants suggests that the independent variable had an effect. A statement of the number of experimental and control participants above the median rank in combination with the results of an appropriate statistical test should demonstrate the effect of the independent variable. You will be able to analyze the results in Table 8-5 after reading Chapter 10.

Interval and Ratio Data

The task of describing the results of experiments in which interval or ratio data are obtained is more involved than with a lower level of measurement because of the need to compute measures of central tendency and variability. However, such computations are not difficult. Often the problem is deciding what measures to compute and how to present them. Once more, we will use examples to indicate some of the difficulties investigators may encounter.

One Independent Variable. An investigator uses a two-group, random-groups design to assess the effect of a driver education program on subsequent driving performance. The facilities at the school are limited, so only half of the students who want to take the driver education course can be accepted. To be fair, the students are randomly selected. This set of circumstances, though unfortunate from the point of view of those not selected for the program, provides an excellent opportunity to evaluate the program's effectiveness.

The independent variable is whether or not the student has received the driver education program. There are fifty students in each condition. Those not selected for the program learn to drive by other methods such as self-instruction or instruction by a parent or sibling. The dependent measure is the number of arrests for driving violations in the ten-year period after learning to drive. Assume that the investigator has no difficulty learning the number of arrests for each subject. How should the results be described?

The score for each subject is, of course, the number of arrests in the ten-year period. The effect of the independent variable is assessed by comparing the average performance of the two groups. In most experiments in which interval data are obtained, the mean will be selected as the best measure of central tendency. However, if the distribution is markedly skewed, the median is likely to be a better indicator because the mean is influenced greatly by extreme scores. In this case, let us assume that the distribution of scores in each group is fairly symmetrical. Thus, the first task is to obtain the mean number of arrests for the two groups. Assume that the mean was 2.13 arrests for the driver education group and 3.07 for the control group. Is this all the information needed to describe the results of the experiment?

It is necessary to know the mean performance of the two groups, but this information is not sufficient to assess whether the independent variable had an effect. It is not clear whether the obtained result is a common or rare outcome if only chance is operating. Therefore, an appropriate statistical test must be performed to determine whether the null hypothesis can be rejected. The important point is that the results of many experiments in which interval data are obtained can be adequately described by presenting the mean for each treatment condition and the results of an appropriate statistical test.

It is also a good idea to present a measure of variability, usually the standard deviation, for each condition. By comparing the standard deviations one can determine whether the treatments influenced the fluctuations within conditions, make predictions about the effect of treatments on variability as well as on mean performance, and estimate chance fluctuation. Statistical tests can be used to assess whether the conditions differ significantly, but many investigators prefer to present a measure of the variability within each condition as well. There is no set rule about presenting measures of variability. Some readers prefer to see a measure of variability for each condition. Others are satisfied with a measure of central tendency (usually a mean) and the results of statistical tests. It is a good idea to present measures of variability whenever convenient, since some readers will appreciate having this information.

Factorial Design Example. You believe that the important variable determining the accident rate on the highways is alcohol, not driver education. To be sure, you have nothing against driver education, but you believe that alcohol consumption is a much more important consideration. Statistics from law enforcement agencies support your view in that a large percentage of traffic accidents (usually 50 percent or more) are alcohol-related. The task is, therefore, to convince people that alcohol and driving is a very dangerous combination. This is hardly new; the relationship between drinking and traffic accidents has been known for years.

The problem, you believe, is that most people do not appreciate how alcohol influences their ability to drive. Driving is, after all, a relatively simple task in many instances. Under ideal conditions we can daydream while driving and still manage to keep our car on the road. You have probably had the experience, perhaps while driving on a superhighway under ideal conditions (dry pavement, light traffic, good visibility), of suddenly realizing that you have no recollection of the driving experiences of the past twenty minutes or so because you were deeply engaged in daydreaming. We can, you argue, drive under some conditions with little or no mental effort, although if conditions are not good (heavy fog, icy roads) we cannot daydream while driving and still manage to keep the car on the road or avoid accidents. It is difficult to convince many drinkers not to drive, you reason, because driving frequently does not require much mental effort. When it does, the drinker is more likely to have an accident because alcohol influences the amount of mental capacity he or she has available to allocate to the driving task. It is known, for example, that the eye movements of the drunk behind the steering wheel are considerably different from those of the nondrinker. The nondrinker scans the environment whereas the drunk is more likely to fixate on a single object such as the car ahead.

You perform a 2 by 2 factorial experiment in which you vary the amount of alcohol as one independent variable and the difficulty of the driving task as the second independent variable. You measure the number of errors on the driving tests as your dependent measure. You randomly assign forty adults to the four conditions of your experiment with the only restriction being that ten participants will be in each condition. Once you have completed the experiment, how do you describe the results? There should be little doubt that you need to compute measures of central tendency — in this case means — and variability. You want to know the mean performance for each condition so that you can determine whether your independent variables actually had an effect. The results for the hypothetical experiment are presented in Table 8-6.

An examination of the results reveals that, indeed, the difficult task was more difficult for the drivers than the easy task and that alcohol influenced the number of errors on the driving tests. Moreover, it appears that the effect of alcohol depended on the difficulty of the driving test because the effect was considerably greater for the difficult than for the easy test. The point here is that an examination of the mean performance for each condition frequently provides us with a clear picture of the results. If there are big differences between conditions and relatively small variability within conditions, as is the case here, it is likely that significant differences will be obtained. A statistical test is needed to test for significance in most cases, however. Even with the clear results presented in Table 8-6 we would still perform a statistical test to determine the likelihood of the particular outcome (the experimental results) if only chance were operating. We will consider a statistical test appro-

TABLE 8-6

The Mean Number of Errors and the Standard Deviations for the Four Conditions of the Alcohol and Driving Experiment (fictitious data)

Alcohol	Statistic	Type of driving test	
		Easy	Difficult
Yes	$\overline{X}$	5.00	30.00
	s	2.25	4.85
No	$\overline{X}$	4.50	8.00
	s	1.00	1.50

priate for this hypothetical experiment in Chapter 11. The results presented in Table 8-6 could also be presented in the form of a graph, as in Figure 8-4. Notice that mean performance is plotted in the figure.

Evaluation cannot be clearly separated from description. One can argue that the evaluation of a particular result is one step in the description process; that is, determining whether a particular outcome is a rare or common event if chance only is operating can be considered a descriptive task. However, some readers will prefer to distinguish between the procedures involved in obtaining descriptive measures, which are discussed in this chapter, and the statistical tests involved in deciding to reject or not to reject the null hypothesis. Bear in mind, however, that it may not be necessary to use statistical tests to evaluate a particular outcome. The distinction between describing and evaluating results is not always clear.

SUMMARY

There are four levels of measurement: nominal, ordinal, interval, and ratio. A nominal classification system is one in which the categories are qualitatively related. An ordinal scale is one in which the scale values are quantitatively related, but the differences between successive values are not necessarily equal. An interval scale has the properties of an ordinal scale *and* equal differences between successive scale values. A ratio scale has all the properties of an interval scale plus an absolute zero. The level of measurement determines how data can be described and evaluated.

There are two major sets of descriptive measures: measures of central tendency and measures of variability. The mode, median, and mean are

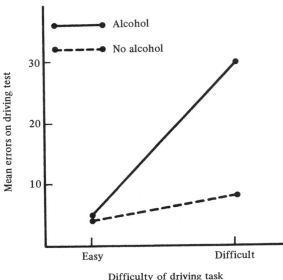

FIGURE 8–4

*The mean errors on the driving test for the four
conditions of the experiment*

measures of central tendency. The mode is the most frequently occurring score. The median is the value that divides the distribution in half after the scores are placed in ascending or descending rank order. The mean is the arithmetic average. For most investigators the mean is the most useful and the mode the least useful measure of central tendency. The range, variance, and standard deviation are measures of variability. The range is the difference between the smallest and the largest score. The variance is the average squared deviation from the mean. The standard deviation is the square root of the variance. Standard deviations are useful as units of measurement.

We can express relative standing by indicating the number of standard deviation units above or below the mean of the distribution that a particular score is. Many distributions have similar properties in that scores pile up around the mean and decline symmetrically on both sides of the mean so that there are about as many scores above as below the mean and the same percentage of scores at various distances from the mean when standard deviation units are used. For example, 34 percent of the scores fall between the mean and 1 standard deviation above the mean. Distributions with these properties are labeled as normal or, when expressed in terms of z-scores, as standard normal. Normal distributions are important because many frequency distributions and sampling distributions are normal or nearly so. If raw scores from a normal distribution are transformed to z-scores, the distribution of the z-scores will be the same as the original distribution. If raw scores are transformed to percentile ranks, the shape of the original distribution will be changed.

The type of descriptive measure that is computed and the way the data are reported depend on the level of measurement. If nominal data are obtained, the results can be described by indicating the number of subjects assigned to each category. If ordinal data are obtained, the results can frequently be described by indicating the number of experimental subjects above the median rank plus the results of an appropriate statistical test. If interval data are obtained, it is usually necessary to compute mean scores for each treatment. Tables are particularly useful when there are many means *and* measures of variability (such as standard deviations) to report. Investigators who prefer to present measures of variability usually use tables instead of figures because tables allow them to present measures of variability more easily.

QUESTIONS

(The answers to most of the questions and problems are given in Appendix D.)

1. What level of measurement is obtained in each of these examples? Why?
    a. Three hundred subjects are asked to give their political party preference: Republican, Democratic, or Independent.
    b. The thirty members of a class are ranked according to height. The shortest person is assigned the number 1; the second shortest, the number 2, and so on.
    c. A thirty-item questionnaire designed to measure altruism is administered to 100 people. A score from 1 to 30 is obtained for each person.
    d. The independent variable is whether subjects use the new "hair grower" scalp treatment. The dependent variable is the number of hairs in a square-inch patch on the top of each subject's head.
    e. A free association test is administered. The amount of time each person takes to respond to each word is the performance measure. An average responding time is computed for each subject.
    f. Three judges rate twenty subjects on cooperation. Each judge rates each subject on a nine-point scale from 1 (very uncooperative) to 9 (very cooperative). The median of the three judgments is used as the score for each subject.
2. Each of ten subjects was given a twenty-item current events test. The number of correct responses for each subject is given below. What are the mode, median, and mean scores? The scores are: 8, 13, 16, 14, 12, 13, 19, 6, 10, and 9.
3. What are the mode, median, and mean for the following scores: 10, 14, 16, 16, 14, 16, 14, 14, 16, 14, 16, 20?

4. What are the mode, median, and mean for the following scores: 18, 19, 3, 4, 8, 15, 2, 3, 3, 5? Is one measure of central tendency preferred over the others?

5. If you were interested in buying a new home, would you be more interested in the median or mean price of homes for your particular geographical area? Why?

6. Assume that you have the money and the inclination to sponsor a young golfer on the professional tour. Golfer A has a mean score of 72 and a standard deviation of 4 for 100 rounds. Golfer B has a mean score of 71.5 and a standard deviation of 2 for the same 100 rounds. Which golfer would you sponsor and why? (There is no right or wrong answer to this question.)

7. Compute the range, variance, and standard deviation for each set of scores given in questions 2, 3, and 4.

8. What is the advantage of using the standard deviation as a unit of measurement?

9. Jane has taken two tests of self-esteem. On the first test she had a score of 25. The mean for the first test was 20 and the standard deviation was 4. On the second test she scored 78. The mean for the second test was 70 and the standard deviation was 9. Which test indicates that Jane has higher self-esteem? Assume that the scores on both tests are normally distributed.

10. What are z-scores and why are they important?

11. What are the properties of normal distributions?

12. What is the probability of obtaining a z-score of +2.00 or greater given random selection and a standard normal distribution?

13. Give an example of a linear transformation and a nonlinear transformation and indicate what is meant by linearity.

14. Why is the level of measurement an important consideration when determining how the results of experiments should be described?

15. The numbers that athletes wear on their uniforms are best classified at the _____ level of measurement. (1) nominal   (2) ordinal   (3) interval   (4) ratio

16. If differences between categories are of kind (such as political parties), the categories are best classified as _____ measurement. (1) nominal   (2) ordinal   (3) interval   (4) ratio

17. Ordinal scales and interval scales differ in that   (1) the interval scale has an absolute zero   (2) the ordinal scale is used only for categorical data   (3) ordinal scales reflect qualitative changes whereas interval scales reflect quantitative changes   (4) the distance between successive units is equal for interval scales

18. If we rank-order the students in a class of fifteen according to leadership potential, we would have an example of _____ measurement.   (1) nominal   (2) ordinal   (3) interval   (4) ratio

19. The median is   (1) the score that appears most frequently   (2) the middle score   (3) the arithmetic average   (4) the modal score

20. Several extreme scores in a distribution are likely to affect the value of the   (1) median more than the mean   (2) mean more than the median   (3) median and the mean equally   (4) mode the most

21. The measure obtained by subtracting the smallest score from the largest is called the   (1) standard deviation   (2) variance   (3) z-score   (4) range

22. The _____ of a sample is the sum of the squared deviations from the mean divided by the number of scores minus one.   (1) standard deviation   (2) variance   (3) range   (4) z-score

$$\frac{\varepsilon(x - \bar{x})^2}{N - 1}$$

23. The variance or standard deviation of a distribution can never be   (1) greater than the mean   (2) less than the mean   (3) less than one   (4) negative

24. The _____ is used as a reference point when computing variance.   (1) median   (2) mode   (3) range   (4) mean

25. The standard deviation is equal to the square root of the   (1) range   (2) z-score   (3) mean   (4) variance

26. A small standard deviation indicates that   (1) scores are equal above and below the mean   (2) the median is greater than the mode   (3) scores are grouped closely around the mean   (4) the distribution is normal

⑨ Correlation

Our interest in this unit is in the relationship between two variables (bivariate data). We have bivariate data any time we obtain two measures for each object or event considered (for example, two measures for each person). In Chapter 2 we learned that the correlational approach makes it possible to specify the degree of relationship between variables, to predict performance, and to test rival hypotheses about the relationships among variables. Now it is time to consider correlation in greater detail. We will look primarily at the steps in computing three correlation coefficients: the phi coefficient, and the rank-order and product-moment correlations. Scattergrams are used in the second section, where we discuss possible relationships between variables and the role of correlational techniques in studying these relationships. The final section is devoted primarily to a variance view of correlation in which the product-moment correlation is emphasized.

COMPUTING CORRELATION COEFFICIENTS

The procedures that can be used to assess the degree of relationship between variables depend on the level of measurment for each variable. The phi coefficient can be computed if both variables are nominal. The rank-order correlation is appropriate if both variables are ordinal. The Pearson product-moment is appropriate if interval or ratio data are obtained.

Nominal Data and the Phi Coefficient

The phi (ϕ) coefficient is useful for assessing the degree of relationship between two variables when each variable is at the nominal level of measurement and dichotomous (that is, there are only two levels of each variable).

214

TABLE 9–1

The Number of Defendants in Each of the Four Classifications Determined by Verdict and Sex (fictitious data)

Sex	Verdict Convicted	Acquitted	Row total
Female	a 20	b 45	j = 65
Male	c 30	d 25	k = 55
Column total	l = 50	m = 70	

For example, we can evaluate the relationship between a number of subject variables and the outcome of court trials. You might be interested in whether there is a relationship between the sex of the defendant and the outcome of jury trials. You consider 120 consecutive jury trials in which the defendant was acquitted or found guilty. Thus, one variable is the verdict (acquitted versus convicted), and the other is sex (male versus female). Imagine that you obtain the results presented in Table 9-1. We can assess the degree of association between these two variables by computing the phi coefficient.

The formula for the phi coefficient is

$$\phi = \frac{(bc - ad)}{\sqrt{(j)(k)(l)(m)}}$$

where a, b, c, and d refer to the frequencies in the four cells of the 2 by 2 contingency table. In this case, $a = 20$, $b = 45$, $c = 30$, and $d = 25$. The letters j and k refer to the two row totals, and the letters l and m refer to the two column totals. In this case, $j = 65$, $k = 55$, $l = 50$, and $m = 70$. If we insert these values in the formula for the phi coefficient we obtain the following result:

$$\phi = \frac{(45)(30) - (20)(25)}{\sqrt{(65)(55)(50)(70)}}$$

$$\phi = \frac{1350 - 500}{\sqrt{12,512,500}}$$

$$\phi = \frac{850}{3537}$$

$$\phi = .24$$

There is a low positive relationship between sex and verdict. Females are more likely to be acquitted than males. (Remember that these data are fictitious.) Yet the relationship is not strong because the correlation is only .24. The phi coefficient value and the other correlation coefficients to be considered shortly can assume any value from −1.00 to +1.00. Now let us assume that we obtained the results in Table 9-2 instead of those in Table 9-1. A comparison of the results presented in the two tables reveals that the degree of relationship between the two variables is considerably higher in Table 9-2. If all the females are acquitted and all the males are convicted, the relationship between the verdict variable and sex is as high as it can be. We can predict the verdict accurately if we know the sex of the defendant; if we know the verdict, we can predict the sex of the defendant. In short, the accuracy of prediction is related to the degree of relationship. We are not able to accurately predict verdict from sex if the correlation is .24, as is the case for the results presented in Table 9-1. Given the results in Table 9-1, we are more likely to be correct if we predict that a male will be convicted than if we predict that he will be acquitted, but we are likely to be wrong some of the time.

The value of the phi coefficient for the results presented in Table 9-2 is 1.00. The value for the phi coefficient would be −1.00 if either the rows or the columns were interchanged (for example, if males were placed in the *a* and *b* categories and females in the *c* and *d* categories). The sign of the phi coefficient (plus or minus) does not have any meaning. You should expect this because nominal measurement indicates a qualitative distinction not a quantitative one. The sign for the phi coefficient depends on how we arrange the 2 by 2 contingency table. The magnitude of the phi coefficient depends, of course, on the actual relationship between the two variables.

It is possible to examine the relationship between a number of subject variables (sex, wealth, race, education) and the verdict variable, but caution

TABLE 9–2

The Number of Defendants in Each of the Four Classifications Determined by Verdict and Sex (fictitious data)

Sex	Verdict		Row total
	Convicted	Acquitted	
Female	*a* 0	*b* 65	*j* = 65
Male	*c* 55	*d* 0	*k* = 55
Column total	*l* = 55	*m* = 65	

should be exercised when interpreting the results. A high phi coefficient might mean that the judicial system is biased, but other interpretations are also possible. For example, if your results indicate that males are more likely to be convicted than females, it may be that more males are actually guilty. A high phi coefficient should be viewed as a phenomenon to be explained.

Ordinal Data and the Rank-order Correlation   *quantitative* 1-5

Computation of the Rank-order Correlation. Assume that you are interested in the relationship between self-esteem and alcohol consumption. You believe that at least some people drink to escape reality and that they "need" to escape because they have a low opinion of themselves. You decide to check your view by assessing the degree of relationship between these two variables. Clearly, there are likely to be numerous problems involved in obtaining valid measures of self-esteem and alcohol consumption, but we will ignore these problems. Instead, we will assume that you managed to rank order twelve individuals according to alcohol consumption and self-esteem to obtain the results presented in Table 9-3.

The numbers in the table indicate the individual's relative ranking on alcohol consumption and self-esteem with the number 1 assigned to the person with the lowest rank and the number 12 to the person with the highest. For example, Mary has the rank of 1 on alcohol consumption and 8 on self-esteem, meaning that she consumes less alcohol than any of the twelve and has more self-esteem than seven of the twelve individuals. There are no tied ranks in Table 9-3, but in some cases there might be. For example, judges may be unable to decide whether Millie or Gloria consumes more alcohol. In this case, the two ranks in question can be added $(11 + 12 = 23)$ and both participants given the mean of the tied ranks (11.5). If there are a large number of tied scores on a particular measure, the formula given below would not be appropriate. For the present example, we might anticipate a high negative relationship, as we expect self-esteem to decrease as alcohol consumption increases. Since rank data are obtained, a rank-order correlation can be computed. The formula for computing the rank-order correlation is

$$r_s = 1 - \frac{6(\Sigma d^2)}{N(N^2 - 1)}$$

In this formula r_s is used to designate the rank-order correlation. The sigma (Σ) is a symbol for the summing operation. The symbol d refers to the difference between the ranks for each subject. In this case d^2 follows the summation sign, so the squared difference scores are added. The N refers to the number of pairs of scores, in this case 12. The 1 and 6 are always used in this formula and therefore they are called constants. Investigators use the

TABLE 9-3

The Two Sets of Rankings for Twelve Adults and the Computation of the Rank-Order Correlation

Person	Alcohol	Esteem	d	d^2
Mary	1	8	−7	49
Pete	2	3	−1	1
Sam	3	10	−7	49
Larry	4	6	−2	4
Bertha	5	7	−2	4
Gwen	6	1	5	25
Richard	7	12	−5	25
Jean	8	11	−3	9
Dean	9	5	4	16
Fred	10	9	1	1
Millie	11	2	9	81
Gloria	12	4	8	64

Sum of d^2 = 328

$$r_s = 1 - \frac{6(\Sigma d^2)}{N(N^2 - 1)}$$

$N = 12$

$$r_s = 1 - \frac{6(328)}{12(144 - 1)}$$

$$r_s = 1 - \frac{1968}{1716}$$

$$r_s = 1 - 1.147$$

$$r_s = -.147$$

Note: The symbol *d* is used to indicate the difference between the rankings for each person.

symbol r_s for the rank-order correlation when it is computed for a sample and the Greek letter rho (ρ) when it is computed for the population.

Magnitude of the Rank-order Correlation. The magnitude of the rank-order correlation indicates the degree of relationship between two variables. It is free to fluctuate between −1.00 and +1.00. Notice that if the two sets of rankings were identical, all the difference scores would be zero and, of course, the sum of the squared differences would also be zero. Since six multiplied by zero is zero, the numerator would be zero. And since zero divided by any number is zero, the second term of the equation would be zero. Thus the value of r_s when the two sets of ranks are identical is equal to +1.00.

When you have a set of rankings as in the present example, only the sum of the squared difference scores is free to vary. You should experiment with different sets of rankings, computing the sum of the squared difference scores until you are convinced that r_s tends to be close to $+1.00$ when subjects with a high rank on one measure have a high rank on the other, middle ranks go with middle ranks, and low ranks with low, and that r_s tends to be close to -1.00 when subjects with a high rank on one measure have a low rank on the other and middle ranks go with middle. The rank-order correlation tends to be about zero when individuals with a high rank on one measure may have a high, middle, or low rank on the other measure. In short, r_s varies from -1.00 to $+1.00$ depending on the degree and type of relationship between the two variables.

For the present example, there appears to be little support for the view that alcohol consumption is related to self-esteem. This may mean that there is actually little relationship between the two measures or that we simply failed to detect a relationship that actually exists. If a high negative relationship had been obtained, this would not necessarily indicate that the relationship was causal. And, if the relationship had, in fact, been causal, the direction of the cause-effect relationship would still be uncertain. Excessive drinking might result in a lowering of self-esteem, or a lowering of self-esteem might cause one to turn to drink. Thus, as before, a high degree of relationship between variables can be viewed as a phenomenon to be explained.

Interval Data and the Product-Moment Correlation

ratio scale   *quantitative & successive values*

In general, the comments made about the rank-order correlation are appropriate for the product-moment correlation except that the rank-order is used for ordinal data and product-moment for interval data. To demonstrate the steps involved in computing the product-moment correlation, we can consider the relationship between decision making and happiness. For the decision-making variable, people are asked to list the number of excellent, important decisions they have made in the past decade. For the happiness rating, you have developed a test which yields a score from 1 to 10. A person who obtains a score of 1 is very unhappy (dissatisfied); a person with a score of 10 is very happy. We will assume that the measures are reliable and valid and yield interval-level data or better. For ease in computation we consider the results for six participants only. The results and the computation of the Pearson product-moment correlation are presented in Table 9–4. A calculator, particularly one that has a square root function, is very useful for computations at this level of difficulty.

Computation of the Product-Moment Correlation. The formula and computations in Table 9-4 require some explanation. The X refers to the number of important, excellent decisions (such as deciding to go to college, choice of spouse) each participant made in the last ten years, the Y to each participant's score on your Happiness Test, and the N to the number of participants

TABLE 9-4

The Happiness Score and the Number of Excellent Decisions for Six Participants and the Product-Moment Correlation for These Measures (fictitious data)

Participant	Decisions (X)	Happiness (Y)	XY
A	5	2	10
B	5	6	30
C	10	4	40
D	10	8	80
E	15	6	90
F	15	10	150
	$\Sigma X = 60$	$\Sigma Y = 36$	$\Sigma XY = 400$
	$\Sigma X^2 = 700$	$\Sigma Y^2 = 256$	

$$r = \frac{N\Sigma XY - (\Sigma X)(\Sigma Y)}{\sqrt{N\Sigma X^2 - (\Sigma X)^2]\ [N\Sigma Y^2 - (\Sigma Y)^2]}}$$

$$r = \frac{6(400) - (60)(36)}{\sqrt{[6(700) - (60)^2]\ [6(256) - (36)^2]}}$$

$$r = \frac{2400 - 2160}{\sqrt{[4200 - 3600]\ [1536 - 1296]}}$$

$$r = \frac{240}{\sqrt{[600]\ [240]}}$$

$$r = \frac{240}{\sqrt{144000}}$$

$$r = \frac{240}{379.47}$$

$$r = .63$$

considered (pairs of scores). The sigma (Σ) indicates that the summing operation is performed. Thus, for ΣX you would sum the X scores. For ΣX^2 you would sum the squared X scores. It is important to distinguish between the ΣX^2 and the $(\Sigma X)^2$. The ΣX^2 means that each score is squared and then the *squared scores* are summed. The $(\Sigma X)^2$ means that the scores are summed and then the *total score* is squared. The same is true for ΣY^2 and $(\Sigma Y)^2$. For ΣXY you would multiply each XY pair and sum the products. This is all done for you in Table 9-4. After completing these computations, you insert the values into the formula and compute the correlation.

Magnitude of the Product-Moment Correlation. Once again, the magnitude of the correlation depends on the pairings of scores. That is, some index is needed of the extent to which high X scores go with high Y scores. The product-moment correlation is an excellent index of this relationship. The magnitude of the correlation indicates whether the number of excellent, important decisions is related to the scores obtained on the Happiness Test.

The magnitude of the correlation is unrelated to the absolute magnitudes of the scores; the correlation would be unaffected if 25 were added to the score of each participant. The important consideration is whether the high scores for one measure (number of excellent decisions) are paired with the high scores of the other measure (score on Happiness Test). If you keep the same set of scores for the decision measure and the same set for the happiness measure and manipulate the pairings, you will, of course, produce marked changes in the obtained product-moment correlation. These changes will, however, influence only one term in the product-moment correlation formula, namely $N\Sigma XY$. The values for the other terms will remain the same. Thus, to demonstrate that the product-moment correlation assesses the extent to which high scores go with high scores, just manipulate the pairings and note the result. The sum of the X times Y cross-products is the largest when high scores of X are paired with high scores of Y.

SCATTERGRAMS AND CORRELATION

Nature of Scattergrams

The computation of the correlation coefficient provides a single measure of the degree of relationship between two variables, but this measure, by itself, may not provide a complete picture of the relationship between the variables. For cases in which interval data are obtained, we can usually get a better understanding of the relationship between two variables if we make a scattergram *and* compute the correlation. A scattergram (sometimes called a scatterplot) is a plot of the scores made by the same individuals on two different variables presented in the form of a figure. Four scattergrams are presented in Figure 9-1. The values for one variable are presented on the abscissa and the values for the second on the ordinate. Since each subject has a score for each measure, each subject's performance can be represented as a dot. The location of the dot for each person is determined by his or her score on the two measures being considered. Figure 9-1A shows the name of the person represented by each dot. For example, Alice has a score of 40 on the attractiveness measure and 90 on the academic success measure. Pete has a score of 18 on the attractiveness measure and 23 on the academic success measure.

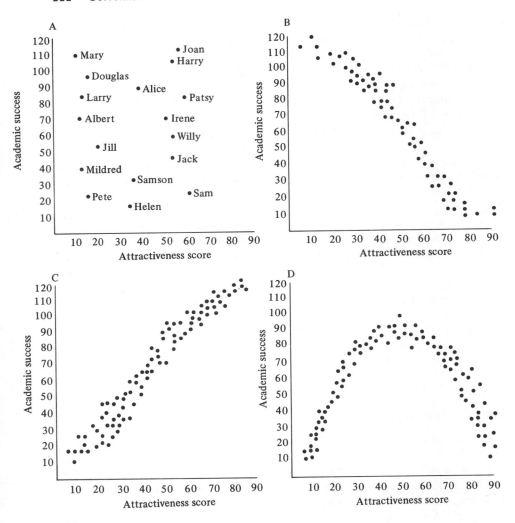

FIGURE 9-1

The scattergram for four relationships between physical attractiveness and academic success (fictitious data)

The first three scattergrams in Figure 9-1 represent, respectively, a zero, a negative, and a positive correlation between the two variables. The fourth plot represents a more complex relationship, to be discussed shortly. You may wish to examine the plot that corresponds to each of these three relationships. Remember that a high positive correlation is obtained when high scores go with high scores, low with low, and middle with middle. When high scores go with low scores and middle scores with middle, a high negative correlation is obtained. In a zero correlation, individuals with high scores on one measure may have high, medium, or low scores on the second measure, or the relationship may be nonlinear. What is the real relationship between attractiveness and academic success? Can you think of reasons why each of the four relationships depicted in Figure 9-1 might be obtained? After we know the facts, it is usually a relatively simple matter to "justify" any obtained result.

The Relationship Between Variables

The scattergrams in Figure 9-1 show linear and nonlinear relationships between the two variables. When two variables are linearly related, an increase in one is accompanied by a constant increase (or a decrease if the variables have a negative relationship) in the other for the entire range of both variables. The effect of an increase in one variable on the other variable does not depend on the value considered. For example, if $Y = 2X$, the variables Y and X are linearly related. If X increases one unit, Y always increases two units.

When two variables have a *perfect* linear relationship, all the dots of the scattergram can be connected by a single straight line. The scattergrams in Figure 9-1B and C do not depict a perfect linear relationship, but they do describe a linear relationship because a single straight line could be drawn that would describe the relationship between the two variables reasonably well. Such a line could be drawn in Figure 9-1B, for example, because an increase in X (attractiveness) is, in general, accompanied by a constant decrease in Y (academic success) for the entire range of both variables. The scattergram in Figure 9-1D, on the other hand, is not linear. A single straight line would not describe the relationship between the two variables.

Let us consider another figure in order to discuss linearity and monotonicity. Four relationships between variables X and Y are plotted in Figure 9-2. Figure 9-2A depicts a linear relationship. Linear relationships are also monotonic, but monotonic relationships are not necessarily linear. When two variables have a positive monotonic relationship an increase in one is accompanied by an increase in the other, but the increase is not necessarily the same for the entire range of both variables. For example, if $Y = X^3$, the two variables X and Y are monotonically but not linearly related. An increase in X is accompanied by an increase in Y, but each increase in X will not increase Y by the same amount. This relationship is depicted in Figure 9-2B. A relationship is nonmonotonic if an increase in one variable is sometimes accompanied by an increase and sometimes by a decrease in the other variable. For example, in Figure 9-2C and D an increase in X is sometimes accompanied by a decrease in Y and sometimes by an increase in Y.

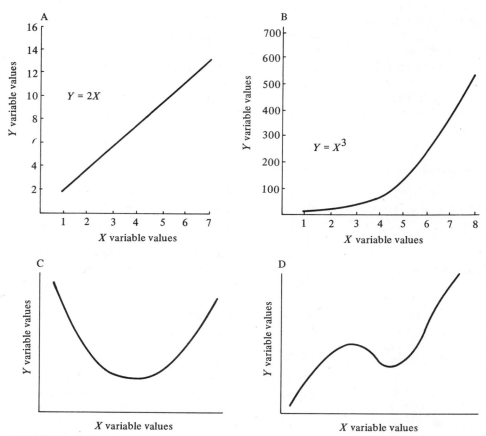

FIGURE 9–2

The relationship between variables X and Y is linear in A and nonlinear in B, C, and D. (The curves in A and B both represent monotonic relationships between variables X and Y. The curves in C and D are nonmonotonic.)

Correlation and the Relationship Between Variables

The Pearson product-moment correlation is useful for assessing the degree to which two variables are linearly related. The magnitude of the correlation, when all else is equal, is related to the extent to which the dots of the scatter-gram cluster around a straight line. The correlation for the results depicted in Figure 9-1C is higher than for the results depicted in Figure 9-1D because we can draw a single straight line that will be close to the data points in the former case but not in the latter. Since the product-moment correlation is designed for assessing the extent to which two variables are linearly related, it is usually not useful for assessing nonmonotonic or nonlinear relationships.

The Spearman rank-order correlation allows us to (assess the monotonicity) of two variables because we ignore the amount of increase in *Y* accompanying an increase in *X* when we rank order. For example, if we rank fifteen people on the basis of height, we do not measure the difference in height for people assigned successive ranks. The difference in height between subjects 3 and 4 may be much greater than the difference between subjects 14 and 15. Because we ignore the absolute difference (or we do not assess it in the first place) between successive ranks, we cannot say whether an increase in one variable is accompanied by a *constant* increase in the other. All we assess is the extent to which an increase in one variable means an increase in the other. Thus, a high rank-order correlation can be obtained if the two variables are monotonically related, even though they are not linearly related. It follows that investigators should not claim that two variables are *linearly* related just because a high rank-order correlation is obtained. They *may* be linearly related, but some monotonic relationships are nonlinear. A scattergram is a useful means of assessing whether the relationship is linear, monotonic, or nonmonotonic. (None of the correlational techniques discussed allows us to assess nonmonotonic relations.) A consideration of these is beyond the scope of this text; we can, however, plot the results in a scattergram to gain a pictorial representation of the relationship.

Regression

The regression line is the straight line drawn so that the sum of the squared deviations from each point to the line is a minimum. That is, we select the line that gives us the smallest sum when we add all the squared deviations from each point to the line. If the correlation is not perfect we can draw two regression lines: one to minimize the sum of the squared deviations when considering horizontal distance and one to minimize the sum of the squared deviations when considering vertical distance. We can consider whether individuals with the same score on *X* differ in their performance on the *Y* variable, or we can consider whether individuals with the same score on *Y* differ in their performance on the *X* variable. Fortunately we only need to discuss one of the regression lines because the principles to be considered are the same for both. We will consider the extent to which people with the same score on *X* differ in their performance on the *Y* variable. That is, we will consider how accurately we can predict a person's score on the *Y* variable if we know the person's score on *X*. We can always define the known score as *X* and the score we want to predict as *Y*.

The magnitude of the correlation, all else being equal, is determined by the extent to which the data points hug the regression line. If all the points fall on the regression line, the correlation is either +1.00 or −1.00, as in

Figures 9-3A and B. When this correlation is obtained, we can predict Y accurately if we know X. If the points do not cluster around the regression line, the correlation will be low, as in Figure 9-3C. Then, knowing X will not tell us very much about Y. We can still predict a Y score given X, but we cannot expect our prediction to be accurate. It is better to use the regression line to make the prediction than to simply predict the mean score for the Y variable (that is, predict the mean score for Y regardless of the value of X) because X and Y are still related. Subjects who have high scores on X will still have higher Y scores than those who have low scores on X. A moderately high correlation is depicted in Figure 9-3D. Our predictions about Y when we know X should be more accurate for Figure 9-3D than for Figure 9-3C because the data points are closer to the regression line.

The scattergrams presented in Figure 9-3 should enable you to see that the accuracy of prediction is related to the extent to which the data points fall on the regression line. However, you should *not* conclude that scattergrams are

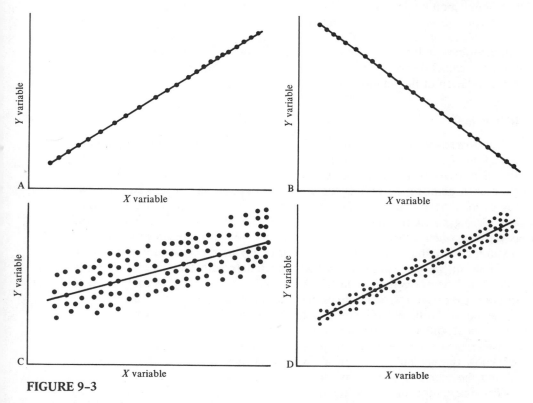

FIGURE 9–3

The scattergrams and regression lines for four different relationships between variables X *and* Y

used for making these predictions or that regression lines are determined by simply drawing the straight line that appears to minimize the sum of the squared deviations from each point to the regression line. A procedure called the method of least squares is used to determine the *equation* for the regression line, and the accuracy of prediction is quantified by calculating the standard error of estimate. We will not consider these statistical methods because the methods, though of interest to investigators who use correlation for prediction, are not essential for computing and understanding correlation.

In summary, we can make scattergrams to represent pictorially the relationship between two variables. The scattergram provides information about the linearity and monotonicity of the relationship and about its magnitude. The magnitude of the correlation, when all else is equal, is directly related to the extent to which the data points hug the regression line. When all the data points are on the line, the correlation is perfect ($+1.00$ or -1.00). Correlation can be used for prediction because we can predict performance if we know a subject's score on one variable (X-score) and the regression line for the two variables (obtained from the data of other subjects, of course). The accuracy of our prediction is directly related to the magnitude of the correlation between the two variables.

UNDERSTANDING CORRELATION

Estimation

The correlation obtained with a sample (a statistic) can be used to estimate the correlation between two variables (a parameter) when the sample is randomly selected from the larger population. The accuracy of the estimate should increase, all things being equal, as the size of the sample increases. If the sample is not randomly selected, then using the sample correlation to estimate the correlation in the population is not warranted. Even when the sample is random, a correlation of considerable magnitude may be due to chance; that is, it may be obtained even though the two variables are unrelated in the population.

When the two variables are unrelated, subjects with a high score on one variable may have a high, medium, or low score on the other. If, by chance, the investigator selects more individuals who have similar scores on the two variables than dissimilar scores, she may conclude, erroneously, that the two variables are related. A table to assess the statistical significance of rank-order correlation is presented in Appendix C-7, and a table to assess the statistical significance of product-moment correlations is presented in Appendix C-8. These tables allow us to determine whether an obtained correlation can reasonably be attributed to chance. If the correlation exceeds the table value, we can reject the null hypothesis that the population correlation is zero.

Variance and Correlation

In our earlier statement — the magnitude of the correlation, all else being equal, is directly related to the extent to which the data points hug a straight line—the qualifier *all else being equal* is necessary because the magnitude of the correlation is not determined solely by the closeness of scores to the regression line. It is determined by their closeness relative to the total fluctuation in *Y*-scores, computed by calculating the variance. When we have scores on two variables (an *X*-score and a *Y*-score) for each subject, we can split the *Y* variance into two components: the variance that does not depend on changes in *X* (variance around the regression line) and the variance that does depend on changes in *X* (variance of the *Y'* or predicted scores).

To keep the computations as simple as possible, let us reconsider our earlier example of the relationship between decision making (*X*) and happiness (*Y*). A scattergram and regression line are presented in Figure 9-4. The first step is to compute the variance for the *Y*-scores.

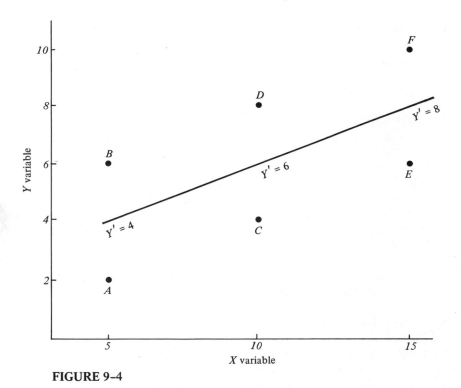

FIGURE 9-4

The scattergram for the hypothetical data presented in Table 9-5 and the regression line for predicting Y *given* X

The Variance for Y-scores. It is important that you keep in mind that our overall interest is in accounting for individual differences in performance, in this case happiness. Why is it that some people are happier than others? Our first step is to quantify the individual differences by computing the variance of the Y-scores. We want to know the extent to which people obtain different scores on the Happiness Test — the greater the fluctuation of these scores the more the individual differences in performance. The variance of the Y-scores is computed by the deviation method in Table 9-5. We determine the mean for the Y-scores, subtract the mean from each score, square each difference score, sum the squared scores, and divide by the number of scores minus one. Since we have both X- and Y-scores we use the symbol $\overline{Y}$ to indicate the mean for the Y-scores and Y to indicate any Y-score. We can now partition the fluctuations in Y into our two components.

Variance of Y-scores Independent of X. If fluctuations in Y are unrelated to or independent of changes in X, then the value of X is not responsible for the fluctuations in Y. If two individuals have the same X-score (that is, report having made the same number of excellent decisions) but different Y-scores (scores on the Happiness Test), we cannot attribute the difference between their Y-scores to X because their X-scores are the same. Something besides the number of excellent decisions must be responsible for the fact that they obtained different scores on the Happiness Test. We can determine the amount of variance in Y that is independent of changes in X by determining the fluctuation of the Y-scores around the regression line.

The computation of the variance in Y that is independent of changes in X is presented in Table 9-6. It is basically the same as that used for the total

TABLE 9–5

The X-scores and Y-scores for Each of Six Subjects and the Computation of the Variance for the Y-scores

Subject	X-scores	Y-scores	$(Y - \overline{Y})$	$(Y - \overline{Y})^2$
A	5	2	−4	16
B	5	6	0	0
C	10	4	−2	4
D	10	8	2	4
E	15	6	0	0
F	15	10	4	16
		Sum = 36		Sum = 40
		$\overline{Y} = 6$		

$$s^2 = \frac{\Sigma(Y - \overline{Y})^2}{n - 1} = \frac{40}{5} = 8$$

TABLE 9-6

*The Computation of the Variance in Y-scores That Is
Independent of Changes in the X-score for the Results
Presented in Table 9-5*

Subject	Y-score	Y'-score	(Y - Y')	(Y - Y')^2
A	2	4	-2	4
B	6	4	2	4
C	4	6	-2	4
D	8	6	2	4
E	6	8	-2	4
F	10	8	2	4
				Sum = 24

$$s^2 = \frac{\Sigma(Y - Y')^2}{n - 1} = \frac{24}{5} = 4.80$$

variance in Y. The difference is that we use Y' (called Y prime) instead of the mean for Y (Y' instead of $\overline{Y}$). Y' is the Y-score you would predict when you know X. Thus, if we obtain X-scores for additional subjects and use these scores to predict Y, we should expect subjects with a score of 15 on X to have higher Y-scores than subjects with a score of 5 on X. The predicted score is the point on the regression line. Over the long haul it results in the most accurate prediction of Y-scores. To determine the fluctuation of Y-scores for subjects with the same X-score, we determine the amount of fluctuation around the predicted score (regression line). The use of Y' in place of $\overline{Y}$ yields this variance. Notice that the variance in Y independent of changes in X is 4.80 (Table 9-6), less than the total variance in Y (8.00). The next step is to compute the variance in Y that is related to changes in X.

Variance of Y-*scores Related to* X. If we say that people get different Y-scores because they have different X-scores or that different Y-scores are related to different X-scores, we are saying that fluctuations in Y can be accounted for or "explained" in terms of X. The abilities necessary to do well on the Y test are the same as the abilities required to do well on the X test. Or the X variable might be directly responsible for the differences in the Y-scores. In our present example, the number of excellent decisions a person makes (going to college, selecting a good spouse) might be directly responsible for the amount of happiness he or she enjoys. If this is the case, we might expect that people who report having made a large number of excellent decisions will also have generally high scores on the Happiness Test. Those who report having made a low number of excellent decisions, in general, should have low scores on the Happiness Test. The interesting question is how much of the fluctuation of Y-scores (individual differences in happiness) we can relate to the quality of decision making.

If we want to account for individual differences in performance (happiness) we need to find the variables that account for the most fluctuation. An X variable that accounts for a large portion of the variance in Y-scores is, obviously, more important than an X variable that accounts for a small amount of the variance. The amount of variance accounted for is thus a "meterstick" by which we can evaluate the importance of X variables. The quality of decision making is more important if it accounts for 50 percent of the variance of the happiness scores than if it accounts for only 4 percent.

The computation of the variance in Y-scores related to changes in X-scores for our hypothetical example is presented in Table 9-7. If the variance of Y-scores is related to changes in X, we should predict different Y-scores when we know the X score. If we predict the same Y-score for all values of X, it should be clear that the X variable does not account for differences in performance on the Y variable. The amount of variance in Y-scores that is related to the X variable is a function of the variance of Y' (the predicted scores). The computation of the variance of Y'-scores is a simple matter in this case. Each subject has a Y'-score because there is a Y'-score for each of the three scores for the X variable; that is, a Y'-score can be assigned to each subject on the basis of his score on the X variable. The symbol $\overline{Y'}$ is used for the mean of the Y' scores. The variance in Y-scores related to changes in X is equal to 3.20. Notice that the variance in Y-scores related to changes in

TABLE 9-7

The Computation of the Variance in Y-scores That Is Related to Changes in the X-score for the Results Presented in Table 9-5

Subject	Y' score	$(Y' - \overline{Y'})$	$(Y' - \overline{Y'})^2$
A	4	−2	4
B	4	−2	4
C	6	0	0
D	6	0	0
E	8	2	4
F	8	2	4
	Sum = 36		Sum = 16
	$\overline{Y'} = 6$		

$$s^2 = \frac{\Sigma(Y' - \overline{Y'})^2}{n-1} = \frac{16}{5} = 3.20$$

X-scores is less than the total variance of the *Y*-scores. The variance in *Y*-scores related to changes in *X*-scores (3.20) plus the variance in *Y*-scores independent of changes in *X*-scores (4.80) is equal to the variance of the *Y*-scores (8.00). This is *always* the case. The ratio of the variance in *Y*-scores related to changes in *X* divided by the total variance of *Y*-scores gives us the portion of the *Y*-score variance that is accounted for (the explained variance). We can assess the relative importance of *X* variables if we know this ratio. Fortunately it is easily obtained when we know the correlation between the *X* and *Y* variables. The amount of *Y*-score variance that is related to the *X*-score is 3.20, and the total variance of the *Y*-scores is 8.00. Thus the amount of *Y*-score variance accounted for is 3.20/8.00 or .40. Forty percent of the *Y*-score fluctuations is related to changes in *X*-scores.

The Coefficient of Determination

The ratio of the *Y*-score variance related to *X* divided by the total *Y*-score variance is equal to r^2. As you will remember, the symbol r is used for the product-moment correlation. The square of r (r^2) is called the coefficient of determination. You can think of r^2 as the coefficient that allows us to determine how much of the variance of *Y*-scores is related to changes in *X*-scores. If we know the correlation it is very simple to compute the coefficient of determination; all we have to do is square r. For example, if $r = .30$, than $r^2 = .09$. In this case 9 percent of the variance of the *Y*-scores can be accounted for in terms of changes in *X*-scores.

Earlier we computed the correlation for the example we have been considering and obtained a correlation coefficient equal to .63 (see Table 9-4). Once we obtain the correlation, we simply square it to obtain the coefficient of determination. In this case r^2 is equal to .40. The point is that you do not have to perform the computations as we did in Tables 9-5, 9-6, and 9-7 to obtain the coefficient of determination. All you have to do is compute the Pearson product-moment correlation and then square the correlation coefficient that you obtain. This value is the amount of the fluctuation in *Y* related to changes in *X*. We discussed the fluctuation of *Y*-scores in terms of the two components in order to enable you to understand the usefulness of the coefficient of determination.

The coefficient of determination allows us to compare the importance of *X*-variables. We can say that a variable that accounts for 40 percent of the *Y*-score variance is more important than a variable that accounts for only 10 percent. Many investigators find the coefficient of determination a more useful measure than the correlation because the interpretation is clear. Although the two measures are closely related, the correlation has to be quite large before very much variance is accounted for. This can be seen by examining Table 9-8, but it can be seen most dramatically by comparing correlations of .00 and .10 with correlations of .90 and 1.00. A correlation of .10

TABLE 9-8

The Relationship Between the Magnitude of the Product-Moment Correlation and the Amount of Variance Accounted for (coefficient of determination)

Correlation	Variance accounted for (%)
.00	0
.10	1
.20	4
.30	9
.40	16
.50	25
.60	36
.70	49
.80	64
.90	81
1.00	100

accounts for 1 percent more variance than a correlation of zero. A correlation of 1.00 accounts for 19 percent more variance than a correlation of .90.

Range Restriction and Correlation

Our final task is to discuss factors that influence the magnitude of the correlation. There are three variances to consider: the total variance of the Y-scores, the Y-score variance related to changes in X-scores, and the Y-score variance unrelated to changes in X-scores. Because the total variance of the Y-scores is equal to the sum of the other two, it follows that once we know two we can determine the third. That is, we can compute the correlation if we know two of these variances. We cannot compute the correlation if we know only one. It is not completely correct to say that the magnitude of the correlation is a function of the extent to which the data points hug the regression line; that is true only if we assume that the total variance of the Y-scores does not change. Only when the total variance of the Y-scores (the variance to be accounted for) does not change can we say that the magnitude of the correlation is a function of the extent to which the data points hug the regression line.

It is also true, however, that the magnitude of the correlation is a function of the total Y-score variance if the variance of the data points around the regression line remains constant. Let us consider two situations, A and B. Assume that the variance of the Y-scores is 500 for situation A and 300 for situation B. Yet in both cases the Y-score variance that is independent of

X-scores is the same (say, 150). That is, the variance of the data points around the regression line is the same for both situations. The correlations are not the same, however, because there is more *Y*-score variance related to changes in *X*-scores in situation A $(500 - 150 = 350)$ than in situation B $(300 - 150 = 150)$. Thus, the coefficient of determination is equal to .70 in situation A $(350/500 = .70)$ and equal to .50 in situation B $(150/300 = .50)$. The respective correlations are 0.84 for situation A and 0.71 for situation B.

The point is that factors that reduce the total variance of *Y*-scores can reduce the correlation even though the variance of the data points around the regression line is unaffected. The total variance of the *Y*-scores can be reduced by the selection procedures used to obtain subjects. For example, we might expect less total variance in *Y*-scores if subjects from a select population are chosen (such as college students at the University of Massachusetts) than if subjects are selected from the general population. The selection of subjects from a homogeneous population is likely to result in a lower correlation if there is a significant (nonzero) correlation between the two variables in the population.

In general, it is not a good idea to select subjects from a homogeneous group if you want to study the degree of relationship between two variables. The extreme case of range restriction is obtained when all subjects have the same score on the *Y* variable. When this result is obtained it does not make any sense to compute a correlation. We must remember that the purpose of correlation is to account for the variance of *Y*-scores. When there is no variance to account for, there is no reason to compute the correlation.

SUMMARY

Correlations are extremely useful measures because they allow a precise indication of the degree of relationship between two variables. The procedures that can be used depend on the level of measurement. The phi coefficient, rank-order correlation, and product-moment correlation are appropriate for nominal, ordinal, and interval data, respectively. Correlation coefficients are free to fluctuate between -1.00 and $+1.00$. The rank-order correlation indicates the degree to which two variables are monotonically related; the product-moment correlation indicates the degree to which they are linearly related.

Scattergrams are useful in describing pictorially the relationship between two variables. We can view correlation in terms of the accuracy with which a regression line describes the relationship between two variables. The regression line is defined as the straight line for which the sum of the squared deviations from each point to the line is a minimum. The magnitude of the correlation, all else being equal, is related to the extent to which the data points hug the regression line.

When we have two scores (an *X*-score and a *Y*-score) for each subject, we can split the variance of Y-scores into two components. One component is the amount of variance in Y independent of changes in X (variance around the regression line). The second component is variance in Y-scores related to changes in X (the variance of the predicted scores). We are primarily interested in the ratio between the Y-score variance related to X-scores and the total Y-score variance. This ratio is equal to r^2, the coefficient of determination. This is the coefficient that allows us to determine how much of the variance of Y-scores is related to changes in X-scores. It thus allows us to compare the importance of X-variables. Restrictions in the range of one or both variables can reduce the correlation.

QUESTIONS

(The answers to most of the questions and problems are given in Appendix D.)

1. Imagine that an investigator interviewed ten Republicans and ten Democrats to assess the views of each participant concerning national health insurance. Of the ten Republicans, three favored national health insurance and seven were against it. Of the ten Democrats, six favored it and four were against it. Compute a phi coefficient to determine the relationship between political party affiliation and attitude toward national health insurance.
2. An investigator sampled 150 registered voters to determine their positions on handgun legislation. Of the 75 males, 50 opposed and 25 favored the legislation. Of the 75 females, 15 opposed and 60 favored the legislation. Compute a phi coefficient to determine the relationship between sex and attitude toward handgun legislation.
3. Ten people randomly selected from the student body of a small liberal arts college were rated on aggressiveness and leadership ability. The ten participants were rank ordered on aggressiveness and they were rank ordered on leadership with the rank of 1 given to the participant with the least aggressiveness and 10 to the participant with the most. Perform a rank-order correlation to determine the degree of association between these two variables. What size correlation would you expect if twenty-five students had been selected?

Student	Leadership	Aggressiveness
A	1	3
B	2	2
C	3	5
D	4	1
E	5	4
F	6	8
G	7	6
H	8	10
I	9	7
J	10	9

4. Assume that eight students were rank ordered according to attractiveness and personality. What is the degree of association between these two variables?

Student	Attractiveness	Personality
A	1	4
B	2	6
C	3	5
D	4	3
E	5	2
F	6	8
G	7	1
H	8	7

5. What size product-moment correlation would you obtain using the results given in question 4? Is it necessary to compute this correlation?
6. Do a product-moment correlation for the following results.

Student	Leadership score	Height score
A	3	5
B	10	9
C	4	3
D	3	3
E	8	9
F	12	6
G	5	10
H	2	4

7. What would you have to do to the scores given in question 6 before you would be able to compute a rank-order correlation?
8. Assume that you test each of fifteen subjects randomly selected from a larger population on two tests and then compute the correlation between the tests. Will the correlation you obtain be the same as if you had tested the whole population instead of a sample of fifteen? What would be your best guess of the relationship between the two variables if you tested only fifteen subjects? What should happen to the accuracy of the estimate of the population correlation as the sample size increases?
9. Assume that two variables you are interested in (beauty and intelligence) are unrelated. That is, the real correlation is 0; the null hypothesis of no relationship between the variables is true. If you were to randomly select a sample of forty subjects, administer the tests, and compute the correlation, would you expect to obtain a correlation of 0? If you were to repeat this procedure 100,000 times with a new sample each time, what would you call the distribution of results you obtain? How would the distribution of results be influenced by the size of the sample?
10. What factors are likely to influence the magnitude of a correlation?

11. What is the difference between linearity and monotonicity?

12. What is a regression line? What is it used for?

13. What is the coefficient of determination? Why is it an important measure? 237

14. Why is it useful to partition the *Y*-score variance into two components? What are the two components? How large is each component when the correlation is 0, +1.00, and −1.00? 235

15. Explain why a range restriction usually results in a lower correlation. 224

16. The _____ is useful for assessing the degree of relationship between two variables when each variable is at the nominal level of measurement and is dichotomous. (1) product-moment correlation (2) rank-order correlation (3) phi coefficient (4) standard deviation

17. A research study has shown that the knowledge of an individual's score on test A gives no information whatsoever about her score on test B. This means that the correlation between test A and test B is probably (1) −1.00 (2) .00 (3) .50 (4) 1.00

18. If two variables are _____ related, then an increase in one is accompanied by a constant increase or a constant decrease in the other for the entire range of both variables. (1) monotonically (2) nonmonotonically (3) linearly (4) nonlinearly

19. If two variables are _____ related, they are also _____ related. (1) linearly, monotonically (2) linearly, nonmonotonically (3) monotonically, linearly (4) monotonically, nonlinearly

20. As the magnitude of the correlation increases the (1) amount of variance in *Y* independent of changes in *X* increases (2) amount of variance in *Y* related to changes in *X* increases (3) total variance in *Y* increases (4) total variance in *Y* decreases

21. Given that everyone in the class received a perfect score of 50 on a statistics test, the correlation between age (say 18–35) and performance on the statistics test would be _____ since there is no variance in test scores to account for. (1) +1.0 (2) −1.0 (3) 0.0 (4) undefined (meaningless)

22. One of the major reasons for doing psychological research is to account for individual differences in behavior. If we obtain a correlation of .50 between aggression and socioeconomic status, then (1) 50 percent of the variance in aggression scores is related to differences in socioeconomic status (2) 50 percent of the variance in aggression scores is not accounted for (3) 25 percent of the variance in aggression scores is related to differences in socioeconomic status (4) both 1 and 2

23. The coefficient of determination is (1) r (2) r^2 (3) the amount (percent) of *Y* variance that is related to changes in *X* (4) the amount (percent) of *Y* variance that is unrelated to changes in *X* (5) both 2 and 3

10 Statistical analysis of between-subject comparisons: Nominal and ordinal data

In the last chapter we discussed the degree of association between two variables with only brief mention of the statistical significance of the obtained correlation coefficient. When all else is equal, the degree of association is directly related to statistical significance, but since all else is rarely equal, we need to discuss how statistical significance is assessed. In Chapters 10 through 12 we will consider a number of tests for analyzing the statistical significance of data.

STATISTICAL TESTS

Need for Statistical Tests

Statistical tests allow us to evaluate whether a particular outcome is rare or common if only chance is operating. There are numerous situations in which it is very useful to have this information. One common use for statistical tests is to evaluate the results of experiments in which one or more independent variables have been manipulated. Different treatment conditions are compared to assess whether differences between treatments are likely or unlikely to occur if only chance is operating (if the treatments do not have any influence on the dependent measure). If the results are unlikely when only chance is operating, it is reasonable to conclude that more than chance is operating — that the treatment is actually responsible for the differences between the treatment conditions. Although a few investigators may obtain only experimental results that are obviously common or obviously rare, thus rendering statistical tests unnecessary, most investigators in the social sciences have frequent use for statistical tests. When an investigator needs to perform a statistical test on a particular experimental result, the first task is to select an appropriate test.

Selecting a Statistical Test

Selecting an appropriate test is crucial because only then will the results of the statistical analysis be meaningful. Notice that the task is to select *an* appropriate test and not *the* appropriate test. It is often possible to use more than one test. Our goal, however, is not to discuss the relative merits of different statistical tests but to provide a scheme for selecting an appropriate one. Then we will consider the steps involved in performing each of the selected tests.

The type of test that is appropriate depends on the type of design used and the level of measurement obtained. Two main designs and three levels of measurement are of interest to social scientists; there are six possible combinations of measurement level and design type. We can select an appropriate statistical test for each using the information in Table 10-1. To use the table we must determine what kind of design was used and what level of measurement was obtained. For example, if a within-subject design was used and ordinal data were obtained, the Wilcoxon test would be suitable.

The structure of Table 10-1 should help you recall what you know about the two major types of design. A between-subject analysis is used with random-groups designs and with subject-variable comparisons (such as comparing males and females). In both cases it is necessary to compare the performance of different subjects to assess the effect of a treatment or differences between participants grouped according to some characteristic such as age, sex, or occupation. The comparison is between subjects. For within-subject comparisons each subject is tested in more than one treatment condition or subjects are matched so that they can be treated as if they were a single subject for the purpose of the analysis. For within-subject comparisons we are interested in chance fluctuations within individuals; for between-

TABLE 10–1

Statistical Tests for the Two Major Types of Comparison and Three Levels of Measurement Combinations

Type of comparison	Level of measurement		
	Nominal	*Ordinal*	*Interval or ratio*

Between-subject
  a. Random-groups
  b. Subject variables
  c. Matched-groups
	Chi square test	Median test or Wilcoxon-Mann-Whitney test	Analysis of variance

Within-subject
  a. Within-subject
  b. Matched-groups
	Cochran Q test	Wilcoxon test	Analysis of variance

subject comparisons we are interested in chance fluctuations between individuals.

qualitative yes or no [handwritten annotation]

THE CHI SQUARE TEST

The chi square test is an extremely useful tool for analyzing between-subject comparisons in which nominal data are obtained. This is the case because there are numerous instances in which we classify subjects into different categories (success or failure, Democrat or Republican, favor or oppose, cured or not cured, wealthy or poor) to assess whether individuals prefer one alternative to another or whether there is a relationship between two or more variables. For the chi square test to be appropriate, each subject can be placed in one and only one category. Since the categories that we use can be viewed as qualitatively different (such as political party preference), the dependent measure is best viewed as nominal data. The characteristics of the chi square test are best demonstrated with specific examples.

One Variable

Imagine that you are interested in the views of college students concerning legalizing marijuana. You select a random sample of 100 students at a large Midwestern university and ask each person selected whether he or she favors or opposes legalizing marijuana. You obtain the results presented in Table 10-2. Our interest is in whether the obtained results are a common or rare outcome if only chance is operating. If only chance is operating, the students, as a whole, will not have a clear preference for or against the legalization of marijuana; that is, if the entire population is considered, the number of students who favor legalization will be equal to the number who oppose it. The question, then, is whether the obtained results are better described as a common or rare outcome if only chance is operating (there is no real preference in the general population).

Obtained and Expected Frequencies. The chi square test allows us to compare the obtained frequencies in each category (the frequencies we obtain by collecting data) with the expected frequencies (the frequencies we should expect if only chance is operating). The expected frequencies are usually computed by accepting the null hypothesis (no treatment effect, no real preference). For the present example (see Table 10-2) the obtained frequency (O) for the favor category is 60, since 60 of the 100 people interviewed indicated that they favor the legalization of marijuana. The obtained frequency for the oppose category is 40, since 40 of the 100 people interviewed indicated that they oppose the legalization of marijuana. If only chance were

TABLE 10-2

*The Number of Students Who Favor
and Oppose the Legalization of Marijuana
(fictitious data)*

View on marijuana legalization	
Favor	*Oppose*
$O = 60$	$O = 40$
$E = 50$	$E = 50$

Computation of the chi square value

$$\chi^2 = \Sigma \frac{(O - E)^2}{E}$$

$$\chi^2 = \frac{(60 - 50)^2}{50} + \frac{(40 - 50)^2}{50}$$

$$\chi^2 = \frac{100}{50} + \frac{100}{50}$$

$$\chi^2 = 4$$

operating, we should expect as many people to favor the legalization of marijuana as to oppose it ("only chance" means no preference in this case). Since there are 100 people to assign to the two categories, we should expect about 50 in each.

Computation of Chi Square. The formula for computing the chi square is

$$\chi^2 = \Sigma \, \frac{(O - E)^2}{E}$$

where O is the obtained frequency of a given category and E is the expected frequency. The actual computation is simple. The expected frequency is subtracted from the obtained frequency for each category; the difference is squared and divided by the expected frequency. This is done for each category. The chi square value is the sum of the values obtained with each category. Note that as the discrepancy between the obtained and expected frequencies increases, the value of chi square will increase. The computation of the chi square test for our present example is presented in Table 10-2. The next step is to consider whether the chi square value of 4.00 is statistically significant.

Evaluation of Chi Square. To assess the significance of the chi square value, one must refer to a table of chi square values. However, since it is necessary to understand degrees of freedom to use the table of chi square values properly, we will first consider this question. The degrees of freedom are calculated by determining the number of obtained category frequencies that are "free to vary" when the total number of subjects is determined. In our present example, in which participants were assigned to two categories, there is 1 degree of freedom. Once the obtained frequency is determined for one category it is known for the other. That is, if 60 people favor the legalization of marijuana, 40 must oppose it, given that we have a sample of 100 people and each person must be in one category or the other. For now, degrees of freedom can be defined as the number of categories in which the obtained frequencies are free to vary when the size of the total sample is determined. If 100 people are assigned to three categories, there would be 2 degrees of freedom. Once the number of people in two of the categories is determined, the number in the third is known.

A table of chi square values is presented in Appendix C-2. The table values are based on chi square sampling distributions that would occur if only chance were operating. Given the chi square distribution, we can determine the probability of obtaining a chi square of a particular magnitude. If only chance is operating, the probability of obtaining a large value for the chi square test is less likely than obtaining a small value.

In general, the table value that is appropriate for evaluating a statistical test is determined by the significance level, degrees of freedom, and whether a one-tailed or two-tailed test is desired. You will probably remember from the discussion in Chapter 3 that in most cases two-tailed tests should be preferred over one-tailed tests. When a two-tailed test is used, the results can be evaluated regardless of their direction. For example, the investigator does not have to predict whether the experimental subjects will be better or worse than the control subjects, just that the independent variable will influence behavior. Table values are a little higher for two-tailed than for one-tailed tests for any significance level and degrees of freedom value.

All the values in the chi square table in Appendix C-2, however, are for two-tailed tests because it is not meaningful to use a one-tailed test for a chi square value if there is more than 1 degree of freedom. The use of the table is very simple. One selects a significance level (usually .05) and determines the appropriate degrees of freedom. For the present example we have already determined that there is 1 degree of freedom. By referring to the table, we can see that a value of 3.841 is needed to reject the null hypothesis at the .05 level of significance. Since the obtained chi square value is equal to 4.00, the null hypothesis can be rejected. The obtained results would be a rare outcome if there were no preference in the larger population, so we reject the view that students do not have any real preference (null hypothesis) and accept the view that a majority believe that marijuana should be legalized.

— data in frequency form
— entries given in categories 75
mutually exclusive

Two Variables

The chi square test is a particularly useful way to assess whether there is a relationship among variables when the nominal level of measurement is obtained. This is fortunate because we are frequently interested in the relationship between variables. For example, you might be interested in whether different "categories" of participants have similar or different views on controversial questions, such as the legalization of marijuana. To test your view you obtain a sample of 100 students, 100 professors, and 100 administrators and ask them whether they favor or oppose the legalization of marijuana. You are interested in whether there is a relationship between the type of participant (one variable) and views on marijuana such that different participants (people classified into different categories) take different positions on the legalization of marijuana. You can obtain an answer by computing a chi square test.

Obtained and Expected Frequencies. Imagine that you obtained the results presented in Table 10-3. Note that each participant is placed in one, and only one, category as a function of his or her view on marijuana legalization and classification as a student, professor, or administrator. The categories are mutually exclusive. Although some professors are also administrators, for the purposes of this analysis they would have to be classified in one or the other of the two categories, not both. As before, the letter O is used for observed or obtained frequencies, and the letter E is used for expected frequencies. We get the observed frequencies in each category by asking people their views (data collection). But how do we obtain the expected frequencies?

In computing the expected frequencies, we assume that only chance is operating and that there is no relationship between the two variables; our basic concern is whether students, professors, and administrators hold similar views on the legalization of marijuana. For the purpose of calculating the expected frequencies, we assume that they do hold the same views. We want to determine whether the obtained result (obtained frequencies) is a rare or common outcome if the null hypothesis is true. Our interest is no longer in whether a majority of each type of participant favors marijuana legalization, but in whether each type of participant has similar views.

To determine the expected frequency for each category in the body of the table we need to calculate the probability that an individual will be classified in each row *and* in each column when the row and column totals are determined. If the two variables of interest are unrelated, chance only should determine the obtained frequencies in each of the six categories. There are two ways to compute the expected frequencies, a hard way and an easy way.

The hard way to compute each expected frequency is to use the fact that the probability of an outcome is the number of favorable outcomes divided by the total number of possible outcomes if only chance is operating. In this

TABLE 10–3

The Number of Students, Professors, and Administrators Who Favor and Oppose the Legalization of Marijuana (fictitious data)

Type of participant	View on marijuana legalization		Row total
	Favor	Oppose	
Student	$O = 60$ $E = 50$	$O = 40$ $E = 50$	100
Professor	$O = 50$ $E = 50$	$O = 50$ $E = 50$	100
Administrator	$O = 40$ $E = 50$	$O = 60$ $E = 50$	100
Column total	150	150	300

Computation of the chi square value

$$\chi^2 = \Sigma \frac{(O - E)^2}{E}$$

$$\chi^2 = \frac{(60 - 50)^2}{50} + \frac{(40 - 50)^2}{50} + \frac{(50 - 50)^2}{50} + \frac{(50 - 50)^2}{50}$$

$$+ \frac{(40 - 50)^2}{50} + \frac{(60 - 50)^2}{50}$$

$$\chi^2 = 2 + 2 + 0 + 0 + 2 + 2$$

$$\chi^2 = 8$$

case the probability of an outcome in each row is .333 (100/300). The probability for each of the two columns is .50 (150/300). When we are given the probability for each row and column, we can obtain the probability for each category (cell) in the body of the table by multiplying the row probability by the column probability. If we assume that type of participant and view on marijuana legalization are unrelated, the probability that an individual will be placed in a particular category will be equal to the probability of her being in the row of the particular category multiplied by the probability of her being in the column of the category. To get the expected frequency for each category, the probability for each is multiplied by the total frequency, in this case 300.

The easy way to compute each expected frequency is to multiply the column total by the row total and divide by the total number of participants. For example, to compute the expected frequency for the student-favor cell, the row total of 100 is multiplied by the column total of 150 and the product is divided by 300, the total number of participants. This is far easier than the procedure discussed above and the result is exactly the same. It skips the needless step of multiplying and dividing by the total number of subjects. The more complicated procedure was presented to demonstrate that the expected frequencies are obtained by determining what is probable if only chance is operating (that is, if the two variables are actually unrelated). The present example is somewhat unusual in that the three row totals are the same and the two column totals are the same, which results in all cells having the same expected frequency. Often the row and column totals are not the same, and, consequently, the expected frequencies for the catgories also differ. This should cause you little difficulty as long as you remember that the expected frequency for each cell can be obtained by multiplying the row total (for the cell) by the column total (for the cell) and dividing the product by the number of total participants or subjects.

Computation of Chi Square. The computation of the chi square is presented in Table 10-3. As you can see, the expected frequency is subtracted from the obtained frequency for each category; the difference is squared and divided by the expected frequency. The same procedure is used for each category, and then the values obtained for each are summed. In this case the obtained chi square value is equal to 8.00. The next step is to evaluate this result.

Evaluation of Chi Square. The question is whether the chi square value of 8.00 is large enough for the hypothesis that the observed results are due to chance to be rejected. If the chi square value is significant, the results suggest that there is a relationship between type of participant and view on marijuana legalization such that different types of participants hold different views. The chi square value is assessed by referring to the table in Appendix C-2.

The problem of determining degrees of freedom for chi square causes little difficulty if you can appreciate the fact that we are not particularly interested in the totals for the rows and columns. We are not asking whether a majority favors the legalization of marijuana, and the number of participants we select for each type of participant classification (row total) is arbitrary. Our concern is the number of category (cell) frequencies that are free to vary if the totals for the rows and columns are "fixed" (not free to vary). The frequencies in the cells tell us whether the two variables are related; the row and column totals do not. The row and column totals are only the starting points for assessing whether the two variables are related.

You compute the number of degrees of freedom for the chi square simply by counting the number of obtained category frequencies that are free to vary when the row and column totals are determined. In the present case, there are 2 degrees of freedom. Once the values for two cells are obtained, the remaining cell frequencies are determined if the row and column totals are fixed. If you do not see how there are only 2 degrees of freedom, prepare a few 2 by 3 contingency tables similar to Table 10-3. Fill in the totals for each row and column and then fill in the "obtained" category frequencies. If you do this you should soon prove to yourself that you have 2 degrees of freedom; that is, once you have filled in the obtained values for two of the cells, the values in the remaining four are determined. If you compute the degrees of freedom for tables that have different numbers of categories, you should soon realize that the number of degrees of freedom for a chi square with two variables is always equal to the number of rows minus one times the number of columns minus one.

An examination of the table of chi square values in Appendix C-2 reveals that a value of 5.991 is needed to reject the null hypothesis at the .05 level given 2 degrees of freedom. Since the obtained chi square value of 8.00 is greater than the table value of 5.991, the null hypothesis is rejected. The hypothetical results support the view that views on the legalization of marijuana are dissimilar for different types of participants. Although investigators tend to select the .05 significance level, they usually report the highest significance level obtained simply because more information is conveyed when the highest level is reported. For example, if an investigator reports that a chi square is significant at the .01 level, it is, of course, also significant at the .05 level. The reverse is not true. For the present example, the results are significant at the .02 level because the obtained value of 8.00 exceeds the table value of 7.824 for the .02 level of significance. The results are not significant at the .01 level because the obtained value of 8.00 is less than the table value of 9.210 needed for significance at the .01 level.

Chi Square and the Phi Coefficient

We can reconsider our example in Chapter 9 of the relationship between sex of the defendant and verdict in a trial to demonstrate the relationship between the phi coefficient and chi square. As you may remember, it is possible to compute a phi coefficient when both variables are at the nominal level of measurement and dichotomous. The results presented in Table 10-4 are the same results we considered earlier (see Table 9-1). When the phi coefficient is computed for these results, a value of .24 is obtained (see Chapter 9). The computation of the chi square value for these results is presented in Table 10-4.

The steps in computing the chi square value are the same for this example as for the previous examples. We need to determine the expected frequencies for each cell, calculate the chi square value by using the formula, and evaluate the obtained results. The computation of the expected frequencies is

TABLE 10-4

The Number of Defendants in Each of the Four Classifications Determined by Verdict and Sex and the Computation of the Chi Square Value (fictitious data)

Sex	Verdict		Row total
	Convicted	*Acquitted*	
Female	$O = 20$ $E = 27.08$	$O = 45$ $E = 37.92$	65
Male	$O = 30$ $E = 22.92$	$O = 25$ $E = 32.08$	55
Column total	50	70	120

Computation of the chi square value

$$\chi^2 = \Sigma \frac{(O - E)^2}{E}$$

$$\chi^2 = \frac{(20 - 27.08)^2}{27.08} + \frac{(45 - 37.92)^2}{37.92} + \frac{(30 - 22.92)^2}{22.92}$$

$$+ \frac{(25 - 32.08)^2}{32.08}$$

$$\chi^2 = 1.85 + 1.32 + 2.19 + 1.56$$

$$\chi^2 = 6.92$$

done as previously. It may look more complicated in this case since the row totals and the column totals are not the same; however, the procedures are identical. For example, to calculate the expected frequency for the female-convicted cell, we multiply the row total for that cell (65) by the column total for that cell (50) and divide the product by the total number of participants (120), which yields an expected frequency of 27.08. The chi square value of 6.92 is significant at the .01 level because it exceeds the table value (see Appendix C-2) of 6.635 needed with 1 degree of freedom. The results are a rare outcome if only chance is operating (no real relationship between sex and verdict), so it is reasonable to conclude that more than chance is operating and that sex and verdict are related.

The phi coefficient tells us the degree of relationship between the two variables, and the chi square allows us to assess whether the results are significant (a rare outcome if only chance is operating). The phi coefficient for this example is .24 and the chi square value is 6.92. Are they related? Yes, we can obtain one when we have the other because $\chi^2 = n\phi^2$. In this case $n = 120$, so chi square $= 120(.24)^2 = 6.91$. Except for a slight rounding error, this value is the same as what we obtained (6.92) when we computed the chi square value directly (see Table 10-4).

The Median Test: A Special Chi Square

Converting Ordinal to Nominal Data. The median test can be used to evaluate between-subject designs when ordinal data are obtained. It requires, however, that the ordinal data be treated as nominal data since the median test is a special application of the chi square test. A single example should be sufficient to familiarize you with this test. Assume that an investigator is interested in the effect of vitamin C on general health. The investigator is particularly concerned with whether or not vitamin C helps to prevent colds, so cold symptoms are given a high weighting by the judges who assess the general health of each subject. Thirty army recruits in basic training who volunteered for the experiment are randomly assigned to two groups with the restriction that there be fifteen subjects in each group. Each subject in the experimental group takes massive doses of vitamin C each day for three months. Each subject in the control group takes massive doses of a placebo.

The dependent measure is the general health of the subjects for the three months during which experimental subjects take vitamin C. The judges, who are unaware of the condition each subject is in, rank the subjects on the basis of general health for the entire three-month period. The rank of 1 is assigned to the subject with the best health, the rank of 30 to the subject with the worst health. Initially the experimenter hoped it would be possible to rank the thirty subjects without allowing ties, but the judges, after several attempts to make fine discriminations, decide that ties are permissible.

The ranking of the thirty subjects is presented in Table 10-5. Although each subject's score is a rank in this particular experiment, it is not necessary to rank subjects directly on the dependent measure in order to use the median test. One could obtain a score for each subject and then rank the scores. In any case, it is necessary to arrive at one overall ranking of the thirty subjects. Given the results in Table 10-5, we must decide whether the results should be attributed to chance or to the effect of the manipulation.

Computing and Evaluating the Chi Square. One way to assess the significance of the results is to use the chi square test. The results can be analyzed in essentially the same way as if nominal data had been obtained. The only difference is that it is necessary to categorize subjects on the basis of their group (experimental or control) and on whether they are above or below the median rank. Then there will be four categories for the thirty subjects. Each subject can be counted in only one of the four.

The obtained and expected frequencies in each category are presented in Table 10-6. The chi square value is computed in exactly the same way that it

TABLE 10–5

*The Rank for Each Subject in the Experimental (E) and Control (C)
Conditions for the Vitamin C Experiment (fictitious data)*

Subject	Condition	Rank	Subject	Condition	Rank
A. B.	E	1	R. M.	E	16
T. B.	E	2	C. B.	C	17
C. S.	C	3	P. D.	E	18
K. P.	E	4.5	C. W.	C	19
L. W.	E	4.5	G. C.	E	20
S. B.	C	6	D. H.	C	21
W. C.	E	7	R. F.	E	22
C. C.	E	8	K. Z.	C	23
J. K.	E	9	J. F.	C	24
F. S.	C	10.5	J. P.	C	25
E. T.	E	10.5	L. W.	C	26
J. D.	C	12	L. S.	C	27
B. B.	E	13	J. M.	C	28
A. D.	E	14	A. M.	C	29
G. D.	E	15	R. R.	C	30

is for nominal data. After computing the chi square value and determining
the degrees of freedom, the table in Appendix C-2 is used to assess whether
the obtained value (with 1 degree of freedom) is large enough to reject the
null hypothesis. In this case the chi square value of 6.53 is greater than the
table value (3.841) with 1 degree of freedom and the .05 level of significance, so the null hypothesis is rejected. It appears that vitamin C tends to
improve health. (You should remember that the results are fictitious.)

You should now understand how to compute a chi square and evaluate it
for statistical significance. If you do much research in the social sciences, you
are very likely to use the chi square sooner or later. It is probably used as
much as any other single statistical tool. It is one of the few good tools for
analyzing nominal data. Another reason for its popularity is that it is easy to
compute and evaluate. Even though the use of the chi square is generally
straightforward, there are some pitfalls to be avoided in using this tool.

Restrictions on the Use of Chi Square *Include*

There are three restrictions to be aware of in using the chi square test.
First, the test is appropriate only if the frequency measures are independent.
In simplest terms this means that only one measure is obtained for each subject. Each subject can be placed in one and only one category. Second, the
data must be in frequency form. There is little problem with this restriction
as long as the chi square test is understood to be appropriate when individuals

TABLE 10-6

The Obtained and Expected Frequencies for the Four Categories in the Experiment on the Effect of Vitamin C on General Health (fictitious data)

Condition	General health		Row total
	Above median	Below median	
Vitamin C (Experimental)	$O = 11$ $E = 7.5$	$O = 4$ $E = 7.5$	15
Control	$O = 4$ $E = 7.5$	$O = 11$ $E = 7.5$	15
Column total	15	15	30

Computation of the chi square value

$$\chi^2 = \Sigma \frac{(O - E)^2}{E}$$

$$\chi^2 = \frac{(11 - 7.5)^2}{7.5} + \frac{(4 - 7.5)^2}{7.5} + \frac{(4 - 7.5)^2}{7.5} + \frac{(11 - 7.5)^2}{7.5}$$

$$\chi^2 = 1.633 + 1.633 + 1.633 + 1.633$$

$$\chi^2 = 6.532$$

are assigned to categories. The data of interest are the number of individuals assigned to each.

Third, the test should not be used if the expected frequencies are too small. What is considered too small will vary somewhat with the number of variables and the total number of subjects. In any case, the test can be used with confidence as long as none of the expected frequencies is equal to or less than five. When there are expected frequencies of less than five the number of subjects should be increased so that the expected frequencies increase. Or it may be possible to combine categories so that those which have expected frequencies of less than five are eliminated. If neither of these options is suitable, another test of significance (such as the Fisher-Yates Exact Probability test) should be used.

WILCOXON-MANN-WHITNEY TEST

A disadvantage of the chi square test (median test) when ordinal data are obtained is that all the available information is not used in the rather crude classification of above versus below the median. Any two ranks above the median count the same, and any two ranks below the median count the same. That is, ordinal data are treated like nominal data. The Wilcoxon-Mann-Whitney test takes into account the differences between ranks on the same side of the median.

Computational Steps

Let us return to the example of the effect of vitamin C on general health and use the Wilcoxon-Mann-Whitney test. The first step is to obtain a ranking of the subjects similar to that in Table 10-5. The principal concern is the sum of the ranks for the experimental subjects and for the control subjects. The sum of each of these ranks is presented in Table 10-7. You should compute the sum of the ranks for each group and then select the smaller sum. In this case the sum of the ranks for the experimental group is selected because it is less than the sum of the control group.

The two groups have the same number of subjects, so it is reasonable to expect that the sums should be about the same if only chance is operating. As one sum decreases the other must increase because together they must equal the sum for all the subjects regardless of group. Because the two sums are directly related, the results of a two-group experiment can be evaluated

TABLE 10-7

The Sum of the Ranks for the Experimental and Control Subjects for the Results Presented in Table 10-5

Experimental	Control
1	3
2	6
4.5	10.5
4.5	12
7	17
8	19
9	21
10.5	23
13	24
14	25
15	26
16	27
18	28
20	29
22	30
Sum = 164.5	Sum = 300.5

by considering the sum of ranks for just one group; that is, the effect of the manipulation can be assessed by considering the magnitude of the sum of ranks for one group. The issue is whether the smaller sum is small enough that the obtained results would be a rare event if only chance were operating.

A complication arises if there is an unequal number of subjects in the two groups because we cannot simply add the ranks for each group and take the smaller sum. We must compute the sum for the smaller group (called T) and then compute another value, T' (called T prime), by using the following formula:

$$T' = N_1(N_1 + N_2 + 1) - T$$

where N_1 is the number of subjects in the smaller group, and N_2 is the number of subjects in the larger group. We then select T or T', whichever is *smaller*. The formula is necessary because the sum of the ranks is related to the number of subjects in each group. For example, all else being equal, the sum for a group of twenty subjects will be higher than the sum for a group of ten subjects. The formula allows us to remove the bias inherent in having a different number of subjects in the two conditions so that our totals (T and T') yield performance measures uninfluenced by differences in group size. The symbols T and T' are shorthand for total. They should not be confused with the t-test, a significance test used for interval data that is briefly considered in the next chapter.

Evaluating the Test

The smaller sum is evaluated by referring to Appendix C-3. To determine the appropriate table value, you must decide on a level of significance (say, .05) and determine the number of subjects in each group (in this case fifteen). If the two groups are of unequal size, then you must refer to the appropriate column for the smaller group and the appropriate row for the larger group. If the groups are the same size, of course, it doesn't make any difference. For the present example the correct table value is 184 for the .05 level of significance and fifteen subjects per group.

If the smaller of the two group sums is *equal to or less than* the table value, the null hypothesis is rejected. In this case the null hypothesis is rejected because the obtained sum of 164.5 is less than 184. The Wilcoxon-Mann-Whitney test is consistent with the median test in revealing that the probability of obtaining these results by chance is less than .05. (On the basis of chance a value smaller than the table value should be obtained about 5 times in 100 attempts. Since this is an unlikely event, it is reasonable to conclude that the results are not attributable to chance.) The investigator can conclude that the manipulation was responsible for the obtained difference between groups.

Characteristics of the Test

The Wilcoxon-Mann-Whitney test is easy to compute and evaluate for significance. The table that is used to evaluate the obtained sum of ranks for the smaller of the two samples is appropriate only if each group has twenty or fewer subjects. This should not be a problem, however, because it is unlikely that you will have more than twenty subjects in one group. If you do you can refer to Kruskal and Wallis (1952) to learn how to evaluate the sum of ranks for larger groups. Also, note that the obtained value must be smaller than the appropriate table value in order to be significant. This is unusual; in most significance tests the obtained value has to be larger than the table value to be significant.

If there are many tied scores the value of the sum of ranks may be affected. Obviously, tied scores will not have any effect when the subjects with the tied scores are in the same group, since the ranks are summed for each group. However, when the ties are between groups, the smaller sum of ranks tends to decrease and, therefore, the likelihood of rejecting the null hypothesis increases. When there are many tied ranks between groups you may want to adopt a more stringent significance level (say, the .01 instead of the .05) or resolve the ties in a way that affords a more conservative test of the research hypothesis. For example, if you have predicted that the experimental subjects will have lower ranks than the control subjects, in the case of a between-group tie you should give the control subject the lower of the two ranks and the experimental subject the higher, instead of giving both subjects the average.

SUMMARY

The type of statistical test that is appropriate depends on the type of design and the level of measurement obtained. Appropriate tests for the six major combinations of measurement level and design type are presented in Table 10-1.

The chi square test is used to analyze between-subject designs in which nominal data are obtained. The basic task is to determine whether the obtained frequencies in a set of categories differ significantly from the expected frequencies. Expected frequencies are calculated by assuming the null hypothesis is true.

Chi square value is computed by subtracting the expected frequency from the obtained frequency for a category, squaring the difference, and dividing by the expected frequency. This is done for each category. The chi square value is the sum of the values obtained for each category. The obtained chi square is evaluated by comparing it with the appropriate value in the chi square table. If the obtained value exceeds the table value, the chi square is significant.

The median test is a special application of the chi square test. All sub-jects are ranked and then split into two categories — above the median and below the median. A chi square test is used to determine whether the number of experimental subjects above the median is greater or less than what can be expected on the basis of chance.

There are three restrictions on the use of the chi square test. The test is appropriate only if frequency measures are independent. The data must be in frequency form. And the test should not be used if the expected frequencies are too small.

The Wilcoxon-Mann-Whitney test is appropriate for between-subject de-signs in which ordinal data are obtained. Like the median test this test is only appropriate for evaluating two conditions at a time. All subjects are rank ordered and the sums of ranks for both groups are obtained. The smaller sum is then evaluated by comparing it with the appropriate table value. If the obtained sum is equal to or less than the table sum, the results are significant.

QUESTIONS

(The answers to most of the questions and problems are given in Appendix D.)

1. Determine the expected frequency for each category (cell) in the following table. In determining the expected frequencies you should assume, of course, that the two variables are unrelated. There are 400 subjects in this experiment.

Variable 1

	Poor	Good	
A			100
B			150
C			150
	100	300	

Variable 2 (row label)

2. A sample of fifty Democrats, fifty Republicans, and fifty Independents is obtained to check the view that wealth and political preference are related. An annual income of $18,000 is used as the criterion of wealth. It is possible to classify each individual according to political party and income. Each can be placed in one category only. Do a chi square test to determine if the two variables are related.

Political party

	Republicans	Democrats	Independents
Below $18,000	$O = 15$	$O = 30$	$O = 25$
Above $18,000	$O = 35$	$O = 20$	$O = 25$

Wealth (row label)

3. Is there any similarity between deciding whether two subject variables are related by using a chi square test and computing a correlation between the two subject variables?

4. Let us assume you are interested in the relationship between parental smoking (one or both parents smoke or neither parent smokes) and whether their children smoke when they become adults. In order to test your view you randomly select 200 adults between the ages of 21 and 30 and assess whether they smoke and whether their parents smoked when they were children. One variable is whether the parents smoked; the second is whether the subject smokes. The hypothetical results for this experiment are presented below. Do a chi square test to determine whether the variables are related.

Subject

	Smokes	Does not smoke
One or both parents smoke	70	40
Neither parent smokes	37	53

Parents

5. Assume that you analyze the fictitious results presented in question 4 further by considering the results for male and female subjects separately. The results of this breakdown of the data are presented below. Do a chi square test for the female subjects only. Are the variables related? Do a chi square test for the male subjects only. Are the variables related?

Male subjects

	Smokes	Does not smoke
Smoke	50	10
Do not smoke	10	25

Parents

Female subjects

	Smokes	Does not smoke
Smoke	20	30
Do not smoke	27	28

Parents

6. What are the limitations of the chi square test?
7. Assume that you want to evaluate a new program of instruction. You ran domly assign twelve subjects to the treatment (experimental) condition and twelve to the control condition. After the treatment, judges who are not aware of the treatment manipulation rank the subjects according to their performance on a criterion test. You obtain the results given below. Did the treatment have an effect? Use the median test to evaluate your results.

Subject	Condition	Rank
a	E	1
b	E	2
c	E	3
d	C	4
e	E	5
f	C	6
g	E	7
h	E	8
i	C	9
j	C	10
k	E	11
l	E	12
m	E	13
n	E	14
o	E	15
p	C	16
q	E	17
r	C	18
s	C	19
t	C	20
u	C	21
v	C	22
w	C	23
x	C	24

8. Repeat the above analysis, but this time use the Wilcoxon-Mann-Whitney test.

Statistical analysis of between-subject comparisons: Interval data

In this unit we compare the performance of different groups when interval or better measurement is obtained. Each subject is included in one and only one group, so the comparison of groups is a between-subject comparison. We will limit our discussion to the analysis of variance because this test is useful at many levels of complexity. It can be used to analyze complex experiments, but it is also very useful for simple experiments or comparisons. Beginning students can use it to make comparisons of two or more groups without concerning themselves with how more complex comparisons can be made. Since many useful comparisons can be made by considering only two groups, we begin with this comparison.

COMPARING TWO GROUPS

Imagine that you are interested in possible sex differences in depression. You use a test for depression which yields a score from 1 to 10, with a higher number indicating greater depression. We will assume that the test yields interval data. Further imagine that you administered the test to ten women and eight men seeking help at a counseling center and obtained the results presented in Table 11-1. Your interest is in whether there are sex differences in the amount of depression. Are the obtained results a rare or common outcome if only chance is operating, that is, if there are no real sex differences in depression?

Sum of Squares

The basic task in performing an analysis of variance for this type of comparison is to compute the sum of squares total (SS_{tot}), the sum of squares between groups (SS_{bg}), and the sum of squares within groups (SS_{wg}). The task

TABLE 11-1

Scores on a Depression Test for
Eight Males and Ten Females
(fictitious data)

Male	Female
	5
	4
3	7
2	6
4	3
1	9
3	8
4	6
4	5
2	3
$\Sigma X = 23$	$\Sigma X = 56$
$\Sigma X^2 = 75$	$\Sigma X^2 = 350$
$n = 8$	$n = 10$

is simplified somewhat in that the SS_{tot} is equal to the SS_{bg} plus the SS_{wg}. Thus, given two values, we can obtain the third by subtraction.

Computation of the Sum of Squares Total. The first step is to compute the SS_{tot}. The formula for the computation of SS_{tot} is

$$SS_{tot} = \Sigma\Sigma X^2 - \frac{(T)^2}{N}$$

The summation signs (sigmas) mean that you add; the numbers denoted by the symbol following the sigmas are added. The X in the formula refers to any score. In this case each score is squared and then all the squared scores are added. It is important to note that the scores are squared *before* they are added. There are two summation signs because the squared scores in each group are added and then the group totals are added (i.e., this can be regarded as two separate adding operations). If all the scores are squared and added, the obtained value is 425 (see computations in Table 11-2). The T in the formula (the total for all the scores) is squared and then divided by N (the total number of scores, in this case 18). The computation of the sum of squares total, the sum of squares between groups, and the sum of squares within groups is presented in Table 11-2.

Computation of the Sum of Squares Between Groups. The formula for the SS_{bg} is

$$SS_{bg} = \Sigma \frac{(\text{group total})^2}{n} - \frac{(T)^2}{N}$$

TABLE 11-2

Computation of the Analysis of Variance for the Data Presented in Table 11-1

$$SS_{tot} = \Sigma\Sigma X^2 - \frac{(T)^2}{N}$$

$$SS_{tot} = 425 - \frac{(79)^2}{18}$$

$$SS_{tot} = 425 - 346.72$$

$$SS_{tot} = 78.28$$

$$SS_{bg} = \Sigma \frac{(\text{group total})^2}{n} - \frac{(T)^2}{N}$$

$$SS_{bg} = \frac{(23)^2}{8} + \frac{(56)^2}{10} - \frac{(79)^2}{18}$$

$$SS_{bg} = 66.13 + 313.60 - 346.72$$

$$SS_{bg} = 33.01$$

$$SS_{wg} = SS_{tot} - SS_{bg}$$

$$SS_{wg} = 78.28 - 33.01$$

$$SS_{wg} = 45.27$$

or

$$SS_{wg} = \left[75 - \frac{(23)^2}{8} \right] + \left[350 - \frac{(56)^2}{10} \right]$$

$$SS_{wg} = 8.87 + 36.40$$

$$SS_{wg} = 45.27$$

The n is the symbol for the number of scores in each group. Each group total is squared and divided by the number of scores in that group. If there are the same number of subjects in each group, each group total can be squared and all the totals can be summed before dividing by the number of subjects in each group. If there is an unequal number of subjects in each group, each group total is squared and divided by the number of subjects in that group before summing the values across groups. Having an unequal number of subjects in each group does not necessarily cause problems if only one independent variable is studied, especially if the number in each group is about the same. The last term in the formula is identical to the last term in the formula for the SS_{tot}. Since this value has already been computed, it is not necessary to do it again.

Computation of the Sum of Squares Within Groups. The computation of the SS_{wg} is very easy, since the value can be obtained by subtracting the SS_{bg} from the SS_{tot}. This follows because $SS_{tot} = SS_{bg} + SS_{wg}$. Obviously, if a mistake is made in computing the SS_{tot} or the SS_{bg} it is not possible to obtain the correct SS_{wg} by subtraction, so it is a good idea to compute the SS_{wg} directly as well. If the results are the same with both methods, you can proceed with confidence. To compute the SS_{wg} directly, each group is taken individually and SS is computed for that group only. After this is done for all the groups, the values that were obtained are summed. The total is equal to the SS_{wg}. If the work is done correctly, the SS_{tot} will be equal to the SS_{bg} plus the SS_{wg}. A sum of squares value can be 0 (for example, if the total for each group is the same), but never negative. A negative sum of squares indicates a mistake.

Analysis of Variance Table

Source of Variance. The next step is to prepare the analysis of variance table. An analysis of variance table for our example is Table 11-3. The first column is labeled *source*. This is shorthand for *source of variance*. Our interest is in between-group and within-group sources of variance.

Degrees of Freedom. The second column is labeled degrees of freedom (df). The degrees of freedom for analysis of variance can be understood in about the same way as degrees of freedom for the chi square. The task is to determine the number of scores that are free to vary when the total is determined. To determine the degrees of freedom between groups, each group total and the overall total are considered. When the overall total is fixed, all the group totals except one are free to vary. Thus, the degrees of freedom between groups is one less than the number of groups. Since the symbol k is used to denote the number of groups, the degrees of freedom between groups is $k - 1$.

To compute the degrees of freedom within groups it is necessary to consider the number of scores in each group and the group total. When the

TABLE 11-3

Analysis of Variance Table for the Sex Differences in Depression Example (fictitious results)

Source	df	SS	MS	F
Between groups	1	33.01	33.01	11.66
Within groups	16	45.27	2.83	
Total	17			

group total is fixed, all the scores in each group except one are free to vary. If you refer to Table 11-1 and count the number of scores in each group that are free to vary when the group total is fixed, it should be clear that the degrees of freedom for each group is one less than the number of subjects in each group. When n is used to denote the number of subjects in each group, the degrees of freedom for each group is equal to $n - 1$. If there is an unequal number of subjects in each group, as in the present example, the degrees of freedom within groups must be computed separately for each group and then summed. Thus, there are seven scores that are free to vary for the male group (that is, $n - 1$ where $n = 8$) and nine that are free to vary for the female group ($n - 1$ where $n = 10$), yielding 16 degrees of freedom for within groups. If there is the same number of subjects in each condition, the number of degrees of freedom within groups is equal to $k(n - 1)$. The total number of degrees of freedom is equal to the total number of scores minus one. Note that the degrees of freedom for within groups plus the degrees of freedom for between groups is equal to the total degrees of freedom.

The SS, MS, *and* F *Columns.* The third column is for the sum of squares. Because these values have already been determined, it is only necessary to record them in the table.

The fourth column is labeled *mean square (MS)*. The mean square is obtained by taking the *SS* for each source, in this case that between groups and within groups, and dividing by the degrees of freedom for that source. When chance only is operating, each mean square is an independent estimate of population variance. If the independent variable manipulation had an effect, the between-group mean square should be larger than the within-group mean square.

The two are compared by dividing the between-group mean square by the within-group mean square. The value obtained is called an F value. It is recorded in the fifth column of the analysis of variance table. (The value is labeled F after Sir Ronald Fisher, who is largely responsible for developing the analysis of variance significance test.) In this case the F value is recorded in the between-group row because the size of the F is used to assess whether the differences between groups are greater than should be expected if only chance is operating. After completing the analysis of variance table, there is only one more step. It is necessary to determine whether the obtained F value of 11.66 is statistically significant.

Evaluating the Obtained *F* Value

By now you have probably guessed that the obtained F value is evaluated for statistical significance by comparing it with a table value. If the between-group estimate is so much larger than the within-group estimate that the obtained F value is a rare event if only chance is operating, the results can be attributed to the independent variable. The table in Appendix C-4 is used to assess the likelihood of the obtained *F* value occurring if only chance is operating.

In order to find the appropriate table value for comparison, we must know the number of degrees of freedom for each variance estimate and select a significance level. The number of degrees of freedom for the between-group estimate indicates the appropriate column to refer to in the table, and the number of degrees of freedom for the within-group estimate indicates the appropriate row. In this case there is 1 degree of freedom for the between-group estimate, and there are 16 degrees of freedom for the within-group estimate. The table value for the .05 level is 4.49; the table value for the .01 level is 8.53 (see Appendix C-4). Since the obtained *F* value of 11.66 is greater than both of these values, we can reject the null hypothesis at the .01 level of significance. The chances are less than one in a hundred that the results in Table 11-1 would be obtained if only chance were operating. If our obtained *F* value had been smaller but still larger than 4.49 (say 6.00), we would still reject the null hypothesis, but at the .05 level of significance. If the obtained *F* value had been smaller than 4.49, we would not be able to reject the null hypothesis.

Relationship Between the *t*- and *F*-Tests

A number of students may have been introduced to another test, called the *t*-test, which can also be used to compare the performance of two groups. The *F*-test, which we have just considered, is comparable to the *t*-test in that in both tests the same conclusion will always be reached about whether to reject the null hypothesis when comparing two groups. This is because whenever two-group comparisons are made, $F = t^2$, and the *appropriate* table values for the *F*-test are equal to the square of the appropriate table values for *t*. Given this relationship, the conclusion reached is totally unaffected by which of the two tests is used. We will *not* consider the *t*-test.

The *F*-test we have considered is no more difficult to compute than the *t*-test, so there is little solid justification for using the *t*-test other than tradition. The major advantage of the analysis of variance is that you can use it to analyze more complex experiments. Students who are only interested in making two-group comparisons now have a statistical tool every bit as useful as the *t*-test. You may go directly to the end of the chapter to work a few practice problems using your new statistical tool. Students interested in additional ways of using the analysis of variance may continue reading.

COMPARING THREE OR MORE GROUPS

The analysis of variance allows us to consider three or more groups in a single analysis. Suppose, for example, that you are interested in the relationship between depression scores and age. You administer your depression test to females seeking therapy and then categorize the participants by age: under twenty, between twenty and forty, and over forty. You decide to select, randomly, ten participants in each age category because you know there are advantages to having an equal number of participants in each group. Imagine that you obtain the results presented in Table 11-4. How would you analyze these results to determine if there is a significant difference between the groups? The procedure is virtually identical to the one considered earlier. We need to compute the appropriate sums of squares, construct the analysis of variance table, and evaluate the obtained F value.

Sum of Squares

The computation of the SS_{tot}, SS_{bg}, and SS_{wg} for the results presented in Table 11-4 is presented in Table 11-5. An examination of this table reveals that we use the same formulas to compute these values as we did earlier, with the exception of a slight modification of the formula for the SS_{bg}. In cases of an equal n in each group, in this case ten participants per group, it is easier to square each group total and add all the squared scores before dividing by n. The formulas for the SS_{bg} presented in Table 11-5 and Table 11-2 are equivalent, of course.

Once again, the summation signs (sigmas) mean that you add; the numbers denoted by the symbol following the sigmas are added. The X in the formula for the SS_{tot} refers to any score. Each score is squared and then all the squared scores are added — that is, the scores are squared before they are added. This is done for each group, and then the totals for each group

TABLE 11-4

Scores on a Depression Test for Thirty Females Classified According to Age (fictitious data)

	Under 20	20–40	Over 40
	1	4	3
	3	2	8
	2	5	7
	5	7	9
	2	4	2
	3	3	5
	1	2	7
	2	6	2
	2	3	5
	2	3	4
ΣX	23	39	52
ΣX^2	65	177	326

TABLE 11-5

*Computation of the Analysis of Variance for
the Data Presented in Table 11-4*

$$SS_{tot} = \Sigma\Sigma X^2 - \frac{(T)^2}{N}$$

$$SS_{tot} = 568 - \frac{(114)^2}{30}$$

$$SS_{tot} = 568 - 433.20$$

$$SS_{tot} = 134.80$$

$$SS_{bg} = \frac{1}{n}\Sigma(\text{group total})^2 - \frac{(T)^2}{N}$$

$$SS_{bg} = \frac{1}{10}\left[(23)^2 + (39)^2 + (52)^2\right] - \frac{(114)^2}{30}$$

$$SS_{bg} = 475.40 - 433.20$$

$$SS_{bg} = 42.20$$

$$SS_{wg} = SS_{tot} - SS_{bg}$$

$$SS_{wg} = 134.80 - 42.20$$

$$SS_{wg} = 92.60$$

are added to yield a value of 568. The total for all the scores, 114 in this case, is squared and then divided by the number of scores (30). The computation of the SS_{bg} should not cause you any difficulty if you note that each group total is squared and all the squared scores are added before you divide by the number of scores in each group, 10 in this case. We can obtain the SS_{wg} by subtraction, since the SS_{tot} is equal to the SS_{bg} plus the SS_{wg}.

Analysis of Variance Table

The analysis of variance table for the present example is presented in Table 11-6. Note that there is nothing particularly new here. Once again we have a column for *source, df, sum of squares, mean squares,* and a final column for *F.* Once again, we have two sources of variance of interest, between-groups and within-groups. Since there are three groups, we have two degrees of freedom. That is, if the overall total is fixed, two group totals are still free to vary. Since we have the same number of participants in each condition, we can compute the degrees of freedom within groups by using the formula $k(n - 1)$, where k is equal to the number of groups and n is equal to the number of participants per group. Note that the total degrees of freedom is equal to one less than the number of participants.

The values for the sum of squares have already been computed, so it is a simple matter to record them in the table. The mean square is obtained by dividing the sum of squares by the appropriate degrees of freedom — that is, for the between-group mean square we divide the sum of squares between groups by the degrees of freedom for between groups, yielding a value of 21.10. The same procedure is used to obtain the mean square for within groups. We obtain the F value by dividing the mean square between groups by the mean square within groups, which yields a value of 6.15.

Evaluating the Obtained F Value

We evaluate the obtained F value of 6.15 by comparing it with the appropriate table value in Appendix C-4. There is no table value corresponding to 2 and 27 degrees of freedom, so it is necessary to use the next *smaller* degree of freedom for the within-group estimate. An examination of column 2 and row 26 reveals a table value of 3.37 corresponding to the .05 significance level and 5.53 for the .01 significance level. Since the obtained F value of 6.15 is greater than both of these values, the results are significant at the .01 level. We can conclude that there is a relationship between age and scores on the depression test for our hypothetical example. In this case we can reject the null hypothesis.

Note that in this case the analysis of variance performed by considering all three groups tells us exactly what we want to know, that there is a relationship between age and depression scores. We are not especially interested in whether there is a significant difference between any two particular groups. Our interest is in a relationship between age and depression scores. If we were interested in comparing two groups, we could, of course, have computed an analysis of variance using only two of the groups. A significant F value obtained when three or more groups are compared does not tell us which groups differ significantly; it simply tells us that the obtained results are a rare outcome if only chance is operating. Frequently, this is all we want to know. If we care to make additional specific comparisons, we can do so.

TABLE 11–6

Analysis of Variance Table for the Age and Depression Test Score Example

Source	df	SS	MS	F
Between groups	2	42.20	21.10	6.15
Within groups	27	92.60	3.43	
Total	29			

Before we proceed, it is important that you have a firm understanding of the steps used in performing an analysis of variance. The easiest way to gain this understanding is to do the actual computations. You can use a calculator to compute the analysis of variance for the results in Table 11-1 by referring to the text material and Table 11-1 only. You can also perform the analysis of variance for the results in Table 11-4. If you can follow these examples or, better, perform the analysis independently, you should be ready to continue. This is also a good time to turn to the problems at the end of the chapter and work those that require an analysis of variance to be performed with just one independent variable. Such practice will facilitate your understanding of the next section.

ANALYSIS OF VARIANCE WITH TWO INDEPENDENT VARIABLES

Two by Two Factorial Design

For the sake of simplicity, assume, once again, that we are interested in the score of each participant on a depression test in which 1 indicates minimal depression and a score of 10 indicates profound depression with intermediate values indicating intermediate amounts of depression. In this case, however, you are interested in using the depression test as a means of assessing the effectiveness of your therapy to increase self-esteem. Your therapy consists of a variety of approaches. For example, you explain that nondepressed people are more likely to give themselves the "benefit of the doubt" than depressed people, that nondepressed people tend to rate themselves higher than they actually are (that is, higher than others rate them), that positive self thoughts are very important, and so on. In brief, your therapy consists of numerous strategies to increase the individual's self-esteem.

You decide to use a 2 by 2 factorial design to evaluate the effectiveness of your therapy. You are interested in the effectiveness of the therapy for individuals who complain about being depressed as well as for those who are not depressed. Thus, one independent variable (a subject variable in this case) is the type of participant, depressed versus nondepressed. The depressed participants are people who seek help for their depression at your clinic; the nondepressed participants are those who seek help for problems other than depression. The therapy manipulation is properly classified as a nonsubject variable manipulation because you have complete control over who receives the therapy and who does not. Half of the depressed participants are randomly assigned to the therapy condition and half to the no-therapy condition. A similar procedure is used for the nondepressed participants. Ten weeks after the completion of the manipulation, you administer a depression test to each of the forty participants. The score that each participant obtained on the test is presented in Table 11-7. Our interest is in how these results should be evaluated. The analysis of variance is an appropriate statistical test. The level of measurement is interval, and a between-subject design is used.

Computing Analysis of Variance

The procedure for analyzing this experiment is very similar to that used for the previous example. In fact, the initial steps are identical to the steps used when only one independent variable is manipulated. The basic task is to compute the SS_{tot}, SS_{bg}, and SS_{wg}, in that order. It is necessary to compute the sum of the scores and the sum of the squared scores for each group in order to compute the three sums of squares. In computing the ΣX for each group, we simply add all the scores. In computing the ΣX^2 it is important to remember to square each score *before* you add the squared scores. These values are computed in Table 11-7.

TABLE 11-7

The Score of Each of the Forty Participants on the Depression Test Ten Weeks After the Therapy Manipulation (fictitious data)

Type of participant	Esteem therapy			
	Yes		No	
Depressed	3 6 4 1 0 3 2 1 4 1	ΣX = 25 ΣX^2 = 93	7 4 8 6 3 7 8 9 5 4	ΣX = 61 ΣX^2 = 409
Not depressed	0 1 1 2 1 3 2 1 2 0	ΣX = 13 ΣX^2 = 25	1 3 4 5 1 0 2 4 3 1	ΣX = 24 ΣX^2 = 82

Computing the SS_{tot}, SS_{bg}, *and* SS_{wg}. The formula for the computation of the SS_{tot} is

$$SS_{tot} = \Sigma\Sigma X^2 - \frac{(T)^2}{N}$$

As we know, the first term is obtained by squaring the score for each subject and then adding all the squared scores. To obtain the value for the second term, the total for all the scores is squared and then divided by the total number of scores (40 in this case). The formula for the SS_{bg} is

$$SS_{bg} = \frac{1}{n}\,\Sigma(\text{group total})^2 - \frac{(T)^2}{N}$$

Thus, to obtain the first term each group total is squared and the squared group totals are added and then divided by the number of subjects in each group (10 in this case). The second term was already computed when the SS_{tot} was computed. Since the SS_{tot} is equal to the SS_{bg} plus the SS_{wg}, the SS_{wg} can be obtained by subtraction (or by computing an SS for each group separately and then adding these values). The next step is to assess each independent variable separately. To do this we must look at the experiment in a slightly different manner. One independent variable has to be ignored while the other is evaluated. The computations are presented in Table 11-8.

Computing a Sum of Squares for Each Independent Variable. This step in the analysis requires a little flexibility or imagination on the part of the student. The formula for the SS_{bg} is used extensively, but the definition of a group changes as the effect of each independent variable is assessed. The first term in the SS_{bg} formula is obtained by squaring each group total, adding the squared scores, and dividing by the number of scores in each group. The same procedure is used to evaluate the effect of each independent variable separately, but the way the groups are defined changes. Therefore the student has to look at the experiment from several points of view. The way the groups are defined will also determine the label given to the SS_{bg}. The SS_{bg} is very useful because it can be used to evaluate the effect of each independent variable separately. These points should become clear shortly.

The effect of the therapy manipulation can be evaluated by viewing the experiment as a two-group experiment in which there are depressed and nondepressed participants in each of the two therapy conditions (that is, therapy versus no therapy). We totally ignore the type of participant variable in order to evaluate the effectiveness of therapy. If we ignore the type of participant independent variable, there are twenty participants in the therapy condition and twenty participants in the no-therapy condition. We can simply imagine that the type of participant variable was not manipulated so that we have a simple two-group experiment. Our task, then, is to obtain an SS_{bg} for the two groups being considered (therapy versus no therapy). If these two groups differ significantly, the difference can be attributed to the therapy

TABLE 11-8

*Computation of the Analysis of Variance for the Data
Presented in Table 11-7*

$$SS_{tot} = \Sigma\Sigma X^2 - \frac{(T)^2}{N}$$

$$SS_{tot} = 609 - \frac{(123)^2}{40}$$

$$SS_{tot} = 609 - 378.23$$

$$SS_{tot} = 230.78$$

$$SS_{bg} = \frac{1}{n}\Sigma(\text{group total})^2 - \frac{(T)^2}{N}$$

$$SS_{bg} = \frac{1}{10}\left[(25)^2 + (61)^2 + (13)^2 + (24)^2\right] - \frac{(123)^2}{40}$$

$$SS_{bg} = \frac{5091}{10} - 378.23$$

$$SS_{bg} = 509.10 - 378.23$$

$$SS_{bg} = 130.87$$

$$SS_{wg} = SS_{tot} - SS_{bg}$$

$$SS_{wg} = 230.78 - 130.87$$

$$SS_{wg} = 99.91$$

$$SS_{therapy} = \frac{1}{n}\Sigma(\text{group total})^2 - \frac{(T)^2}{N}$$

$$SS_{therapy} = \frac{1}{20}\left[(38)^2 + (85)^2\right] - \frac{(123)^2}{40}$$

$$SS_{therapy} = \frac{8669}{20} - 378.23$$

$$SS_{therapy} = 433.45 - 378.23$$

$$SS_{therapy} = 55.22$$

(Continued on next page)

TABLE 11–8 continued

$$SS_{type\ of\ participant} = \frac{1}{n}\Sigma(\text{group total})^2 - \frac{(T)^2}{N}$$

$$SS_{type\ of\ participant} = \frac{1}{20}\left[(86)^2 + (37)^2\right] - \frac{(123)^2}{40}$$

$$SS_{type\ of\ participant} = \frac{8765}{20} - 378.23$$

$$SS_{type\ of\ participant} = 438.25 - 378.23$$

$$SS_{type\ of\ participant} = 60.02$$

$$SS_{therapy\ \times\ participant} = SS_{bg} - SS_{therapy} - SS_{participant}$$

$$SS_{therapy\ \times\ participant} = 130.87 - 55.22 - 60.02$$

$$SS_{therapy\ \times\ participant} = 15.63$$

---

manipulation. It is not reasonable to attribute the differences to the type of participants since both depressed and nondepressed participants are included in each group.

Although the SS_{bg} formula is used to assess the therapy effect, it is more appropriate to label the sum of squares obtained the $SS_{therapy}$ to minimize confusion. A between-group sum of squares is obtained, but it is of a particular kind. It is the sum of squares obtained by comparing the people who received therapy with the people who did not, so it makes good sense to label it the $SS_{therapy}$. The computation of the $SS_{therapy}$ is presented in Table 11-8, as are the other computations. A similar procedure is used to obtain a sum of squares for the type of participant effect. In this case, one group consists of twenty depressed participants and the other of twenty nondepressed participants. Once again the SS_{bg} formula is used. Now consider the differences among all four groups.

Computing the Sum of Squares for the Interaction. Let us consider the factors, besides chance, that might cause the four group totals to differ. If the therapy and type of participant manipulations are related to the scores obtained on the depression test, we should expect the four group totals to vary. Yet, the $SS_{therapy}$ and the $SS_{type\ of\ participant}$ may not account for all the differences among the groups. Determining these main effects does not afford an assessment of the extent to which the effect of one of the manipulations (such as therapy) depends on the level of the other independent variable (type of participant). If the effectiveness of the therapy manipulation depends on the type of participant, the two variables are said to interact.

The interaction effect is assessed by determining the extent to which the $SS_{therapy}$ and $SS_{type\ of\ participant}$ account for all the differences among the four groups — that is, the sum of squares for therapy by type of participant is computed by subtracting the $SS_{therapy}$ and $SS_{type\ of\ participant}$ from the SS_{bg}. The interaction effect is the difference among the four groups that is not accounted for by the overall effect of each of the two independent variables. Now that all the sums of squares have been computed, the analysis of variance table can be considered.

The Analysis of Variance Table

Source of Variance. The analysis of variance table for this example is Table 11-9. The principal difference between this table and the one for the earlier example is that the between-group source of variance is replaced with a therapy, a type-of-participant, and therapy by type-of-participant interaction. It is simply more useful to consider the between-group differences in terms of these three *independent* effects than in terms of an overall between-group effect. The effects are independent in that the statistical significance of any one of them does not depend on the significance, or lack of it, of any other. The within-group variance is used in the same way that it was when only one independent variable was considered.

Degrees of Freedom. The degrees of freedom is determined in essentially the same way as when there is only one independent variable. The degree of freedom for the therapy effect is equal to one because there are only two therapy groups (that is, therapy and no therapy). When calculating the therapy effect, the type-of-participant variable was collapsed. This left two groups of twenty subjects each. Because the overall total is fixed, only one group total is free to vary. By the same reasoning, the degree of freedom for the type-of-participant effect is also equal to 1.

A simple way to remember how to compute the degrees of freedom for any interaction is to keep in mind that a multiplication sign is used to label an interaction (for example, therapy $\times$ type of participant). The degrees of freedom for any interaction effect can be obtained by multiplying the degrees of freedom for the variables involved. In this case there is 1 degree of free-

TABLE 11-9

Analysis of Variance Table for the Experiment Investigating the Effect of Therapy and Type of Participant on the Scores Obtained on a Depression Test

Source of variance	df	SS	MS	F
Therapy (T)	1	55.22	55.22	19.86
Type of participant (P)	1	60.02	60.02	21.59
T $\times$ P	1	15.63	15.63	5.62
Within groups	36	99.91	2.78	
Total	39	230.78		

dom for the interaction because the product of the degrees of freedom for the two variables is equal to 1.

Note that the sum of the degrees of freedom for the three effects is equal to that which would have been obtained if the overall between-group effect had been assessed. Since there were four independent groups, there would be 3 degrees of freedom for the between-group effect. There are 36 degrees of freedom for the SS_{wg} because there are four groups and ten subjects per group $[k(n-1) = 4(9) = 36]$.

The SS, MS, *and* F *Columns.* The column for SS should not cause any difficulty because the sum of squares for each effect has been computed. The task is simply to record the values in the table. The values for the MS column are obtained by dividing the SS values for each effect by the degrees of freedom for that effect. The F value for each effect is obtained by dividing the mean square for the effect by the within-group mean square. In this case there are three separate effects. Each effect is evaluated by comparing the obtained F value with the appropriate table value. You will recall that in this case there are 1 and 36 degrees of freedom for each effect. If the .05 significance level is adopted, an obtained F value of 4.12 or greater (see Appendix C-4) is needed in order to have a statistically significant effect. Note that the value of 4.12 is obtained by interpolation. We select the value that is slightly more than midway between the values for 1 and 30 degrees of freedom (4.17) and 1 and 40 degrees of freedom (4.08). In this case all three effects, the two main effects and the interaction, are statistically significant.

Interpretation of the Results

The results are plotted in Figure 11-1. An examination of this figure in combination with the statistical analysis we have just considered should provide a clear picture of the results. In evaluating the results, we take one effect at a time. If you examine the figure you will note that the scores for the depressed patients are higher than for the nondepressed patients. This is not particularly surprising, of course, given that we are examining scores on a depression test. Yet, it should be reassuring to find that the depressed-nondepressed classification made on the basis of self-report statements is supported by the more objective results obtained with a test. The statistical analysis reveals that the difference is significant, that is, it is an unlikely outcome if only chance is operating. An examination of the figure also reveals that the people who received therapy had lower scores, on the average, than the people who did not receive therapy. This difference is also statistically significant (see Table 11-9). This result is important because it tells us that our treatment (therapy in this case) is an effective way of changing behavior, as reflected by the scores obtained on the depression test.

An examination of the figure also reveals that the effectiveness of therapy is dependent on the type of participant. Effectiveness is greater for people

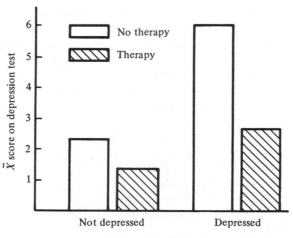

FIGURE 11-1

The mean score on the depression test for the four conditions of the experiment

who complain about being depressed than for those who do not; that is, the benefit obtained from therapy appears to be related to the type of participant. This is a logical expectation in that there would seem to be greater room for improvement for people who complain about being sad than for those who do not. We describe this result by saying that there is an interaction between the therapy independent variable and the type-of-participant variable. We use a figure to describe the results. We perform an analysis of variance to assess statistical significance. In this case the interaction is statistically significant (see Table 11-9), so we can conclude that the effectiveness of the therapy does depend on the type of participant, provided the experiment is methodologically sound. The greater effectiveness of the therapy for depressed than nondepressed participants would be a rare outcome if only chance were operating, so we are willing to conclude that more than chance is operating.

In brief, the analysis of variance with two independent variables is a useful way of assessing the statistical significance of independent variables considered singly as well as the interaction of independent variables. It is frequently useful to be able to determine whether the effectiveness of one independent variable (for example, therapy) depends on the level of another independent variable (such as type of participant). Main effects are independent of each other and independent of interactions — that is, you can have an interaction without having any main effects, and you can have one or more main effects without having an interaction. Yet, all effects need to be considered to interpret a set of results properly. If you have main effects and no interaction, the results can be said to be general. The effect of one independent variable does not depend on the level of the other. However, when an interaction is obtained we must be cautious in interpreting our main effects, if any, because the interaction tells us that we do not have a general result. The effectiveness of our treatment depends on other factors, such as the level of a second independent variable.

ASSUMPTIONS OF THE ANALYSIS OF VARIANCE

The assumptions underlying the analysis of variance depend on the model used. Only the fixed effects model is considered in this text. Conclusions are drawn only about the levels of the independent variable actually manipulated. For the fixed effects model, one makes two assumptions: that the variances of the samples are homogeneous and that the distributions within each sample are normal.

Homogeneity of Variance

The independent variable is expected to influence the extent to which the groups differ but not the fluctuations within a particular group. The within-group fluctuations are expected to be about the same regardless of the treatment. If, however, the manipulation influences the within-group variance (that is, there is significantly greater fluctuation within one group than within another), the assumption of homogeneity of variance has been violated. Our task is to assess whether the within-group fluctuations (variance) are greater than should be expected on the basis of chance. This task can be accomplished by dividing the variance of the group having the greatest variance by that of the group having the smallest variance. The resultant quotient is called the F_{max} value.

The F_{max} value can be evaluated by referring to Appendix C-6. To find the correct table value the number of groups and the size of each group must be considered. The number of groups is used to determine the correct column, and the degrees of freedom for each group (that is, the number of subjects minus one) is used to determine the correct row. The values are given for both the .05 and .01 level of significance. For example, if there are six groups and sixteen subjects in each group, the F_{max} value has to be equal to or greater than 4.68 in order to conclude that the variances are heterogeneous. If the table does not include the value for your degrees of freedom, you should use the next lower value (for example, 10 instead of 12) if you are interested in obtaining a significant F_{max} value, and the next highest (12 instead of 10) if you are interested in obtaining a nonsignificant F_{max} value. Since investigators are usually interested in obtaining an F_{max} value that is not significant, the next highest degree of freedom is usually used whenever the table does not include the value for your degrees of freedom. If the variances are heterogeneous, that is, if a significant F_{max} value is obtained, then the assumption of homogeneity of variance has not been met.

Assume that an investigator performs the F_{max} test and obtains a significant value. There is good reason to believe that the population variances are not homogeneous. The question then is what investigators should do when heterogeneous variances are obtained. Although there is some disagreement on this point, most statisticians think that violating the assumption of homogeneity of variance is not too serious a problem. If this assumption is violated the experimenter is likely to reject the null hypothesis more often than is justified. The likelihood of error is a function of the size of the sample and the extent of the heterogeneity of the variances. Yet there is usually little cause for concern in that the violation of this assumption tends to have very little effect on the accuracy of the analysis of variance test. If the assumption has been violated, a more stringent significance level (say, .01 instead of .05) should probably be used.

On the other hand, the significant F_{max} value may be a very interesting finding. If the independent variable influenced the within-group variance for some groups and not others, this suggests that subjects in the group(s) with the high variance were influenced differentially by the treatment. If the performance of some subjects and not of others is influenced, then the task for the experimenter is to determine why. In short, the fact that a treatment influences variance can be viewed as a finding *to be explained,* not merely as a failure to meet the assumption of the analysis of variance test.

Normality of Each Sample Distribution

The fact that the analysis of variance is so robust (that is, insensitive) with respect to violations of homogeneity of variance has led many investigators to ignore the assumption and not to test for homogeneity of variance. Because the analysis of variance test is also robust with respect to the assumption of the normality of the distribution within each sample, many investigators ignore this assumption as well. Violations of the normality assumption do not have much effect on the validity of the test. However, some readers may want to know how to determine whether this assumption has been met.

The assumption can be evaluated by plotting the deviation of each score from its *group* mean. If the frequency distribution of these deviation scores for all groups combined is fairly normal (symmetrical and mesokurtic), the assumption is satisfied. If the assumption is not satisfied (that is, if the distribution is markedly skewed), the investigator may elect to use a statistical test that does not require this assumption (see Siegel, 1956).

SUMMARY

The analysis of variance is a useful test to evaluate the statistical signifi-cance of between-subject comparisons in which interval data are obtained. The steps involved in obtaining the F value are straightforward. The com-putation of the analysis of variance involves obtaining two estimates of pop-ulation variance. The between-group estimate of population variance (mean square) is obtained by dividing the sum of squares between groups by its degrees of freedom. The within-group estimate of population variance (mean square) is obtained by dividing the sum of squares within groups by its degrees of freedom. The mean square between groups is divided by the mean square within groups to obtain an F value for the effect of the independent variable. The F value is evaluated by comparing it with the appropriate table value. If the obtained value exceeds the table value, the null hypothesis is rejected.

The analysis of variance for experiments in which more than one inde-pendent variable is manipulated is similar to that used for one independent variable. The major difference is that the sum of squares between groups is broken up to assess the effect of each independent variable and the interaction of the independent variables separately. It is not necessary to obtain a signifi-cant main effect to obtain a significant interaction.

The two major assumptions of the analysis of variance are homogeneity of variance and normality of each sample distribution. Slight violations of these assumptions do not have much effect on the accuracy of the analysis of variance test.

QUESTIONS

(The answers to most of the questions and problems are given in Appendix D.)

1. Perform an analysis of variance to assess whether beer consumption is re-lated to smoking. The numbers indicate the number of beers consumed per day, on the average, for each individual.

Smoker	Nonsmoker
3	2
4	2
0	1
0	6
3	0
5	1
6	3

2. Perform the analysis of variance given the following results.

Smoker	Nonsmoker
5	3
4	1
10	2
6	0
5	1
3	2
3	

3. The investigator was interested in whether the attitude of the experimenter toward a child would affect the child's ability to perform a manual dexterity task. While meeting the child and introducing him to the task, the experimenter was either very friendly to the child or very businesslike. The child's task was to drop as many marbles as possible into a jar. The dependent measure was the number of marbles in the jar after one minute. The random-groups design was used. Analyze the results of the experiment and state the conclusions.

Friendly experimenter	Businesslike experimenter
2	6
4	2
6	4
3	3

4. Do an analysis of variance to determine whether the level of the independent variable influenced performance. Present the analysis of variance table. A random-groups design was used and interval data were obtained.

Group I	Group II	Group III
2	4	6
3	5	8
1	4	7
2	6	8
4	5	7
2	4	6
4	6	9
3	6	7
5	5	5
2	4	6

5. Perform an analysis of variance for the results in question 4 using only groups I and II.

6. An investigator was interested in the relationship between the type of appeal and judgments about guilt or innocence for two types of participants: humanitarians and lawyers. (Those who qualified for both categories were not used in the study.) The emotional appeal consisted of a description of the plight of poor George Grimley and his family of fifteen children. The judicial approach was based on legal precedents. The dependent measure was obtained by asking each participant to indicate guilt or innocence on a scale from 1 to 10 with 1 being "definitely guilty" and 10 being "definitely innocent." Perform an analysis of variance for these results.

Type of participant

		Humanitarian	Lawyer
Type of appeal	Emotional	10	2
		9	3
		8	2
		9	1
		10	4
		7	2
		5	1
	Judicial	3	3
		4	7
		6	5
		5	4
		4	6
		5	5
		4	3

7. Do an analysis of variance to determine whether the effect of two independent variables — type of task and anxiety level — influence performance (see table at top of page 280). Do the two variables interact? The random-groups design was used for the type-of-task manipulation. Anxiety level is a subject variable. Interval data were obtained.

Type of task

		Easy	Difficult
Anxiety	Low	9 10 8 7 9 10 11 9	6 5 7 8 6 5 6 7
	High	10 11 9 10 12 13 14 12	2 3 4 3 4 3 5 4

8. Draw a figure for the results obtained in question 7.
9. A 2 by 2 factorial design was used to assess the effects of two drugs, marijuana and alcohol, on memory ability. The score for each participant was the number of words remembered after one presentation of the list of twelve words. Perform the appropriate analysis.

Marijuana

		Yes	No
Alcohol	Yes	3 5 2 4 3 1	6 5 6 7 4 6
	No	4 6 8 7 3 1	6 8 10 8 11 8

10. What are the assumptions of analysis of variance?

12 Analysis of within-subject and matched-groups designs

A few words need to be said about matched-groups designs and between-subject analyses before we consider statistical tests for within-subject and matched-groups designs. A matched-groups design can be considered a half-way step between a within-subject and a between-subject design. The way the matching is carried out determines which type of analysis is appropriate. When groups are matched by equating the group means and variances on the matching variables, the between-subject analyses discussed in Chapters 10 and 11 should be used. If they are matched on a subject by subject basis, then the analyses discussed in this chapter are appropriate.

The major purpose of this chapter is to acquaint you with statistical tools for analyzing experiments in which related samples are obtained. The samples may be related in that each subject is tested under each treatment condition (within-subject design), or the subjects in each treatment condition may be matched with subjects in the other treatment conditions on a subject by subject basis. As in the previous two chapters, the type of statistical tool will depend on the level of measurement of the dependent variable. The levels of measurement are examined in the same order as before, namely, nominal, ordinal, and interval. The steps in computing each test are considered in the context of an example.

NOMINAL DATA

Nominal Data Example

Imagine that an experimenter is interested in how to persuade people to stop smoking. An experiment is conducted to test the effectiveness of two treatments relative to no treatment. For one treatment condition an aversive stimulus is paired with smoking in an attempt to make smoking unpleasant.

The stimulus is an electric shock of sufficient intensity to be annoying but weak enough that no physical damage is done. The second treatment condition combines emotional and intellectual appeals intended to convince subjects that it would be in their own best interest to stop smoking. This approach involves presenting the evidence that smoking causes lung cancer, familiarizing subjects with the consequences of lung cancer, and so on. The third is a no treatment condition. The three conditions are labeled *shock, verbal,* and *control,* respectively.

The two treatment conditions are administered for a two-hour period, four times a week for one month. The control subjects are also seen for the same amount of time, but their sessions are spent discussing issues unrelated to smoking, such as community problems. At the conclusion of the treatment period the experimenter checks periodically with the subjects and with their associates to determine whether they have, in fact, quit smoking. Success is defined as smoking a mean of five or fewer cigarettes a day for two months. The dependent measure requires classifying each person into the success or failure category. Assume that the experimenter has little difficulty classifying the subjects. For our purposes the success and failure categories are qualitatively different. That is, the dependent measure is to be treated as nominal data even though it could be viewed as an instance of a higher level of measurement.

The experimenter believes that the length of time a person has been smoking prior to treatment and the amount of smoking per day prior to treatment are likely to be related to the difficulty of breaking the cigarette habit. Therefore he decides to match the three groups on the basis of prior smoking habits. From the sample of smokers he identifies groups of three persons who have essentially the same smoking history. He then *randomly assigns* them to the three conditions in such a way that one subject from each group is in each condition. This process is repeated until three groups of twenty subjects each are obtained.

The results of the experiment are presented in Table 12-1. Notice that there are twenty subjects in each condition and that the three subjects in the same row are matched with respect to prior smoking history. Each subject has a score of 0 (failure) or 1 (success). The issue is whether the three groups differ significantly in the number of successes. A significance test is used to assess whether the obtained differences are greater than can reasonably be expected on the basis of chance. In this case a test is needed that can be performed with a matched-groups (or within-subject) design which yields nominal data. The Cochran Q test (Cochran, 1950) is suitable.

Cochran Q Test

Computing the Q Value. The data in Table 12-1 are in the correct form for the use of the Cochran Q test in that each subject is placed in either a

TABLE 12-1

The Results of an Experiment Investigating the Effect of Two Treatments,
Relative to a Control, in Reducing the Incidence of Smoking (fictitious data)

Row	Control	Verbal approach	Shock approach	Total
a	0	1	1	2
b	1	1	0	2
c	0	0	1	1
d	0	1	1	2
e	0	0	0	0
f	1	1	1	3
g	0	0	0	0
h	1	1	1	3
i	0	1	1	2
j	0	0	1	1
k	1	0	1	2
l	0	1	0	1
m	1	1	0	2
n	0	0	0	0
o	0	1	1	2
p	0	0	0	0
q	1	1	1	3
r	0	0	0	0
s	0	1	1	2
t	1	1	1	3
Condition total	7	12	12	$T = 31$
(Condition total)^2	49	144	144	$\Sigma(\text{row total})^2 = 71$

$$Q = \frac{(k-1)[k\,\Sigma(\text{condition total})^2 - (T)^2]}{k(T) - \Sigma(\text{row totals})^2}$$

$$Q = \frac{2[3(49 + 144 + 144) - (31)^2]}{3(31) - 71}$$

$$Q = 4.55$$

success or failure category. To make possible the use of the Cochran Q test, the dependent measure must be dichotomous (success or failure, yes or no, pass or fail, consent or refuse). A 0 is always assigned to individuals in one category and a 1 to individuals in the other. Also, the data in Table 12-1 are in correct form in that the treatment conditions are represented in the columns, and the number of observations in each condition is equal to the number of rows.

The value of Q can then be computed by the formula

$$Q = \frac{(k-1)\ [k\ \Sigma(\text{condition total})^2 - (T)^2]}{k(T) - \Sigma(\text{row totals})^2}$$

As in earlier examples, k is equal to the number of treatment conditions and T is equal to the total of all the scores. The condition totals refer, of course, to the totals for each treatment condition. The computation of the Q value is presented in Table 12-1. Following the computation of Q, the next step is to evaluate Q to determine whether the obtained value is statistically significant.

Evaluating the Q *Value.* The obtained Q value is evaluated for significance in essentially the same way as the chi square. That is, since the two are essentially equal, the chi square distribution can be used to evaluate Q. The number of degrees of freedom for the Cochran Q test is equal to $k - 1$. The value in the chi square table with $k - 1$ degrees of freedom is the appropriate table value with which to evaluate the obtained Q value. If the .05 significance level is adopted, a Q value of 5.991 or higher (see Appendix C-2) is needed to reject the null hypothesis. In this case the obtained value of 4.55 is less than the value needed, so it is not possible to reject the null hypothesis. The probability of this particular outcome is greater than 5 percent if chance only is operating.

Uses of the Cochran Q *Test.* To use the Cochran Q test the number of observations per condition should not be too small (not less than, say, ten). Note also that the Cochran Q test can be used with a within-subject as well as a matched-groups design. For example, a perception experiment could be performed in which each subject receives three conditions of illumination. The condition of illumination is the independent variable. The task is to determine whether the subject is a success or failure under each of the three conditions. In this case there would be three observations from each subject, and therefore the observations in each row would be one subject's data. The Cochran Q test could be used to analyze this experiment in the same way that it was used to analyze the matched-groups experiment. However, if it is possible to do more than classify subjects into one of two categories, information is wasted by classifying them into two categories and using the Cochran Q test.

ORDINAL DATA

Ordinal Data Example

Assume that an experimenter is interested in the effect of a training program to reduce or eliminate shyness. The investigator has a test for shyness that we will assume to be reliable and valid. The test scores are treated as ordinal measurement because it is not clear that the intervals between successive units are equal. It is clear, however, that the test scores are at least at the ordinal level of measurement and that differences between test scores are ordinal. We can rank the differences between test scores obtained by testing each individual twice. All subjects are given a pretest, the treatment, and then a posttest. You may wish to consider the methodological weaknesses of this nonexperimental design (see Chapter 6) and perhaps suggest how the design might be changed to remove the weaknesses. Our task will be to consider a significance test for evaluating the pretest-posttest difference.

The results of this hypothetical experiment are presented in Table 12-2. Twelve subjects are randomly selected for the treatment from a population of introductory psychology students who indicated that they were shy. The question of interest is whether the pretest-posttest differences, if any, can be attributed solely to chance fluctuations or whether something besides chance (the treatment, regression, history) is operating. The Wilcoxon test can be used to evaluate the statistical significance of the results.

The Wilcoxon Test

Computations for the Wilcoxon Test. The computation of the Wilcoxon test for the results of the experiment on shyness is presented in Table 12-2. As shown in the table, each subject has two scores, in this case a pretest and posttest score. We want to examine the two sets of scores to assess whether the obtained differences between the two sets is a rare or common event if chance only is operating. The first step is to subtract one score from the other for each subject to obtain a difference score. It does not matter which score is subtracted (pretest score minus posttest score or vice versa) as long as we are consistent. However, we cannot use any subject who has the same score on the two tests; a difference score of zero is not permitted. Subjects with a difference score of zero are dropped from the analysis completely. We keep the sign of the difference and the amount of the difference separate because we want to rank the difference scores independent of sign. The ranked difference scores are presented in the sixth column of Table 12-2. When there are tied scores we assign the average of the tied ranks. The last column is obtained by taking the sign (column 4) and placing it next to the rank difference (column 6) to obtain the signed rank difference (column 7). Then we add the positive ranks and the negative ranks. We compare the smaller sum with a tabled value to determine whether the results are statistically significant.

Evaluation of the Wilcoxon Test. The smaller sum, in this case the sum of the negative ranks, is called the W value (for Wilcoxon). In this case W is 12. We need to determine whether this value is a rare or common occurrence

TABLE 12–2

The Pretest and Posttest Shyness Scores for the Twelve Subjects Who Received the Treatment and the Computations for the Wilcoxon Test (fictitious data)

Subject	Pretest	Posttest	Sign	Difference	Rank difference	Signed rank difference
A	45	38	+	7	8.0	+8.0
B	34	23	+	11	10.0	+10.0
C	31	35	−	4	4.0	−4.0
D	50	48	+	2	1.5	+1.5
E	22	19	+	3	3.0	+3.0
F	39	45	−	6	6.5	−6.5
G	42	30	+	12	11.0	+11.0
H	25	20	+	5	5.0	+5.0
I	50	30	+	20	12.0	+12.0
J	42	44	−	2	1.5	−1.5
K	36	30	+	6	6.5	+6.5
L	23	14	+	9	9.0	+9.0

Sum of positive ranks = 66

Sum of negative ranks = 12

if chance only is operating. In order to do this we compare the obtained value with a distribution of W values obtained by referring to Appendix C-5. To find the appropriate tabled value we need to adopt a significance level and know the number of subjects (that is, the number of pairs of scores). Let us adopt the .05 significance level (two-tailed). Because there are twelve subjects, the tabled value is 13. Our W value of 12 is lower than the tabled value of 13 so we can reject the null hypothesis. For the Wilcoxon test the obtained value must be less than or equal to the tabled value in order to be significant.

In this case we can reject the null hypothesis, but it does not follow necessarily that we can attribute the results to chance fluctuation *plus* the treatment effect. There may be variables other than the treatment that are responsible for the statistically significant reduction in the shyness scores from pretest to posttest. The significance test allows us to conclude that more than chance is operating, but it does not allow us to specify exactly what "more than chance" means. We can attribute statistically significant results to the effect of the treatment only when we have used experimental procedures that make alternative interpretations unlikely. There are several other plausible interpretations for a statistically significant result obtained with a pretest-posttest, nonexperimental design.

INTERVAL DATA

Interval Data Example

Assume that an investigator is interested in evaluating a theory of aggression in which aggressive behavior is viewed in relation to survival. The view is simply that aggressive behaviors are necessary for the survival of those species that kill other animals for food. Perhaps hunger in lower animals results in increased aggressiveness; that is, the internal stimuli associated with hunger may also be associated with aggressiveness. Our investigator decided to assess whether aggressiveness is related to hunger in children.

Assume that the investigator has access to young children at a summer camp. The investigator has control over the time each child eats because it is necessary to stagger the eating times at the dining hall. The children eat their evening meal at 5:00, 6:00, or 7:00 P.M. Children who eat early (5:00 P.M.) are free to play afterward; children who eat late (7:00 P.M.) are free to play before eating. Thus it is possible to observe the play behavior of children at 6:00 P.M. to determine the relationship between aggressive behaviors and time since the last meal. Each child is observed for one hour, starting at 6:00 P.M., on two days. On one day the child eats at 5:00 P.M., on the other day at 7:00 P.M. The order of the conditions (5:00 P.M. versus 7:00 P.M.) is counterbalanced across conditions so that the nature of the treatment is not confounded with the order of the treatments. A within-subject design is used and interval data (number of aggressive acts) are obtained.

One can ponder the methodological, ethical, and interpretational problems inherent in an experiment of this nature. One can consider the problems of defining hunger and aggressiveness, demand characteristics, possible differential transfer, and so on. Or one may want to consider other approaches that could be used to investigate the relationship between hunger and aggression. Our concern will be with the analysis of results obtained with a within-subject design in which interval data are obtained. In this case the level of measurement is ratio because there is an absolute zero and one can argue that there are equal intervals between successive units of measurement. We are not interested in differences between interval and ratio measures because this distinction is not important for the statistical procedures considered. Here, interval data can mean interval or ratio.

Analysis of Variance

The results of our hypothetical, within-subject design experiment are presented in Table 12-3, along with the analysis of variance. Note that the analysis differs somewhat from that performed for a between-subject design. The first step is to obtain the SS_{tot}. This value is obtained in exactly the same

TABLE 12-3

The Results and Analysis of a Hypothetical Experiment Investigating the Effect of Hunger on Aggressiveness

Subject	Hungry	Not hungry	Total
A	8	4	12
B	22	18	40
C	9	1	10
D	4	7	11
E	6	6	12
F	14	12	26
G	17	3	20
H	12	13	25
I	9	2	11
J	11	8	19
K	19	14	33
L	2	1	3
X	133	89	222
X^2	1877	1013	5390

$$SS_{tot} = \Sigma\Sigma X^2 - \frac{(T)^2}{N}$$

$$SS_{tot} = 2890 - \frac{(222)^2}{24}$$

$$SS_{tot} = 2890 - 2053.50$$

$$SS_{tot} = 836.50$$

$$SS_{conditions} = \Sigma \frac{(\text{group total})^2}{n} - \frac{(T)^2}{N}$$

$$SS_{conditions} = \frac{(133)^2 + (89)^2}{12} - \frac{(222)^2}{24}$$

$$SS_{conditions} = 2134.17 - 2053.50$$

$$SS_{conditions} = 80.67$$

(Continued on next page)

Table 12-3 continued

$$SS_{subjects} = \Sigma \frac{(\text{subject total})^2}{\# \text{ of conditions}} - \frac{(T)^2}{N}$$

$$SS_{subjects} = \frac{5390}{2} - \frac{(222)^2}{24}$$

$$SS_{subjects} = 641.50$$

$$SS_{subjects \times conditions} = SS_{tot} - SS_{conditions} - SS_{subjects}$$

$$SS_{s \times c} = 836.50 - 80.67 - 641.50$$

$$SS_{s \times c} = 114.33$$

Source	df	SS	MS	F
Conditions (C)	1	80.67	80.67	7.76
Subjects (S)	11	641.50	58.32	
$C \times S$	11	114.33	10.39	
Total	23	836.50		

way as for a between-subject design. Next the $SS_{conditions}$ is obtained. *Conditions* is a label for the independent variable. For example, if the independent variable is type of social setting, *social setting* could be substituted for *conditions*. This value is obtained in the same way that the main effects for the independent variables were obtained for the between-subject design. The $SS_{subjects}$ is obtained after the $SS_{conditions}$ and it is obtained in the same way except that the totals for each subject (row totals) are used instead of the column totals. After the subject totals are squared and then added, the sum is divided by two because there are two scores for each subject. The next step is to obtain the sum of squares for the interaction of conditions by subjects by subtracting the $SS_{conditions}$ and $SS_{subjects}$ from the SS_{tot}.

The analysis of variance table for the present example is also presented in Table 12-3. The degrees of freedom and the mean square values are obtained in the same manner as for a between-subject analysis. Note that the F value for conditions is obtained by dividing the mean square for conditions by the mean square for the conditions-by-subjects interaction. An F value for subjects is not computed because there is no appropriate error term (estimate of chance fluctuation). Our sole concern is with whether the conditions produced a significant effect.

The evaluation of the obtained F value is accomplished by comparing the obtained value of 7.76 with the appropriate tabled value. In this case there are 1 and 11 degrees of freedom, so the tabled value (see Appendix C-4) corresponding to the .05 significance level is equal to 4.84. Because the obtained value is greater than the tabled value, we can reject the null hypothesis.

In performing the above analysis, we have to assume that the mean square of conditions by subjects provides a suitable estimate of chance fluctuation only. The extent to which this assumption is justified frequently depends on the research area considered. Investigators who do not have to be particularly concerned about interactions between subject and nonsubject variables can usually use the above analysis. If there is reason to believe that the effect of the treatment depends on the type of subject, the above analysis may not be appropriate. An investigator who is concerned about the differential effect of treatments on subjects can, of course, combine subject variable with nonsubject variable manipulations to determine whether the two kinds of variables interact.

SUMMARY

The statistical tests discussed in this chapter are appropriate for within-subject designs and for matched-groups designs if the matching is done on a subject by subject basis. The Cochran Q test is appropriate for nominal data, the Wilcoxon test for ordinal data, and the analysis of variance for interval data. The steps in computing the Cochran Q and Wilcoxon tests are straightforward.

Using the analysis of variance to analyze experiments with matched-groups or within-subject designs is quite similar to using it with between-subject designs. The major difference is that fluctuations within subjects or within matched sets of subjects are used to evaluate the effect of the independent variable. This estimate of chance fluctuation is the interaction of conditions by subjects if a within-subject design is used.

QUESTIONS

(The answers to most of the questions and problems are given in Appendix D.)

1. An experiment was conducted to assess the effects of two treatments. A within-subject design was used and nominal data were obtained. Perform the appropriate statistical test to determine whether the treatments differed in effectiveness. A score of 1 indicates success and a score of 0 indicates failure. The presentation order of the conditions was counterbalanced so that half the subjects were given treatment A first and the other half were given treatment B first.

Subject	Treatment A	Treatment B
a	0	0
b	0	1
c	0	1
d	1	1
e	0	1
f	0	1
g	1	1
h	0	1
i	1	0
j	0	1
k	0	1
l	0	1
m	0	1
n	1	1
o	0	1
p	1	0

2. An experiment was conducted in which a within-subject design was used. Subjects were tested under condition A and condition B. The dependent measure was whether subjects were successful or unsuccessful under each testing condition. They were given a score of 0 if they were unsuccessful and a score of 1 if successful. Do the appropriate analysis to determine if the condition manipulation had any effect. In this case, treat the success-versus-failure categorization as an instance of a nominal classification.

Subject	Condition A	Condition B
a	0	0
b	1	0
c	1	0
d	1	0
e	1	0
f	1	0
g	1	1
h	0	1
i	1	0

3. Assume that the same experiment was conducted as in question 2 but that ordinal data were obtained. Do the appropriate analysis. Then assume that the data are at the interval level of measurement and perform an appropriate statistical analysis.

Subject	Condition A	Condition B
a	6	1
b	10	5
c	6	4
d	8	6
e	9	5
f	7	8
g	5	4
h	10	8
i	9	9
j	4	2

4. An experiment was conducted to assess the effect of three treatments. A within-subject design was used and interval data were obtained. Each subject obtained a score for each of three treatment conditions. A high score indicates good performance. Do an analysis to determine whether the three treatments differed in effectiveness. The order of the treatments was counter-balanced.

Subject	Treatment A	Treatment B	Treatment C
a	3	1	10
b	3	0	15
c	5	1	8
d	7	4	7
e	4	8	8
f	9	9	9
g	4	6	8
h	6	4	10
i	1	10	20
j	6	8	12

13 Evaluating and reporting results

In this chapter we will examine some of the difficulties encountered in evaluating and reporting results. Our task is to consider whether the results are worth reporting and, if they are, where and how they should be reported. This is not easy. There is no accepted standard for evaluating research, no prescribed place to send the manuscript, and no single set of principles to follow in writing the report. The experimenter has to make decisions. Deciding whether his results are worth reporting means that he will have to consider their psychological significance.

THE PSYCHOLOGICAL SIGNIFICANCE OF RESULTS

Statistical Versus Psychological Significance

Statistical significance refers to the likelihood that an event can be attributed to chance effects. Psychological significance refers to whether or not a particular finding is a contribution to knowledge. The fact that a result is statistically significant does not mean, necessarily, that it is of psychological significance. The psychological significance of a study is determined by the quality of the idea, the adequacy of the test, and the clarity of the results. All three are important.

To evaluate the results for psychological significance, you should reconsider your research idea. You probably considered your idea at length while planning and conducting your research, but now you have information that you did not have previously. Now you can reevaluate your idea in light of the results to assess whether the idea still has merit.

Evaluating the Quality of Ideas

It is difficult to make general statements about the process of evaluating ideas. In some cases evaluation will be easy because the idea is clearly important or unimportant. For example, if you demonstrate a finding that has already been demonstrated numerous times, you have not made a contribution to knowledge. On the other hand, if you establish a new phenomenon or provide an explanation for a previously unexplained phenomenon, your contribution is probably worthwhile. Several people usually participate in judging whether a particular finding makes a contribution to knowledge. The investigator assesses the value of his work at various stages in the investigation, particularly the planning stage. He usually asks colleagues to participate in this evaluation. When the results are submitted for publication, the work is usually evaluated by specialists in the same area. Most journal editors insist that research findings pass a contribution to knowledge test as one step in determining whether the findings should be published.

Adequacy of the Test

If the idea passes the quality evaluation, the next step is to consider the adequacy of the test. Did the experimental manipulation provide a fair test of the prediction? Were there any confounding variables? Could the results have turned out in such a way that the idea would have been proved incorrect? An adequate test of an idea is obtained only if the results can refute as well as support the assertions to be tested.

Sometimes an experimental design fails to yield an adequate test of the idea owing to unforeseen problems. For example, an investigator may decide to test the effectiveness of different learning strategies by manipulating the strategy instructions to each group. If differences are obtained between the groups, there is no problem. However, if differences are not obtained, it will be very difficult to determine whether the strategies actually do not differ in effectiveness or the subjects simply failed to use the strategy they were told to use. If the test is inadequate there is little choice but to start over by devising a better test. If the test is adequate the next task is to consider the clarity of the results.

Definitiveness of the Results

Evaluating the results for clarity involves both statistical and nonstatistical considerations. If statistically significant, easily interpreted results are obtained, the investigator is very fortunate. Interpretational problems arise when the results are not as clear as the experimenter would have liked. For example, when two predictions are made and one is clearly supported and the other is not, there will be interpretational problems. If both predictions follow from the theoretical view the investigator is likely to be ambivalent about the results. In evaluating the clarity of results one should consider whether it is possible to draw firm conclusions from the findings. If the predictions received firm support and the experiment was a fair test of the predictions and the research idea was equal to or better than ideas already reported in refereed scientific journals, then it is fair to conclude that the findings are psychologically significant.

We can distinguish between nonsignificance, which refers to the lack of statistical significance, and insignificance, which refers to the lack of psychological significance. Let us assume that the results lack psychological significance. At this point the investigator may be very discouraged. He has spent a lot of time and energy on an insignificant result. Clearly he has reason to be discouraged, but it may be incorrect to conclude that he gained nothing but a few more gray hairs and a higher hostility level. He may now be in a good position to redesign the experiment and conduct it properly, having discovered some of the pitfalls in conducting research.

It is not uncommon for an investigator to make mistakes that invalidate the results of the experiment. His task is then to decide whether the test was inadequate or the idea was wrong. If the test was inadequate, the experimenter may have some firm notions about how a better test could be made. If the idea was wrong, perhaps an alternative theoretical notion is now worthy of testing. The point is that experimenters should not be surprised if their first attempts at research do not come out as well as they had hoped. Many research projects do not yield the anticipated results. Let us assume, however, that the results are clear and important. The next task is to report the findings.

REPORTING THE FINDINGS

The Decision to Report Research Findings

Importance of the Findings. It would appear that the only factor in deciding whether to report research findings is their psychological significance. If you have something important to report you are likely to be eager to have it in print. If you have rather uninteresting results there is usually little reason to bother reporting them. However, there may be situations that make it necessary to report insignificant or nonsignificant results. For example, an instructor may insist that his students report the less-than-exciting results of a laboratory experiment in order to gain skill in making and evaluating reports.

Graphic Phobia. There is at least one additional factor that may influence the decision whether to report findings. For lack of a better term, let us call this factor *graphic phobia* (fear of writing). In some cases anxiety about writing may be related to the lack of psychologically significant findings. Yet many people experience anxiety about writing even when they are convinced that the finding should be reported or even when they have excellent "external justification" (such as being required to report a laboratory experiment). You can expect to be a little anxious about reporting the findings because writing can be both a reinforcing and a punishing experience. This point requires further elaboration.

We have said before that one should attempt to find a research problem of genuine personal interest. An experimenter is not likely to derive much satisfaction from research unless it is intrinsically rewarding. Let us assume that you did find a problem of personal interest. You generated an idea that you believe to be excellent, designed an experiment to test it, and obtained statistically significant results. You evaluate all that you have done and conclude that the findings are psychologically significant. You are extremely excited by this chain of events. Now it is time to report the findings so that others can evaluate the work.

If the experiment required a large commitment, you will undoubtedly want the finished manuscript to reflect this. Perhaps friends and relatives know that you have been conducting a research project, and they are interested in learning the results. How, you may ask, can one possibly communicate all the excitement, frustration, confusion, depression, and insight that went into the research project? The answer is that one cannot, and should not, as this would detract from the major goal of reporting the findings. Perhaps the objective approach that investigators convey on the printed page has led some students to conclude that scientists are a cool, unemotional lot. However, the reader who has experienced some of the rewards and punishments of doing research should know better. In short, don't be overly concerned if you sweat a little while preparing the manuscript.

Factors to Consider Before Writing

Selecting the Audience. If the findings are worth reporting, the next task is to consider what audience to reach and how to reach it. Scores of journals publish research findings about behavior and mental activity. Your task is to select the most appropriate journal or other medium. To determine the proper audience it is necessary to assess the extent to which the finding is of general interest.

If the finding has broad significance it may be reasonable to inform the major communications networks. If it is likely to be of interest to scientists in other disciplines a journal should be selected that is widely read among scientists (such as *Science* or *Scientific American*). If it is of interest mainly to psychologists, a psychological journal should be selected. If it is of interest to psychologists working on a particular problem only, a specialized psychological journal would be appropriate. If the finding is unimportant it may only be necessary to notify the one other person in the world who is interested. You accomplish this by calling your mother.

It is important to take care in selecting the place to submit the manuscript because if an inappropriate journal is chosen your time and that of the journal editor will be wasted. The manuscript will be returned and you will be advised to send it elsewhere. Since the format varies for different journals it will then be necessary to make changes in the manuscript so that it conforms to the style of a second journal. Investigators often decide where they want to submit their articles by the time they are ready to start writing. If you have not familiarized yourself with the journals that publish articles in your area of interest, you should do so before starting to write.

Following the Correct Format. After you have selected a journal you should study recent issues to learn the style used in that journal. Often there will be instructions for investigators who plan to submit manuscripts to the journal. It is also a good idea to obtain a copy of the most recent edition of the publication manual of the American Psychological Association (1200 Seventeenth Street, N.W., Washington, D.C., 20036). This manual provides useful information for preparing a manuscript. It is still necessary to examine recent issues of the journal you are interested in, however, because each journal usually has slight deviations from the general style.

Now let us turn to general problems encountered in manuscript preparation. We will examine the four major sections of a research article: introduction, method, results, and discussion.

The Introduction Section

The four major sections of the manuscript correspond roughly to the four major stages of experimentation. One can conceptualize experimentation as involving an idea stage in which the problem area is selected and testable ideas are generated, a testing stage in which data are collected, a results stage in which the effects are determined and evaluated for statistical significance, and an overall evaluation stage in which the possible value of the finding to the state of knowledge in the field is considered.

The introduction corresponds to the idea stage. The goal in the introduction should be to familiarize the reader with the problem, the insights for problem solution, and the procedure for testing the insights. One should say why the predictions, if supported, will be of psychological significance. The task of writing an introduction is usually more difficult than it first appears, often because of poor organization and a failure to assess accurately how much background information is needed.

Selecting the Relevant Prior Research. The amount of background information needed will depend on the nature of the problem, the audience, and the journal. Obviously, if the readers of the journal already know a great deal about the problem, it is not necessary to present much background information in the introduction. To do so would be to waste journal space and the reader's time. Yet the investigator does have an obligation to consider the earlier work most directly related to his study. He should realize that it is extremely unlikely that the idea is completely new. The chances are that someone investigated a similar idea but not in quite the same way or in the same context or for the same purpose. At the very least the reader should be informed about the previous work that is most closely related to the study to be reported. Planning the organization of the introduction should be relatively easy after a decision has been made about how much background information to provide. (Many instructors will insist that their students present a more extensive literature review than would be found in the introduction of a journal article.)

Organizing the Introduction. At the risk of laboring the obvious, it should be pointed out that one should plan the introduction before writing it. In many cases, unfortunately, little or no thought goes into planning. One needs to consider how much background material to present, the order in which to present it if there is more than one relevant study, the specific problem, the solution, and how the solution is to be tested. If the reader does not learn from the introduction what is going to be done and why, the introduction has not been written properly.

Indicating the Importance of the Problem. The introduction is the place to persuade the reader of the importance of the experiment. If you are ashamed of your idea you should not bother to report the study. If you are not ashamed of it you should talk about its psychological significance in the introduction. The reader should be told the basic plan for testing the idea, the results to be expected, and how the results will support or refute the predictions. The specific details of the testing procedure, however, should be left for the method section.

The Method Section

The major task in the method section is to explain how the predictions were tested. If elaborate equipment or complicated materials were used it may be helpful to discuss this in a special subsection. If the experiment was extremely simple, no subheadings may be needed. In general, however, subheadings for design and procedure are useful.

Design. The reader should be told in the design subsection what was manipulated, correlated, or observed and what was measured. If the experimental method was used, it is necessary to specify the independent variable(s) and dependent variable(s). In general the method section should proceed from the more overall aspects of the experiment (independent and dependent variables) to the more specific procedures employed. After reading the discussion of design, the reader should have a clear view of what was manipulated and the type of design used to test the predictions. The specific procedures used in making the tests are reported in the procedure subsection.

Procedure. The task in the discussion of procedure is to tell exactly how the experiment was conducted so that the reader could repeat the experiment in essentially the same way. After writing the procedure subsection you should ask yourself whether the experiment could be completed by referring only to the information presented in the method section. The reader has to be told how subjects were obtained, how they were assigned to conditions, what materials were used, how much time was needed for each phase of the experiment, what the subjects were told, how the dependent measure was obtained, and so on. One way to present this information is to describe the procedure used to test the subjects in each of the conditions. It is a good idea to study the method sections of published journal articles to see how this is done. After the procedure is presented, the next step is to consider the results of the experiment.

The Results Section

It is important to plan the results section before starting to write it. When you have completed all the statistical analyses, you should have a clear notion of what aspects of the results are interesting and what aspects are not. For example, if there are two or more independent variables and only one produced a statistically significant effect, this variable, all things being equal, is going to be more interesting than the others. It is also important to double-check calculations to be sure that the reported results are identical to the obtained results.

Organizing the Results. The major task is to lead the reader through the results, pointing out what is significant and what is not. Your role is like that of a guide taking visitors through a museum. Make sure that the reader is made aware of the important results. The results have to be organized in such a way that the reader is not confronted with a large mass of data. The task is to give a simple, clear, and reasonably complete account of the results. Although the specific organization will depend on the particular study considered, there are a few points that need to be emphasized.

Presenting Data. There is usually no reason to present the raw data to the reader. You should simplify the data by presenting descriptive measures (for example, measures of central tendency such as the mean) for each group. You may have to decide whether it would be better to present the descriptive measures in the text, in a figure, or in a table. There is no rule that can be applied in all circumstances. However, if there are many numbers to present (say, ten or more), probably a table or figure should be used. Often a figure cannot be used because there are too many means to present. In such a case the tabular presentation should be preferred. The choice between a table and a figure will often depend on the nature of the data.

If you are unsure of which way to present the measures of central tendency, frequency, or whatever, prepare them in different forms. Then it may become clear which mode of presentation is best. If you are still unsure which method is the clearest for the reader, ask a few friends or colleagues to judge. Do not present the same measures in two different ways in the manuscript as this may confuse or insult the reader.

Leading the Reader Through the Results. A very common mistake experimenters make in reporting results is presenting a measure of central tendency in a figure or table and then leaving the readers to their own devices. This is analogous to an unguided trip through a museum. If the results are merely presented in a table and the reader is expected to decide which values are important and which are unimportant, the investigator is not assuming the responsibilities of the guide. After all, by the time you report the results you should have thought about them for a long time and should be in a good position to point out what is important.

Amount of Data Presented. You should avoid, if possible, presenting a large amount of data. If you have an exceptionally interesting study in which there are many important measures, there is little choice but to present a great deal of information. However, if a large amount of data is to be reported, the burden on the guide is increased.

You should accept the fact that you are in a better position than the reader is to judge the importance of your data and should organize the results section to emphasize what is important. It is reasonable to ignore completely or just give passing notice to unimportant results. As long as your view of what is important is reasonably consistent with what others think, you should have little difficulty with instructors, journal editors, or readers.

After presenting the basic descriptive measures, you need to indicate what comparisons the reader should consider and whether they are statistically significant. If a complex analysis of variance was conducted, you may decide to present the analysis of variance table. However, it is generally better to present the F values of interest without bothering to present the entire table. Once again, the task is to decide which method of presentation is easier for the reader. The plan of the results section, then, is to present the basic descriptive measures, point out the important comparisons, and indicate whether the differences between conditions are statistically significant.

Discussing the Results. Another question is how much discussion of the results is desirable in the results section. Some investigators prefer to present the bare results and save all discussion of them for the discussion section. Others prefer to say more about them in the results section. The nature of the experiment and the preferences of the investigator may influence the choice. If it would be clearer to discuss each finding right after presenting it, then it would be better to combine the discussion section with the results section.

Let us assume, however, that you do not want to eliminate the separate discussion section because it is necessary to provide an overall evaluation of the present findings and relate them to previous research. Yet you would still like to say something about each finding immediately after presenting it. Is it permissible to do so? The answer is *yes* if the discussion does not take you too far afield. In general you should avoid comparing your results with the results of earlier work as this may confuse the reader. It is usually best to concentrate on making concise remarks about the interesting aspects of *your* results. A consideration of the relationship of the findings to other findings, their psychological significance, and the overall state of the problem is usually best left for the discussion section.

The Discussion Section

The discussion section is similar to the introduction in that it is a place to consider the broader problem area of interest. The introduction can be regarded as the *before* and the discussion section as the *after*. In the introduction the state of the art before the investigation was examined. In the discussion section you should consider the state of the art after the investigation (how the investigation influenced knowledge about the phenomenon in question). The introduction offered the idea or insight that was expected to further the understanding of a particular phenomenon or produce a particular result. The insight is testable since certain predictions follow from it. In the discussion section, presented after the reader has been informed about the accuracy of the prediction, all the cards are on the table so it is time to assess the degree of success or failure.

Reporting an Important Finding. The ease of writing the discussion section will be determined in large part by the psychological significance of the findings and the quality and thoroughness of the introduction. If the understanding of a particular phenomenon has changed drastically because of your contribution, then, of course, you will want to emphasize the impact of your finding. The discussion section should be very enjoyable to write. Perhaps the finding has implications for further research, or perhaps it makes possible the reinterpretation of earlier work within a different theoretical framework. If the finding has practical application, this may be emphasized in the discussion. The specific nature of the discussion will depend, of course, on the particular contribution.

Reporting a Finding of Some Interest. Another possibility is that the results, although clear, are not entirely consistent with earlier findings. Your task, therefore, is to compare your findings with those of other investigators and try to resolve the differences. Because you have the most recent evidence bearing on a particular problem, you should be in a good position to evaluate the current state of knowledge. The experiment may provide evidence which suggests that one view is to be preferred over the others. In order to write this kind of discussion you may need to spend a lot of time studying the results of other investigators in an attempt to integrate the results. Yet the attempt at integration may result in additional insights that can be tested experimentally. Even if the results do not provide a complete solution to the problem of interest, they may suggest avenues for additional research.

Reporting Findings of Little Interest. Another possibility is that the results did essentially nothing to clarify the problem, but you still have to report the findings in order to gain experience. This kind of discussion is painful to write. It is not feasible to concentrate on the extent of your contribution because this would only depress you. You cannot concentrate on a comparison of your results with those of other investigators because yours were not sufficiently clear to warrant the comparison. Thus there is little choice but to admit that your predictions were not supported and consider the possible reasons for the failure. The state of knowledge is the same as it was before your "contribution" except that you may be convinced that one idea, yours, is not a particularly useful insight. You have the unpleasant task of considering a problem for which you were unable to offer a good solution. However, since you probably learned a great deal about the problem, or at least thought a great deal about it, you may have a number of new ideas to present in the discussion section. If you can generate sufficiently interesting ideas, you may wish to put them to an experimental test.

General Comments About Writing

After you have completed a draft of the four major sections you may be tempted to decide on a title, write an abstract or summary as required, prepare the tables or figures, list the references, and then type the manuscript for publication. This would be a mistake. There is almost no chance that the first draft would measure up to the standards of a professional journal. It is necessary to polish the manuscript. You polish it by recasting unclear statements, eliminating redundancy, correcting faulty organization, and remedying any other defects you can find. After you believe the manuscript is in fine shape it is a good idea to ask someone to read it and make criticisms.

One has to be very careful in choosing a critic. It is important to find someone who will criticize constructively. You are likely to be ego-involved in your work and, therefore, somewhat reluctant to accept even constructive criticism. If you are offered nonconstructive criticism ("I can't believe you passed freshman English!"), the only thing you gain is a feeling of animosity toward the critic. There is also the danger of finding a critic who is so picayune that you doubt the value of the criticism. On the other hand, there is the danger of finding someone who is unwilling to make any criticism for fear of offending. What is needed is someone with a knowledge of language to tell you objectively how your paper reads. It may be difficult to find such a person, but you should know at least one who qualifies.

Once you have found this rare person you need to treat him with extreme care. It is important to take his comments seriously. If he says a statement is unclear, you have to be willing to clarify it. It is irrelevant that the statement is clear to you. The important thing is that it be clear to others. After all, your purpose is to communicate your findings.

You may be frustrated by the criticism. You would probably prefer the critic to say that the manuscript is in excellent shape so that you could prepare it for publication. Task completion is usually a rewarding state of affairs so anything that delays it may be frustrating. Yet it is necessary to fight the urge to get the job over with at any cost. Once a manuscript is published there is no way to change it.

Preparing the Manuscript for Publication

As we have said, you should check recent issues of the journal you have in mind and any instructions for authors — such as instructions on the inside covers of the journal or in the publication manual of the American Psychological Association — before preparing the manuscript for publication. Unless you have special drawing talents you should find a professional draftsman to prepare the figures. The manuscript should be typed according to the specifications of the journal and the appropriate number of copies made. Then it is important to proofread carefully. After any errors are eliminated, the manuscript is sent to the journal editor along with a covering letter asking that it be considered for the journal. After a reasonable length of time (in some cases an unreasonable length of time) you will receive a reply from the editor. The manuscript will be accepted as is, accepted subject to certain revisions, or rejected.

SUMMARY

It is important to distinguish between statistical and psychological significance. Statistical significance refers to the likelihood than an event can be attributed to chance effects. Psychological significance refers to whether a finding is a contribution to knowledge. The psychological significance of a study is determined by the quality of the idea tested, the adequacy of the test, and the clarity of the results.

The decision to report research findings should be based solely on their importance, but other factors frequently enter in. Some people are reluctant to report their findings because writing makes them nervous. One should expect to experience some anxiety while preparing a manuscript because research usually involves a tremendous personal commitment.

The four major sections of the manuscript correspond roughly to the four major stages of experimentation. The introduction corresponds to the idea stage, the method section to the testing stage, the results section to the evaluation of the obtained findings, and the discussion section to the overall evaluation.

The problems in writing the introduction are selecting the relevant prior research, organizing the introduction, and explaining how the proposed idea should contribute to knowledge. The reader should be told in the method section about how the idea was tested. It should be possible to repeat the experiment by referring to the information presented in the method section. The problems in writing the results section include organizing the results and deciding what to present and how to present it. The nature of the discussion section will be influenced by whether the finding is of little interest, some interest, or great interest.

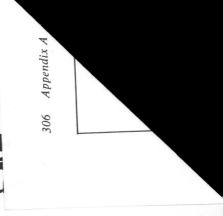

Appendix  Sam
rese
manu

This appendix is included to give the student preparing a laboratory report or the beginning researcher preparing a research article an example of a manuscript as submitted for publication. For this example each page of the manuscript is outlined and, when applicable, numbered so it is clear what sections require a new page and what sections do not. The cover page, abstract, tables, and figures are each on a separate page. Reference notes, references, footnotes, and figure captions are *started* on a new page. The running head on the first page (title page) is a short title (maximum of 60 spaces including punctuation and spaces between words). If the title is already short, then the running head and the title will be identical.

Weapons as Aggression-Eliciting Stimuli

Leonard Berkowitz and Anthony LePage

University of Wisconsin

Running head: Weapons as Aggression-Eliciting Stimuli

Reprinted by permission of the senior author and publisher from the *Journal of Personality and Social Psychology,* vol. 7 (1967), pp. 202–207.

Abstract

An experiment was conducted to test the hypothesis that stimuli commonly associated with aggression can elicit aggressive responses from people ready to act aggressively. One hundred male university students received either one or seven shocks, supposedly from a peer, and were then given an opportunity to shock this person. In some cases a rifle and revolver were on the table near the shock key. These weapons were said to belong, or not to belong, to the available target person. In other instances there was nothing on the table near the shock key, while for a control group two bad- minton racquets were on the table near the key. The greatest number of shocks was given by the strongly aroused Ss (who had received seven shocks) when they were in the presence of the weapons. The guns had evidently elicited strong aggressive responses from the aroused men.

Weapons as Aggression-Eliciting Stimuli[1]

Human behavior is often goal directed, guided by strategies and influenced by ego defenses and strivings for cognitive consistency. There clearly are situations, however, in which these purposive considerations are relatively unimportant regulators of action. Habitual behavior patterns become dominant on these occasions, and the person responds relatively automatically to the stimuli impinging upon him. Any really complete psychological system must deal with these stimulus-elicited, impulsive reactions as well as with more complex behavior patterns. More than this, we should also be able to specify the conditions under which the various behavior determinants increase or decrease in importance.

The senior author has long contended that many aggressive actions are controlled by the stimulus properties of the available targets rather than by anticipations of ends that might be served (Berkowitz, 1962, 1964, 1965). Perhaps because strong emotion results in an increased utilization of only the central cues in the immediate situation (Easterbrook, 1959; Walters & Parke, 1964), anger arousal can lead to impulsive aggressive responses which, for a short time at least, may be relatively free of cognitively mediated inhibitions against aggression or, for that matter, purposes and strategic considerations. This impulsive action is not necessarily pushed out by the anger, however. Berkowitz has suggested that appropriate cues must be present in the situation if aggressive responses are actually to occur. While there is still considerable uncertainty as to just what characteristics define aggressive cue properties, the association of a stimulus with aggression evidently can enhance the aggressive cue value of this stimulus. A variety of observations can be cited in support of this reasoning (cf. Berkowitz, 1965).

Direct eivdence for the present formulation can be found in a study conducted by Loew (1965). His subjects, in being required to learn a concept, either aggressive or neutral words, spoke either 20 aggressive or 20 neutral words aloud. Following this "learning task," each subject was to give a peer in an adjacent room an electric shock whenever this person made a mistake in his learning problem. Allowed to vary the intensity of the shocks they administered over a 10-point continuum, the subjects who had uttered the aggressive words gave shocks of significantly greater intensity than did the subjects who had spoken the neutral words. The aggressive words had evidently evoked implicit aggressive responses from the subjects, even though they had not been angered beforehand, which then led to the stronger attacks upon the target person in the next room when he supposedly made errors.

Cultural learning shared by many members of a society can also associate external objects with aggression and thus affect the objects' aggressive cue value. Weapons are a prime example. For many men (and probably women as well) in our society, these objects are closely associated with aggression. Assuming that the weapons do not produce inhibitions that are stronger than the evoked aggressive reactions (as would be the case, e.g., if the weapons were labeled as morally "bad"), the presence of the aggressive objects should generally lead to more intense attacks upon an available target than would occur in the presence of a neutral object.

The present experiment was designed to test this latter hypothesis. At one level, of course, the findings contribute to the current debate as to the desirability of restricting sales of firearms. Many arguments have been raised for such a restriction. Thus, according to recent statistics, Texas communities having virtually no prohibitions against firearms have a much higher homicide rate than other American cities possessing stringent firearm regulations, and J. Edgar Hoover has maintained in *Time* magazine that the availability of firearms is an important factor in murders (Anonymous, 1966). The experiment reported here seeks to determine how this influence may come about. The availability of weapons makes it easier for a person who wants to commit murder to do so. But, in addition, we ask whether weapons can serve as aggression-eliciting stimuli, causing an angered individual to display stronger violence than he would have shown in the absence of such weapons. Social significance aside, and at a more general theoretical level, this research also attempts to demonstrate that situational stimuli can exert "automatic" control over socially relevant human actions.

Method

Subjects

The subjects were 100 male undergraduates enrolled in the introductory psychology course at the University of Wisconsin who volunteered for the experiment (without knowing its nature) in order to earn points counting toward their final grade. Thirty-nine other subjects had also been run, but were discarded because they suspected the experimenter's confederate (21), reported receiving fewer electric shocks than were actually given them (7), had not attended to information given them about the procedure (9), or were run while there was equipment malfunctioning (2).

Procedure

General design. Seven experimental conditions were established, six organized in a 2 x 3 factorial design, with the seventh group serving essentially as a control. Of the men in the factorial design, half were made to be angry with the confederate, while the other subjects received a friendlier treatment from him. All of the subjects were then given an opportunity to administer electric shocks to the confederate, but for two-thirds of the men there were weapons lying on the table near the shock apparatus. Half of these people were informed the weapons belonged to the confederate in order to test the hypothesis that aggressive stimuli which also were associated with the anger instigator would evoke the strongest aggressive reaction from the subjects. The other people seeing the weapons were told the weapons had been left by a previous experimenter. There was nothing on the table except the shock key when the last third of the subjects in both the angered and nonangered conditions gave the shocks. Finally, the seventh group consisted of angered men who gave shocks with two badminton racquets and shuttlecocks lying near the shock key. This condition sought to determine whether the presence of any object near the shock apparatus would reduce inhibitions against aggression, even if the object were not connected with aggressive behavior.

<u>Experimental manipulations</u>. When each subject arrived in the laboratory, he was informed that two men were required for the experiment and that they would have to wait for the second subject to appear. After a five-minute wait, the experimenter, acting annoyed, indicated that they had to begin because of his other commitments. He said he would have to look around outside to see if he could find another person who might serve as a substitute for the missing subject. In a few minutes the experimenter returned with the confederate. Depending upon the condition, this person was introduced as either a psychology student who had been about to sign up for another experiment or as a student who had been running another study.

The subject and confederate were told the experiment was a study of physiological reactions to stress. The stress would be created by mild electric shocks, and the subjects could withdraw, the experimenter said, if they objected to these shocks. (No subjects left.) Each person would have to solve a problem knowing that his performance would be evaluated by his partner. The "evaluations" would be in the form of electric shocks, with one shock signifying a very good rating and 10 shocks meaning the performance was judged as very bad. The men were then told what their problems were. The subject's task was to list ideas a publicity agent might employ in order to better a popular singer's record sales and public image. The other person (the confederate) had to think of things a used-car dealer might do in order to increase sales. The two were given 5 minutes to write their answers, and the papers were then collected by the experimenter who supposedly would exchange them.

Following this, the two were placed in separate rooms, supposedly so that they would not influence each other's galvanic skin response (GSR) reactions. The shock electrodes were placed on the subject's right forearm, and GSR electrodes were attached to fingers on his left hand, with wires trailing from the electrodes to the next room. The subject was told he would be the first to receive electric shocks as the evaluation of his problem solution. The experimenter left the subject's room saying he was going to turn on the GSR apparatus, went to the room containing the shock machine and the waiting confederate, and only then looked at the schedule indicating whether the subject was to be angered or not. He informed the confederate how many shocks the subject was to receive, and 30 seconds later the subject was given seven shocks (angered condition) or one shock (nonangered group). The experimenter then went back to the subject, while the confederate quickly arranged the table holding the shock key in the manner appropriate for the subject's condition. Upon entering the subject's room, the experimenter asked him how many shocks he had received and provided the subject with a brief questionnaire on which he was to rate his mood. As soon as this was completed, the subject was taken to the room holding the shock machine. Here the experimenter told the subject it was his turn to evaluate his partner's work. For one group in both the angered and nonangered conditions the shock key was alone on the table (no-object groups). For two other groups in each of these angered and nonangered conditions, however, a 12-gauge shotgun and a .38-caliber revolver were lying on the table near the key (aggressive-weapon conditions). One group in both the angered and nonangered conditions was informed the weapons belonged to the subject's partner. The subjects given this treatment had been told earlier that their partner was a student who had been conducting an experiment. They now were reminded of this, and the experimenter said the weapons were being used in some way by this person in his research (associated-weapons condition); the guns were to be disregarded. The other men were told simply the weapons "belong to someone else" who "must have been doing an experiment in here" (unassociated-weapons group), and they too were asked to disregard the guns. For the last treatment, one group of angered men found two badminton racquets and shuttlecocks lying on the table near the shock key, and these people were also told the equipment belonged to someone else (badminton-racquets group).

Immediately after this information was provided, the experimenter showed the subject what was supposedly his partner's answer to his assigned problem. The subject was reminded that he was to give the partner shocks as his evaluation and was informed that this was the last time shocks would be administered in the study. A second copy of the mood questionnaire was then completed by the subject after he had delivered the shocks. Following this, the subject was asked a number of oral questions about the experiment, including what, if any, suspicions he had. (No doubts were voiced about the presence of the weapons.) At the conclusion of this interview the experiment was explained, and the subject was asked not to talk about the study.

Results

Effectiveness of Arousal Treatment

Analyses of variance of the responses to each of the mood scales following the receipt of the partner's evaluation indicate the prior-shock treatment succeeded in creating differences in anger arousal. The subjects getting seven shocks rated themselves as being significantly angrier than the subjects receiving only one shock, $F(1,84) = 20.65$, $p < .01$). There were no reliable differences among the groups within any one arousal level.

Aggression Toward Partner

The mean number of shocks administered in each experimental condition are given in Table 1. The hypothesis guiding the present study receives good support. The strongly provoked men delivered more frequent electrical attacks upon their tormentor in the presence of a

----
Insert Table 1 about here
----

weapon than when nonaggressive objects (the badminton racquets and shuttlecocks) were present or when only the shock key was on the table. An analysis of variance of the shock data for the six groups in the 3 x 2 factorial design (i.e., exclude the badminton racquets condition) revealed two significant effects. The subjects who received seven shocks delivered more shocks to the confederate than the subjects who received one shock $F(1,84) = 104.62$, $p < .001$. And, the Number of Shocks by Weapons Association interaction was significant,

$\underline{F}(2,84) = 5.02$, $\underline{p} < .01$. The significant interaction means that the effect of the presence of the weapons on the dependent measure was influenced by whether subjects were given one or seven shocks.

Discussion

Common sense, as well as a good deal of personality theorizing, both influenced to some extent by an egocentric view of human behavior as being caused almost exclusively by motives within the individual, generally neglect the type of weapons effect demonstrated in the present study. If a person holding a gun fires it, we are told either that he wanted to do so (consciously or unconsciously) or that he pulled the trigger "accidentally." The findings summarized here suggest yet another possibility: The presence of the weapon might have elicited an intense aggressive reaction from the person with the gun, assuming his inhibitions against aggression were relatively weak at the moment. Indeed, it is altogether conceivable that many hostile acts which supposedly stem from unconscious motivation really arise because of the operation of aggressive cues. Not realizing how these situational stimuli might elicit aggressive behavior, and not detecting the presence of these cures, the observer tends to locate the source of the action in some conjectured underlying, perhaps repressed, motive. Similarly, if he is a Skinnerian rather than a dynamically oriented clinician, he might also neglect the operation of aggression-eliciting stimuli by invoking the concept of operant behavior, and thus sidestep the issue altogether. The sources of the hostile action, for him, too, rest within the individual, with the behavior only steered or permitted by discriminative stimuli.

Alternative explanations must be ruled out, however, before the present thesis can be regarded as confirmed. One obvious possibility is that the subjects in the weapons condition reacted to the demand characteristics of the situation as they saw them and exhibited the kind of behavior they thought was required of them. ("These guns on the table mean I'm supposed to be aggressive, so I'll give many shocks.") Several considerations appear to negate this explanation. First, there are the subject's own verbal reports. None of the subjects voiced any suspicions of the weapons and, furthermore, when they were queried generally denied that the weapons had any effect on them. But even those subjects who did express any doubts about the experiment typically acted like the other subjects.

Setting this aside, moreover, it is not altogether certain from the notion of demand characteristics that only the angered subjects would be inclined to act in conformity with the experimenter's supposed demands. The nonangered men in the weapons group did not display a heightened number of attacks on their partner. Would this have been predicted beforehand by researchers interested in demand characteristics? The last finding raises one final observation. Recent unpublished research by Allen and Bragg indicates that awareness of the experimenter's purpose does not necessarily result in an increased display of the behavior the experimenter supposedly desires. Dealing with one kind of socially disapproved action (conformity), Allen and Bragg demonstrated that high levels of experimentally induced awareness of the experimenter's interests generally produced a decreased level of the relevant behavior. Thus, if the subjects in our study had known the experimenter was interested in observing their aggressive behavior, they might well have given less, rather than more, shocks, since giving shocks is also socially disapproved. This type of phenomenon was also not observed in the weapons conditions.

Nevertheless, any one experiment cannot possibly definitely exclude all of the alternative explanations. Scientific hypotheses are only probability statements, and further research is needed to heighten the likelihood that the present reasoning is correct.

References

Anonymous. A gun-toting nation. Time, August 12, 1966.

Berkowitz, L. Aggression: A social psychological analysis. New York: McGraw-Hill, 1962.

Berkowitz, L. Aggressive cues in aggressive behavior and hostility catharsis. Psychological Review, 1964, 71, 104-122.

Berkowitz, L. The concept of aggressive drive: Some additional considerations. In L. Berkowitz (Ed.), Advances in experimental social psychology. Vol.2. New York: Academic Press, 1965, pp. 301-329.

Easterbrook, J. A. The effect of emotion on cue utilization and the organization of behavior. Psychological Review, 1959, 66, 183-201.

Loew, C. A. Acquisition of a hostile attitude and its relationship
   to aggressive behavior. Unpublished doctoral dissertation, State
   University of Iowa, 1965.

Walters, R. H., & Parke, R. D. Social motivation, dependency, and
   susceptibility to social influence. In L. Berkowitz (Ed.),
   <u>Advances in experimental social psychology</u>. Vol.1. New York:
   Academic Press, 1964, pp. 231-276.

Footnotes

[1]The present experiment was conducted by Anthony LePage under
Leonard Berkowitz's supervision as part of a research program sponsored
by Grant G-23988 from the National Science Foundation to the senior
author.

Table 1

Mean Number of Shocks Given in Each Condition

Condition	Shocks received	
	1	7
Associated weapons	2.60	6.07
Unassociated weapons	2.20	5.67
No object	3.07	4.67
Badminton racquets	----	4.60

Appendix $\mathbb{B}$ Research topics

The purpose of this appendix is to present a few research topics that can be used as starting points for further research. Suggestions for research are made for each of the topics, but the task of selecting, planning, and executing a project is left to you. Planning and executing your own research project is an excellent way to gain an understanding of the various stages of experimentation and the relationships among them. Moreover, any student who becomes actively involved in a research project which is of personal interest is likely to find that research can be fun. If you do not find a topic to your liking in this appendix, you should examine the journals that report research findings in psychology and the other social sciences. The topics in this appendix are not representative of the research areas investigated by social scientists because it was necessary to exclude those topics which require special skills, equipment, or an extensive knowledge of the area. Instructors who elect to emphasize a particular content area can offer alternative research topics.

TOPIC 1. THE LOST LETTER TECHNIQUE

Milgram (1969) describes a technique that can be used to assess public opinion and that avoids some of the problems inherent in the survey technique. The survey technique typically entails selecting a representative sample from a larger population and then questioning each subject in the sample. Its success is demonstrated by the fact that political polls tend to predict accurately the outcome of elections. The survey technique is a reactive measure, of course, because the person being interviewed is aware that some sort of "evaluation" is occurring.

The lost letter technique yields a nonreactive measure. The subjects are not aware, presumably, that their performance is being assessed, because the investigator does not select or make direct contact with them. The only contact between the investigator and the subjects is through a "lost letter." The investigator plants a number of self-addressed, stamped letters at various locations. The dependent measure is the number of letters that are mailed by the people who find them. Thus, the lost letter technique differs from the survey technique in that it assesses the willingness of individuals to carry out a particular act — to mail or not mail a letter — instead of assessing opinion directly.

In one of Milgram's studies, 400 letters were addressed in exactly the same way (to the same address in New Haven, Connecticut) except that they were directed either to Mr. Walter Carnap, to the Friends of the Communist Party, to the Friends of the Nazi Party, or to the Medical Research Associates. The words "Attention: Mr. Walter Carnap" were typed at the lower left on each of the 300 envelopes addressed to one of the organizations. The contents of every letter were the same. Walter Carnap was told that the plans for the meeting had changed because the speakers could not arrive in time. The letter was straightforward but suggestive in light of the organization involved. That is, the reader would be likely to infer that the sender (Max Thuringer) and addressee (Walter Carnap) were actively involved in the affairs of the organization, particularly in the recruitment of new members. The envelopes were distributed in various locations (sidewalks, shops, telephone booths) in ten preselected districts of New Haven. In addition, each envelope had been sealed so that, if the letter was posted, the investigator would be able to determine whether it had been opened.

The results were striking. The percentage of the 100 letters posted was very high for the letters to the Medical Research Associates (72 percent) and for the personal letters (71 percent), but very low (25 percent) for letters to the other two organizations. There was a greater tendency to open the letters addressed to the organizations, particularly the Communist (40 percent) and Nazi (32 percent) ones, than the personal letters (10 percent).

The Milgram technique can be used in several ways. It can be used to assess public opinion on a controversial issue by varying the name of the organization that is placed on the lost letters. If the issue is one about which people tend to be highly emotional, it may be interesting to compare the results of the lost letter technique with the results obtained through a survey technique. The technique could be used to study how subject variables or location variables influence whether individuals will carry out a particular act. For example, if you lost a textbook that was clearly marked with your name, address, and telephone number, do you believe the probability of having it returned would be influenced by whether it was left in a chapel, dormitory, or classroom?

Reference

Milgram, S. The lost-letter technique. *Psychology Today,* June 1969, 30–33; 66–68.

TOPIC 2. CORRELATION OF ABILITIES

Many problems can be investigated only by correlational and observational techniques. For example, beginning in 1921, Terman and his associates studied over fifteen hundred children who had IQs of 140 or above. The progress of the children was followed through the middle years of their adult lives. The major finding was that the gifted children were above average in characteristics other than intelligence. That is, there is a positive correlation between intelligence and health, social adaptability, and leadership. In general, the gifted children continued to be superior to their own generation as they grew older.

You are encouraged to design a correlational study which would yield data of personal interest. For example, you may be interested in whether performance in a methodology course is related to performance in nonmethodology courses, whether quantitative abilities are related to verbal abilities, or whether the amount of study time is related to course performance. Or you could select a test of ability such as the Remote Associates Test (Mednick & Mednick, 1967), a memory test, or a vocabulary test and correlate performance on the test with another variable of interest.

The Remote Associates Test can be described as a search task. Each item consists of three stimulus words. The subject's task is to find a word that is related to all three of the stimulus words. For example, *party* is an acceptable solution to the stimulus triad of *line, birthday,* and *surprise.* A remote associates test similar to the Mednick test is published in the paperback entitled *Involvement in Psychology Today.* There are a number of ways to construct a memory test. For example, you could select a list of twenty-five common nouns, read it aloud to subjects at the rate of one word every five seconds, and then have them recall as many words as they can from the list in any order. A vocabulary test can be constructed by selecting words which differ in degree of difficulty. It is important to select enough words of intermediate difficulty so that individual differences among the subjects will be detected.

After the test has been constructed, the next step is to establish the reliability of the measure. Reliability can be assessed by correlating the performance of subjects on even-numbered items with their performance on odd-numbered items, by correlating the scores obtained by testing each subject twice with a time lag between the two testing sessions, or by correlating the performance of subjects on two comparable tests. For example, for the memory test, you could select fifty common nouns and randomly assign each noun to list 1 or list 2 with the restriction that there be twenty-five nouns in each list. Then you could test each subject on both lists. Half the subjects would receive list 1 and then list 2, and the other half would receive them in the reverse order. The performance for each subject on the two lists could then be correlated.

If you have attempted to establish the reliability of a test, you are likely to appreciate the fact that it is not a simple matter to construct a reliable test. A number of attempts may be necessary. After a reliable test has been constructed, it is reasonable to question whether test performance is related to other measures. Keep in mind that there should be logical or theoretical grounds for correlating variables. For example, one might ask whether performance on a memory test can predict performance in a course which requires extensive memorization. Unfortunately, it is still not uncommon for psychologists to construct a test and then correlate it with everything in sight. On the positive side, it should be noted that psychologists have developed very sophisticated correlational techniques. These techniques, which are beyond the scope of this text, allow investigators to "explain" correlations. And, if it is possible to obtain correlations between measures at different points in a subject's life, such data can be used to assess whether variables are causally related.

References

Crano, W. D., Kenny, D. A., & Campbell, D. T. Does intelligence cause achievement? A cross-lagged panel analysis. *Journal of Educational Psychology,* 1972, 63, 258–275.

Involvement in Psychology Today. Del Mar, Calif.: CRM Books, 1970.

Mednick, S. A., & Mednick, M. T. *Examiner's Manual: Remote Associates Test.* Boston: Houghton Mifflin, 1967.

Oden, M. H. The fulfillment of promise: Forty year follow up of the Terman gifted group. *Genetic Psychology Monographs,* 1968, 77, 3–93.

Terman, L. M., & Oden, M. H. *The Gifted Child Grows Up.* Stanford, Calif.: Stanford University Press, 1947.

TOPIC 3. MNEMONIC SYSTEMS

There are slight variations among mnemonic systems, but the basic components are essentially the same. The first phase of most systems involves the memorization of a series of "pegs." Generally, words are used as pegs and each word is numbered, with associations between numbers and words. A frequently used peg list is: 1-bun, 2-shoe, 3-tree, 4-door, 5-hive, 6-stick, 7-heaven, 8-gate, 9-line, 10-hen. Following the memorization of the peg words, new words can be memorized by using bizarre imagery to connect the new words to peg words. For example, if *automobile* is the first to-be-recalled word, the task is to conjure up a bizarre image connecting the first peg, *bun,* and *automobile.* A possible image might be a 5-foot bun driving an automobile. The same principle is used for the remaining to-be-recalled words. At recall, the peg words, which are accessible because they have been well memorized, are presumed to elicit the visual images formed during the study trial and thus make the to-be-recalled words accessible.

The effectiveness of providing subjects with a plan for improving memory can be demonstrated by performing an experiment. The experimental subjects are given the list of peg words to memorize. It is important that they have the list extremely well memorized. Then they are told to use the peg list items to recall new items by linking each peg word with a to-be-recalled word by conjuring up a bizarre image of the two words. The control subjects do not receive a peg list. They are told to study the words so that they can recall them during the subsequent recall trial. The list of to-be-recalled words is read to subjects at a rate of one word every 5 seconds. Concrete words such as *automobile, paper, tiger,* and *football* are used. The typical finding (for example, Bugelski, Kidd, & Segman, 1968) is that the experimental subjects perform much better than controls.

There is reason to believe that the way information is represented in images is related to the size of the image. Kosslyn (1975) had subjects conjure up images at the correct relative size next to a fly or an elephant. For example, subjects might be asked to conjure up an image of a cat next to an elephant or a cat next to a fly. The image was to be projected flush up against a large surface (such as a tennis backboard) so that the projected images "covered" most of the surface while still maintaining the relative size relationship between the two animals imagined. For our example, we can expect the image of a cat to be larger when paired with a fly than when paired with an elephant. Kosslyn found that more information was represented in large images than small images.

A number of experiments can be performed to study mnemonic systems and the role of imagery in mnemonics. For example, one could assess the effect of image size. If large images yield better performance than small images, can we attribute the results to the size of the image? Do large images take longer to construct than small images? Does the effectiveness of a mnemonic system depend on the material to be memorized? Can children use imagery more effectively than adults?

References

Bower, G. H. Analysis of a mnemonic device. *American Scientist,* 1970, 58, 496–510.

Bugelski, B. R., Kidd, E., & Segman, J. Image as a mediator in one-trial paired-associate learning. *Journal of Experimental Psychology,* 1968, 76, 69–73.

Kosslyn, S. M. Information representation in visual images. *Cognitive Psychology,* 1975, 7, 341–370.

Wood, G. Mnemonic systems in recall. *Journal of Educational Psychology,* 1967, 58 (6, Pt. 2), 1–27.

TOPIC 4. INFORMATION PROCESSING

If you have thought about the acquisition of skills, you have probably noted that voluntary control is required during the early stages of skill acquisition. For example, in the early stages of learning to type, one has to think about the letters that are being typed. As greater proficiency is developed it is no longer necessary to think about each individual letter. In fact, thinking about individual letters tends to result in more mistakes and a slower rate of typing. One explanation for this phenomenon is that the skilled typist processes units larger than single letters (words or phrases). The processing may only appear to be controlled by involuntary mechanisms because the use of larger units does not require all the capacity of the voluntary processing system.

It is possible to study the size of the unit or the nature of the unit that the skilled typist processes. Suppose, for example, that you were interested in determining whether a typist processes the meaning of the material to be typed. That is, you are interested in determining whether meaning units or nonmeaning units are processed. One way to answer this question is, of course, simply to ask skilled typists whether they pay attention to the meaning of the passage they are typing. Or you could select two passages of equal difficulty and change the ordering of the nouns so that the meaning is disrupted without affecting the syntax and grammar. The normal and distorted versions of each passage are used equally often. Each typist receives the distorted version of one passage and the normal version of the other. The distortion should have a negative effect on typing performance only if the typist is processing the meaning of the passage being typed. If this manipulation has such an effect, it is possible to conclude that meaning units are being processed.

The size of the units being processed can be studied by taking a passage and varying the presentation order of its parts. For one condition the passage could be presented without any changes. For a second condition the sentences could be presented in a random order. For a third condition the sentences and the phrases within each sentence could be presented in a random order. For a fourth condition all the words could be ordered randomly. For a fifth condition the letters of each word could be scrambled. The effect of the various disruptions can then be used to determine the size of the unit that the typist is processing. For example, if there are no differences between the first four conditions and the fifth condition is the poorest, it is possible to conclude that the typist is processing word units.

References

Annett, J. Acquisition of skill. *British Medical Bulletin*, 1971, 27, 266–271.

TOPIC 5. AGGRESSION

There are several studies of aggression in which nonhumans are used as subjects. Animals have a strong tendency to attack each other if they are shocked on the feet (Ulrich & Azrin, 1962) or if a positive reinforcer is withdrawn (Azrin, Hutchinson, & Hake, 1966). In the Azrin et al. study, pigeons were trained to peck a disk, in a schedule that included both reinforcement and extinction. For the reinforcement periods food was delivered as a reward for pecking. For the extinction periods no food was delivered when the pigeons pecked the disk. When the two periods of reinforcement and extinction were alternated, the investigators found that the pigeons would attack a nearby pigeon during the extinction periods. Some of the pigeons attacked even when the "bystander" pigeon was a stuffed model.

The length of the attack on the other pigeon decreased as the length of the time since the last reinforcement increased, and it increased as the number of prior reinforcements increased. It was necessary to alternate reinforcement with extinction in order to get attack, and attack was produced only if the food delivered during the reinforcement period was eaten. That is, satiated pigeons were less likely to attack. The extinction-produced attacks were not attributable to a past history of aggression because the same effect was obtained with socially deprived pigeons. The authors concluded that the change from food reinforcement to extinction produced aggression. The reader who has recently been denied an anticipated reward should empathize with the pigeons in the Azrin et al. study. Yet, it is difficult to demonstrate that the findings obtained with lower animals are applicable to the understanding of human aggression.

Aggression in humans cannot readily be studied through procedures comparable to those used with lower animals because of practical and ethical considerations. Investigators have demonstrated that human subjects tend to be aggressive after witnessing an aggressive act (Bandura, Ross, & Ross, 1963), but it is difficult to determine whether these effects are long-lasting or applicable to more "real-life" situations. The student who is interested in studying human aggression in natural situations is limited primarily to observational and correlational techniques. There are at least two problems that may be of interest. One is determining the level of aggression. Another is determining the antecedents of aggressive behavior.

The investigator who wants to assess the level of aggression can use a number of approaches. One approach is to obtain the incidence of violent crimes per 100,000 population over a period of years. It should be easy to obtain this data because law enforcement agencies keep records of violent crimes. If these records can be accepted as accurate (if there is no reason to believe the relationship between *actual* and *reported* crimes varied from year to year) *and* there is a trend toward more or less violence, the incidence of crime can be used as a starting point for determining the antecedent conditions. For example, if there is an increase in actual violence as inferred from police records and an increase in the incidence of violence in magazines, newspapers, movies, and television, it is reasonable to ask whether the relationship between depicted and actual violence is causal. If it is possible to obtain measures on actual and depicted violence at various times, it is possible to use correlational techniques that allow a cause-effect interpretation. The reader who is interested in this approach can refer to Eron, Huesmann, Lefkowitz, and Walder's (1972) article on television violence and aggression.

The suggestions made above are not realistic for the student who is interested in studying aggression but does not have the time or resources for an elaborate project. Instead, she may elect to study aggression using an observational technique. For example, one could design a questionnaire or interview people to assess attitudes toward violence. Why do some people enjoy watching movies that depict beatings, rapes, killings, shootouts, and slaughters? Is watching violence a novel experience? Is it a safety valve that allows people to release violence rather than commit violent acts? Do people learn to like violence? Another procedure would be to assess individual differences in preference for violence. How do people who enjoy watching violence differ from those people who do not? Or one could assess whether people are satiated quickly on violence. For example, one could determine whether the repeat rate (people who see a particular movie more than once) is greater for violent or nonviolent movies. Marler (1976) considers the role of strangeness and familiarity on animal aggression and suggests that this may be the single most important variable for controlling animal aggression. You may be able to think of ways to assess the importance of the strangeness-familiarity variable for human aggression.

References

Ardrey, R. *The Territorial Imperative.* New York: Atheneum, 1966.

Azrin, N. H., Hutchinson, R. R., & Hake, D. F. Extinction-induced aggression. *Journal of the Experimental Analysis of Behavior,* 1966, 9, 191–204.

Bandura, A., Ross, D., & Ross, S. A. Imitation of film mediated aggressive models. *Journal of Abnormal and Social Psychology,* 1963, 66, 3–11.

Berkowitz, L. Experimental investigations of hostility catharsis. *Journal of Consulting and Clinical Psychology, 1970, 35,* 1–7.

Eron, L. D., Huesmann, L. R., Lefkowitz, M. M., & Walter, L. O. Does television violence cause aggression? *American Psychologist, 1972, 27,* 253–263.

Lorenz, K. *On Aggression.* New York: Harcourt Brace Jovanovich, 1966.

Marler, P. On animal aggression: The roles of strangeness and familiarity. *American Psychologist, 1976, 31,* 239–246.

Smith, D., King, M., & Hoebel, B. Lateral hypothalamic control of killing: Evidence for a cholinoceptive mechanism. *Science, 1970, 167,* 900–901.

Ulrich, R. E., & Azrin, N. H. Reflexive fighting in response to aversive stimulation. *Journal of the Experimental Analysis of Behavior, 1962, 5,* 511–520.

Zimbardo, P. G. The human choice: Individuation, reason, and order versus deindividuation, impulse, and chaos. *Nebraska Symposium on Motivation, 1969,* 1970, *18,* 237–307.

TOPIC 6. THE COCKTAIL PARTY PHENOMENON

The cocktail party phenomenon (Cherry, 1957) is the label given to the observation that it is possible to select a message to listen to and ignore other messages. Thus, at a cocktail party you can eavesdrop on the conversation behind you or attend to a different conversation, but not both. It is possible to switch back and forth between the two conversations but very difficult to comprehend both if the level of discourse is complex. The phenomenon of selective attention can be investigated using earphones that make it possible to send one message to one ear and a different message to the other ear. The subject has to repeat (shadow) the message in one ear. The message to be shadowed must be difficult enough to require full attention. Usually the material to be shadowed is made more difficult by presenting it faster.

The shadowing procedure makes it possible to study some interesting aspects of selective attention. One can consider whether subjects process any of the unattended message by varying the relationship between the attended and unattended message (Treisman, 1964) and by presenting high-priority information (such as the subject's name) in the unattended message (Moray, 1959). The results of these studies reveal that subjects do process some of the unattended message.

The study of selective attention is usually performed with special equipment that makes it possible to control the messages presented to each ear, but elaborate equipment is not essential for all studies of selective attention. The student can study selective attention by presenting two messages simultaneously to both ears and requiring subjects to attend to only one. This is similar to the situation faced by the student who wants to study while a roommate is playing the stereo. A similar procedure could be used to investigate whether the ability to attend selectively is influenced greatly by the similarity of the two messages. For example, are some kinds of music more disruptive of reading than others? Does music interfere with ability to work mathematical problems? Is it more difficult to attend selectively to one message when both messages are in the same modality (verbal) than when they are in different modalities (one verbal and one visual)? Are there other variables that influence a subject's ability to attend selectively?

One such variable is prior attention habits. The effect of trying to ignore well-learned habits can be demonstrated by constructing a task similar to one developed by Stroop (1935). Pens or pencils with different color inks or leads — say, red, black, green, yellow, and brown — are used to print the words *red, black, green, yellow,* and *brown* in rows. Each word should appear once in each row and the order of the words in each row should be random. Each word is printed in a color other than the color for which it is the label; for example, the word *red* could be printed in black, green, yellow, or brown, but not in red. The color for each word is changed each time the word is presented. The task for the subject is to name the color of each word (that is, the color of the ink) as quickly as possible. The amount of time needed to complete the task can be the performance measure. The student who performs this task is likely to notice the interference. The interference results from the fact that there is a very strong tendency to respond (attend) to the word instead of to the color of the word. A test of this nature may be used to study individual differences in selective attention. Would you expect to find individual differences in the ability to attend selectively? Do you believe the ability to attend selectively is related to other cognitive abilities?

References

Cherry, C. *On Human Communication.* New York: Science Editions, 1957.

Howarth, C. I., & Bloomfield, J. R. Search and selective attention. *British Medical Bulletin,* 1971, 27, 253–257.

Lindsay, P. H., & Norman, D. A. *Human Information Processing: An Introduction to Psychology.* New York: Academic Press, 1972.

Moray, N. Attention in dichotic listening: Affective cues and the influence of instructions. *Quarterly Journal of Experimental Psychology,* 1959, 11, 56–60.

Neisser, U., & Becklen, R. Selective looking: Attending to visually specified events. *Cognitive Psychology,* 1975, 7, 480–494.

Stroop, J. R. Studies of interference in serial verbal reactions. *Journal of Experimental Psychology,* 1935, 18, 643–662.

Treisman, A. M. Monitoring and storage of irrelevant messages in selective attention. *Journal of Verbal Learning and Verbal Behavior,* 1964, 3, 449–459.

TOPIC 7. BETTER THAN AVERAGE

Are you a better-than-average student? Are you more honest than the average student? Are you of better-than-average attractiveness? Myers and Ridl (1979) discuss what they refer to as the better-than-average phenomenon, which has been investigated in one way or another by a variety of investigators. As we discussed at various points in the text, there is evidence that we give ourselves the benefit of the doubt and are guilty of various forms of cognitive conceit, which, in fact, may be an important aspect of adjustment (Mischel, 1979). The important point here is that there are a number of ways that you can investigate these phenomena further. You could, for example, ask groups of people to rate themselves on various characteristics (such as honesty, attractiveness, intelligence, cooperativeness, athletic ability) to determine the generality of the better-than-average effect. And you can consider the robustness of the effect. For example, will self-ratings of honesty be influenced if participants are told about the general bias to give oneself a better-than-average rating?

References

Myers, D. G., & Ridl, J. Can we all be better than average? *Psychology Today,* August 1979, 89, 95, 96, 98.
Mischel, W. On the interface of cognition and personality: Beyond the person-situation debate. *American Psychologist,* 1979, 34, 740–754.

TOPIC 8. THE KNEW-IT-ALL-ALONG EFFECT

When a misfortune occurs for which a culprit can be identified, there is a strong tendency to second-guess the culprit. For example, sports fans are known to second-guess coaches. When a particular strategy or play does not work, the fans may engage in considerable second-guessing, believing that they knew all along that the particular strategy or play was doomed to failure. The issue of interest is whether the process of second-guessing is "fair" to those who are being second-guessed. Once we have knowledge of the outcome, such as a misfortune, can we remember the state of our knowledge prior to the misfortune? Would we have been able to predict the misfortune? Are we likely to believe that the misfortune had to occur? Is hindsight better than foresight or merely different (Fischhoff, 1975)? There are a number of ways that you can investigate the knew-it-all-along effect. You can, for example, ask students to predict the outcome of research studies that have already been conducted and compare these predictions with the results obtained by telling other students the actual results and asking them what they would have predicted. If there is a clear difference between the two groups in the "accuracy" of prediction so that the group given outcome knowledge makes "better" predictions, there is evidence for the knew-it-all-along effect.

References

Fischhoff, B. The silly certainty of hindsight. *Psychology Today,* April 1975, 70–72, 76.
Fischhoff, B. Perceived informativeness of facts. *Journal of Experimental Psychology: Human Perception and Performance,* 1977, 3, 349–358.

TOPIC 9. MACHIAVELLIANISM

It is possible to administer a test to assess whether an individual has a Machiavellian view of others (Christie, 1970). A Machiavellian is someone who believes that people are no good so it is permissible to use guile and deceit to influence and control them. The items in the test are designed to assess how the individual views others (as good, honest, and kind, or as selfish, vicious, and dishonest). The results of the research reported by Christie revealed that people who score high on the Machiavellian scale are more likely to be young, male, from urban environments, and members of professions that manipulate people (lawyers, psychiatrists, and behavioral scientists, as opposed to accountants, surgeons, and natural scientists). The scores were not related to intelligence, personality variables, authoritarianism, occupational status, education, marital status, or birth order.

Christie reported a study conducted by Dorothea Braginsky in which children were given a Machiavellianism test designed for elementary school children. The children who had high scores on the test were compared with children who had low scores. The task was to persuade children who had middle scores to eat crackers soaked in quinine. As you probably know, crackers soaked in quinine have a very bitter taste. The subjects who were to be the persuaders were told they would receive one nickel for every quinine-soaked cracker their subject (victim?) ate. The high Machiavellian persuaders outperformed the low Machiavellian persuaders.

There are a number of possible experiments that a student could perform to study Machiavellianism. For example, it is possible to assess the effect of flattery on behavior to determine whether it "pays" to be a Machiavellian. Or Machiavellianism could be studied by using factorial experiments in which Machiavellianism (a subject variable) and a nonsubject variable are manipulated. For example, one could manipulate the reasons subjects are given for complying with a request. In one case the reasons are subject-based (that is, gains for the subject) and in the other case the reasons are altruistic (that is, gains for others). The effect of the reasons manipulation can be expected to be different for high and low Machiavellians. For example, the experimenter could manipulate the reasons given for donating blood (money versus an altruistic appeal). The effectiveness of the two appeals should depend on whether high or low Machiavellians are asked to donate blood. You may be able to think of other nonsubject variables that will interact with Machiavellianism.

References

Christie, R. The Machiavellis among us. *Psychology Today,* November 1970, 82–86.

Geis, F., & Christie, R. (eds.). *Studies in Machiavellianism.* New York: Academic Press, 1970.

TOPIC 10. THE PRISONER'S DILEMMA

The prisoner's dilemma game has been used to study conflict and conflict resolution. The name of the game is believed to be based on the conflict situation that two individuals could face when picked up on suspicion of committing a crime (see Lindsay & Norman, 1972). The district attorney can interrogate each suspect separately and offer each a special deal for confessing. He may promise that the person who confesses will be set free and the person who does not will be prosecuted on the maximum charge. If both confess, then they will be prosecuted on a lesser charge. If neither confesses, then the district attorney will not have a good case, so the probability of either of the suspects being convicted is quite small. In this case the most reasonable procedure is for neither suspect to confess. This poses a dilemma, however, in that it is necessary for the two suspects to trust each other for this strategy to work.

The game is played by two players. Each player has to select one of two alternatives on each trial. They have to choose simultaneously, usually by writing their choices on pieces of paper, so that neither player knows what the other will do. The amount that one player gains or loses is determined both by his own choice and the choice of the other player. This can be seen by examining a typical payoff matrix presented in Table B-1. If both players choose B, they both receive only one cent. If they both choose A, they both receive ten cents. If player 2 chooses B and player 1 chooses A, then player 2 receives fifty cents and player 1 loses five cents. The reverse is true if player 1 chooses B and player 2 chooses A. The game is usually played for a number of trials.

Several variables can be studied with the prisoner's dilemma game. For example, one could compare choices when subjects are playing for keeps or when they have to return the money. One could look at performance over different stages of practice. That is, do the players arrive at a cooperative strategy or not? A confederate of the experimenter could be one of the players so that the choices of one player (the confederate) could be manipulated. The effect of the confederate's strategy on the selections of the subject could then be systematically investigated. A questionnaire could be given at the end of the experiment to determine how the subjects view each other; the actual subject would not know, of course, that the other "subject" is actually a confederate of the experimenter.

TABLE B-1

A Payoff Matrix for the Prisoner's Dilemma Game

		Player 1	
		Selects A	*Selects B*
Player 2	*Selects A*	+10¢ / +10¢	+50¢ / −5¢
	Selects B	−5¢ / +50¢	+1¢ / +1¢

References

Lindsay, P. H., & Norman, D. A. *Human Information Processing: An Introduction to Psychology*. New York: Academic Press, 1972.
Wrightsman, L. S., O'Connor, J., & Baker, N. J. (eds.). *Cooperation and Competition: Readings on Mixed-Motive Games*. Belmont, Calif.: Brook/Cole, 1972.

TOPIC 11. CLOTHES AND BEHAVIOR

There have been a number of experiments which demonstrate that clothes influence the way people are treated. In general, well-dressed people are treated better than poorly dressed people because most people associate clothes with social status. Bickman (1974) reported a series of experiments demonstrating that clothing influences honesty, willingness to sign petitions, and obedience. Uniforms are particularly effective in eliciting obedience even when the uniformed person is seeking obedience in an area outside his normal role. In one experiment, for example, a passerby was stopped and instructed to give a dime to a confederate standing by a parking meter. Participants were much more likely to comply if the person making the demand was in a guard uniform than if he was not in uniform, but well dressed.

A student can perform a number of experiments to assess further the relationship between clothes and behavior. Are there situations in which poorly dressed persons are treated better than well-dressed persons? Does clothing influence all aspects of interpersonal relations or just those requiring obedience and honesty? Do we assess a person's clothing when making judgments about intelligence, political views, morals, and personality? Does a person's clothing become an unimportant consideration once we get to know the person? Is the probability of "interacting effectively with members of the opposite sex" influenced by the nature of one's dress? Is it possible to investigate these problems without violating the ethical principles discussed in Chapter 1?

References

Bickman, L. Social roles and uniforms: Clothes make the person. *Psychology Today*, April 1974, 48–51.

TOPIC 12. THE EYEWITNESS

There is considerable evidence to support the view that eyewitness testimony frequently leaves much to be desired. This point can be demonstrated by staging an incident in front of several observers (confederates could attack a professor while she is lecturing) and then question the witnesses. The usual result is that the witnesses do not agree about what happened. Let us consider why eyewitness testimony tends to be inaccurate.

One problem with eyewitness testimony is that the phrasing of the question can influence the response that is given. In one study (Loftus & Palmer, 1974) subjects were shown a short movie in which two cars collided. Later, subjects were asked how fast the two cars were going when they smashed, collided, bumped, hit, or contacted. That is, the verb was manipulated to determine if the phrasing of the question influenced the speed estimates that subjects gave. It did. The average speed estimate was 40.8 miles per hour when smashed was used and 31.8 miles per hour when contacted was used. And, although no broken glass was shown in the movie, twice as many subjects reporting seeing broken glass in the "smashed" condition than in the "hit" condition. In another experiment (Loftus, 1975) subjects were shown a movie and then asked questions about the movie. Some subjects were asked questions containing false presuppositions. For example, one of the questions was, "Did you see the children getting on the school bus?" Since there was no school bus in the film, the presupposition of the question was false. A week later all subjects were asked direct questions about the presuppositions. For example, all subjects were asked whether they had seen a school bus in the film. The interesting result is that the subjects in the false presupposition condition were much more likely to respond yes (incorrectly) than subjects in the control conditions. Thus, asking a question with a false presupposition immediately following an event appears to be a particularly effective way to alter a person's memory of an event.

There are a number of ways for a student to study how memory of an event can be altered. One might, for example, assess the effect of time delay between the occurrence of the event and testifying about the event. Is the effect of questions with false presuppositions greater if the questions are asked immediately after an event or several days later? What other approaches could be used to alter a person's memory of an event? Is the use of false presuppositions more effective for altering a child's memory or an adult's memory? Are there ways to improve eyewitness testimony?

References

Loftus, E. F. The incredible eyewitness. *Psychology Today,* December 1974, 116–119.

Loftus, E. F. Leading questions and eyewitness report. *Cognitive Psychology,* 1975, 7, 560–572.

Loftus, E. F., & Palmer, J. C. Reconstruction of automobile destruction: An example of the interaction between language and memory. *Journal of Verbal Learning and Verbal Behavior,* 1974, 13, 585–589.

Appendix C Tables

1. NUMBER TABLES FOR RANDOM ASSIGNMENT

1	2	3	4	5	6	7	8	9	10	11	12	13	14	15	16	17	18	19	20
3	2	8	2	4	6	4	5	5	1	7	6	4	6	1	5	2	8	1	8
1	5	7	8	5	4	1	2	7	3	4	2	8	7	3	2	3	6	7	6
4	8	2	8	8	8	8	3	1	4	6	5	7	5	2	6	1	3	4	4
2	6	1	5	8	1	5	1	3	7	8	1	1	2	6	4	5	1	6	7
8	4	6	7	7	3	6	8	2	6	5	8	2	3	5	1	7	2	3	3
6	3	4	1	1	5	7	4	8	5	1	4	1	4	7	3	8	7	2	5
7	1	3	3	3	7	3	6	6	8	2	7	5	4	8	7	4	4	8	1
5	7	5	6	6	2	2	7	4	2	3	3	3	8	4	8	6	5	5	2

21	22	23	24	25	26	27	28	29	30	31	32	33	34	35	36	37	38	39	40
1	6	3	4	5	1	3	5	5	7	8	2	3	6	8	1	7	1	6	4
3	8	1	6	6	3	6	3	7	1	3	8	3	8	4	6	1	5	3	2
3	4	4	3	8	5	5	8	2	8	2	7	4	7	5	2	5	8	1	6
6	2	4	2	3	2	4	2	6	3	5	6	5	3	7	5	6	4	4	8
2	3	6	7	4	4	8	6	3	2	7	1	8	5	6	3	3	2	5	3
4	7	8	5	2	7	7	7	1	4	6	4	7	4	3	8	4	6	7	7
5	1	5	8	1	8	1	1	8	5	1	3	2	6	1	1	2	7	8	5
8	5	2	1	7	6	2	4	4	6	4	5	6	1	2	4	8	3	2	1

41	42	43	44	45	46	47	48	49	50	51	52	53	54	55	56	57	58	59	60
2	3	3	2	5	1	8	3	2	6	4	7	5	5	2	2	7	8	7	7
7	6	4	1	3	4	6	7	3	1	6	3	6	7	5	3	1	7	6	5
1	8	8	4	4	6	3	4	8	3	3	8	2	2	4	4	5	6	3	6
5	2	1	8	7	8	4	6	1	2	2	5	8	4	1	7	8	4	1	3
6	5	2	7	2	3	5	2	5	8	7	2	4	3	6	8	2	2	8	1
3	4	6	6	6	7	7	1	6	4	1	4	1	8	3	1	4	1	4	2
8	7	7	5	1	2	2	8	7	5	5	6	7	6	7	6	6	3	5	8
4	1	5	3	8	5	1	5	4	7	8	1	3	1	8	5	3	5	2	4

61	62	63	64	65	66	67	68	69	70	71	72	73	74	75	76	77	78	79	80
4	4	2	8	5	7	5	7	2	1	8	4	7	1	8	3	3	5	5	2
5	8	1	5	2	2	6	6	5	3	2	7	5	7	5	8	5	6	2	4
8	7	4	1	7	6	8	3	6	2	5	5	2	4	6	7	8	3	3	8
6	3	3	2	6	5	7	2	7	5	7	1	3	8	7	2	2	4	6	7

	No.	Sequence	No.	Sequence	No.	Sequence
1 3 6 5	100	4 2 1 3 5 6 7 8	120	2 4 3 8 7 1 6 5	140	5 6 7 8 4 1 3 2
7 4 1 8	99	5 7 8 2 1 4 3 6	119	1 3 2 5 4 6 8 7	139	5 3 2 7 6 4 1 8
7 2 1 8	98	2 5 8 3 6 4 1 7	118	2 8 6 7 1 3 5 4	138	2 3 7 4 1 6 8 5
4 6 7 1	97	1 8 2 6 4 7 5 3	117	3 6 4 1 8 7 2 5	137	7 1 3 8 6 5 2 4
4 5 6 1	96	2 6 1 5 8 4 7 3	116	7 8 4 6 2 3 1 5	136	7 4 8 3 1 2 5 6
3 4 2 1	95	3 2 7 6 4 1 8 5	115	6 4 8 2 7 5 3 1	135	2 6 3 8 5 7 4 1
2 6 5 8	94	2 3 6 1 7 4 5 8	114	3 8 2 4 7 6 1 5	134	3 2 7 4 6 5 8 1
6 4 1 3	93	2 7 6 8 3 1 5 4	113	8 6 2 7 5 3 1 4	133	6 7 5 8 3 4 1 2
2 6 3 8	92	7 8 6 2 1 4 3 5	112	6 5 8 1 4 7 3 2	132	4 7 3 8 2 5 6 1
3 4 6 1	91	2 4 6 5 1 3 8 7	111	3 8 4 1 7 6 2 5	131	1 7 8 6 4 5 3 2
8 6 4 7	90	1 4 3 8 5 6 2 7	110	2 1 8 4 7 3 5 6	130	4 8 7 6 2 5 1 3
3 1 8 4	89	7 6 2 5 3 8 4 1	109	4 8 6 5 1 3 2 7	129	2 7 5 4 3 8 6 1
4 1 5 8	88	8 5 6 7 2 1 4 3	108	3 6 4 5 8 1 7 2	128	5 2 8 4 7 6 1 3
2 1 3 4	87	3 8 5 2 4 7 6 1	107	1 2 3 7 8 6 4 5	127	7 5 6 2 4 8 1 3
4 3 1 8	86	6 2 8 1 3 7 4 5	106	3 1 7 4 6 8 2 5	126	8 1 6 4 2 3 7 5
3 1 8 4	85	2 5 6 3 1 8 7 4	105	8 3 4 7 2 5 1 6	125	7 6 4 3 5 8 2 1
6 4 3 7	84	2 1 5 6 4 7 8 3	104	6 4 5 1 2 3 7 8	124	2 8 3 4 1 5 7 6
6 7 5 8	83	1 3 2 8 7 4 5 6	103	1 2 6 5 7 4 8 3	123	5 1 2 6 8 4 7 3
5 1 2 6	82	8 5 3 2 4 1 6 7	102	5 1 3 2 7 8 6 4	122	2 3 1 7 6 4 8 5
7 2 3 1	81	5 8 2 6 7 1 4 3	101	7 3 8 1 6 2 4 5	121	6 8 3 2 7 5 4 1

160	2 6 7 3 1 5 4 8	180	3 7 4 2 6 8 1 5	200	7 5 8 4 3 2 1 6	220	8 2 6 4
159	7 4 1 3 8 6 2 5	179	7 6 8 5 4 1 2 3	199	5 1 8 6 4 7 6 3	219	4 2 8 5
158	6 5 7 8 3 2 1 4	178	3 1 2 4 5 7 6 8	198	6 1 4 3 5 8 2 7	218	5 4 8 7
157	4 7 1 3 6 8 5 2	177	6 4 2 5 1 7 3 8	197	4 5 7 3 2 8 6 1	217	6 1 7 4
156	1 7 2 5 8 3 4 6	176	2 1 6 7 5 4 8 3	196	1 2 4 3 8 6 5 7	216	6 5 1 4
155	6 2 1 7 4 3 8 5	175	6 5 3 2 7 4 8 1	195	7 6 1 5 2 8 4 3	215	7 6 1 8
154	3 5 1 8 7 2 6 4	174	8 5 7 4 2 1 3 6	194	5 3 7 4 8 2 1 6	214	2 1 7 6
153	1 2 6 8 3 4 5 7	173	6 4 2 3 7 1 5 8	193	8 5 6 3 4 2 7 1	213	5 4 7 2
152	8 3 7 2 5 6 1 4	172	7 2 1 6 4 8 5 3	192	8 5 1 7 4 3 6 2	212	2 3 1 6
151	3 4 5 1 7 6 8 2	171	3 1 5 8 4 7 6 2	191	6 5 7 8 1 4 2 3	211	3 1 5 7
150	6 8 3 2 5 4 1 7	170	5 4 7 6 8 3 2 1	190	7 8 2 6 5 3 4 1	210	2 3 1 5
149	2 7 3 5 8 4 6 1	169	1 2 4 7 5 8 6 3	189	4 1 7 3 2 5 6 8	209	4 8 7 6
148	7 1 8 4 2 3 6 5	168	4 3 1 6 7 5 8 2	188	2 8 4 6 3 7 1 5	208	8 2 3 1
147	2 7 5 6 3 8 4 1	167	6 2 1 4 8 5 7 —	187	5 8 4 6 3 7 2 1	207	1 8 7 2
146	5 7 6 1 2 3 8 4	166	4 5 6 8 3 2 1 7	186	4 5 6 1 8 2 7 3	206	7 4 5 3
145	4 8 5 2 3 6 7 1	165	3 1 8 5 6 2 7 4	185	7 6 3 5 1 2 4 8	205	6 3 1 8
144	2 4 7 5 6 1 8 3	164	4 7 8 3 1 6 2 5	184	5 6 3 4 7 2 1 8	204	2 3 4 8
143	7 6 1 4 2 5 3 8	163	8 2 6 3 1 4 5 7	183	2 6 7 4 1 3 8 5	203	8 2 5 7
142	6 4 5 3 7 8 2 1	162	8 7 4 2 3 6 5 1	182	8 3 7 6 2 4 5 1	202	4 1 7 3
141	2 4 7 5 3 8 1 6	161	7 3 4 6 1 8 5 2	181	1 5 6 2 4 7 3 8	201	5 1 2 4

	No.		No.		No.	
7 3 5 1	240	5 4 7 8 3 2 1 6	260	7 5 2 6 3 1 4 8	280	3 2 7 8 1 4 6 5
1 7 3 6	239	6 3 1 7 4 5 2 8	259	4 1 8 2 7 3 5 6	279	3 6 7 4 8 2 1 5
1 2 6 3	238	4 2 7 6 5 1 8 3	258	7 8 5 2 6 3 4 1	278	4 2 1 7 5 3 8 6
5 3 2 8	237	3 2 5 8 1 7 6 4	257	2 4 5 3 7 8 6 1	277	1 8 7 6 4 2 5 3
2 8 7 3	236	6 3 2 1 7 5 4 8	256	3 7 1 5 8 2 4 6	276	8 7 3 6 4 2 1 5
2 4 3 5	235	2 8 6 3 4 5 7 1	255	5 7 6 1 8 3 2 4	275	2 7 8 5 1 4 3 6
8 5 4 3	234	1 4 5 7 8 6 3 2	254	7 8 6 3 2 1 4 5	274	7 3 4 6 1 2 8 5
3 6 1 8	233	5 8 6 1 3 7 2 4	253	6 3 5 8 2 1 4 7	273	2 8 3 4 1 6 7 5
5 7 8 4	232	6 5 2 7 4 1 8 3	252	5 3 6 7 4 1 2 8	272	6 2 8 3 5 7 4 1
8 2 4 6	231	8 4 7 5 3 2 1 6	251	4 1 5 7 6 3 8 2	271	2 3 6 7 8 1 4 5
4 8 7 6	230	6 7 8 2 1 4 5 3	250	1 4 7 2 6 8 5 3	270	2 5 7 6 8 3 4 1
3 2 1 5	229	7 1 6 2 8 4 3 5	249	1 4 5 6 3 8 7 2	269	5 1 4 7 8 3 6 2
7 4 5 6	228	4 3 5 2 7 1 8 6	248	5 4 2 6 7 8 1 3	268	4 8 2 1 3 6 5 7
6 4 5 3	227	6 4 1 7 3 8 5 2	247	8 1 5 3 4 7 2 6	267	3 7 5 1 6 2 8 4
2 6 1 8	226	3 4 2 8 6 7 1 5	246	1 6 3 2 5 7 8 4	266	2 7 6 8 4 3 5 1
5 4 2 7	225	5 1 4 6 7 3 8 2	245	1 8 2 7 6 5 4 3	265	2 6 5 4 8 7 1 3
7 5 6 1	224	3 8 1 6 4 7 2 8	244	4 1 3 2 8 5 6 7	264	4 1 6 5 8 7 2 3
4 1 6 3	223	4 8 7 2 5 1 3 6	243	7 8 3 4 2 5 6 1	263	5 7 3 8 1 6 4 2
5 8 6 2	222	4 2 7 8 1 3 5 6	242	3 6 8 1 5 4 2 7	262	1 6 8 2 3 4 5 7
7 3 6 8	221	7 5 2 6 3 4 8 1	241	8 4 3 6 5 1 2 7	261	7 8 4 3 6 2 1 5

2. TABLE OF CHI SQUARES

Degrees of Freedom df	Two-tail levels			
	p = .10	.05	.02	.01
1	2.706	3.841	5.412	6.635
2	4.605	5.991	7.824	9.210
3	6.251	7.815	9.837	11.341
4	7.779	9.488 —	11.668	13.277
5	9.236	11.070	13.388	15.086
6	10.645	12.592	15.033	16.812
7	12.017	14.067	16.622	18.475
8	13.362	15.507	18.168	20.090
9	14.684	16.919	19.679	21.666
10	15.987	18.307	21.161	23.209
11	17.275	19.675	22.618	24.725
12	18.549	21.026	24.054	26.217
13	19.812	22.362	25.472	27.688
14	21.064	23.685	26.873	29.141
15	22.307	24.996	28.259	30.578
16	23.542	26.296	29.633	32.000
17	24.769	27.587	30.995	33.409
18	25.989	28.869	32.346	34.805
19	27.204	30.144	33.687	36.191
20	28.412	31.410	35.020	37.566
21	29.615	32.671	36.343	38.932
22	30.813	33.924	37.659	40.289
23	32.007	35.172	38.968	41.638
24	33.196	36.415	40.270	42.980
25	34.382	37.652	41.566	44.314
26	35.563	38.885	42.856	45.642
27	36.741	40.113	44.140	46.963
28	37.916	41.337	45.419	48.278
29	39.087	42.557	46.693	49.588
30	40.256	43.773	47.962	50.892

This table is taken from Tables III and VI of Fischer: *Statistical Methods for Research Workers*, and Fischer and Yates: *Statistical Tables for Biological, Agricultural and Medical Research*, published by Longman Group Ltd., London. Reprinted by permission of the authors and publishers.

3. CRITICAL VALUES OF *T* IN THE WILCOXON-MANN-WHITNEY SUM OF RANKS TEST

a. Two-tailed test, *p* = .10; one-tailed test, *p* = .05

N_2	1	2	3	4	5	6	7	8	9	10	11	12	13	14	15	16	17	18	19	20
3			6																	
4			6	11																
5			7	12	19															
6		3	8	13	20	28														
7		3	8	14	21	29	39													
8		4	9	15	23	31	41	51												
9		4	9	16	24	33	43	54	66											
10		4	10	17	26	35	45	56	69	82										
11		4	11	18	27	37	47	59	72	86	100									
12		5	11	19	28	38	49	62	75	89	104	120								
13		5	12	20	30	40	52	64	78	92	108	125	142							
14		5	13	21	31	42	54	67	81	96	112	129	147	166						
15		6	13	22	33	44	56	69	84	99	116	133	152	171	192					
16		6	14	24	34	46	58	72	87	103	120	138	156	176	197	219				
17		6	15	25	35	47	61	75	90	106	123	142	161	182	203	225	249			
18		7	15	26	37	49	63	77	93	110	127	146	166	187	208	231	255	280		
19	1	7	16	27	38	51	65	80	96	113	131	150	171	192	214	237	262	287	313	
20	1	7	17	28	40	53	67	83	99	117	135	155	175	197	220	243	268	294	320	348

N_1 (*Smaller sample*)

This table is taken from Table L in Tate, M. W., and Clelland, R. C.: *Nonparametric and Shortcut Statistics* (1957). Reprinted by permission of The Interstate Printers & Publishers, Inc., Danville, Illinois.

b. Two-tailed test, $p = .05$; one-tailed test, $p = .025$

N_1 (Smaller sample)

N_2	1	2	3	4	5	6	7	8	9	10	11	12	13	14	15	16	17	18	19	20
3																				
4				10																
5			6	11	17															
6			7	12	18	26														
7			7	13	20	27	36													
8			8	14	21	29	38	49												
9			8	14	22	31	40	51	62											
10			9	15	23	32	42	53	65	78										
11			9	16	24	34	44	55	68	81	96									
12			10	17	26	35	46	58	71	84	99	115								
13			10	18	27	37	48	60	73	88	103	119	136							
14			11	19	28	38	50	62	76	91	106	123	141	160						
15			11	20	29	40	52	65	79	94	110	127	145	164	184					
16			12	21	30	42	54	67	82	97	113	131	150	169	190	211				
17			12	21	32	43	56	70	84	100	117	135	154	174	195	217	240			
18			13	22	33	45	58	72	87	103	121	139	158	179	200	222	246	270		
19			13	23	34	46	60	74	90	107	124	143	163	182	205	228	252	277	303	
20			14	24	35	48	62	77	93	110	128	147	167	188	210	234	258	283	309	337

c. Two-tailed test, *p* = .01; one-tailed test, *p* = .005

N_2										N_1 (Smaller sample)										
	1	2	3	4	5	6	7	8	9	10	11	12	13	14	15	16	17	18	19	20
3																				
4																				
5					15															
6				10	16	23														
7				10	16	24	32													
8				11	17	25	34	43												
9			6	11	18	26	35	45	56											
10			6	12	19	27	37	47	58	71										
11			6	12	20	28	38	49	61	73	87									
12			7	13	21	30	40	51	63	76	90	105								
13			7	14	22	31	41	53	65	79	93	109	125							
14			7	14	22	32	43	54	67	81	96	112	129	147						
15			8	15	23	33	44	56	69	84	99	115	133	151	171					
16			8	15	24	34	46	58	72	86	102	119	136	155	175	196				
17			8	16	25	36	47	60	74	89	105	122	140	159	180	201	223			
18			8	16	26	37	49	62	76	92	108	125	144	163	184	206	228	252		
19		3	9	17	27	38	50	64	78	94	111	129	147	168	189	210	234	258	283	
20		3	9	18	28	39	52	66	81	97	114	132	151	172	193	215	239	263	289	315

4. F DISTRIBUTION

df for denom.	p	\multicolumn{10}{c}{df for numerator}									
		1	2	3	4	5	6	7	8	9	10
1	.05	161	200	216	225	230	234	237	239	241	242
2	.05	18.5	19.0	19.2	19.2	19.3	19.3	19.4	19.4	19.4	19.4
	.01	98.5	99.0	99.2	99.2	99.3	99.3	99.4	99.4	99.4	99.4
3	.05	10.1	9.55	9.28	9.12	9.10	8.94	8.89	8.85	8.81	8.79
	.01	34.1	30.8	29.5	28.7	28.2	27.9	27.7	27.5	27.3	27.2
4	.05	7.71	6.94	6.59	6.39	6.26	6.16	6.09	6.04	6.00	5.96
	.01	21.2	18.0	16.7	16.0	15.5	15.2	15.0	14.8	14.7	14.5
5	.05	6.61	5.79	5.41	5.19	5.05	4.95	4.88	4.82	4.77	4.74
	.01	16.3	13.3	12.1	11.4	11.0	10.7	10.5	10.3	10.2	10.1
6	.05	5.99	5.14	4.76	4.53	4.39	4.28	4.21	4.15	4.10	4.06
	.01	13.7	10.9	9.78	9.15	8.75	8.47	8.26	8.10	7.98	7.87
7	.05	5.59	4.74	4.35	4.12	3.97	3.87	3.79	3.73	3.68	3.64
	.01	12.2	9.55	8.45	7.85	7.46	7.19	6.99	6.84	6.72	6.62
8	.05	5.32	4.46	4.07	3.84	3.69	3.58	3.50	3.44	3.39	3.35
	.01	11.3	8.65	7.59	7.01	6.63	6.37	6.18	6.03	5.91	5.81
9	.05	5.12	4.26	3.86	3.63	3.48	3.37	3.29	3.23	3.18	3.14
	.01	10.6	8.02	6.99	6.42	6.06	5.80	5.61	5.47	5.35	5.26
10	.05	4.96	4.10	3.71	3.48	3.33	3.22	3.14	3.07	3.02	2.98
	.01	10.0	7.56	6.55	5.99	5.64	5.39	5.20	5.06	4.94	4.85
11	.05	4.84	3.98	3.59	3.36	3.20	3.09	3.01	2.95	2.90	2.85
	.01	9.65	7.21	6.22	5.67	5.32	5.07	4.89	4.74	4.63	4.54

12	.05	4.75	3.89	3.49	3.26	3.11	3.00	2.91	2.85	2.80	2.75
	.01	9.33	6.93	5.95	5.41	5.06	4.82	4.64	4.50	4.39	4.30
13	.05	4.67	3.81	3.41	3.18	3.03	2.92	2.83	2.77	2.71	2.67
	.01	9.07	6.70	5.74	5.21	4.86	4.62	4.44	4.30	4.19	4.10
14	.05	4.60	3.74	3.34	3.11	2.96	2.85	2.76	2.70	2.65	2.60
	.01	8.86	6.51	5.56	5.04	4.69	4.46	4.28	4.14	4.03	3.94
15	.05	4.54	3.68	3.29	3.06	2.90	2.79	2.71	2.64	2.59	2.54
	.01	8.68	6.36	5.42	4.89	4.56	4.32	4.14	4.00	3.89	3.80
16	.05	4.49	3.63	3.24	3.01	2.85	2.74	2.66	2.59	2.54	2.49
	.01	8.53	6.23	5.29	4.77	4.44	4.20	4.03	3.89	3.78	3.69
17	.05	4.45	3.59	3.20	2.96	2.81	2.70	2.61	2.55	2.49	2.45
	.01	8.40	6.11	5.18	4.67	4.34	4.10	3.93	3.79	3.68	3.59
18	.05	4.41	3.55	3.16	2.93	2.77	2.66	2.58	2.51	2.46	2.41
	.01	8.29	6.01	5.09	4.58	4.25	4.01	3.84	3.71	3.60	3.51
19	.05	4.38	3.52	3.13	2.90	2.74	2.63	2.54	2.48	2.42	2.38
	.01	8.18	5.93	5.01	4.50	4.17	3.94	3.77	3.63	3.52	3.43
20	.05	4.35	3.49	3.10	2.87	2.71	2.60	2.51	2.45	2.39	2.35
	.01	8.10	5.85	4.94	4.43	4.10	3.87	3.70	3.56	3.46	3.37
22	.05	4.30	3.44	3.05	2.82	2.66	2.55	2.46	2.40	2.34	2.30
	.01	7.95	5.72	4.82	4.31	3.99	3.76	3.59	3.45	3.35	3.26
24	.05	4.26	3.40	3.01	2.78	2.62	2.51	2.42	2.36	2.30	2.25
	.01	7.82	5.61	4.72	4.22	3.90	3.67	3.50	3.36	3.26	3.17

df for numerator

df for denom.	p	1	2	3	4	5	6	7	8	9	10
26	.05	4.23	3.37	2.98	2.74	2.59	2.47	2.39	2.32	2.27	2.22
	.01	7.72	5.53	4.64	4.14	3.82	3.59	3.42	3.29	3.18	3.09
28	.05	4.20	3.34	2.95	2.71	2.56	2.45	2.36	2.29	2.24	2.19
	.01	7.64	5.45	4.57	4.07	3.75	3.53	3.36	3.23	3.12	3.03
30	.05	4.17	3.32	2.92	2.69	2.53	2.42	2.33	2.27	2.21	2.16
	.01	7.56	5.39	4.51	4.02	3.70	3.47	3.30	3.17	3.07	2.98
40	.05	4.08	3.23	2.84	2.61	2.45	2.34	2.25	2.18	2.12	2.08
	.01	7.31	5.18	4.31	3.83	3.51	3.29	3.12	2.99	2.89	2.80
60	.05	4.00	3.15	2.76	2.53	2.37	2.25	2.17	2.10	2.04	1.99
	.01	7.08	4.98	4.13	3.65	3.34	3.12	2.95	2.82	2.72	2.63
120	.05	3.92	3.07	2.68	2.45	2.29	2.17	2.09	2.02	1.96	1.91
	.01	6.85	4.79	3.95	3.48	3.17	2.96	2.79	2.66	2.56	2.47
200	.05	3.89	3.04	2.65	2.42	2.26	2.14	2.06	1.98	1.93	1.88
	.01	6.76	4.71	3.88	3.41	3.11	2.89	2.73	2.60	2.50	2.41
∞	.05	3.84	3.00	2.60	2.37	2.21	2.10	2.01	1.94	1.88	1.83
	.01	6.63	4.61	3.78	3.32	3.02	2.80	2.64	2.51	2.41	2.32

*This table is taken from Table 18 in Pearson, E. S. and Hartley, H. O.: *Biometrika Tables for Statisticians*, vol. 1, 2nd Ed. (New York: Cambridge University Press, 1958). Reprinted by permission of Dr. E. S. Pearson.

5. CRITICAL VALUES OF *W* FOR THE WILCOXON TEST[a]

N	Level of significance for a directional (one-tailed) test				N	Level of significance for a directional (one-tailed) test			
	.05	.025	.01	.005		.05	.025	.01	.005
	Level of significance for a nondirectional (two-tailed) test					Level of significance for a nondirectional (two-tailed) test			
	.10	.05	.02	.01		.10	.05	.02	.01
5	0	—	—	—	28	130	116	101	91
6	2	0	—	—	29	140	126	110	100
7	3	2	0	—	30	151	137	120	109
8	5	3	1	0	31	163	147	130	118
9	8	5	3	1	32	175	159	140	128
10	10	8	5	3	33	187	170	151	138
11	13	10	7	5	34	200	182	162	148
12	17	13	9	7	35	213	195	173	159
13	21	17	12	9	36	227	208	185	171
14	25	21	15	12	37	241	221	198	182
15	30	25	19	15	38	256	235	211	194
16	35	29	23	19	39	271	249	224	207
17	41	34	27	23	40	286	264	238	220
18	47	40	32	27	41	302	279	252	233
19	53	46	37	32	42	319	294	266	247
20	60	52	43	37	43	336	310	281	261
21	67	58	49	42	44	353	327	296	276
22	75	65	55	48	45	371	343	312	291
23	83	73	62	54	46	389	361	328	307
24	91	81	69	61	47	407	378	345	322
25	100	89	76	68	48	426	396	362	339
26	110	98	84	75	49	446	415	379	355
27	119	107	92	83	50	466	434	397	373

This table is taken from F. Wilcoxon, S. Katte, and R. A. Wilcox, *Critical Values and Probability Levels for the Wilcoxon Rank Sum Test and the Wilcoxon Signed Rank Test,* New York, American Cyanamid Co., 1963, and F. Wilcoxon and R. A. Wilcox, *Some Rapid Approximate Statistical Procedures,* New York, Lederle Laboratories, 1964 as used in Runyon and Haber, *Fundamentals of Behavioral Statistics,* 3rd edition, 1976, Addison-Wesley, Reading, Mass.

[a]For a given *N* (the number of pairs of scores), if the observed value is *equal to* or *less than* the value in the table for the appropriate level of significance, then reject H_0. The symbol *W* denotes the smaller sum of ranks associated with differences that are all of the same sign.

6. DISTRIBUTION OF F_{max} STATISTICS[a]

n - 1	k = *Number of variances*								
	2	3	4	5	6	7	8	9	10
4	9.60	15.5	20.6	25.2	29.5	33.6	37.5	41.4	44.6
5	7.15	10.8	13.7	16.3	18.7	20.8	22.9	24.7	26.5
6	5.82	8.38	10.4	12.1	13.7	15.0	16.3	17.5	18.6
7	4.99	6.94	8.44	9.70	10.8	11.8	12.7	13.5	14.3
8	4.43	6.00	7.18	8.12	9.03	9.78	10.5	11.1	11.7
9	4.03	5.34	6.31	7.11	7.80	8.41	8.95	9.45	9.91
10	3.72	4.85	5.67	6.34	6.92	7.42	7.87	8.28	8.66
12	3.28	4.16	4.79	5.30	5.72	6.09	6.42	6.72	7.00
15	2.86	3.54	4.01	4.37	4.68	4.95	5.19	5.40	5.59
20	2.46	2.95	3.29	3.54	3.76	3.94	4.10	4.24	4.37
30	2.07	2.40	2.61	2.78	2.91	3.02	3.12	3.21	3.29
60	1.67	1.85	1.96	2.04	2.11	2.17	2.22	2.26	2.30
∞	1.00	1.00	1.00	1.00	1.00	1.00	1.00	1.00	1.00

This table is taken from Table 31 in Pearson, E. S. and Hartley, H. O.: *Biometrika Tables for Statistics*, vol. 1, 2nd Ed. (New York: Cambridge University Press, 1958). Reprinted by permission of Dr. E. S. Pearson.
[a]$p = .05$.

7. CRITICAL VALUES OF r_s (RANK-ORDER CORRELATION COEFFICIENT)

Number of pairs	*Level of significance*		
	.10	.05	.01
5	.900	1.000	—
6	.829	.886	1.000
7	.714	.786–	.929
8	.643	.738	.881
9	.600	.683	.833
10	.564	.648	.794
12	.506	.591	.777
14	.456	.544	.715
16	.425	.506	.665
18	.399	.475	.625
20	.377	.450	.591
22	.359	.428	.562
24	.343	.409	.537
26	.329	.392	.515
28	.317	.377	.496
30	.306	.364	.478

This table is taken from Olds, E. G.: "The 5 percent significance levels of sums of squares of rank differences and a correction," *Annals of Mathematical Statistics*, 20 (1949): 117–118, and from Olds, E. G.: "Distribution of sums of squares of rank differences for small numbers of individuals," *Annals of Mathematical Statistics*, 9 (1938): 113–148. Reprinted by permission of the Institute of Mathematical Statistics.

8. CRITICAL VALUES OF *r* (PEARSON PRODUCT-MOMENT CORRELATION)

Number of pairs minus two	Level of significance		
	.10	.05	.01
1	.98769	.99692	.999877
2	.90000	.95000	.990000
3	.8054	.8783	.95873
4	.7293	.8114	.91720
5	.6694	.7545	.8745
6	.6215	.7067	.8343
7	.5822	.6664	.7977
8	.5494	.6319	.7646
9	.5214	.6021	.7348
10	.4973	.5760	.7079
11	.4762	.5529	.6835
12	.4575	.5324	.6614
13	.4409	.5139	.6411
14	.4259	.4973	.6226
15	.4124	.4821	.6055
16	.4000	.4683	.5897
17	.3887	.4555	.5751
18	.3783	.4438	.5614
19	.3687	.4329	.5487
20	.3598	.4227	.5368
25	.3233	.3809	.4869
30	.2960	.3494	.4487
35	.2746	.3246	.4182
40	.2573	.3044	.3932
45	.2428	.2875	.3721
50	.2306	.2732	.3541
60	.2108	.2500	.3248
70	.1954	.2319	.3017
80	.1829	.2172	.2830
90	.1726	.2050	.2673
100	.1638	.1946	.2540

This table is taken from Tables III and VI of Fischer; *Statistical Methods for Research Workers,* and from Fischer and Yates: *Statistical Tables for Biological, Agricultural and Medical Research,* published by Longman Group Ltd., London. Reprinted by permission of the authors and publishers.

9. RANDOM NUMBERS

22 17 68 65 84	68 95 23 92 35	87 02 22 57 51	61 09 43 95 06	58 24 82 03 47
19 36 27 59 46	13 79 93 37 55	39 77 32 77 09	85 52 05 30 62	47 83 51 62 74
16 77 23 02 77	09 61 87 25 21	28 06 24 25 93	16 71 13 59 78	23 05 47 47 25
78 43 76 71 61	20 44 90 32 64	97 67 63 99 61	46 38 03 93 22	69 81 21 99 21
03 28 28 26 08	73 37 32 04 05	69 30 16 09 05	88 69 58 28 99	35 07 44 75 47
93 22 53 64 39	07 10 63 76 35	87 03 04 79 88	08 13 13 85 51	55 34 57 72 69
78 76 58 54 74	92 38 70 96 92	52 06 79 79 45	82 63 18 27 44	69 66 92 19 09
23 68 35 26 00	99 53 93 61 28	52 70 05 48 34	56 65 05 61 86	90 92 10 70 80
15 39 25 70 99	93 86 52 77 65	15 33 59 05 28	22 87 26 07 47	86 96 98 29 06
58 71 96 30 24	18 46 23 34 27	85 13 99 24 44	49 18 09 79 49	74 16 32 23 02
57 35 27 33 72	24 53 63 94 09	41 10 76 47 91	44 04 95 49 66	39 60 04 59 81
48 50 86 54 48	22 06 34 72 52	82 21 15 65 20	33 29 94 71 11	15 91 29 12 03
61 96 48 95 03	07 16 39 33 66	98 56 10 56 79	77 21 30 27 12	90 49 22 23 62
36 93 89 41 26	29 70 83 63 51	99 74 20 52 36	87 09 41 15 09	98 60 16 03 03
18 87 00 42 31	57 90 12 02 07	23 47 37 17 31	54 08 01 88 63	39 41 88 92 10
88 56 53 27 59	33 35 72 67 47	77 34 55 45 70	08 18 27 38 90	16 95 86 70 75
09 72 95 84 29	49 41 31 06 70	42 38 06 45 18	64 84 73 31 65	52 53 37 97 15
12 96 88 17 31	65 19 69 02 83	60 75 86 90 68	24 64 19 35 51	56 61 87 39 12
85 94 57 24 16	92 09 84 38 76	22 00 27 69 85	29 81 94 78 70	21 94 47 90 12
38 64 43 59 98	98 77 87 68 07	91 51 67 62 44	40 98 05 93 78	23 32 65 41 18
53 44 09 42 72	00 41 86 79 79	68 47 22 00 20	35 55 31 51 51	00 83 63 22 55
40 76 66 26 84	57 99 99 90 37	36 63 32 08 58	37 40 13 68 97	87 64 81 07 83
02 17 79 18 05	12 59 52 57 02	22 07 90 47 03	28 14 11 30 79	20 69 22 40 98
95 17 82 06 53	31 51 10 96 46	92 06 88 07 77	56 11 50 81 69	40 23 72 51 39
35 76 22 42 92	96 11 83 44 80	34 68 35 48 77	33 42 40 90 60	73 96 53 97 86
26 29 13 56 41	85 47 04 66 08	34 72 57 59 13	82 43 80 46 15	38 26 61 70 64
77 80 20 75 82	72 82 32 99 90	63 95 73 76 63	89 73 44 99 05	48 67 26 43 18
46 40 66 44 52	91 36 74 43 53	30 82 13 54 00	78 45 63 98 35	55 03 36 67 68
37 56 08 18 09	77 53 84 46 47	31 91 18 95 58	24 16 74 11 53	44 10 13 85 57
61 65 61 68 66	37 27 47 39 19	84 83 70 07 48	53 21 40 06 71	95 06 79 88 54
93 43 69 64 07	34 18 04 52 35	56 27 09 24 86	61 85 53 83 45	19 90 70 99 68
21 96 60 12 99	11 20 99 45 18	48 13 93 55 34	18 37 79 49 90	65 97 38 20 46
95 20 47 97 97	27 37 83 28 71	00 06 41 41 74	45 89 09 39 84	51 67 11 52 49
97 86 21 78 73	10 65 81 92 59	58 76 17 14 97	04 76 62 16 17	17 95 70 45 80
69 92 06 34 13	59 71 74 17 32	27 55 10 24 19	23 71 82 13 74	63 52 52 01 41
04 31 17 21 56	33 73 99 19 87	26 72 39 27 67	53 77 57 68 93	60 61 97 22 61
61 06 98 03 91	87 14 77 43 96	43 00 65 98 50	45 60 33 01 07	98 99 46 50 47
85 93 85 86 88	72 87 08 62 40	16 06 10 89 20	23 21 34 74 97	76 38 03 29 63
21 74 32 47 45	73 96 07 94 52	09 65 90 77 47	25 76 16 19 33	53 05 70 53 30
15 69 53 82 80	79 96 23 53 10	65 39 07 16 29	45 33 02 43 70	02 87 40 41 45
02 89 08 04 49	20 21 14 68 86	87 63 93 95 17	11 29 01 95 80	35 14 97 35 33
87 18 15 89 79	85 43 01 72 73	08 61 74 51 69	89 74 39 82 15	94 51 33 41 67
98 83 71 94 22	59 97 50 99 52	08 52 85 08 40	87 80 61 65 31	91 51 80 32 44
10 08 58 21 66	72 68 49 29 31	89 85 84 46 06	59 73 19 85 23	65 09 29 75 63
47 90 56 10 08	88 02 84 27 83	42 29 72 23 19	66 56 45 65 79	20 71 53 20 25
22 85 61 68 90	49 64 92 85 44	16 40 12 89 88	50 14 49 81 06	01 82 77 45 12
67 80 43 79 33	12 83 11 41 16	25 58 19 68 70	77 02 54 00 52	53 43 37 15 26
27 62 50 96 72	79 44 61 40 15	14 53 40 65 39	27 31 58 50 28	11 39 03 34 25
33 78 80 87 15	38 30 06 38 21	14 47 47 07 26	54 96 87 53 32	40 36 40 96 76
13 13 92 66 99	47 24 49 57 74	32 25 43 62 17	10 97 11 69 84	99 63 22 32 98

This table is taken from Table XXXIII of Fisher and Yates, *Statistical Tables for Biological, Agricultural and Medical Research*, published by Longman Group Ltd., London (previously published by Oliver and Boyd, Ltd., Edinburgh), and by permission of the authors and publishers.

```
10 27 53 96 23    71 50 54 36 23    54 31 04 82 98    04 14 12 15 09    26 78 25 47 47
28 41 50 61 88    64 85 27 20 18    83 36 36 05 56    39 71 65 09 62    94 76 62 11 89
34 21 42 57 02    59 19 18 97 48    80 30 03 30 98    05 24 67 70 07    84 97 50 87 46
61 81 77 23 23    82 82 11 54 08    53 28 70 58 96    44 07 39 55 43    42 34 43 39 28
61 15 18 13 54    16 86 20 26 88    90 74 80 55 09    14 53 90 51 17    52 01 63 01 59

91 76 21 64 64    44 91 13 32 97    75 31 62 66 54    84 80 32 75 77    56 08 25 70 29
00 97 79 08 06    37 30 28 59 85    53 56 68 53 40    01 74 39 59 73    30 19 99 85 48
36 46 18 34 94    75 20 80 27 77    78 91 69 16 00    08 43 18 73 68    67 69 61 34 25
88 98 99 60 50    65 95 79 42 94    93 62 40 89 96    43 56 47 71 66    46 76 29 67 02
04 37 59 87 21    05 02 03 24 17    47 97 81 56 51    92 34 86 01 82    55 51 33 12 91

63 62 06 34 41    94 21 78 55 09    72 76 45 16 94    29 95 81 83 83    79 88 01 97 30
78 47 23 53 90    34 41 92 45 71    09 23 70 70 07    12 38 92 79 43    14 85 11 47 23
87 68 62 15 43    53 14 36 59 25    54 47 33 70 15    59 24 48 40 35    50 03 42 99 36
47 60 92 10 77    88 59 53 11 52    66 25 69 07 04    48 68 64 71 06    61 65 70 22 12
56 88 87 59 41    65 28 04 67 53    95 79 88 37 31    50 41 06 94 76    81 83 17 16 33

02 57 45 86 67    73 43 07 34 48    44 26 87 93 29    77 09 61 67 84    06 69 44 77 75
31 54 14 13 17    48 62 11 90 60    68 12 93 64 28    46 24 79 16 76    14 60 25 51 01
28 50 16 43 36    28 97 85 58 99    67 22 52 76 23    24 70 36 54 54    59 28 61 71 96
63 29 62 66 50    02 63 45 52 38    67 63 47 54 75    83 24 78 43 20    92 63 13 47 48
45 65 58 26 51    76 96 59 38 72    86 57 45 71 46    44 67 76 14 55    44 88 01 62 12

39 65 36 63 70    77 45 85 50 51    74 13 39 35 22    30 53 36 02 95    49 34 88 73 61
73 71 98 16 04    29 18 94 51 23    76 51 94 84 86    79 93 96 38 63    08 58 25 58 94
72 20 56 20 11    72 65 71 08 86    79 57 95 13 91    97 48 72 66 48    09 71 17 24 89
75 17 26 99 76    89 37 20 70 01    77 31 61 95 46    26 97 05 73 51    53 33 18 72 87
37 48 60 82 29    81 30 15 39 14    48 38 75 93 29    06 87 37 78 48    45 56 00 84 47

68 08 02 80 72    83 71 46 30 49    89 17 95 88 29    02 39 56 03 46    97 74 06 56 17
14 23 98 61 67    70 52 85 01 50    01 84 02 78 43    10 62 98 19 41    18 83 99 47 99
49 08 96 21 44    25 27 99 41 28    07 41 08 34 66    19 42 74 39 91    41 96 53 78 72
78 37 06 08 43    63 61 62 42 29    39 68 95 10 96    09 24 23 00 62    56 12 80 73 16
37 21 34 17 68    68 96 83 23 56    32 84 60 15 31    44 73 67 34 77    91 15 79 74 58

14 29 09 34 04    87 83 07 55 07    76 58 30 83 64    87 29 25 58 84    86 50 60 00 25
58 43 28 06 36    49 52 83 51 14    47 56 91 29 34    05 87 31 06 95    12 45 57 09 09
10 43 67 29 70    80 62 80 03 42    10 80 21 38 84    90 56 35 03 09    43 12 74 49 14
44 38 88 39 54    86 97 37 44 22    00 95 01 31 76    17 16 29 56 63    38 78 94 49 81
90 69 59 19 51    85 39 52 85 13    07 28 37 07 61    11 16 36 27 03    78 86 72 04 95

41 47 10 25 62    97 05 31 03 61    20 26 36 31 62    68 69 86 95 44    84 95 48 46 45
91 94 14 63 19    75 89 11 47 11    31 56 34 19 09    79 57 92 36 59    14 93 87 81 40
80 06 54 18 66    09 18 94 06 19    98 40 07 17 81    22 45 44 84 11    24 62 20 42 31
67 72 77 63 48    84 08 31 55 58    24 33 45 77 58    80 45 67 93 82    75 70 16 08 24
59 40 24 13 27    79 26 88 86 30    01 31 60 10 39    53 58 47 70 93    85 81 56 39 38

05 90 35 89 95    01 61 16 96 94    50 78 13 69 36    37 68 53 37 31    71 26 35 03 71
44 43 80 69 98    46 68 05 14 82    90 78 50 05 62    77 79 13 57 44    59 60 10 39 66
61 81 31 96 82    00 57 25 60 59    46 72 60 18 77    55 66 12 62 11    08 99 55 64 57
42 88 07 10 05    24 98 65 63 21    47 21 61 88 32    27 80 30 21 60    10 92 35 36 12
77 94 30 05 39    28 10 99 00 27    12 73 73 99 12    49 99 57 94 82    96 88 57 17 91

78 83 19 76 16    94 11 68 84 26    23 54 20 86 85    23 86 66 99 07    36 37 34 92 09
87 76 59 61 81    43 63 64 61 61    65 76 36 95 90    18 48 27 45 68    27 23 65 30 72
91 43 05 96 47    55 78 99 95 24    37 55 85 78 78    01 48 41 19 10    35 19 54 07 73
84 97 77 72 73    09 62 06 65 72    87 12 49 03 60    41 15 20 76 27    50 47 02 29 16
87 41 60 76 83    44 88 96 07 80    83 05 83 38 96    73 70 66 81 90    30 56 10 48 59
```

Appendix **D** Answers for selected questions and problems in chapters 1–12

CHAPTER 1

15. 4　16. 4　17. 4　18. 2　19. 4　20. 1　21. 3

CHAPTER 2

14. 3　15. 3　16. 4　17. 3　18. 1　19. 3　20. 3　21. 4　22. 2　23. 5　24. 2
25. 3　26. 2　27. 2　28. 2　29. 2　30. 1　31. 2　32. 3　33. 2　34. 4　35. 4
36. 4　37. 4　38. 2

CHAPTER 3

15. 1　16. 3　17. 4　18. 4　19. 4　20. 2　21. 2　22. 2　23. 4　24. 4　25. 4
26. 4　27. 1　28. 4　29. 1

CHAPTER 4

9. 3　10. 3　11. 3　12. 2　13. 1　14. 3　15. 2　16. 3　17. 4

CHAPTER 5

14. 3　15. 1　16. 3　17. 1　18. 2　19. 3　20. 4

CHAPTER 6

10. 1　11. 3　12. 4　13. 3　14. 1　15. 3　16. 1　17. 4　18. 1

CHAPTER 7

15. 2   16. 3   17. 1

CHAPTER 8

1. a. Nominal
   b. Ordinal
   c. Ordinal or interval
   d. Ratio
   e. Ratio
   f. Ordinal
2. Mode = 13, median = 12.5, mean = 12.0.
3. Mode = 14 and 16, median = 15, mean = 15.0.
4. Mode = 3, median = 4.5, mean = 8.0.
5. Probably the median, since the mean is influenced by extreme scores, in this case very expensive homes.
7. Range = 13, variance = 15.11, and standard deviation = 3.89 for problem 2
   Range = 10, variance = 5.45, and standard deviation = 2.34 for problem 3
   Range = 17, variance = 45.11, and standard deviation = 6.72 for problem 4
12. about 2.1 percent
15. 1   16. 1   17. 4   18. 2   19. 2   20. 2   21. 4   22. 2   23. 4   24. 4   25. 4
26. 3

CHAPTER 9

1. Phi = .30 or −.30
2. Phi = .47 or −.47
3. Rank-order correlation = .81
4. Rank-order correlation = .05
5. r = .05, no
6. r = .546
16. 3   17. 2   18. 3   19. 1   20. 2   21. 4   22. 3   23. 5

CHAPTER 10

1. The expected frequencies are 25, 75, 37.5, 112.5, 37.5, and 112.5.
2. The obtained chi square of 9.37 exceeds the tabled value, so the null hypothesis can be rejected.
4. Chi square = 10.09; you can reject the null hypothesis.
5. Chi square for females = .88; you cannot reject the null hypothesis. Chi square for males = 28.51; you can reject the null hypothesis.
7. Chi square for median test = 2.68 so you cannot reject the null hypothesis.
8. Smaller sum = 108 so you can reject the null hypothesis.

CHAPTER 11

1. $F = .56$; you cannot reject the null hypothesis. You need an F value equal to or larger than 4.75 to reject at the .05 level of significance.
2. $F = 11.68$; you can reject the null hypothesis. The obtained F value exceeds the tabled value of 4.84 for the .05 level of significance.
3. $F = .00$; you cannot reject the null hypothesis.
4. $F = 33.90$; you can reject the null hypothesis.
5. $F = 19.36$; you can reject the null hypothesis.
6. $F = 1.53$ for the type of appeal; you cannot reject the null hypothesis. $F = 31.77$ for the type of participant variable; you can reject the null hypothesis. $F = 38.26$ for the interaction; you can reject the null hypothesis.
7. $F = 0.32$ for anxiety level; you cannot reject the null hypothesis. $F = 146.29$ for the type of task effect; you can reject the null hypothesis. $F = 31.65$ for the interaction; you can reject the null hypothesis.
9. $F = 18.32$ for the marijuana effect; you can reject the null hypothesis. $F = 9.96$ for the alcohol effect; you can reject the null hypothesis. $F = .45$ for the interaction; you cannot reject the null hypothesis.

CHAPTER 12

1. $Q = 5.33$; you can reject the null hypothesis.
2. $Q = 3.57$; you cannot reject the null hypothesis.
3. $W = 1.5$; you can reject the null hypothesis since the W value is smaller than the tabled value of 5 for the .05 level of significance. $N = 9$ in this case because we cannot use any subject who has a tie score for the two conditions, in this case subject i. For the analysis at the interval level of measurement, $F = 12.24$; you can reject the null hypothesis.
4. $F = 9.16$; you can reject the null hypothesis.

References

Alloy, L. B., & Seligman, M. E. P. The cognitive component of learned helplessness. In G. H. Bower (ed.), *The Psychology of Learning and Motivation,* vol. 13. New York: Academic Press, 1979.

Anderson, B. F. *Cognitive Psychology: The Study of Knowing, Learning, and Thinking.* New York: Academic Press, 1975.

Baumrind, D. Child care practices anteceding three patterns of preschool behavior. *Genetic Psychology Monographs,* 1967, 75, 43–88.

Beck, A. T. *Cognitive Therapy and the Emotional Disorders.* New York: International Universities Press, 1976.

Beck, A. T. Cognitive therapy: Nature and relation to behavior therapy. *Behavior Therapy,* 1970, 1, 184–200.

Beck, A. T., & Kovacs, M. A new, fast therapy for depression. *Psychology Today,* January 1977, 94, 100, 102.

Cameron, P. Children's reactions to second-hand tobacco smoke. *Journal of Applied Psychology,* 1972, 56, 171–173.

Campbell, D. T. Factors relevant to the validity of experiments in social settings. *Psychological Bulletin,* 1957, 54, 297–312.

Campbell, D. T., & Stanley, J. C. *Experimental and Quasi-Experimental Designs for Research.* Chicago: Rand McNally, 1963.

Chance, P. Ads without answers make the brain itch. *Psychology Today,* November 1975, 9, 78.

Chapman, L. J., & Chapman, J. P. Illusory correlation as an obstacle to the use of valid psychodiagnostic signs. *Journal of Abnormal Psychology,* 1969, 74, 271–280.

Cochran, W. G. The comparison of percentages in matched samples. *Biometrika,* 1950, 37, 256–266.

Cohen, M., Liebson, I. A., & Faillace, L. A. A technique for establishing controlled drinking in chronic alcoholics. *Diseases of the Nervous System,* 1972, 33, 46–49.

Crano, W. D., & Brewer, M. B. *Principles of Research in Social Psychology.* New York: McGraw-Hill, 1973.

Crano, W. D., Kenny, D. A., & Campbell, D. T. Does intelligence cause achievement? A cross-lagged panel analysis. *Journal of Educational Psychology,* 1972, 63, 258–275.

Cronbach, L. J. Beyond the two disciplines of scientific psychology. *American Psychologist,* 1975, 30, 116–127.

Dabbs, J. M. Sex, setting, and reactions to crowding on sidewalks. *Proceedings of the Annual Convention of the American Psychological Association,* 1972, 7 (Pt. 1), 205–206.

Darley, J. M., Seligman, C., & Becker, L. J. The lesson of Twin Rivers: Feedback works. *Psychology Today,* April 1979, 16, 23, 24.

Dawes, R. M. The robust beauty of improper linear models in decision making. *American Psychologist,* 1979, 34, 571–582.

Dawes, R. M. Shallow psychology. In J. S. Carroll & J. W. Payne (eds.), *Cognition and Social Behavior.* Hillsdale, N.J.: Erlbaum, 1976.

Gibson, E. J., & Levin, H. *The Psychology of Reading.* Cambridge, Mass.: The M.I.T. Press, 1975.

Goodall, J. Chimp killings: Is it the man in them? *Science News,* 1978, 113, 276.

Hanley, C. Personal communication, 1969.

Hebb, D. O. What psychology is about. *American Psychologist,* 1974, 29, 71–79.

Hussar, D. A. Drug interactions 1. *American Journal of Pharmacy,* 1973, 145, 65–116.

Jones, E. E., & Nisbett, R. E. The actor and the observer: Divergent perceptions of the causes of behavior. In E. E. Jones et al. (eds), *Attribution: Perceiving the Causes of Behavior.* Morristown, N.J.: General Learning Press, 1972.

Koch, M. D., & Arnold, W. J. Effects of early social deprivation on emotionality in rats. *Journal of Comparative and Physiological Psychology,* 1972, 78, 391–399.

Kruskal, W. H., & Wallis, W. A. Use of ranks in one criterion variance analysis. *Journal of the American Statistical Association,* 1952, 47, 583–621.

Labovitz, S., & Hagedorn, R. *Introduction to Social Research.* New York: McGraw-Hill, 1971.

Latané, B., & Darley, J. M. *The Unresponsive Bystander: Why Doesn't He Help?* New York: Appleton-Century-Crofts, 1970.

Lewinsohn, P. M., Mischel, W., Chaplin, W., & Barton, R. Social competence and depression: The role of illusory self-perceptions. *Journal of Abnormal Psychology,* 1980, 89, 203–212.

Lindsay, P. H., & Norman, D. A. *Human Information Processing: An Introduction to Psychology,* 2nd ed. New York: Academic Press, 1977.

Maier, S. F., & Seligman, M. E. P. Learned helplessness: Theory and evidence. *Journal of Experimental Psychology: General,* 1976, 105, 3–46.

Mischel, W. On the interface of cognition and personality: Beyond the person-situation debate. *American Psychologist,* 1979, 34, 740–754.

Myers, D. G., & Ridl, J. Can we all be better than average? *Psychology Today,* August 1979, 89, 95, 96, 98.

Nisbett, R. E., & Wilson, T. D. Telling more than we can know: Verbal reports on mental processes. *Psychological Review,* 1977, 84, 231–259.

Norris, D. Crying and laughing in imbeciles. *Developmental Medicine and Child Neurology,* 1971, 13, 756–761.

Orne, M. T. The nature of hypnosis: Artifact and essence. *Journal of Abnormal and Social Psychology,* 1959, 58, 277–299.

Orne, M. T. On the social psychology of the psychological experiment: With particular reference to demand characteristics and their implications. *American Psychologist,* 1962, 17, 776–783.

Rayner, K. Eye movements in reading and information processing. *Psychological Bulletin,* 1978, 85, 618–660.

Rice, B. The SAT controversy: When an aptitude is coachable. *Psychology Today,* September 1979, 30, 33.

Rosenthal, R. *Experimenter Effects in Behavioral Research.* New York: Appleton-Century-Crofts, 1966.

Rosenthal, R. On the social psychology of the psychological experiment: The experimenter's hypothesis as unintended determinant of experimental results. *American Scientist,* 1963, 51, 268–283.

Scarf, M. The more sorrowful sex. *Psychology Today,* April 1979, 44, 45, 47, 48, 51, 52, 89, 90.

Schusterman, R. J., & Gentry, R. L. Development of a fatted male phenomenon in California sea lions. *Developmental Psychobiology,* 1971, 4, 333–338.

Seligman, M. E. P. *Helplessness: On Depression, Development, and Death.* San Francisco: Freeman, 1975.

Siegel, S. *Nonparametric Statistics for the Behavioral Sciences.* New York: McGraw-Hill, 1956.

Tversky, A., & Kahneman, D. Availability: A heuristic for judging frequency and probability. *Cognitive Psychology,* 1973, 5, 207–232.

Wason, P. C. On the failure to eliminate hypotheses — A second look. In P. C. Wason & P. N. Johnson-Laird (eds.), *Thinking and Reasoning.* Baltimore: Penguin, 1968.

Webb, E. J., Campbell, D. T., Schwartz, R. D., & Sechrest, L. *Unobtrusive Measures: Nonreactive Research in the Social Sciences.* Chicago: Rand McNally, 1966.

Wolf, M. M., & Risley, T. M. Reinforcement: Applied research. In R. Glaser (ed.), *The Nature of Reinforcement.* New York: Academic Press, 1971.

Yankelovich, D. Who gets ahead in America? *Psychology Today,* July 1979, 28–34, 40–43, 90–91.

Glossary

Abscissa: the X or horizontal axis in a graph.

Alpha: in hypothesis testing, the probability of rejecting the null hypothesis when the null hypothesis is true; the probability of a type 1 error. The alpha level is equal to the significance level.

Analysis of variance: a statistical test appropriate for analyzing interval data obtained with between-subject and within-subject experimental designs.

Assumption: a basic tenet of a theory that is taken for granted from which other tenets are derived; condition that must be met before certain conclusions are warranted (such as the assumptions of a statistical test).

Bar graph: a frequency distribution in which the height of bars is used to indicate the frequency of each score or each class of scores.

Beta: in hypothesis testing, the probability of failing to reject the null hypothesis when it is false; the probability of making a type 2 error.

Between-group variance: a measure of the fluctuations between groups based on group means.

Between-subject design: an experimental design in which each subject is tested under only one level of each independent variable.

Chance: in probability, the lack of any systematic effect influencing an outcome.

Chi square test: a statistical test appropriate for analyzing nominal data obtained with between-subject designs.

Cochran Q test: a statistical test appropriate for analyzing nominal data obtained with within-subject designs.

Confounding variable: a variable not manipulated as an independent variable that systematically varies with an independent variable so that the effect of the confounding variable and the effect of the independent variable cannot be separated.

Constant: a term in a mathematical formula that does not vary.

Control group: the group that does not receive the treatment. The performance of the no treatment group (control) is compared with the treatment group (experimental) to assess the effect of the treatment.

Correlation: a measure of the extent to which two variables are related, not necessarily in a causal relationship. The magnitude of a correlation can vary from -1.00 to $+1.00$.

356

Counterbalancing: a technique used to distribute order and time-related effects over all conditions equally by systematically varying the order of the conditions within or across subjects.

Criterion: a standard used to assess the predictive validity of a test.

Data: the scores obtained on a dependent variable or performance measure.

Degrees of freedom: the number of values that are free to vary if the sum of the values and the number of values are fixed.

Demand characteristics: those cues available to a subject in an experiment that may enable him to determine the "purpose" of the experiment; the cues that allow the subject to infer what the experimenter "expects" of him; one type of confounding variable.

Dependent variable: the variable the investigator measures to assess the effect of the independent variable; in an experiment, the variable whose level is not determined by the experimenter.

Descriptive statistics: methods for summarizing, organizing, and communicating data.

Determinism: an assumption of science which asserts that events have a finite number of causes that can be discovered.

Dichotomous variable: a variable with two and only two mutually exclusive categories (male-female, yes-no).

Differential transfer: in a within-subject design, differential transfer occurs when the effect of one treatment is dependent on the treatment that preceded it; an interaction of treatment by order of treatment.

Distribution: a set of values for an attribute or variable.

Double-blind: a design in which neither the subject nor the experimenter knows which subjects are in which treatment condition.

Equivalent groups: groups are said to be equivalent if the probability of the obtained group differences if only chance is operating is greater than the significance level.

Experimental design: a plan for obtaining and treating data in which the experimental method is used.

Experimental method: a method used to study phenomena in which one or more independent variables are manipulated and performance on one or more dependent variables is measured.

Explanation: a specification of the antecedent condition necessary to demonstrate a phenomenon.

Factorial design: an experimental design in which each level of each independent variable occurs with each level of every other independent variable.

Fixed effects model: a statistical model that necessitates that the conclusions drawn from the experiment be limited to the actual levels of the independent variable that were manipulated because the levels manipulated have not been randomly selected from the population of possible levels.

Frequency distribution: a set of scores arranged in ascending or descending order. The number of times each score occurs is indicated.

F_{max} *statistic:* a statistical test appropriate for determining whether the probability of the obtained differences between sample variances is less than the significance level.

Generalization: in experimentation, being able to extend the results of an experiment beyond the sample tested to the population from which the sample was drawn. In order to generalize the results to the population the sample must have been randomly selected from the population.

Heterogeneous: dissimilar.

Histogram: a bar graph.

Homogeneous: similar, alike.

Hypothesis: a proposed explanation for a phenomenon.

Independent variable: a variable in an experiment whose level is determined by the experimenter; a variable systematically manipulated by the experimenter in order to determine the effect of one variable on another.

Interval scale: a scale in which the scale values are related by a single, underlying, quantitative dimension and there are equal intervals between successive scale values.

Kurtosis: the degree of peakedness of a distribution.

Leptokurtic: a distribution or curve that is steep.

Linear relationship: a relationship between two variables in which an increase in one variable is always accompanied by a constant increase or is always accompanied by a constant decrease in the other.

Longitudinal study: a method in which individuals are studied over time and measurements are obtained on the individuals at various intervals.

Matched-groups design: a between-subject design in which groups are equated on the variable(s) selected for matching in an attempt to obtain equal groups or to reduce the within-group chance fluctuations.

Mean ($\overline{X}$): a descriptive measure of central tendency appropriate for interval data; the sum of all the scores divided by the number of scores.

Mean square (MS): in analysis of variance, an estimate of population variance if the null hypothesis is true.

Median: a descriptive measure of central tendency; the value that divides the distribution in half.

Median test: a statistical test appropriate for analyzing ordinal data obtained with between-subject designs.

Mesokurtic: a curve or distribution that is neither peaked nor flat. The normal distribution is mesokurtic.

Mnemonic system: a memory-improving system.

Mode: a descriptive measure of central tendency; the most frequently occurring value.

Monotonic relationship: a relationship between two variables in which an increase in one variable is always accompanied by an increase or is always accompanied by a decrease in the other variable.

Nominal measurement: placement of subjects into qualitatively different categories.

Nonreactive measure: a measure of behavior in which the subject is not aware of being observed and the subject's behavior is not changed by the observation process.

Normal distribution: a symmetrical, mesokurtic, bell-shaped curve. If scores on a measure are distributed normally, the greater the difference between a score and the mean, the less the probability of obtaining the score.

Null hypothesis: the assertion that the independent variable will not have an effect on the dependent variable.

Null hypothesis sampling distribution: a distribution of sample values that can be expected if only chance is operating.

Observational techniques: a method of research based on observing behavior of organisms without the systematic manipulation of an independent variable.

One-tailed test: a procedure for testing the null hypothesis in which the entire rejection area is placed at one end of the appropriate sampling distribution.

Operational definition: a definition of a concept in terms of the operations that must be performed in order to demonstrate the concept.

Order: an assumption of science which asserts that events follow each other in regular sequences.

Ordinal scale: a scale in which scale values are related by a single, underlying quantitative dimension but it is not possible to assume that the differences between successive scale values are of equal magnitude.

Ordinate: the Y or vertical axis in a graph.

Phenomenon: a fact or event that is observable.

Placebo: a substance or treatment having no effect that is given to a control group in place of a drug or experimental treatment to minimize demand characteristics.

Platykurtic: a curve or distribution that is flat.

Population: the potential units for observation from which the sample to be observed is drawn.

Probability: an estimate of the likelihood that a particular outcome will occur; the ratio of the number of favorable outcomes to the total number of possible outcomes if only chance is operating.

Random assignment: a procedure used to place subjects in groups or to order events so that only chance determines the placement or ordering.

Random-groups design: a between-subject design in which random assignment is used to assign subjects to conditions.

Random sampling: a procedure used to obtain representative samples from a population. In complete random sampling, each subject in the population must have an equal chance of being selected and the selection or nonselection of one subject cannot influence the selection or nonselection of any other subject.

Range: a descriptive measure of variability; the difference score obtained by subtracting the smallest score in the distribution from the largest score in the distribution.

Ratio scale: a scale in which scale values are related by a single, underlying, quantitative dimension; there are equal intervals between scale values, and there is an absolute zero.

Reliability: the consistency of a test or a measurement instrument, usually determined by computing a correlation between scores obtained by the same subjects on two forms of the test, scores on the same test at two points in time, or scores obtained on each half of the test.

Research hypothesis: the assertion that the independent variable will have an effect on the dependent variable.

Rho (ρ): the rank-order correlation for a population; r_s is an estimate of rho.

Sample: the group of subjects selected from the population.

Scattergram: a plot of the scores made by the same individuals on two different variables, which provides a pictorial representation of the degree of correlation between two variables.

Significance: statistical significance refers to whether the obtained results are a rare or common event if only chance is operating. Psychological significance refers to the quality of the idea, the adequacy of the test of the idea, and the clarity of the results.

Significance level: the probability used to define an experimental outcome as a rare event if only chance is operating and to define what is meant by equivalent groups.

Skewed distribution: a nonsymmetrical distribution. In a negatively skewed distribution, extreme scores are below the mean. In a positively skewed distribution, extreme scores are above the mean.

Standard deviation: a descriptive measure of variability obtained by taking the square root of the variance; a unit of measurement, or a standard way of describing scores in terms of their relation to the mean.

Standard error: the standard deviation of the sampling distribution.

Stereotaxic procedure: a procedure for immobilizing and positioning the head of an organism in order to stimulate or destroy brain tissue.

Subject: the object or organism on which a manipulation or observation is being made.

Subject variable: a characteristic of a subject that can be measured.

Theory: a tentative explanation for a phenomenon or set of phenomena.

Two-tailed test: a procedure for testing the null hypothesis in which the rejection area is placed at both ends of the appropriate sampling distribution.

Type 1 error: an error that occurs if the null hypothesis is rejected when it is true.

Type 2 error: an error that occurs if the null hypothesis is not rejected when it is false.

Validity: the extent to which an instrument measures what it is purported to measure.

Variable: a thing or event that can be measured or manipulated; a symbol and its set of values.

Variance (s^2): a descriptive measure of variability within a sample; the sum of the squared deviations of each score from the mean divided by the number of scores minus one.

Wilcoxon-Mann-Whitney test: a statistical test appropriate for analyzing ordinal data obtained with within-subject designs.

Within-group variance: a measure of the fluctuations between subjects in the same group.

Within-subject design: an experimental design in which each subject is tested under more than one level of the independent variable.

Index